# OBAMA IN OFFICE

# OBAMA IN OFFICE

*Edited by*
*James A. Thurber*

*Paradigm Publishers*
Boulder • London

Copyright © 2011 by Paradigm Publishers

Published in the United States by Paradigm Publishers, 2845 Wilderness Place, Boulder, Colorado 80301 USA.
Paradigm Publishers is the trade name of Birkenkamp & Company, LLC, Dean Birkenkamp, President and Publisher.

Library of Congress Cataloging-in-Publication Data

Obama in office / edited by James A. Thurber.
    p. cm.
  Includes bibliographical references and index.
  ISBN 978-1-59451-986-4 (hardcover : alk. paper) — ISBN 978-1-59451-993-2 (pbk. : alk. paper)
  1. Obama, Barack. 2. United States—Politics and government—2009–. I. Thurber, James A., 1943–.
  E908.O33 2011
  973.932—dc22

                                                                              2011006599

Printed and bound in the United States of America on acid-free paper that meets the standards of the American National Standard for Permanence of Paper for Printed Library Materials.

Designed and Typeset by Straight Creek Bookmakers.

15 14 13 12 11   5 4 3 2 1

*For my wife, Claudia*

*And my family,*
*Mark, Kathryn, Greg, Tristan, Bryan, and Kelsey*

# Contents

*Preface and Acknowledgments*                                                    *ix*

Chapter 1
An Introduction to an Assessment of the Obama Presidency            1
   *James A. Thurber*

## PART I  FROM CAMPAIGNING TO GOVERNING

Chapter 2
Obama and the Polarized Public                                                  19
   *Gary C. Jacobson*

Chapter 3
Obama and the Public Mood                                                       41
   *Richard W. Boyd*

Chapter 4
Obama's Personality and Performance                                          63
   *Stephen J. Wayne*

Chapter 5
Organizing the Obama White House                                             75
   *James P. Pfiffner*

## PART II  ON THE HILL AND OFF

Chapter 6
Congressional Leadership in Obama's First Two Years                     89
   *Barbara Sinclair*

Chapter 7
A "Post-Partisan" President in a Partisan Context                        107
   *John E. Owens*

Chapter 8
Obama's Battle with Lobbyists                                          127
*James A. Thurber*

## PART III  OBAMA AND THE MEDIA

Chapter 9
Fall of the Favorite                                                  145
*Ron Elving*

Chapter 10
Communication Is Destiny                                              167
*Scott Lilly*

## PART IV  OBAMA AND DOMESTIC POLICY

Chapter 11
From Ambition to Desperation on the Budget                           183
*Joseph White*

Chapter 12
The Politics of Regulation in the Obama Administration               199
*Claudia Hartley Thurber, Esq.*

Chapter 13
The Obama Administration and Internet Policy                         211
*Douglas E. Van Houweling*

## PART V  OBAMA AND FOREIGN POLICY

Chapter 14
Structural Challenges for American Foreign Policy
in the Obama Administration                                          227
*Jonathan Wilkenfeld*

Chapter 15
The Obama Administration and Counterterrorism                        243
*Martha Crenshaw*

Chapter 16
Obama's Use of Prerogative Powers in the War on Terrorism            255
*Richard M. Pious*

Chapter 17
Reclaiming and Rebuilding American Power                             269
*Lawrence J. Korb and Alexander H. Rothman*

*References*                                                         *281*
*Index*                                                              *305*
*About the Contributors*                                             *315*

# Preface and Acknowledgments

When Barack Obama was elected in November 2008, he rode to Washington on a wave of hope and change. However, early in his term President Obama was faced with unprecedented economic and political challenges, while still working to pass the major legislative reforms that he campaigned on, including health care, climate change, financial institutional reform, immigration, and changing the way Washington worked. In January 2010, just one year into the Obama administration, Dr. Nada Mourtada-Sabbah, AUS Vice Chancellor for Development and Alumni Affairs and Professor of International Studies at American University of Sharjah (AUS), asked that I assist her in the organization of a convocation of academics, journalists, and practitioners in their respective fields of expertise to give an objective and balanced evaluation of Obama's policies and performance since taking office. That conference led to an ongoing discussion and research, which eventually became the beginning of this book. The research and book took on a life beyond the conference as the Obama administration progressed and authors and topics were added, but this book would not have been written without the support of Dr. Mourtada-Sabbah and the American University of Sharjah. I want to thank AUS for sponsoring and hosting this conference in early 2009. Individually, I want to thank His Highness Sheikh Dr. Sultan Bin Mohammed Al Qassimi, United Arab Emirates Supreme Council Member, Ruler of Sharjah, and President of the American University of Sharjah, under whose aegis the conference was held; AUS Trustee Riad T. Sadik, Chairman of Al Habtoor Leighton Group who, along with the American University of Sharjah, generously co-sponsored and supported the conference; Dr. Peter Heath, Chancellor of AUS, who took time in his busy schedule to attend the various panels of this conference and endorsed it from its inception; and the Center for Congressional and Presidential Studies (CCPS) in the School of Public Affairs at American University for continuing support of the research for this book. Dr. Nada Mourtada-Sabbah deserves special thanks for her creative idea for the conference and for her long-term collaboration with CCPS. I am grateful to Jennifer Knerr, Vice President and Executive Editor and Director of College Publishing at Paradigm Publishers, for her support of this project, creativity, and timely but careful editing. This is the third time I have had a book published with Jennifer. Each time gets better. I want to thank several individuals at Paradigm Publishers for their enthusiasm and editorial and marketing support for this book: Terra A. Dunham, Publishing Associate, College Marketing and Acquisitions; Laura Esterman, Senior Project Editor; and Pete Hammond, Director of Sales and Marketing. I thank Paradigm Publishers for its support of this volume.

I also want to thank my colleagues and staff at the Center for Congressional and Presidential Studies at American University who provided assistance at various stages of this project, especially Rebecca Prosky, Matt Grieg, Laura Uttley, Sarah Heidt, and Aaron Zimmerman. Special thanks go to Dr. Patrick Griffin, whose years of experience in the White House, on the Hill, and as a lobbyist, AU professor, and CCPS's Assistant Director for Programs and Policy Analysis brings new insights, wisdom, and knowledge that help my research and writing about American politics. Thanks to my students at American University, many of whom have worked in the White House, on the Hill, in campaigns, and for interest groups, for their questions, creative ideas, and inspiration. I have been blessed to have such consistently great students for so many years at American University. I owe a special thanks to William LeoGrande, dean of the School of Public Affairs at American University, for the long-term support of the Center for Congressional and Presidential Studies. Neil Kerwin, President of American University has been a close friend and colleague and a strong supporter of CCPS's mission of bringing together the best academic research and applied knowledge about politics and government, which is a central approach of this book.

I thank all the authors of this book for their contributions of original and timely scholarship. The book is clearly a collective effort, but as editor and author, I take full responsibility for errors of fact, interpretation, and omission.

I dedicate this book to my family: Claudia, Mark, Kathryn, Greg, Tristan, Bryan, and Kelsey for the joy, inspiration, and support they give me. Special thanks go to my wife, Claudia, who is a wonderful partner, a patient editor, and sometimes a researcher for my scholarly endeavors. She has been a stalwart supporter of my work from graduate school to this day. I am pleased she finally agreed to share her knowledge and wisdom about the politics of the regulatory process, gained from 25 years in federal government service, by writing a chapter for this volume. Thank you, Claudia.

# CHAPTER 1

# An Introduction to an Assessment of the Obama Presidency

*James A. Thurber*

Following his momentous campaign and inspiring inaugural, Barack Obama faced divisive political confrontations and major economic, social, environmental, and foreign policy challenges. How should his presidency be measured after two years in office? Where will President Obama stand in history? What will be his legacy? How much of his success and failure and the quality of his leadership was shaped by the economic and political realities he inherited? What was the impact of Obama's personality, policy preferences, and political style on governing? More specifically, what was the impact on Obama of governmental and political institutions such as Congress, political parties, public opinion, and elections? How did world politics, two wars and threats from Iran and North Korea, detente with Russia, international economic competition from China and India, and other realities impact his governing style? What were the major constraints on Obama's presidency? What were his major policy and political achievements? What were his failures and what challenges are left for him to address? These are just some of the important questions addressed in this book. The chapter authors here employ a variety of policy and political perspectives, including approaches from history, law, political science, public administration, psychology, sociology, policy analysis, survey research, and media studies, as they assess Obama's presidency.

President Obama has had a major impact on America; voters have reacted to his accomplishments as shown in the historic 2010 midterm election. His major legislative accomplishments are impressive, yet controversial: the Lilly Ledbetter Fair Pay Act, American Recovery and Reinvestment Act (ARRA, the economic stimulus legislation), Affordable Care Act (ACA, health care reform), Wall Street/financial institutional reform, reauthorization and funding the Troubled Asset Relief Program (TARP), funding the deployment of 30,000 more troops to Afghanistan, and several significant legislative victories in the Lame Duck Congress. The tax bill, extension of unemployment compensation, food safety reform, repeal of the "don't ask, don't tell" policy in the military services, and approval of the START II treaty in the Lame Duck session of the 111th Congress are historic policy achievements by themselves. These accomplishments may define President Obama's place in history, but there are other factors to be taken into account when assessing his presidency after only two years.

Because the authors here include presidential and congressional scholars, media and interest group specialists, domestic and foreign policy experts, public administration experts and policy analysts, practitioners and academics, each brings a unique perspective to bear. No single analytic approach or dominant ideology reigns. The chapters focus on public opinion, voting behavior, Obama's personality, his organization of the White House, his relationship with congressional leadership, his legislative strategy, his domestic and foreign policy achievements (and challenges), his relationship with interest groups, lobbyists, and the media, his communications strategy, his regulatory strategies, his focus on the federal debt and deficits, and many other policy accomplishments and failures. Only this diverse group of authors could address such a myriad of issues.

## FACTORS INFLUENCING THE ASSESSMENT OF PRESIDENT OBAMA

An appraisal of President Obama's first two years starts with his 2008 campaign. Presidential campaigns are a test of a candidate's style and leadership and a way for voters to judge what policies they will attempt to implement. Obama's 2008 campaign was the longest, most expensive, and one of the best presidential campaigns in the history of the United States. The first African American president of the United States had a "mandate," but he inherited one of the worst economic crises in the history of the United States. Campaigns and governing do not occur in a vacuum; they are influenced greatly by economic and political circumstances. President Obama's responses—the passage of the $787 billion economic stimulus three weeks into his presidency and his introduction of a transformational $3.6 trillion federal budget a month into his administration—were as swift and historic as was his election.

Obama's campaign had a clear message: "hope and change"—change the failing economy and change the party in the White House. This message mobilized party loyalists, "the base," and swing voters who are often moderate and ideologically in the middle. After taking office, President Obama tried to govern in the same way. He attempted to build a solid base of votes from his party in Congress and then show post-partisanship by reaching out for votes from moderate Republicans.

Starting on Inauguration Day, January 20, 2009, President Obama used his "political capital" from his successful election campaign—the size of his election victory (53 percent), his popularity as shown in early high poll ratings, job approval ratings in the mid-80 percent range in his first few days in office and in the mid-65 percent range after three months, and the natural surge of partisan support inherent in unified party government—to build a strong relationship with the Democratically controlled Congress. However, Obama's presidential "political capital" decayed rapidly, as will be described by several authors in this book. His political momentum was undermined by events, the staggering economic crises in the US and the world, the wars in Iraq and Afghanistan, and the unified and intransigent political opposition of the Republican congressional leadership to his policy agenda.

Well-run governing strategies start with a plan, a theme, and a message. The goal is to maximize resources (particularly the president's time), reduce liabilities by marginalizing opposition, and establish a set of objectives that, when achieved, will maximize the probability of getting the votes needed to pass the president's legislative agenda in Congress. This sounds simple, but the key elements of a presidential leadership strategy and plan are complex and dynamic, as President Obama quickly discovered. Governing must take into account a vast number of factors, such as the president's personality and charisma, the constituencies in the nation and on the Hill, the policies being advocated, the party organization or lack of it, the strength of party leadership, the economic situation, and the political capital available. The authors in this book have analyzed the impact of all these institutions, events, and circumstances.

President Obama's leadership and policy achievements must be viewed in a constitutional context. As with all presidents, the framers of the Constitution set the framework for President Obama. By fragmenting power between the national government and the states, federalism, and among the executive, legislative, and judicial branches (separation of powers), they guaranteed that President Obama would struggle to achieve his policy goals. The framers bequeathed to Americans one of the most enduring rivalries in government: that between the president and Congress. They also divided legislative powers by creating two coequal houses, a bicameral Congress with different constituencies, which further magnifies rivalry and conflict. The effects are shown in the deadlock between the House and Senate on a variety of Obama's policies, including energy cap and trade legislation, which was stopped by the Senate, and health care reform, in which the House bill was stopped until a completely revised Senate version passed using reconciliation. Although divided, Congress was designed to be independent and powerful, able to check the power of the executive and to be directly linked with the people through popular, periodic elections. The Constitution, in the way it divided power between the two branches, created an open invitation for conflict, which President Obama immediately experienced and will likely feel more acutely with the 112th Congress.

Other factors influencing President Obama's relationship with Congress and contributing to his successes were electoral motivations and competitiveness, and different terms of office, both of which are discussed by this book's authors. The Constitution mandates different terms of office: representatives serve for two years, senators hold office for six-year terms, and the president is elected every four years. Constituency bases are different, too, with the president elected by the nation, the senators by their states, and representatives by their districts. Presidents have only four years, possibly eight, in which to establish their programs. They are expected to set the national policy agenda and usually move rapidly in the first year before their inevitable decline in popularity. President Obama has followed this formula. Members of Congress are driven by the short-term motivation to be re-elected rather than long-term goals of a president, and they rightly see their futures as less important to their leader. The "shellacking" Obama and his Democratic colleagues experienced in the 2010 midterm election is a perfect example of these competing goals. The decision-making pace of Congress and of the president is not the same because of their different terms of office, electoral bases, and perceived constituency mandates.

Another dynamic influencing President Obama's relationship with Congress is that of the state-based political parties. These parties allow members of Congress to be independent from the president, but because they are decentralized, they exercise little control over recruitment of candidates who run under their party label. Senators and representatives usually run their own races with their own financing. The way they respond to local conditions has little to do with national party platforms or presidential politics. Members often freely pursue their own interests without fear of discipline from the president. Independence from political parties and the president enables legislators to seek benefits for their own constituents and to serve specialized interests.

President Obama, however, was the beneficiary of exceptionally cohesive party unity among Democrats. The cohesion of the majority Democrats enabled him achieve his legislative goals. Those legislative achievements were even more remarkable because of strong Republican party unity against him and because there were few Republicans in the middle, ideologically, with whom he could work. Although President Obama wanted to be the post-partisan president, reaching out to the opposition party, party-voting patterns revealed the parties to be too unified, ideological, and polarized for the president to achieve that goal.

Whether party government is unified or divided has a major impact on the relationship between the president and Congress, as shown in the first two years of the Obama administration. With the 2008 election of President Obama and a Democratic Congress, unified party government returned to Washington. A major electoral impediment to legislative-executive cooperation is divided government, as shown by the dramatic election of 1994 (and now, 2010). Divided government does not always mean that the two branches will fight. However, it is generally easier for presidents to govern during periods of unified party government, as was shown in the first two years of the Obama administration. The midterm election of 2006 forced President Bush to work with the opposition party in the House and Senate in the 110th Congress, as will the 2010 midterm election for President Obama in the 112th Congress. The 2010 Lame Duck session foreshadowed what may happen in the 112th Congress: more cross-party cooperation. There are two varieties of divided government (the condition that exists when the majority party in either or both houses of Congress differs from the party of the president): divided party control of Congress and split control of Congress and the White House. The outcome of the 2010 midterm election gave President Obama a troublesome split control of Congress with a narrow majority of Democrats in the Senate for the 112th Congress. From 1901 through 2012, the United States has had unified party control of government for 67 years (60 percent of the time) and divided party control of government for 45 years (almost 40 percent of the time), a contextual factor that was not ignored by President Obama. President Obama continued the historic trend of being more successful with his legislative agenda with unified party government (2009–2010) than he will be with divided government (2011–2012). This trend has been especially true since the post-1980 resurgence of party-line voting and party cohesion in Congress.

President Obama's legislation is only part of his story. His successful Supreme Court appointments, organization of the White House and appointment of policy czars, aggressive regulatory actions, management of crises such as the BP oil leak in the Gulf, command of the two wars, and leadership on the international scene are all important parts of his presidency.

What are the challenges facing President Obama in the 112th Congress after losing the House of Representatives to the Republicans? They are monumental and include the economy and job creation, the debt and deficit, tax reform, appropriations allocations, environmental and energy policy, immigration reform, reauthorization of No Child Left Behind, redeployment of troops in Iraq and Afghanistan, threats from Iran and Korea, the revolution in Egypt, trade agreements, and keeping promises to change the way Washington works (ethics, lobbying reform, stopping earmarks, campaign finance [DISCLOSE Act], partisanship, and breaking gridlock), to name just a few. Divided party government will likely include little voter and congressional consensus about the public problems and threats facing the United States, especially the economy, health care reform, education reforms, energy/environmental policy, immigration, and the war in Afghanistan. There may be little consensus on *solutions* to these problems, especially if there is little consensus about the *nature* of the problems. There may be a unified and strong opposition party that is interested in making sure he is a one-term president and strong interest groups that will disagree about problems and solutions. There will be limits on resources in the budget and time to deal with the looming and dangerously large deficits and federal debt. With divided party government and the upcoming 2012 presidential election, President Obama may see his central core of political authority decay very rapidly. Much depends upon his ability to communicate to and persuade the American people to support his politics.

Will the 112th Congress be patterned like 1995–1996, when Clinton and the Republicans worked together, or will it be a continuation of partisan deadlock? Will compromise and moderation rule or will permanent partisan campaigns with wedge issues and mean-spirited confrontation? Presidential-congressional relations in the post-2010 election Lame Duck Congress revealed that cooperation and historic legislative productivity can occur. The authors in this book assess President Obama's performance in the first two years and comment on what it may mean for his leadership and relationship with the American public, the media, interest groups, Congress, and the world during the next two years.

## How the Book Is Organized and What to Look For

This book includes 16 independent assessments of the Obama administration from a variety of perspectives. It is organized around campaigns, public opinion and voting, personality, governmental and political institutions, and domestic and foreign policy in five parts: Part I: From Campaigning to Governing; Part II: On the Hill and Off; Part III: Obama and the Media; Part IV: Obama and Domestic Policy; and Part V: Obama and Foreign Policy.

### Part I: From Campaigning to Governing

This part of the book begins with Gary Jacobson's Chapter 2, "Obama and the Polarized Public," a foundation for understanding his accomplishments and failures. He evaluates President Obama's attempt to bridge the wide partisan and ideological divide that has emerged in American politics. Jacobson argues that Obama has failed to be the post-partisan president he wanted to be in his first two years in office, despite extensive courtship of the Republicans. Congressional Republicans voted almost unanimously against Obama's most important domestic initiatives—his economic stimulus and health care reform packages—and adopted resolute opposition and obstruction as their strategy for party revival. They viewed Obama's failure as a prerequisite for their retaking control of Congress. Jacobson shows that the strategy was largely successful; the 2010 midterm gave Republicans their largest majority in the House of Representatives since 1946. Jacobson concludes that the 2010 election results virtually guarantee even deeper partisan divisions in Washington in the 112th Congress. His analysis reveals that the American public has become thoroughly divided along party lines in evaluations of Obama and his policies. Jacobson shows that after Obama's brief period of post-election popularity, popular assessments of his job performance have trended downward, dipping below 50 percent in early 2010 and ending up at in the mid-40 percentile on Election Day. He describes the wide partisan differences in presidential approval. Democrats continued to rate his performance quite highly, but Republicans approvers dropped by half during Obama's first six months in office and continued to decline rapidly thereafter. Jacobson argues that the partisan divide by the 2010 election had grown wider than under any president prior to President George W. Bush. Jacobson describes how Obama's presidency provoked an increase in conservative populism, represented most prominently by the 2010 Tea Party movement. A majority of the 66 newly elected Republicans were associated in some way with the Tea Party movement. Jacobson predicts that if they remain loyal to their Tea Party roots, the House Republicans' center of ideological gravity will move to the right. The result would be the most polarized House on record. Moreover, the Republicans' principal objective for the new Congress, openly articulated by Senate minority leader Mitch McConnell, is to make Obama a one-term president. Their vow to repeal Obama's signature health care reforms (as well as to roll back financial and environmental regulations) is part of their strategy for doing so. Jacobson concludes that an electorate that detests partisan bickering has unintentionally created the circumstances for intense partisan trench warfare.

Richard Boyd in Chapter 3, "Obama and the Public Mood," analyzes the sources of Obama's victory in 2008 and then extends Jacobson's analysis by interpreting the sharp fall in Obama's job approval rating in terms of two related themes. Boyd's theme concerns the multiple meanings of change in election campaigns. He analyzes the meaning of change in Obama's victory in 2008 and the Republican resurgence in 2010. Boyd argues that legislative success did not improve the public's confidence in Obama, in Congress, or in the congressional parties. He shows that this has been true since the late 1960s. Voters have remained mistrustful and disaffected no matter who is in power. Boyd concludes that Obama hoped he could raise the quality of political discourse and increase trust in leaders and institutions (change Washington), but he has failed. He thinks that the goal of civility and nonpartisanship will likely prove elusive, both for his administration and for his successors.

Shifting from public opinion, voting, and elections to the personality of President Obama, Stephen Wayne in Chapter 4, "Obama's Personality and Performance," evaluates the impact of President Obama's personality on his leadership style. He explores the topic of the influence of Obama's personality on governing. Wayne addresses the question of whether President Obama been a transformational or charismatic leader. A charismatic leader has an ability to draw others to his side and move them to accomplish a cause bigger than themselves. A charismatic approach is transformational if it invokes a permanent change in the people who embrace the leader's vision. Other authors in this book will show that Obama has formulated a more multilateral leadership style with other countries, thinking not only of the US's interests, but also of the interests of the other nations as well. Wayne and other authors show that President Obama at times seems to be a "contingency leader," giving great deference to congressional leaders. Obama has responded to various situations using different types of leadership styles for different challenges. Professor Wayne addresses why Obama took so long to make a policy decision to commit 30,000 more troops in Afghanistan. Why did Obama, who believes vision to be his key policy-making role, delegate the details of his key policy initiatives in health care, energy independence, and environmental improvement first to White House aides and then to members of Congress? Why would a president who advocates major change be so preoccupied with finding common ground? Why would a transformational leader adopt a transactional style of doing business? Wayne argues that the answers to these questions have to do with tensions and contradictions within Obama himself. This chapter discusses those character, environmental, and situational issues and their impact on President Obama's decisions and actions. Wayne argues that we have witnessed a bundle of personal contradictions: a transformational leader with a down-to-earth operating style, a man with lofty visions but a pragmatic outlook, a president who refuses to compromise his major priorities but who is extremely flexible on their policy details, an inspiring public speaker who often appears distant or stoic, a candidate who advocates change and a politician who is preoccupied with finding common ground. Other authors also refer to Obama's personality and leadership style with Congress, the media, and interest groups, and on the international stage.

James Pfiffner evaluates the structure and organization of President Obama's White House in Chapter 5, "Organizing the Obama White House." He describes the challenge of organizing the White House and structuring its relations with the rest of the executive branch. The separation of power, checks and balances, and the enduring institutional tensions carry forward for a president, regardless of partisan control or the changing personnel in the presidency and appointed positions. Pfiffner's shows how President Obama's administration illustrates the enduring tensions between centralized control and the delegation of power to departments and agencies. After examining White House domination of policy making in the Obama presidency, Pfiffner describes the friction with the cabinet. He concludes by describing how President Obama was deeply involved in the details of all of his major policy priorities, particularly economic recovery, health care reform, and Afghanistan strategy.

## Part II: On the Hill and Off

Barbara Sinclair assesses congressional leadership relationship with President Obama in Chapter 6, "Congressional Leadership in Obama's First Two Years." She concludes that a major failure of President Obama and the congressional leaders was in managing expectations. The Obama presidency and the 111th Congress began with extraordinarily high expectations, as described by Jacobson and Boyd. Sinclair states that President Obama should have done a much better job of explaining the problems confronting the country given his political capital. Obama did not use the bully pulpit effectively and has received most of the criticism, including from Democratic members of Congress and sometimes from the leaders themselves, for not framing the choices Democrats faced and persuading the public of the rightness of the policy choices. If Obama had just been a more effective communicator, the public would have understood and so liked the stimulus bill and health care reform better, and congressional Democrats would not have suffered such a big defeat in the 2010 elections, the strongest form of the argument goes. Sinclair concludes that undoubtedly Obama could have done a more effective job communicating, as could members of Congress in their own districts, and that congressional leaders could probably have done more to make the legislative process appear less messy.

Some commentators have argued that if Democrats had put off health care reform and focused on jobs and the economy instead, they would have done much better in the 2010 midterm elections. Sinclair disagrees. She concludes that the congressional Democrats' fate was primarily determined by the state of the economy. There was not much within the realm of political and economic feasibility that could be done to "fix" the economy.

John Owens in Chapter 7, "A 'Post-Partisan' President in a Partisan Context," continues an analysis started by Sinclair of President Obama's interaction with the 111th Congress. Owens first describes the strategic context that Obama inherited and how that context influenced his relationship with Congress. Owens further describes Obama's personal style, perceptions, and approaches and how they influence his workings with Congress. His analysis also identifies Obama's legislative priorities, achievements, and legislative strategies. He assesses the effectiveness of Obama's identification and exploitation of legislative opportunities. Owens argues, as do other authors in this book, that the list of legislative accomplishments of the Obama administration and the 111th Congress is significant. Owens concludes that Obama's legislative successes, particularly the stimulus and the health care legislation, were essentially congressional Democratic products, albeit ones on which the White House helped facilitate congressional agreement. Owens predicts that while Obama's political instincts will remain pragmatic, conciliatory, and bipartisan, he will face an environment whose defining characteristics are not.

James A. Thurber, in Chapter 8, "Obama's Battle with Lobbyists," assesses President Obama's battle with special interests and lobbyists in Washington. This chapter explores the causes, characteristics, and consequences of President Obama's attacks on lobbyists and his attempt to "change the way Washington works." It concludes with a discussion of the barriers President Obama faced in reforming pluralist democracy in Washington. President Obama's lobbying and ethics reforms, his effort to change the way Washington works, boil down to three basic principles of sound government: transparency, accountability, and enforcement. Thurber concludes that President Obama has brought some new transparency, but generally his initiatives have had limited effect. President Obama has called for more accountability and enforcement of the law and rules related to lobbying and ethics. He has made it clear who is responsible for monitoring and maintaining ethical behavior. Thurber shows that Obama's new rules have brought more accountability for lobbyists and executive branch officials, but there are serious problems with lack of enforcement. Thurber concludes that lobbying disclosure has had limited impact on changing the influence industry in Washington. In fact, an unintended consequence of President Obama's attempt to reduce conflicts of interest has seriously limited those with expertise from serving as appointees and on government advisory panels, making it difficult to implement his policy goals. President Obama has changed the rhetoric, but not the way Washington's political culture works. Obama promised change, to be the reform post-partisan president, but he has failed to do that and to meet the expectations of the American public.

## Part III: Obama and the Media

In Part III, Ron Elving and Scott Lilly evaluate Obama's communication strategy and his relationship with the media. Elving begins this part with Chapter 9,

"Fall of the Favorite," a description of how Barack Obama was elected with the implicit support of much of the news, entertainment, and social media, and then that media turned against him. As shown by Jacobson and Boyd, Elving details how after President Obama passed much of his promised policy agenda, he lost significant support of the media and American people. Elving argues that among the factors contributing to this reversal were the president's own priorities in the White House, the rise of an anti-Obama media narrative, rising and amplified criticism of the president from conflicting directions, and the difficulty of using new media techniques to motivate support for policies rather than election objectives. Great expectations had been encouraged by the media as much as by Obama's own campaign rhetoric. Elving shows that the motivations differed, but the pursuit of Obama's narrative had driven the media and the candidate together. The change from campaign to governance broke this bond, especially as competing narratives of resistance and pushback gained currency and power. This change produced a reversal of fortune for President Obama, who had been the ultimate media favorite. Elving concludes that the dynamic relationship between the president and the media will continue to evolve and may look quite different by the time the president himself faces voters again in 2012.

The second chapter in Part III, Chapter 10, "Communication Is Destiny," by Scott Lilly, evaluates Obama's communication style and his achievements in domestic policy. Lilly concludes that the level of miscommunication out of the Obama White House is surprising because Obama was such a good candidate. He thinks it is especially important to understand why Obama's communications problems were not recognized and corrected. Lilly concludes that the lessons learned from the communications miscues of the first six months of the administration could have become a major asset in the remaining months leading up to the midterm elections. He failed to win the public back on key issues, which had disastrous effects in the 2010 election. Lilly concludes that one possible explanation is that the Obama White House clung to the assumption that successful policy would automatically translate into successful governance. While good governance requires good policy outcomes, good policy is not enough by itself. Successful governance also requires an ongoing dialogue between those who govern and those who are governed. Further, the quality of that dialogue must be measured not by what is said, but by what is understood. He also concludes that now that the Obama White House is operating with a more emboldened Republican opposition, success will depend not so much on the magnitude of the compromises offered by Obama, but on how well the administration is able to defend its vision of the future and clearly oppose the vision of its opposition in the court of public opinion.

*Part IV: Obama and Domestic Policy*

Part IV focuses on Obama and his domestic policy with evaluations of his budget priorities, regulatory actions, and Internet policy. Joseph White describes the battle over the budget in Obama's first two years in office in Chapter 11, "From

Ambition to Desperation on the Budget." President Obama's administration found the challenge of pulling the economy out of a recession as well as dealing with the looming deficits and debt particularly difficult. White reminds us that the challenge of government budgeting is how to make hard choices between policy preferences about total spending to specific program spending that keeps government running and meeting program commitments. The budget and its effects on the economy were at the center of President Obama's first two years in office. White concludes that Obama's early policy choices were ambitious and successful: the stimulus bill and health care reform. Performance of the economy affects spending for some programs, such as unemployment insurance and Medicaid, interest rates on federal borrowing, and the profits and earnings that are available for taxes. White shows that budget decisions about spending, taxes, and debt were a major way that Obama sought to influence the economy. The Obama administration's budget decisions were driven by the economic crisis it inherited, yet the economic and political results could be and were overwhelmed by the same economic risks that the budget sought to address, as is shown by Sinclair. The crisis was bad enough to help elect him but, unlike Franklin Delano Roosevelt, President Obama took office when the consequences of the financial system breakdown had only begun to spread through the rest of the economy. White also concludes that all of Obama's budget and policy preferences caused more spending or reduced revenues, making the deficit and debt significantly worse than before the recession hit. President Obama viewed deficit reduction, after the stimulus, as an essential part of the "new era of responsibility" he announced in his inaugural address. He promised to "get serious about fiscal discipline," which meant to "get serious about entitlement reform" using a special commission on debt and deficits to help set the policy agenda to do something about entitlements. White concludes that making such a pledge might be popular, but following up on it proved to be difficult. White predicts more conflict and deadlock over appropriations and the budget.

Claudia Thurber, in Chapter 12, "The Politics of Regulation in the Obama Administration," assesses the role of federal regulations in achieving President Obama's policy goals. She describes the federal regulatory process and argues that the final two years of the president's (first) term will be marked by significant regulatory initiatives, because of the major legislation passed in the first two years, including the stimulus package, health care reform, and financial reform, all of which will require rulemaking in some form, but also because with a divided government and the potentially low presidential support scores in the 112th Congress, he will have to command the one sector of the government over which he has control—the federal bureaucracy. The federal regulatory agencies, all presidents' tools for honing their policy or in some cases creating it, are laden with legal requirements, making each rulemaking a cumbersome and time-consuming process. It is not cheap, either. The 95 major rules, promulgated between October 1999 and September 2001, were estimated to cost between $42,700,000 and $54,597,000 and to generate benefits of between $127,962,000 and $616,282,000 (in 2001 dollars). President Obama, like all presidents before him (and certainly those who will follow), inherited his predecessor's regulatory policy, including regulations in progress and completed, deregulations, and midnight regulations. As Ms. Thurber notes, no president wants to have his policies dictated by his predecessor's policies, so focus must be kept on moving forward on all regulatory fronts, which is exactly what the major regulatory agencies such as the Environmental Protection Agency, Occupational Safety and Health Administration, Mine Safety and Health Administration, Department of Health and Human Services, Securities and Exchange Commission and its new Office of Credit Ratings, Department of Treasury and the new Office of National Insurance, and Federal Deposit Insurance Corporation with its new Consumer Financial Protection Bureau, Federal Communications Commission (see Van Houweling's chapter), and others are doing. Regulatory agencies have already begun, continued, or completed rulemaking projects reflecting his policies. Major new initiatives have been brought forth in all the agencies. President Obama is also administering the federal government through more than 64 substantive Executive Orders, with more to follow. President Obama is poised to use all the regulatory tools at his disposal. He has ample statutes on the books to put his policies into practice. As Ms. Thurber concludes, "Let us pay close attention to rulemaking and see if he succeeds."

Claudia Thurber's chapter on regulation is paired with Chapter 13, "The Obama Administration and Internet Policy," by Douglas E. Van Houweling. He points out that Barack Obama is the first president of the United States for whom the Internet has played an important personal and political role. His election was very much aided by utilizing the Internet to build the community that supported him. As his administration developed its policy toward the Internet, though, it needed to take into account the history of Internet development and policy. Van Houweling summarizes the history of government support for the Internet from Clinton through Bush to the Obama administration. President Obama has recognized the key role of the federal government in ensuring the nation's ability to continue to provide global leadership in Internet technology and make the investments required to support business and citizen applications of that technology. Van Houweling argues that throughout the short history of the Internet, the core question has been whether the Internet is a key element of societal infrastructure worthy of public investment or just another service best provided by private enterprise. Van Houweling concludes that the Obama administration's first two years have resulted in a major step forward for Internet capabilities in the United States. A more active FCC, the investment and accompanying activity resulting from the ARRA stimulus program, and the increased investments in network capability for science and research have all reenergized America's Internet development community. Van Houweling finds that while the competing political forces surrounding the Internet in the United States will continue to cloud the future, there is no question that the first two Obama years have provided substantial impetus for the development of the Internet infrastructure. President Obama recognizes the Internet as an important public good.

*Part V: Obama and Foreign Policy*

Part V includes four interrelated chapters on foreign, defense, and anti-terrorism policy achievements and future challenges. Jonathan Wilkenfeld evaluates the foreign policy challenges facing Obama in Chapter 14, "Structural Challenges for American Foreign Policy in the Obama Administration." Wilkenfeld describes the complex, dynamic, and dangerous world inherited by President Obama. He concludes that as the Obama administration passes the midpoint of its first term in office, it appears to have settled on the broad outlines for dealing with some of the more vexing immediate foreign policy issues that it inherited from the previous administration. It now faces the development and implementation of broad policy on key global issues that will define its own unique foreign policy agenda. We know a lot about the headline issues—how the administration is dealing with the aggression and expanding nuclear programs in North Korea and Iran, resetting ties with Russia and reaching a new balance with China, a new START treaty with Russia, and the war in Afghanistan. But a central question posed by Wilkenfeld has to do with whether the Obama administration will recognize and address some of the longer-term critical underlying issues facing the international system—those factors that are likely to define the nature of the international system for our children and grandchildren, long after President Obama leaves office. Wilkenfeld asks what tools the US has to deal with such long-term threats to the stability and prosperity of the world and what measures might be developed to help the Obama administration begin to address these threats. Wilkenfeld identifies the sources of several threats to world stability and prosperity facing President Obama: ethnic diversity, inconsistent governance, ineffective conflict resolution, and poor development strategies. His analysis also addresses deceptive myths and often uncomfortable realities in the international system. The chapter concludes with several prescriptions for the Obama administration about how best to deal with the more dangerous consequences of these threats.

Martha Crenshaw in Chapter 15, "The Obama Administration and Counterterrorism" focuses on the Obama administration's aspirations for counterterrorism policy and evaluates the results. She describes Obama's framing of policy in terms of repudiation of a generalized war on terror, rejection of the idea that security requires weakening of legal and moral standards, and positive outreach to Muslims as a break with the past. However, President Obama's implementation of these aims has not so far lived up to promise. Crenshaw finds that it has proved difficult to undo the domestic security apparatus in terms of both structure and practice. Many of these frustrations are to be expected, because every president who has had to deal with the threat of terrorism has confronted them. Crenshaw concludes that the emphasis on military force as a solution to international terrorism has not been explained in terms that make it a logical means to the ends the administration has prescribed.

Richard Pious complements Crenshaw's findings in Chapter 16, "Obama's Use of Prerogative Powers in the War on Terrorism." This chapter assesses President Obama's terrorism policy from a legal and constitutional basis. Pious shows that President Obama laid out much of the strategy in the struggle against terrorists in a speech at the National Archives Museum on May 21, 2009: "For the first time since 2002, we are providing the necessary resources and strategic direction to take the fight to the extremists who attacked us on 9/11 in Afghanistan and Pakistan." Obama claimed that the decisions of his predecessor had taken the nation "off course" and promised that he would deal with the terrorism threat "with an abiding confidence in the rule of law and due process; in checks and balances and accountability." He noted that he had banned "enhanced interrogation" techniques, ordered the closing of the prison camp at Guantánamo and a review of all pending cases there, and took credit for developing due-process standards to apply to those the government would wish to detain indefinitely. Pious argues that Obama's speech and actions raise the question of whether his policies involved fundamental changes from those of the Bush administration. John Brennan (an assistant to former President George W. Bush) called Obama's decisions "Bush's third term." Bush's CIA director, General Michael Hayden, praised Obama's "continuity" of policy, observing "to President Obama's credit, he has used many of the tools that we used to continue to take the fight to the enemy." He cited renditions to other nations for interrogation, indefinite detention of detainees, limited definition of habeas corpus rights, use of military commissions, and reliance on state secrets defenses in court proceedings. Pious documents that Obama chose continuity, and in some cases he chose significant changes in policy. Pious concludes that Obama has not yielded any grounds in his claims of constitutional prerogatives, and in some respects he has gone even farther in than his predecessors. He ends his analysis with the question: What accounts for Obama's choices?

The book ends with an assessment of President Obama's overall foreign and defense policy in Lawrence J. Korb and Alexander H. Rothman's Chapter 17, "Reclaiming and Rebuilding American Power." As all the authors in this book have emphasized, Obama inherited a massive spread of domestic and foreign policy challenges unmatched by any president in recent history. Korb and Rothman describe the wars in Iraq and Afghanistan as stretching the American military almost to the breaking point. They argue that in both of these conflicts, "victory" remained difficult to define. They conclude that our invasion of Iraq has alienated not only the Muslim world but also traditional allies such as Germany and Turkey. They also conclude that waterboarding, Guantánamo Bay, and Abu Ghraib had compromised US credentials on human rights. US-Russian relations were at their lowest point since the end of the Cold War. At a time when Iran and North Korea appeared determined to continue their nuclear weapons programs, the Bush administration's incoherent nonproliferation policy had seriously undermined the global nonproliferation regime. And in the midst of a global recession, the United States faced record deficits, fueled by the cost of the wars and a tax policy that had neither grown the economy nor created jobs. The authors conclude that Obama was propelled into office by an electorate frustrated with the disastrous policies of the Bush administration; President Obama faced the prospect of picking up the pieces. Korb and Rothman argue that since taking office, President Obama has been forced to balance his own foreign policy goals, such as focusing international attention on the threat of nuclear terrorism, with a need to respond to crises inherited from President Bush. The authors describe Obama's most important foreign policy initiatives as winding down the US military presence in Iraq; refocusing American attention and resources on the war in Afghanistan; combating the spread of weapons-usable nuclear material and technology (e.g., the New START treaty); and crafting a defense policy that sustains, rather than simply expends, American political, economic, and military power. They deduce that change in foreign and defense policy has been neither quick nor easy, and significant challenges remain in all four of these efforts. Overall their assessment is that President Obama deserves credit for fulfilling his campaign promises in Iraq and Afghanistan, recommitting the United States to nuclear disarmament, and reorienting US defense policy to better handle the threats of the 21st century—significant accomplishments in two years.

## The Book Ahead

The following chapters offer a scholarly assessment of President Obama, focusing on his relationship with voters, Congress, interests groups, the media, the bureaucracy, foreign nations, and wide variety of domestic and foreign policy communities. The authors evaluate the results of the 2010 elections, the Tea Party movement, the Lame Duck Congress, the economy, the media, and other factors on the prospects for President Obama in 2011 and 2012.

A major collective conclusion of this book is that President Obama's domestic and foreign policy achievements have been monumental, yet highly controversial and not yet accepted by a large number of Americans. With the leadership of President Obama, the 111th Congress has been one of the most productive congresses in decades, probably since President Lyndon Johnson. The Recovery Act policy achievements alone are more than most presidents can claim in an entire term. President Obama substantially altered the course of the economy. His management of the TARP program, which was passed by Bush but translated into policy by Obama, was controversial but immensely successful. Wall Street/banking reform was also historic in scope and impact. The health care reform legislation was one of the monumental accomplishments of our lifetime. The post-election 2010 Lame Duck Congress saw President Obama shift and coalesce with the Republicans to pass a comprehensive tax bill with an extension of unemployment compensation, the repeal of "don't ask, don't tell," a major food safety bill, the START II treaty, the 9/11 first responders health care act, and dozens of others appointments and legislative actions. President Obama described the Lame Duck session "as the most productive post-election period we have had in decades." The following chapters discuss many other achievements and some major policy and communications failures.

Although President Obama has had major achievements, several authors in this book have concluded that President Obama did not draw the lines between policy and governance and campaigning and governance clearly enough, causing major problems for his administration and the Democrats in Congress. Sound policy linked to public problems is necessary for successful governance, but not sufficient. Announcing policy preferences is only part of the equation. Governance is leadership; it requires interaction with those who are governed and it requires a dialogue, clear and sometimes simple communication, which explains what a president is trying to accomplish and why the citizenry needs to get behind it. Citizens must hear what the leader is saying. There is a consensus among the authors in this book that President Obama failed to clearly communicate to the American public what the problems and solutions were in a simple and reinforcing way. Obama had a clear strategy theme and message in his campaign, but he did not have that in governing. He did not successfully explain the problems facing America and his policies to solve those problems in the innumerable ways necessary until the message was understood by the American public. One consequence of this failure was the outcome of the 2010 election, and another might be a one-term presidency for him. President Obama expended his political capital and has little left to fight for further change. In fact, he has little left to defend what he has already accomplished. Obama did not realize that presidents rarely set the rules of American politics. They are established by the components of our constitutional structure, attitudes among the American public, the composition of Congress, the nature of the media, and the role of interest groups who fight every day for power over the policy directions of the country. An opportunity to change the rules comes only to those who play with extraordinary skill under the existing rules. Obama believed that he would change the rules ("change the way Washington works") and operate on a higher plane by willing our political system to be what he believed it should be. After two years, President Obama failed to do that, even though he was enormously successful with his policy agenda.

# PART I
## FROM CAMPAIGNING TO GOVERNING

CHAPTER 2

# Obama and the Polarized Public

*Gary C. Jacobson*

Barack Obama, like his immediate predecessor, George W. Bush, entered the White House with aspirations to bridge the wide partisan divide that had emerged in American politics during the final decades of the twentieth century.[1] So far he has also failed conspicuously to do so. Despite considerable courtship, congressional Republicans voted almost unanimously against Obama's most important domestic initiatives—his economic stimulus and health care reform packages—and adopted resolute opposition and obstruction as their strategy for party revival, viewing Obama's failure as a prerequisite for their retaking control of Congress. The strategy was largely successful; the 2010 midterm gave Republicans their largest majority in the House of Representatives since 1946 (243–192) and increased their share of Senate seats from 41 to 47, putting them within striking distance of majority control in 2012, when Democrats will be defending 23 of the 33 seats in play. The election results virtually guarantee even deeper partisan divisions in Washington during the second Congress under Obama than during the first.

The American public, too, has become thoroughly divided along party lines in evaluations of Obama and his policies. After a brief moment of post-election euphoria, during which substantial majorities of Americans celebrated the passing of the Bush administration and the historically remarkable election of an African American president, popular assessments of Obama's job performance have trended downward, dipping below 50 percent in early 2010 and ending up at about 48 percent on Election Day (Figure 2-1). Moreover, the extraordinarily wide partisan differences in presidential approval typical of Bush's final five years in office soon reappeared under Obama (Figure 2-2). Democrats continued to rate his performance quite highly, but the proportion of Republican approvers dropped by half during Obama's first six months in office and continued to decline thereafter, falling to about 10 percent by the midterm election. Although the partisan divide has yet to reach the record levels inspired by Bush, by the 2010 election it had grown wider than under any president prior to Bush (Jacobson 2011a). More important for Obama's party's midterm electoral fortunes, the trend among independents paralleled the downward Republican trend, and by the election the proportion of independents approving of Obama's performance was below 40 percent.[2]

In some circles, antipathy toward Obama has far exceeded ordinary partisan disdain. His presidency has provoked a upsurge of conservative populism, represented most prominently by the Tea Party movement, an assortment of conservative activists, the more unhinged of whom display in classic form the "paranoid style in American politics" (Hofstadter 1964).[3] To this faction, Obama is not merely an objectionable liberal Democrat, but a tyrant (of the Nazi, fascist, communist, socialist, monarchist, or racist variety, depending on the critic[4]) bent on subjecting Americans to, variously, socialism, communism, fascism, concentration camps, or control by United Nations, Interpol, international bankers, the Council on Foreign Relations, or the Trilateral Commission (Barstow 2010). Not all Tea Party supporters (13–18 percent of the public) or sympathizers (about a third of the public[5]) entertain such notions, but they are nearly unanimous in their hostility toward Obama and belief that his policies are moving the country toward socialism. They are also overwhelmingly white,

### Figure 2-1: Barack Obama's Job-Approval Ratings, 2009–2010

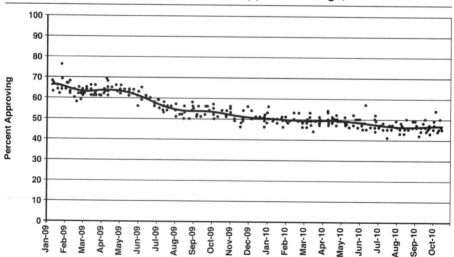

Source: 279 ABC News/*Washington Post*, CBS News/*New York Times*, CNN, CNBC, NBC News/*Wall Street Journal*, AP-GfK, *Newsweek*, Gallup, Ipsos *Los Angeles Times*, *Time*, Bloomberg, Marist, and Pew surveys

**Figure 2-2: Approval of Obama's Performance, by Party**

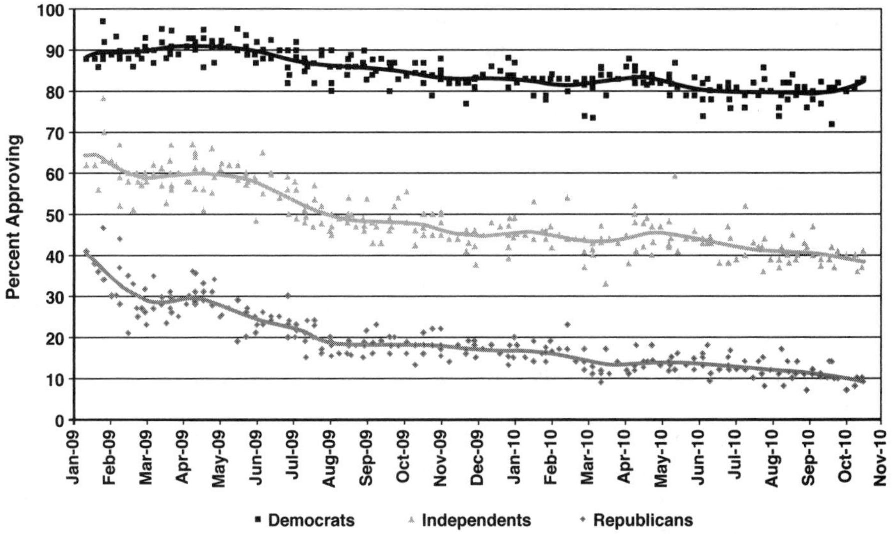

■ Democrats ▲ Independents ♦ Republicans

Source: 224 ABC News/*Washington Post*, CBS News/*New York Times*, CNN, NBC News/*Wall Street Journal*, AP-Ipsos, *Newsweek*, Gallup, and Pew surveys

conservative, and Republican or independent leaning Republican (83–88 percent, depending on the survey). A very large majority of Tea Partiers who voted in 2008 supported John McCain; about two-thirds deny that global warming is occurring or is a threat.[6] Such people would be expected to take a jaundiced view of any Democratic president, but the intensity of their antipathy toward Obama is certainly remarkable.

Tea Party sympathizers join the sizable fraction of Republicans who believe that Obama is not a native-born American and thus is ineligible to be president. The April, 2010, CBS News/*New York Times* poll found 32 percent of Republicans and 30 percent of Tea Party activists saying Obama was foreign born, with only 41 percent saying he was born in the United States.[7] An ABC News/*Washington Post* survey from the same month reported similar results. Responding to a CNN poll taken in July, 14 percent of Republicans said Obama was definitely foreign born, and another 27 percent said he was probably foreign born; only 23 percent said he was definitely born in the United States.[8]

The flames of anti-Obama populism have been fanned vigorously by the conservative voices on talk radio, Fox News, and the Internet. Glenn Beck, a demagogic conspiracy theorist who in calmer times would be dismissed as a street-corner crank, is now a star performer on Fox, with a nightly audience of millions.[9] According to the April, 2010, CBS News/*New York Times* survey, Fox News is the preferred news source for 63 percent of the Tea Party supporters, and 59 percent of them view Glenn Beck favorably (the equivalent figures for the general public are 23 and 18 percent, respectively).[10]

How did a president characterized (accurately) by a moderately conservative columnist as a "center-left pragmatic reformer" advocating "a moderately activist government constrained by a sense of trade-offs" (Brooks 2010)[11] polarize Congress and the country so quickly and so thoroughly? In this chapter, I argue that this has happened for several complementary and related reasons. First, Americans were polarized from the start in their opinions of Obama and his agenda. The outline of the current configuration of political attitudes was plainly visible during the 2008 campaign, and the coalitions supporting and opposing the Obama administration look remarkably like the rival electoral coalitions of 2008 (Jacobson 2011c). Tea Party activists display the same inchoate anger at Obama first observed at campaign rallies for John McCain and Sarah Palin.[12] The attacks on Obama by Republican leaders and conservative pundits basically replay the 2008 Republican presidential campaign, now freed of the burden of Bush's unpopularity and responsibility for the economy.

Second, the economy itself is an important part of the explanation, for the collapse of real estate values, a deep recession, and stubbornly high unemployment have fueled a combination of anger and anxiety that has left many Americans looking for someone to blame and susceptible to conspiracy theories fingering various culprits. Others simply give low marks to all political leaders, including Obama, for bailing out the big banks and other corporations while failing to alleviate the economic distress of ordinary Americans.

Third, Republican leaders made the strategic decision to court the Tea Party enthusiasts and sympathizers rather than trying to broaden their party's appeal to moderates, counting on the anger and energy emanating from the right to revive their electoral fortunes. Obama's health care reform initiative became their focal target on the theory that, as Republican Senator Jim DeMint put it, "If we're able to stop Obama on this, it will be his Waterloo" (Seelye 2009a). Although the legislation passed, it left the public badly divided, with most independents joining Republicans in opposing it. Fourth, inverting the pattern of the Bush administration, Obama's policies toward Iraq and Afghanistan attracted considerable bipartisan support, and his handling of the two wars generated his least polarized popular performance evaluations. But this has done nothing to narrow partisan differences in evaluations of his overall performance, which have been dominated by reactions to his domestic initiatives.

In this chapter, I develop these points through an analysis of public reactions to Obama during his election campaign and through the first two years of his presidency, and I consider how the configuration of public attitudes regarding his administration paved the way for a major Republican victory in the 2010 midterm elections, which is likely to generate even more intense partisan polarization during the remaining two years of Obama's term.

## THE 2008 ELECTIONS

The 2008 elections accurately foreshadowed the configuration of popular responses to the Obama administration. First, Republican identifiers were never attracted to Obama in significant numbers. Party line voting was very high in 2008—at 89.1 percent, surpassed only by 2004's 89.9 percent in the American

National Election Studies (ANES) series going back to 1952—and Obama's electoral coalition contained the smallest share of opposite-party identifiers of any winning candidate in elections covered by the ANES series, just 4.4 percent.[13] Obama won, despite having very little crossover appeal, by inspiring unusually high turnout among Democrats, particularly African Americans and younger voters, and by winning a majority of independents, most of whom had thoroughly rejected the Bush administration. Obama also benefited from a notable decline in Republican Party identification during Bush's second term (Jacobson 2009a, 2009b, 2010a).

Second, a large proportion of voters who were not part of Obama's coalition became convinced during the campaign that he was an extreme, dishonest leftist. This was of course a central theme of the campaign conducted by John McCain, Sarah Palin, and their allies, who sought to offset what was a toxic political environment for Republicans by portraying Obama as a '60s-style radical plotting to turn the United States into a socialist country (Drogan and Barabak 2008; Johnson 2008; Conroy 2008). Although the campaign failed to win the election, it did succeed in shaping Obama's image among people who did not vote for him. The 2008 Cooperative Congressional Election Study (CCES)[14] asked respondents to place themselves and the presidential candidates on a scale where 0 was the most liberal location and 100 was the most conservative location. As Figure 2-3 indicates, the McCain and Obama voters surveyed expressed sharply divergent views of Obama's location on the ideological spectrum. Three quarters of the McCain voters placed him on the extreme left (0–9 points), with a mean placement of 8. Obama voters, in contrast, tended to place him to the left but considerably closer to the center, with a mean placement of 37. McCain voters among the 2008 American National Election Study respondents were not quite so lopsided in their views of Obama's ideology; 41 percent judged him "extremely liberal" and another 34 percent "liberal" on the ANES's 7-point liberal-conservative scale; only 23 percent put him in the middle three categories (slightly liberal, middle of the road, slightly conservative). In contrast, 49 percent of Obama voters in this survey put him in the middle three categories; 7 percent rated him extremely liberal, 32 percent, liberal, and 12 percent, conservative or extremely conservative.

Placements of Obama on these scales were strongly influenced by the respondent's presidential preference and self-designated ideological location (Figure 2-4). The more conservative the McCain voter, the further left he or she tended to place Obama. Among Obama supporters, the relationship between placement of self and Obama was positive; liberals viewed him as a liberal, moderates as a moderate, and conservatives as a conservative. An identical pattern appears among ANES voters (Jacobson 2010c). Obviously, the psychological processes of contrast (among McCain voters) and assimilation (among Obama voters) were powerfully at work here (Sherif and Hovland 1961).[15] One consequence is that conservative McCain voters (comprising 71 percent of McCain voters in the CCES, 73 percent in the ANES) perceived a huge ideological gulf between themselves and Obama: averages of 75 points apart on the 100-point CCES scale, and 4.1 points apart on the 7-point ANES scale. The comparable figures for moderate and liberal McCain supporters were 45 points and 1.1 points, respectively.

# Figure 2-3: Ideological Placement of Obama, by Presidential Vote

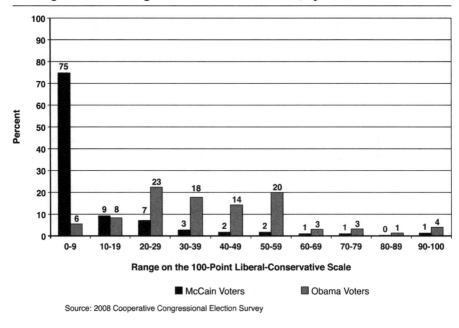

Range on the 100-Point Liberal-Conservative Scale

■ McCain Voters   ▦ Obama Voters

Source: 2008 Cooperative Congressional Election Survey

# Figure 2-4: Perceptions of Obama's Ideology, by Respondent's Ideology (100-Point Scale)

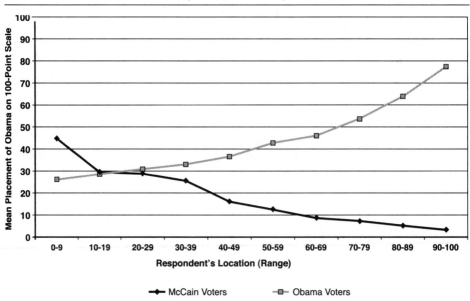

Respondent's Location (Range)

◆— McCain Voters   —□— Obama Voters

Source: 2008 Cooperative Congressional Election Survey

Voters who came to see Obama as an extreme liberal were much more likely to express negative opinions of him. For example, the 41 percent of McCain voters in the ANES survey who pegged him as an extreme liberal rated him on average a chilly 31 degrees on the 100 point feeling thermometer scale, whereas other Republicans rated him at a nearly neutral 48 degrees.[16] (Few Obama voters considered him an extreme liberal, and those who did rated him a couple of degrees warmer on the scale, 89 compared with 87.) McCain voters who considered Obama an extreme liberal were also more inclined to doubt his honesty. The ANES survey asked respondents one of two versions of the usual ANES "trait" battery question asking if "honest" described Obama.[17] Combining the questions, 73 percent of Republicans who considered him an extreme liberal said the word "honest" described him not too well, only slightly well, or not at all well. Among other Republicans, the figure was 46 percent. Altogether, 52 percent of the McCain voters in the ANES considered Obama a dishonest liberal. McCain voters in the CCES were even more likely to see Obama this way. Among those who placed Obama below 10 points on the 100-point liberal-conservative scale (75 percent did so; see Figure 2-3), 95 percent also said they thought he was not honest, compared to 70 percent of McCain voters who thought him more moderate.[18] Altogether, 74 percent of McCain voters (and 68 percent of all Republicans) in the 2008 CCES regarded Obama as dishonest and at the extreme left of the ideological spectrum.

There was also a racial component in negative views of Obama, although its magnitude is difficult to pin down precisely. Racial attitudes, regardless of how they are measured, had a significant effect on voters' preferences in 2008 (Weisberg and Devine 2009), and more so than in previous elections covered by the ANES (Tesler and Sears 2010). The unusually strong relationship between the racial resentment scale—a commonly used measure of racial attitudes developed by Kinder and Sanders (1996)[19]—and the vote in 2008 meant that racial resentment was comparatively high among McCain voters. On a scale of 0 (least resentful, most racially liberal) to 1 (most resentful, most racially conservative), the average McCain voter was at .73 compared to .51 for the average Obama voter. According to Tesler and Sears (2010), racially resentful Democrats strongly favored Hillary Rodham Clinton in the primary, and a large proportion defected to John McCain in the general election.

Among McCain voters, racial resentment was positively related to assessments of Obama as dishonest and as an extreme liberal, and all three of these attitudes were significant predictors of their ratings of Obama on the feeling thermometer scale. According to the regression equation in Table 2-1, McCain voters rated Obama 10 degrees lower if they doubted his honesty, 16 degrees lower if he was considered an extreme liberal rather than a moderate, and 32 degrees lower if the respondent was at the maximum compared to the minimum on the racial resentment scale. Racial resentment also affected ratings of Obama among his own voters, but to smaller degree than for McCain voters; the other variables made little substantive difference.

In sum, a large proportion of voters on the losing side in 2008—the vast majority of them Republicans or conservative independents leaning Republican—

**Table 2-1: Ratings of Obama on the 100-Point Thermometer Scale, 2008 ANES**

| | McCain Voters | | Obama Voters | |
|---|---|---|---|---|
| | Coefficient | Robust S.E. | Coefficient | Robust S.E. |
| Doubt Obama's honesty (1,0) | −10.8*** | 2.1 | −2.1 | 1.6 |
| Obama's perceived ideology (7-point scale, 7 is extreme liberal) | −5.2*** | 1.1 | −.9** | .3 |
| Racial resentment scale (0.0–1.0) | −32.3*** | 5.2 | −12.9*** | 2.4 |
| Constant | 101.7*** | 6.3 | 97.9*** | 2.08 |
| Adjusted R² | .27 | | .06 | |

**p<.01; ***p<.001

had by Election Day come to regard Obama as the McCain-Palin campaign had portrayed him: as an untrustworthy leftist radical with a socialist agenda.[20] There was also an undertone of racial animosity, broadened in Obama's case by the spread of rumors that he was not even born in the United States and was a Muslim. As noted earlier, the former belief evidently remains quite common among Republicans. The latter belief was expressed by an average of 16 percent of McCain supporters in eight surveys taken during the campaign season and remained at that level among Republicans respondents when the question was asked again in March, 2009.[21] Since then it has actually risen, reaching 31 percent and 46 percent, respectively, in Pew and *Time* surveys taken in July and August, 2010.[22]

Obama's victory naturally rattled people subject to such beliefs. One notable reaction was a sharp increase in the purchase of guns and ammunition, leading to reported national shortages of both (McGreal 2009). Requests to the FBI for background checks (required for new gun purchases) were 29 percent higher in the year following Obama's election than in the year preceding it.[23] Although Obama took pains during the campaign to pledge support for Second Amendment rights—Democrats have long since learned that gun control is a losing issue in some important swing states—a majority of gun owners have come to believe that he will try to ban gun sales during his presidency (Newport 2009a).

## OBAMA AND THE ECONOMY

These attitudes and beliefs were not conjured out of thin air by Obama's Republican opponents. The combination of Obama's own background and traits, and the nature of the economic crisis and the government's actions to manage it, could hardly have been better designed to incite a right-wing populist antipathy and anger. An African American (his father Kenyan, his mother a white American) carrying a foreign-sounding name with "Hussein" in its middle, Obama also has an Ivy League education, a detached manner, and a cerebral approach to politics. As a child he lived for several years in predominantly Moslem Indonesia. He began his political career as a community organizer on Chicago's South Side and maintained links with local black activists and leaders, some with fairly radical views, including his long-time minister, Rev. Jeremiah Wright. Obama thus vibrated the racist, xenophobic, anti-intellectual, and anti-elitist as well as the anti-liberal strands lurking within right-wing populism. In short, it was almost guaranteed that Obama would become an object of derision and fear among identifiable segments of the American public. But it took the economic crisis and deep recession to expand the ranks of the intensely anti-Obama camp beyond this endemic fringe.

The banking crisis and ensuing recession, along with the government's response to it, were bound to provoke anger among ordinary Americans. The housing price deflation that began in late 2006 left millions of families with negative equity in their homes, rendering billions of dollars in sub-prime mortgages worthless; by the summer of 2008, financial institutions heavily invested in mortgage-backed bonds were on the brink of collapse. The credit markets froze, hammering stocks and eventually plunging the economy into a deep recession with massive job losses, particularly in manufacturing and construction. Millions of Americans saw their homes, jobs, small businesses, and much of their wealth and retirement savings lost or threatened.

The government responded in September, 2008, with a bipartisan plan to shore up the financial system (and eventually Chrysler and General Motors) with a $700 billion rescue package, the Troubled Assets Relief Program (TARP), that gave the federal government unprecedented authority over the financial sector. TARP was not at all popular. Propping up the very institutions whose greed and recklessness had provoked the crisis proved a tough sell. Most Democrats thought it would mainly benefit Wall Street, not ordinary Americans.[24] Republicans objected to its cost and expanded government role in the banking sector. A month after the bill passed, only 32 percent of respondents to the October 19–22 CBS News/*New York Times* poll approved of the bailout, with Republicans only slightly more supportive (35 percent) than Democrats (31 percent). In the 2008 CCES, the bailout was approved by only 18 percent of Republicans, 25 percent of Democrats, and 14 percent of independents.[25]

TARP seems to have worked as planned, but success has not made it any more popular. It stabilized the financial sector, saved Chrysler and GM, and is projected to end up costing taxpayers a small fraction of the $700 billion authorized, if anything.[26] The stock market also rebounded, and by November 2010 the S&P 500 stock index was up 75 percent from its March 2009 low. But with unemployment stuck at high levels and millions of homeowners still underwater on their mortgages, the revival of the banks and Wall Street (along with handsome bonuses for their executives) not only was galling, but fed suspicions that that big business and big government had colluded to stick ordinary Americans with the bill for elite greed and ineptitude. Notwithstanding a broad consensus among economists that failure to rescue the banks would have been much more devastating for jobs, housing, and small businesses, the costs appeared to out-weigh the benefits to much of the public. People who had lost their jobs, homes, and businesses did not see the bailout as benefiting them; people who had kept them because the economic contraction hadn't been even more severe could see no direct evidence that TARP had anything to do with their good fortune. An April 2010 Pew survey found that only 42 percent of Americans believed the "loans to troubled banks" prevented "a more severe crisis," while 49 percent did not.[27] Only 26 percent of respondents in an October 2010 *Newsweek* survey thought the bailout had been good for the country, while 63 percent thought it had been bad for the country.[28]

Because of its origin during the Bush administration, TARP was a bipartisan program, although most congressional Republicans who supported it did so reluctantly.[29] Once they no longer shared responsibility for governing, they were free to disown the unpopular bailout. When Obama turned to dealing with the recession sparked by the banking crisis, partisan lines on economic policy were already firmly drawn. His $787 billion stimulus package—a combination of tax cuts; expanded unemployment and other social welfare benefits; and spending on infrastructure, energy development, education, and health care—passed in February 2009 with no Republican votes in the House and only three in the Senate. The action reinforced the already sizable partisan divisions in public opinion on the bill. In three polls taken before the vote, an average of 70 percent of Democrats and 27 percent of Republicans said they favored it. In four surveys taken in the month after it passed, an average of 86 percent of Democrats but only 25 percent of Republicans favored it.[30]

As with the bank bailout, the benefits of the stimulus package for ordinary Americans were at best ambiguous. It may have saved from 1.4 to 3.0 million jobs, as the Congressional Budget Office concluded,[31] but the unemployment rate was higher in October 2010 (9.6 percent) than it had been when the bill was passed (8.2 percent). Only 33 percent of respondents to a June 2010 Pew survey thought the stimulus had helped the job situation, while 60 percent thought it had not.[32] Most Democrats continued to look favorably on the stimulus legislation as the midterm election approached, with 69 percent of Democrats but only 10 percent of Republicans judging that it had generally been good rather than bad for the country. Independents, however, tended to express negative assessments (40 percent good, 49 percent bad).[33]

## REPUBLICANS' STRATEGIC DECISIONS AND THE HEALTH CARE REFORM BATTLE

After back-to-back electoral losses in 2006 and 2008, the remaining Republican leaders divided into two camps as they debated how to revive their party's fortunes. Minnesota governor Tim Pawlenty articulated the "big tent" alternative: "We've got to be a party that's about addition and not subtraction," fielding candidates who could attract moderate Democrats and independents (Wilson 2009). Presumably, this might include cooperating with Obama and congressional

Democrats on occasion to address the nation's many problems. South Carolina senator Jim DeMint emphatically rejected that approach: "I would rather have 30 Republicans in the Senate who really believe in principles of limited government, free markets, free people, than to have 60 that don't have a set of beliefs" (Leibovich 2010). Those on DeMint's side of the debate argued that the party's real problem was that it had betrayed its conservative principles by allowing government to expand during the Bush administration; salvation would come through a return to small-government fundamentalism. This would require root-and-branch opposition to the domestic initiatives of the Obama administration and Democratic congressional majorities.

The anger and energy manifested by the Tea Party movement, and, more importantly, the election of Republican Scott Brown in January 2010 to the late Edward Kennedy's Senate seat in Massachusetts on a platform opposing Obama's health care plan, effectively settled the debate. Republican House and Senate leaders adopted a strategy of all-out opposition, exemplified by their united opposition to changes in the health care system that, as its Democratic defenders were fond of pointing out, look very much like those Republican presidential aspirant Mitt Romney had pushed through when he was governor of Massachusetts and that Republicans had proposed as alternatives to Bill Clinton's plan in 1993. Republican leaders even adopted some of the Tea Party's apocalyptic rhetoric in denouncing the legislation: House minority leader John Boehner called the struggle over the final vote "Armageddon" because the bill would "ruin our country."[34] His Republican colleague, Devin Nunes of California, declared that with this "Soviet"-inspired bill, Democrats "will finally lay the cornerstone of their socialist utopia on the backs of the American people."[35]

Like other important strands of public opinion during Obama's first 18 months in office, Republican opposition to health care reform was prefigured by opinions on the issue expressed during the 2008 campaign. The 2008 CCES asked, "Do you favor or oppose the US government guaranteeing health insurance for all citizens, even if it means raising taxes?" About 62 percent of respondents said they supported the idea and 38 percent opposed it, so it was generally popular at the time. Partisan divisions were substantial, however, with 88 percent of Democrats, 61 percent of independents, but only 23 percent of Republicans supporting such a plan. More importantly, the distribution of opinion across House voters and districts provided little reason for congressional Republicans to support such a policy. The 2008 CCES, with 32,800 respondents, allows estimates of opinion at the House district level. Figure 2-5 displays the kernel densities for the distribution of district-level opinion on the health care question among four sets of respondents: The dotted lines show the distribution of district-level opinion among all constituents across the set of districts won by Republicans (black line) or Democrats (gray line). The solid lines show the distributions for those respondents who said they voted for Republican or Democratic winner—that is, the voters who formed the electoral constituencies of each party's House delegation.

Taken as a whole, the two parties' constituencies differed only modestly on this question; in the median Democratic district, 65 percent of respondents supported this kind of health care reform, in the median Republican district, it

### Figure 2-5: Distribution of Support for Health Care Reform Across US House Districts, 2008

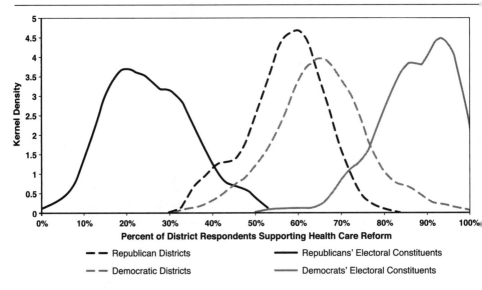

Percent of District Respondents Supporting Health Care Reform

- - Republican Districts          —— Republicans' Electoral Constituents

- - Democratic Districts          —— Democrats' Electoral Constituents

*Note*: The question was, "Do you favor or oppose the US government guaranteeing health insurance for all citizens, even if it means raising taxes?"

was 58 percent. Their electoral constituencies, in contrast, were thoroughly polarized on the issue; a large majority of House Democrats' electoral constituencies strongly favored the idea, while few of the Republicans' electoral constituencies gave it more than minimal support. Partisan divisions that emerged in Congress on the health care issue were thus firmly rooted in district opinion and electoral politics, and it is therefore not surprising that both elite and popular reactions to Obama's health care reform proposals split sharply along partisan lines.

The public as a whole was fairly evenly divided on the extraordinarily complicated legislative package, but people with unfavorable views generally outnumbered those with favorable views of the legislation; on average in 69 surveys taken between the bill's enactment in March 2010 through November of that year, 43 percent favored the legislation, 47 percent opposed it—although some of the latter were unhappy that the legislation did not go far enough (wanting it to include, for example, a "public option"). Partisans' views solidified early and changed little over the months the legislation was working its way through Congress. After its passage, Republicans remained overwhelmingly opposed to the legislation (12 percent in favor, 81 percent opposed), Democrats, predominantly but somewhat less lopsidedly in favor of it (72 percent to 18 percent opposed). The most politically consequential response came from self-identified independents (37 in favor, 51 opposed), whose lack of enthusiasm for the bill was to pose major problem for the Democrats in the 2010 election.[36]

The opposition to the health care package among independents represents a substantial shift from the distribution of opinions expressed on the issue during the 2008 campaign. The 2008 CCES asked a generic question about support for a policy guaranteeing coverage for everyone, even if it meant raising taxes, and the 2009 CCES asked about support for the House-passed version of the bill a year later. Democrats' support for the actual bill was 7 points lower than for the earlier hypothetical proposal (down from 87 to 82); among Republicans, the level of support was essential the same in both surveys (22 and 23 percent, respectively). Among independents, however, support for the actual bill was 17 points lower (dropping from 61 percent to 44 percent), turning a solid majority favoring such a policy in 2008 into a solid majority opposing it 2009.

A review of the extensive polling data on the health care issue suggests an explanation for the bill's low support among independents. Although Americans remain rather evenly divided over the reform package, opinions on its most important elements range from solid approval to solid disapproval. Predictably, majorities tend to like its benefits but dislike its costs. Thus, for example, most people favor requiring insurance companies to cover pre-existing conditions and to continue to cover people who become sick, providing subsidies so that poor families can buy insurance, and requiring employers to provide health insurance to workers. The idea of universal coverage also generally wins majority support. But majorities also tend to oppose components necessary to pay for these features: taxing the most generous health care policies (the so-called "Cadillac" policies), limiting some Medicare reimbursements and increasing some Medicare taxes, and requiring everyone to buy health insurance (so that the risk pool is large enough) and enforcing this requirement through fines.[37] In addition, most people do not see whole package of changes as improving their own health care coverage, even if they believe it will improve the health care delivery system more generally.

However, the most important reservation, at least for people not reflexively opposed to any government action, is that whatever its virtues, the legislation would cost too much, leading to tax increases and adding to the national debt. And it is the prevalence of these reservations among independents that seems to have turned a majority of them against the bill. Observe, for example, their responses to questions regarding the legislation's financial effects in the Quinnipiac poll taken just before the legislation passed (Table 2-2). The views of independents on these questions are much closer to those of Republicans than to those of Democrats; three quarters thought that the reforms would increase their taxes, increase the deficit, and not be worth the cost. Obama thus generally succeeded in persuading his own partisans that the legislation was a good thing (some of them, of course, wanted reform to go further, with a government insurance program to compete with private providers or even a Canadian-style single-payer system), but lost most independents on this issue. Obama "went public" on the issue several times, but his efforts to increase overall public support for his health care proposals were not successful, an outcome consistent with a skeptical view of the bully pulpit's alleged potency (Edwards 2009, 2010).

The health care debate contributed to a more general loss of support for Obama among independents, which was the most significant change in his public standing since the election. Obama had won a majority of independent voters in 2008,[38] but as Figure 2-2 indicates, his approval rating among independents fell

### Table 2-2: Opinions on Costs of Obama's Health Care Reform Package (Percentages)

| Proposed changes in the system: | Democrats | Republicans | Independents |
|---|---|---|---|
| Are too expensive | 27 | 82 | 62 |
| Will increase my health care costs | 27 | 81 | 60 |
| Will increase the taxes I pay | 51 | 93 | 77 |
| Will increase the federal budget deficit | 52 | 90 | 74 |
| Will hurt the quality of my health care | 10 | 68 | 46 |
| Will help the quality of my health care | 36 | 3 | 12 |
| Will not be worth the cost | 25 | 93 | 74 |

*Source:* "Obama Gets Small Bounce from Health Care Win, Quinnipiac University National Poll Finds; Net Disapproval Drops 9 Points," at http://www.quinnipiac.edu/x1295.xml?ReleaseID=1437 (accessed March 27, 2010).

below 50 percent in the summer of 2009 and was down to about 40 percent in November 2010. Like health care reform, Obama's economic stimulus package was eventually opposed by most independents, including about a quarter of the independents who had voted for Obama in 2008, and unhappiness with these bills cost Obama some support from this group. Obama's approval rate among independents in the 2009 CCES who said they had voted for him was 61 percent for those who opposed either bill and 41 percent for those who opposed both bills; those favoring both bills gave him an 89 percent approval rating, and those supporting at least one, 83 percent.

The debates over Obama's two most important domestic initiatives evidently persuaded the more conservative independents that he was an extreme liberal, which had not typically been their view while he was running for president. Figure 2-6 shows the relationship between the independent respondent's own location on the 7-point ideology scale and the mean placement of Obama on the scale in the 2008 ANES and the 2009 CCES surveys.[39] In 2008, regardless of their own ideology, independents typically considered Obama to be a moderate leaning slightly left of center. A year later, however, independents displayed the same pattern as McCain voters in 2008 (Figure 2-4): the more conservative the independent, the more liberal the placement of Obama; 87 percent of conservative or very conservative independents (comprising 32 percent of independents in this survey) considered him an extreme liberal. And among independents who did consider Obama an extreme liberal—about 47 percent of the independents in this survey—his approval rate was only 5 percent, compared to 68 percent among the other independents. At least within this segment of the public, then, the Tea Partiers' perspective on Obama came to prevail.

## Obama's Wars

Although Americans have become nearly as divided along party lines about Barack Obama as they were about George W. Bush during most of his presidency, the sources of polarization are quite different. For Bush, the strongest polarizing

**Figure 2-6: Perceptions of Obama's Ideology by Independents, 2008 and 2009**

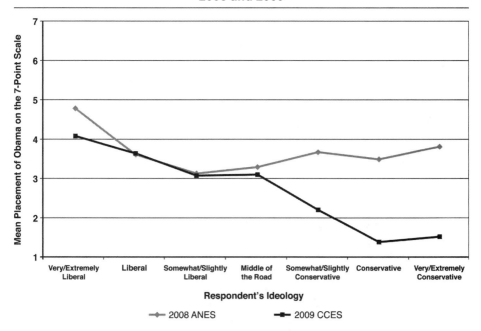

force was his foreign policy, particularly the Iraq War (Jacobson 2011b). For Obama, it has been his domestic initiatives, particularly regarding the health care system; his foreign and military policies have proven notably less divisive. Table 2-3 displays the distribution of opinions on Obama's handling of four policy domains as well as his overall performance in office in polls taken between January and October 2010. Partisan divisions have been widest on health care and economic management, and these are also the domains where Obama receives lowest marks from independents.

**Table 2-3: Approval of Obama's Job Performance, by Party and Domain, January–October 2010  (Percentages)**

|  | All Respondents | Democrats | Republicans | Independents | Partisan Differences |
|---|---|---|---|---|---|
| Overall (120) | 49 | 82 | 14 | 44 | 68 |
| Economy (33) | 42 | 74 | 13 | 37 | 61 |
| Health care (19) | 40 | 70 | 10 | 35 | 60 |
| Afghanistan (20) | 48 | 63 | 33 | 45 | 30 |
| Iraq (10) | 50 | 70 | 33 | 44 | 37 |

*Note:* The number of surveys averaged is in parentheses.

*Sources:* ABC News/*Washington Post,* CBS News/*New York Times,* NBC News/*Wall Street Journal,* Gallup, Quinnipiac, CNN, Pew, Ipsos, *Newsweek,* Marist, and Franklin and Marshall polls.

Divisions are narrowest on Obama's handling of Iraq and Afghanistan, no doubt because his policies toward both have pleased Republicans as much (Iraq) or more (Afghanistan) than Democrats. In keeping with the plan announced early in his term, Obama withdrew most American combat troops by late summer 2010, leaving about 50,000 to train Iraqi security forces, protect US personnel, and hunt down terrorists. Those units are scheduled to leave by December 2011 in accordance with the Status of Forces agreement the Bush administration negotiated with the Iraqi government in late 2008 (Baker 2009b). Republicans had little reason to object to the drawdown because it follows the path laid out by the Bush administration and is consistent with their assessment of Bush's "surge" of 2007–2008 as a great success (Jacobson 2010c). Democrats were generally happy with a trajectory that would extract the US from a war most of them now consider a monumental mistake, although enough Democrats preferred a hastier departure to account for their comparatively tepid approval ratings in this domain.

Obama's Afghan policy has been to expand US involvement. Early in his administration, Obama ordered 24,000 combat and training troops to Afghanistan to supplement the 36,000 American and 32,000 allied NATO forces already there (Colvin 2009). In December 2009, after weeks of well-publicized deliberation, he committed an additional 30,000 troops to the fight, although he also pledged to begin withdrawing US forces in mid-2011 (Stolberg and Cooper 2009). The initial buildup in Afghanistan, fulfilling a Democratic campaign promise, was more popular among Republicans than among Democrats, although at least 60 percent in each partisan category approved (Jacobson 2010b). Republicans were equally supportive of the second escalation in December, but Democrats were not; only a bare majority of them, 50 percent, favored the move. Still, overall public support for the escalation was high, and Obama's approval rating on handling Afghanistan rose from an average of 41 percent in October and November before the buildup was announced to 50 percent over the next six months. His biggest bounce came from Republicans, up 16 points to 36 percent. Among independents, approval was up 11 points to 47 percent, but among Democrats, it was up only a point, to 61 percent.

Obama's Afghan policies left partisans internally conflicted. Republicans' support for the December escalation averaged 70 percent in polls taken in the months after it was announced, 33 points higher than their approval of his handling of the Afghan war, while Democrats' approval of the escalation averaged 49 percent, 14 points lower than their approval of his handling of the war (Jacobson 2010c). Thus many Republicans approved of the president's decisions but not his handling of the war, while many Democrats approved of his handling of the war but not his decisions, a nice illustration of reflexive partisan bias in responses to approval questions. In neither case, however, did opinions on Obama's performance in this domain (or regarding Iraq) have an appreciable effect on his overall approval ratings. According to the entries in Table 2-3, Republicans' approval of Obama's overall job performance averaged 19 points lower than their approval of his handling of Afghanistan and Iraq, while Obama's overall approval among Democrats averaged 19 to 22 points higher than his ratings on the wars. In sharp contrast to evaluations of Bush, then, overall assessments of Obama's job performance were driven by reactions to his domestic rather than his foreign policies, reflecting both his agenda and the economic crisis that dominated American politics during his first two years.

## THE 2010 ELECTIONS AND THEIR IMPLICATIONS

Barack Obama's election to the American presidency was a remarkable historical event, but not all Americans were ready for it. Public reactions to the first two years of his presidency strongly echoed the divisions that emerged during the campaign. Those predisposed to think of him as a radical leftist—mainly Republicans, but now joined by some conservative independents—have taken his economic stimulus and health care initiatives as cases in point. Their intense opposition shaped the strategies of Republicans congressional leaders, who effectively exploited right-wing populist anger in their 2010 campaign to retake Congress. His Democratic supporters, meanwhile, suffered inevitable disappointments with the compromises needed to enact his domestic agenda and with the continuing military involvements in Iraq and Afghanistan. More important, they, like many of the more moderate independents, were also unhappy about the slow pace of the economic recovery and worried about the rising national debt.

The economy was obviously Obama's and the Democrats' biggest problem going into election. Although as late as July 2010, Americans were still twice as likely to blame Bush as to blame Obama for the recession,[40] Obama nonetheless received poor ratings on his handling of the economy (Table 2-3), which a large majority of Americans (62 percent in the exit poll) saw as the most important issue in the 2010 election. If Obama was not blamed for the economy's problems, he clearly failed to convince ordinary Americans that his government's efforts to mitigate them had helped them. Asked in an August 2010 Pew survey who had been helped by the "federal government's economic policies since the recession began in 2008," respondents ranked the beneficiaries (helped "a great deal" or "a fair amount") this way: large banks and financial institutions, 74 percent; large corporations, 70 percent; wealthy people, 57 percent; poor people, 31 percent; middle-class people, 27 percent; and small businesses, 23 percent.[41] Partisan differences on this question are comparatively small, on the order of 20 percentage points or so; only slightly more than a third of Democrats, for example, think the administration's policies have helped the poor, middle class, and small businesses. With unemployment at 9.6 percent and home foreclosures continuing at record levels, these views are understandable; the administration's argument that the economic contraction and unemployment rates would have been much worse without its actions did little to mollify people continuing to face bleak economic realities.

The configuration of public opinion regarding Obama and his policies posed severe problems for Democrats in the 2010 midterm elections. Although the country as a whole was quite evenly divided about Obama, his disapprovers tended to be more adamant in their views and more motivated to vote than his approvers.[42] This was the reverse of 2006 and 2008, when antipathy to Bush and the Iraq War were powerful motivators for Democrats. Moreover, Obama's success in 2008 was driven by unusually high turnout among black voters, his large majorities among younger voters, and majority support among independents, with positive spillover effects for Democratic congressional candidates (Jacobson 2009b). Young and minority voters tend to be less committed to voting and thus more likely to drop out of the electorate at the midterm, and as we have seen, most independents had turned against Obama.

Democrats faced additional problems in 2010. Presidents have a powerful effect on popular attitudes toward their parties (Jacobson 2009b); one of George W. Bush's contributions to Obama's victory in 2008 was the damage done to the Republican Party image during his second term. By the time Obama took over, his Democrats enjoyed a wide lead on the favorability question ("Do you have a favorable or unfavorable view of the Republican [Democratic] Party?"). Since then, Republican favorability has undergone a modest rebound from its low point while views of the Democratic Party have become substantially less favorable. The Democrats' 19 point advantage on this measure during the first half of 2009 (53–34) had shrunk to 2 points during the second half of 2010 (43–41; for details, see Jacobson 2010c). Marginal changes in mass party identification also track presidential approval quite closely (Jacobson 2009b); with Bush's exit and Obama's approval ratings falling into the middling range, the gains Democrats made in party identification during Bush's second term have been largely erased, at least according to the Gallup party identification series (Jacobson 2010b). Thus the electorate appearing at the polls in 2010 was considerably more favorable to the Republicans than were the electorates in 2006 and 2008.

Together, these circumstances produced a major Republican victory in 2010 that is almost certain to polarize national politics further. A disproportionate share of the House seats Republicans took from Democrats had been held by moderates; Democrats lost 61 of the 123 districts represented by members whose roll call votes placed them to the right of the party's mean ideological location, but they lost only 5 of the 132 districts represented by members ideologically to the left of the party's House mean. Thus the Democrats' center of ideological gravity will move to the left.[43] A majority of the 66 newly elected Republicans were associated in some way with the Tea Party movement, whose supporters hold attitudes that place them solidly in the right wing of the Republican Party (Jacobson 2011c). If they remain loyal to their Tea Party roots, the House Republicans' center of ideological gravity will move to the right. The result would be the most polarized House on record. Moreover, the Republicans' principal objective for the new Congress, openly articulated by Senate minority leader Mitch McConnell, is to make Obama a one-term president. Their vow to repeal Obama's signature health care reforms (as well as to roll back financial and environmental regulations) is part of their strategy for doing so, as they foresee using the issue in their 2012 campaigns to take control of the White House and Senate.[44] Such a strategy would preclude any efforts to improve the complex legislation or, indeed, to cooperate with the Obama administration on anything that might enhance the president's standing with the public. Thus an electorate that professes to detest partisan bickering has unwittingly created the conditions for all-out partisan trench warfare during the remainder of Obama's term.

## APPENDIX: THE CCES

The 2008 Cooperative Congressional Election Study involved 30 teams, each purchasing 1,000 cases, yielding a Common Content sample of 32,800 cases (some additional cases were otherwise provided). For each survey of 1,000 persons, the content of half of the questionnaire was controlled by the individual research team, and half of the questionnaire was devoted to Common Content. Most of the questions analyzed in this paper were taken from the Common Content.

The 2008 CCES survey was conducted over the Internet by YouGov/Polimetrix. The Common Content was asked of 32,800 adults interviewed in August and September 2008 (for the profile data), in October 2008 (for pre-election data), and in November 2008 (for post-election data). The sampling was conducted via YouGov/Polimetrix's matched random sample methodology. It involves a two-stage process. First, a random sample is drawn from the target population. Second, for each member of the target sample, one or more matching members is chosen from an Internet pool of opt-in respondents. Matching is accomplished using a large set of variables that are available in consumer and voter databases for both the target population and the opt-in panel. The idea is to find an available respondent who is as similar as possible to the selected member of the target sample. The result is a sample of respondents who have the same measured characteristics as the target sample. Polimetrix employs the proximity matching method. For each variable used for matching, *distance function*, d(x,y), is defined, which describes how close the values x and y are on a particular attribute. The overall distance between a member of the target sample and a member of the panel is a weighted sum of the individual distance functions on the variables used for matching. For additional details on sample matching see Rivers (2006) and Ansolabehere (2009b).

The 2009 CCES was conducted in November and December using the same methodology as the 2008 CCES; the module used in the analyses reported here included 6,000 interviews. I am obliged to Steve Ansolabehere for providing access to this study.

## NOTES

1. In his election-night victory speech, Obama declared, "In this country, we rise or fall as one nation, as one people. Let's resist the temptation to fall back on the same partisanship and pettiness and immaturity that has poisoned our politics for so long." (http://edition.cnn.com/2008/POLITICS/11/04/obama.transcript/, accessed March 16, 2010.) He subsequently appointed three Republicans to his cabinet, held a number of meetings with congressional Republicans during his first months in office, and actively sought bipartisan support for his major initiatives to stimulate the economy and restructure the health care system. Republicans ended up unanimously opposing both.

2. When regressed on time, the slopes of the independent and Republican trends are identical and nearly 75 percent steeper than the slope for Democrats.

3. Richard Hofstadter, "The Paranoid Style in American Politics," *Harper's Magazine,* November 1964, pp. 77–86.

4. Google "Obama" in conjunction with any of these labels to see how routinely they are used—and defended—on the Internet.

5. In 19 surveys taken between January and October 2010, between 18 and 41 percent said they had a favorable view of the Tea Party movement (average, 32 percent), and 12–50 percent had an unfavorable view of it (average, also 32 percent); the rest were uncertain or did not know enough about it to have an opinion; from NBC News/*Wall Street Journal,* CBS News/*New York Times,* Quinnipiac, Fox News, AP-GfK, and ABC News/*Washington Post* polls available at http://www.pollingreport.com/politics.htm (accessed November 7, 2010).

6. Quinnipiac survey, March 16–21, 2010, at http://www.quinnipiac.edu/x1295.xml?ReleaseID=1436 (accessed March 26, 2010); "Tea Party Shows Prospects; Less So for Sarah Palin," news release, ABC News/*Washington Post,* February 11, 2010, at http://abcnews.go.com/images/PollingUnit/1102a3TeaPartyandPalin.pdf (accessed March 22, 2010); Mark Blumenthal, "A Teacup is 80% (or More) Full," April 6, 2010 (citing CNN and Gallup polls), at http://www.quinnipiac.edu/x1295.xml?ReleaseID=1436 (accessed April 6, 2010); "Tea Party Movement: What They Think," report of CBS News/*New York Times* poll, April 5–12, 2010, at http://www.cbsnews.com/htdocs/pdf/poll_tea_party_041410.pdf (accessed April 15, 2010).

7. "Polls: 'Birther' Myth Persists Among Tea Partiers, All Americans," at http://www.cbsnews.com/8301-503544_162-20002539-503544.html?tag=contentMain;contentBody (accessed April 15, 2010).

8. The ABC News/*Washington Post* findings are reported at http://abcnews.go.com/images/PollingUnit/Birthers_new.pdf; the CNN results are at http://i2.cdn.turner.com/cnn/2010/images/08/04/rel10k1a.pdf (both accessed November 7, 2010).

9. For a sample of Beck's flights of rhetoric, see http://politicalhumor.about.com/library/bl-glenn-beck-quotes.htm (accessed March 24, 2010); by one count reported in July, 2010, since Obama's inauguration, Beck transcripts included "202 mentions of Nazis or Nazism, … 147 mentions of Hitler, 193 mentions of fascism or fascist, and another 24 bonus mentions of Joseph Goebbels. Most of these were directed in some form at Obama—as were a majority of the 802 mentions of socialist or socialism" (Milibank 2010).

10. "Tea Party Movement: What They Think," report of CBS News/*New York Times* poll, April 5–12, 2010, at http://www.cbsnews.com/htdocs/pdf/poll_tea_party_041410.pdf (accessed April 15, 2010).

11. See also Ornstein (2010).

12. For examples, see "Rage rising on the McCain campaign trail," CNN report, October 11, 2008, at http://www.cnn.com/2008/POLITICS/10/10/mccain.crowd (accessed June 22, 2010).

13. If independent leaners are included as partisans, the figure rises to 8.0 percent; only John F. Kennedy attracted fewer (7.1 percent).

14. See the appendix for a description of the 2008 and 2009 Cooperative Congressional Election Studies.

15. "Contrast" occurs when people perceive someone they dislike as having opinions more distant from their own than is actually the case; "assimilation" occurs when people perceive someone they like as having opinions closer to their own than is actually the case.

16. The ANES uses the feeling thermometers to rate all sorts of political figures and groups; the prompt reads, "I'll read the name of a person and I'd like you to rate that person using something we call the feeling thermometer. Ratings between 50 degrees and 100 degrees mean that you feel favorable and warm toward the person. Ratings between 0 degrees and

50 degrees mean that you don't feel favorable toward the person and that you don't care too much for that person. You would rate the person at the 50 degree mark if you don't feel particularly warm or cold toward the person."

17. The variables are V083099f and V083100f in the 2008 ANES.

18. The question stem was, "Do you consider this candidate to be honest?" followed by a list that included Obama.

19. *Racial Resentment* is a summary measure of four 5-point scales (strongly agree to strongly disagree) responding to the following statements: "Irish, Italians, Jewish and many other minorities overcame prejudice and worked their way up. Blacks should do the same without any special favors." (V085143); "Generations of slavery and discrimination have created conditions that make it difficult for blacks to work their way out of the lower class." (V085144); "Over the past few years, blacks have gotten less than they deserve." (V085145); and "It's really a matter of some people not trying hard enough; if blacks would only try harder they could be just as well off as whites." (V085146). Response are coded from most to least supportive of blacks and rescaled to range from 0 (least racially resentful) to 1 (most racially resentful).

20. In a *Newsweek* poll taken October 22–23, 2008, 72 percent of the prospective McCain-Palin voters said that the possibility that Obama's policies might lead to "socialism or redistribution of wealth" was a "major concern," and only 8 percent said it was "not a concern" (the position taken by 73 percent of the Obama voters).

21. The comparable average for Obama supporters was 7.9 percent; from *Newsweek* polls taken May 21–22, June 18–19, and July 9–10, 2008, and Pew polls taken March 19–22, June 19–29, September 9–14, and October 16–19, 2008, and March 9–12, 2009, available through the Roper Center, University of Connecticut.

22. Pew survey, July 24–August 5, reported at http://people-press.org/report/645/; the *Time* poll, August 16–17, 2010, archived at the Roper Center, University of Connecticut available at http://webapps.ropercenter.uconn.edu/CFIDE/cf/action/catalog.

23. Calculated from data at http://www.fbi.gov/hq/cjisd/nics/Total%20NICS% 20Background%20Checks.htm (accessed March 26, 2010).

24. In a CBS News/*New York Times* poll taken September 27–30 2008, 56 percent of Democrats said they thought the bill would benefit "mostly just a few big investors and people who work on Wall Street," while only 37 percent thought it would help "homeowners and people throughout the country." Republicans were split, 48 percent to 46 percent, on this question. Most Democrats wanted the government to provide financial help to homeowners (75 percent), while only 43 percent of Republican agreed.

25. Sixty percent of Republicans, 44 percent of Democrats, and 56 percent of independents opposed the bill; the rest were unsure.

26. Perhaps as little as $89 billion—a modest price for avoiding a replay of the 1930s (Solomon 2010); as of February 2010, the Treasury had already gotten back $162 billion, nearly a third of the total that went to rescuing financial institutions; see Reynolds (2010).

27. Partisans were not particularly far apart on the question; the breakdown for Democrats was 54–37, for independents, 37–58, for Republicans, 35–56; see "Pessimistic Public Doubts Effectiveness of Stimulus, TARP," Pew report, April 28, 2010, at http://people-press.org (accessed April 28, 2010).

28. Critics included a plurality of Democrats and large majorities of independents and Republicans; results of the October 20–21 *Newsweek* poll are reported at http://www .pollingreport.com/business.htm (accessed October 28, 2010).

29. In the House the Democrats split 263–171 for the bill, Republicans 91–108 against. The respective partisan votes in the Senate split 39–3 and 34–15.

30. CBS News/*New York Times* poll, February 2–4, 2009; Gallup poll, February 4, 2009; Pew Center for the People & the Press survey, February 8, 2009; CNN polls February 18–19

and March 12–15, 2009; NBC News/*Wall Street Journal* poll, February 26–March 1, 2009, and ABC News/*Washington* Post poll, February 19–22, 2009.

31. The CBO estimated that the stimulus bill increased the number of full-time-equivalent jobs by between 1.4 million to 3.0 million compared to what employment would have been without it; see Congressional Budget Office.

32. The partisan breakdown was 53–40 for Democrats, 34–59 for independents, 15–80 for Republicans (Dick 2010).

33. October 20–21 *Newsweek* poll at http://www.pollingreport.com/budget.htm (accessed October 28, 2010); the sample is of registered voters.

34. "Boehner: It's 'Armageddon,' Health Care Bill Will 'Ruin Our Country'," The Speaker's Lobby, Fox News, March 20, 2010, at http://congress.blogs.foxnews.com/2010/03/20/boehner-its-armageddon-health-care-bill-will-ruin-our-country/comment-page-3/?action=late-new (accessed April 2, 2010).

35. Speech on the House floor, March 21, 2010, video available at http://vodpod.com/watch/3280104-devin-nunes-health-care-the-ghost-of-communism-a-socialist-utopia (accessed April 10, 2010).

36. Data are averages of 38 Gallup, Gallup/*USA Today*, Quinnipiac, CBS News/*New York Times*, Kaiser Family Forum, NBC/*Wall Street Journal*, *Newsweek*, and Ipsos polls taken between during the first 10 months of 2010.

37. See the extensive compilation of survey questions and responses at http://www.pollingreport.com/health.htm (accessed April 4, 2010).

38. In the CCES survey, 52 percent of independents favored Obama, 44 percent, McCain; in the ANES survey, 56 percent of independents favored Obama, 40 percent, McCain; in the national exit poll, it was 52 percent Obama, 42 percent McCain.

39. Note that the categories are not quite identical (the ANES uses "slightly," the CCES "somewhat" for categories 3 and 5); there is no evidence that this makes any substantive difference.

40. On average in the four surveys that have asked the question this year, 57 percent blame Bush, 28 percent blame Obama; results from the January Quinnipiac and NPR polls and the March Democracy Corps poll reported at the Roper Center's iPoll facility at http://webapps.ropercenter.uconn.edu (accessed April 10, 2010) and the April ABC News/*Washington Post* poll at http://www.washingtonpost.com/wp-srv/politics/documents/postpoll_042810.html (accessed April 26, 2010).

41. "Gov't Economic Policies Seen as Boon for Banks and Big Business, Not Middle Class or Poor," Pew Survey Report, July 19, 2010, at http://people-press.org/report/637 (accessed July 26, 2010).

42. For example, in the three ABC News/*Washington Post* polls taken during the first quarter of 2010, 75 percent of respondents who disapproved of Obama's performance said they disapproved strongly, compared with 59 percent of approvers who said they approved strongly; the comparable figures for disapprovers and approvers of his handling of health care were 84 percent and 60 percent, respectively. In four Gallup polls taken in March, an average of 44 percent of Republicans but only 28 percent of Democrats said they were very enthusiastic about voting for Congress this year; at http://www.gallup.com/poll/127073/Republicans-Move-Ahead-2010-Vote-Congress.aspx (accessed April 14, 2010).

43. Based on the McCarty-Poole-Rosenthal DW Nominate scores for the first year of the 111th Congress; the average DW Nominate score for departing members was -.20, for the remaining members, -0.40 on a scale where -1 is most liberal and 1 is most conservative.

44. Noam Levy, "Republicans Spoiling for a Health Care Fight," *Los Angeles Times*, 15 November 2010, at http://articles.latimes.com/2010/nov/15/nation/la-na-health-congress-20101115 (accessed November 17, 2010).

CHAPTER 3

# Obama and the Public Mood

## Richard W. Boyd

Almost a year to the day after the November 2008 presidential election, a front page story in *The New York Times* reported on the second thoughts of many Iowans about their votes for Obama.[1] My muse is this article, which begins,

> Pauline McAreavy voted for President Obama. From the moment she first saw him two years ago, she was smitten by his speeches and sold on his promise of change. She switched parties to support him in the Iowa caucuses, donated money and opened her home to a pair of young campaign workers.
>
> But by the time she received a fund-raising letter last month from the Democratic National Committee, a sense of disappointment had set in. She returned the solicitation with a handwritten note, saying, "Until I see some progress and he lives up to his promises in Iowa, we will not give one penny."
>
> "I'm afraid I wasn't realistic," Ms. McAreavy, 76, a retired school nurse, said on a recent morning on the deck of her home here in east-central Iowa.
>
> "I really thought there would be immediate change," she said. "Sometimes the Republicans are just as bad as Democrats. But it's politics as usual, and that's what I voted against."

President Obama began his presidency with great expectations and a robust job approval rating of 67 percent in the Gallup poll.[2] Of the nine newly elected first-term presidents in the post–World War II period, only Eisenhower and Kennedy began their presidencies with a higher favorability rating than Obama. By the end of 2009, however, Obama's approval rating had fallen to 51 percent. This 16 percentage point decline in his first year exceeded that of all of

41

the other seven first-term presidents. On the eve of his first midterm election in 2010, Obama's job approval stood at 45 percent. Only Ronald Reagan's approval rating of 42 percent in 1983 was lower at midterm than Obama's. By comparison, Eisenhower's approval rating in October 1954 was 61 percent; Kennedy's in 1962, 61 percent; Nixon's in 1970, 58 percent; Carter's in 1978, 49 percent; George Bush in 1990, 54 percent; Clinton in 1994, 48 percent; and George W. Bush in 2002, 67 percent.

In the 2010 elections, voters swung strongly Republican in congressional and state elections. The November 2010 Political Report of the American Enterprise Institute (AEI 2010) presents a composite measure of seat losses in the Senate, House, gubernatorial races, and state legislative elections for midterm elections since 1914. The 2010 election represents the sixth largest composite defeat for the presidential party during this period. Incumbency offered little protection against this tide in 2010. Strategic votes by moderate Democratic members of Congress against health care reform, the stimulus, or financial regulation may have marginally improved their election prospects (Nyhan 2010), but the scope of the Democratic defeat reflected a national swing against the party. Nate Silver (2010) calls the 2010 election an "aligning election," in that the Democratic congressional candidate's share of the vote in each district in 2010 was highly correlated with Obama's share of the vote in that district in 2008, but with a consistent swing in all districts toward the Republicans. Silver concludes "we have entered a period in which races for Congress have become highly nationalized, and in which few potentially competitive races are conceded by either party and few incumbents are given a free pass. That could mean that we'll continue to see some wild swings over the next several election cycles."

This chapter first analyzes the sources of Obama's victory in 2008. I then interpret the sharp fall in Obama's job approval rating in terms of two related themes. The first theme concerns the multiple meanings of change in election campaigns. What concretely do Obama's victory in 2008 and the Republican resurgence in 2010 imply about American's hopes and fears in domestic and foreign policy and about their judgments on contemporary campaigns and governance? What do Americans really want?

**Theme 1: Four Types of Political Change.** One meaning of change is simply the public's sense that "it's time for a change," as expressed in Obama's campaign slogan, "Change We Can Believe In." Even if George Bush was not on the 2008 ballot, his economic and foreign policies were. By the end of his administration, fewer than 30 percent of the public approved of Bush's job performance. In *The American Voter* (Campbell et al. 1960: 240–244) argued that about a quarter of all voters evaluated the parties and candidates in 1956 merely in terms of "the nature of the times." Alan Abramowitz (2008) has developed a simple "time-for-change" model for predicting presidential elections well in advance of an election. Abramowitz's model incorporates only three predictor variables (p. 211): "the growth rate of the economy in the first half of the election year, the incumbent president's approval rating at mid-year, and the length of time the incumbent president's party has controlled the White House." His explanation includes no information about the policy preferences or qualifications of the contending candidates or the political views of voters, but it is nonetheless useful in anticipating the most likely outcome of an upcoming election. This is a "time for a change" model at its most basic.

Voters who are especially responsive to such a call for change are typically less cognitively sophisticated and knowledgeable than voters who consider the contending policy prescriptions of the candidates. Their resolve to vote against the candidate of the incumbent party is principally a retrospective judgment about the performance of the party in office. Such voters typically do not share any considered views on alternative policies. As V. O. Key, Jr. (1964, 544) described time-for-a-change voters, "The vocabulary of the people consists mainly of the words 'yes' and 'no'; and at times one cannot be certain which word is being uttered." Retrospective performance judgments communicate little useful information to an incoming administration and imply the most limited kind of policy mandate. This description presumably does not characterize Pauline McAreavy or her disillusionment with Obama. She appears, like many other Obama voters, to have expected more rapid progress in concluding the war in Iraq as well as improvements on other policy fronts.

More interesting for our purposes is a second type of desired political change, when voting decisions reflect policy preferences sharpened by the contested stances of opposing campaigns. Health care reform, financial regulation, energy policy, and the Iraq War in the 2008 campaign are prime examples. Such issues move the votes of more sophisticated citizens and more clearly communicate their policy views to a new administration. The newly elected may heed the calls for more policy purism from their party's base, or they may be attentive to policy moderates and party independents, but voters' messages can be clearly ascertained by the newly elected. If these policy-based opinion shifts are durable and favor one party, then the long-term balance of partisan strength will also change. In this chapter, I present evidence that Obama's victory in 2008 did turn on highly contested domestic and foreign policy issues, but also that independents and policy moderates still hold the balance of electoral power in American politics.

A third desire for change may be an aspiration for less negative campaigns and less polarized and partisan governance (Thurber, Nelson, and Dulio 2000). While the white-hot temperature of contemporary politics pleases the party bases, it may be repellant to independents and to policy moderates in both parties. The public may also view the president or one or both of the congressional parties as corrupt and resolve to "throw the rascals out." In the 2008 Cooperative Congressional Election Study (CCES), over half of the respondents marked the economy as the most important problem facing the country. But in second place, ahead of all policy issues from abortion to terrorism, was "corruption in government."

A fourth form of change is a shifting balance of demographic groups in the mass party coalitions. When groups such as Hispanics or Evangelicals sense that their growing numbers increase their political leverage with the parties, demographic change affects political consciousness.

**Theme 2: Party Polarization, Policy Moods, and Public Trust.** A second theme is the tension between the public's expectations about the possibilities of political change and the partisan polarization of policy beliefs in America. On the one hand, Lloyd Free and Hadley Cantril (1967) famously argued that Americans are ideological conservatives, but operational liberals. That is, while Americans identify themselves predominantly as conservatives, they support many liberal social policies. To be sure, Free and Cantril were measuring the political beliefs of Americans during a very liberal policy mood in the mid-1960s (Stimson 1999).[3] A nation that had just witnessed the Johnson administration's achievements in securing the Civil Rights Act in 1964, the establishment of Medicare in 1964, and the Voting Rights Act in 1965 had every reason to believe that the federal government could successfully shepherd major policy change. As James Stimson (1999) shows, the US has subsequently moved through cycles of conservative and liberal policy moods.

The 1960s was also the period in which Americans faith in the competence and trustworthiness of its political leaders began its long erosion. (See, for example, the trust in government index from the American National Election Studies.[4]) Trust in the federal government, which had peaked in 1966, fell sharply in the 1970s, and, except for brief revivals in Reagan's first term, Clinton's second term, and George Bush's first term, Americans have remained largely cynical about the character and competence of national leaders.

Reflecting at the time on this erosion of political trust, William A. Gamson (1968) and Philip E. Converse (1972) noted that what was new about popular attitudes in the 1960s and 1970s was the emergence of many voters who felt politically competent and effective but who also mistrusted public officials. Such voters, Converse suggested (pp. 334–337), created a "prime setting for the mobilization of discontent." To this epiphany, Arthur Miller (1974) added that the growth of disaffection was centered among voters who were well to the left or well to the right on such major policy issues as Vietnam, the economy, race, and social welfare issues. Miller labeled these voters as "cynics of the right" and "cynics of the left." The cynics of the left, Miller noted, preferred more social change; the cynics of the right, more social control. Disaffection was thus rooted in the opposition of both the left and the right to centrist government policies (Boyd 1974). Political activism and mistrust were mutually reinforcing. Gerald Pomper (1972) showed convincingly that voters' political beliefs had become increasingly joined to their partisan identification from 1956 to 1968 on a range of domestic policy issues, including medical care, school integration, job guarantees, and federal aid to education.

The themes in these early analyses of the relation of policy dissatisfaction to political disaffection have resurfaced the contemporary debate on whether American voters are increasingly polarized on intractable economic and social policies. Fiorina, Abrams, and Pope's engaging *Culture War?* (2006) argues that the center of political gravity is located in the moderate middle, even on such hot-button issues as abortion and homosexuality. While elites may be polarized on these issues, most Americans have, he argues, views that are contingent, qualified, and largely unconnected to the highly politicized combat among the elite "political class."

Taking up Fiorina's challenge, Pietro Nivola and David Brady (2006, 2008) have edited two volumes on whether the political beliefs of American voters are increasingly polarized. The contributors present persuasive evidence that even though most Americans are not to be found on the policy extremes, they are nonetheless well sorted out into the two major party camps. Gary Jacobson (2008) and Alan Abramowitz (2010) offer extended evidence that on a range of domestic and foreign policy issues, the political beliefs of self-identified Democrats are now predominately liberal, just as those of Republicans are conservative.

Are Free and Cantril correct in describing Americans as operational liberals who support many federal policy initiatives? And with what political consequences? Marc Hetherington (2005) contends that declining trust in political leaders and institutions undermines popular support for liberal policy initiatives. Ruy Teixeira (2010) and Karlyn Bowman (2008) have reviewed a large number of recent surveys that expose the contradictory feelings that Americans express about their national government. Teixeira's conclusion is captured in his report's title, "The Public Opinion Paradox: An Anatomy of America's Love-Hate Relationship with Its Government." As operational liberals (pp. 1–2), "Americans want more government action in key areas such as health, poverty, law enforcement, and improving the environment." But, "polls reveal the U.S. public lacks trust and confidence in government, and believes it is inefficient, unresponsive to ordinary citizens, and often hurts more than it helps."

The public's ambivalence about its government is evident in its continued skepticism about Obama's most important achievements in domestic policy: health care reform, the economic stimulus package, and the new financial regulation law. A June 2010 survey by the Pew Research Center[5] shows that Obama's job approval ratings were positive only for energy policy and for foreign policy, the latter typically a strength of Republican presidents. His approval ratings were negative for his handling of the economy, health care, the budget deficit, and immigration policy (p. 6). On issue after vexed issue, the public disapproves of current federal policy but is ambivalent about any alternatives. For example, 81 percent of the respondents agree that "there need to be stricter laws and regulations to protect the environment" and 52 percent oppose "allowing more offshore oil and gas drilling in U.S. waters." However, only 49 percent agree that "people should be willing to pay higher prices to protect the environment" (p. 2). Moreover, the region most opposed to the Obama administration's moratorium on offshore drilling includes the Gulf states most affected by the BP oil spill.

Similarly, the Pew survey respondents approve by nearly a two-to-one margin Arizona's new immigration law that "requires police to verify the legal status of someone they have already stopped or arrested if they suspect that the person is in the country illegally." However, these respondents also favor by the same two-to-one margin "providing a way for illegal immigrants in the U.S. to gain citizenship if they pass background checks, pay fines and have jobs." A majority opposes amending the constitution "so that the parents must be legal residents of the U.S. in order for their newborn child to be a citizen" (p. 2). The Pew survey also shows a growing partisan division on whether "immigrants are a burden on the country" and whether "immigrants threaten U. S. customs and values" (p. 21). In a climate in which policy views are so conflicted and confidence in the good faith and competence of presidents and members of Congress has so eroded, Americans may no longer support controversial policy initiatives even when the "national mood" may be increasingly supportive of such policy changes.

## The 2008 Cooperative Congressional Election Study

I examine Obama's victory through an analysis of the 2008 Cooperative Congressional Election Study.[6] The Internet-based CCES survey combines a very large sample of 32,000 respondents with a two-wave, pre- and post-election interview design.[7]

The vote decision model is adapted from the Michigan School's "funnel of causality" (Campbell et al. 1960, 24–32), as subsequently refined by Miller and Shanks (Miller and Shanks 1996, 192). In this model, voters' socioeconomic and demographic characteristics influence their long-term partisan and ideological self-identifications, which in turn influence their policy preferences. Voters' policy views affect their judgments of the performance of the current administration and help determine their final vote decisions. A fuller analysis with supporting statistics is available at the author's web page.[8] In this chapter, I highlight the findings that bear most directly on the public's reactions to the Obama candidacy and his first two years as president.

## Social, Economic, and Demographic Characteristics

**Sex.** Sixty percent of women voted for Obama, compared to only 48 percent of men.[9] This gender gap first emerged in the Reagan victories, when the Republican Party platform embraced its pro-life position and withdrew support for the Equal Rights Amendment. This gap persists even when the differing incomes and marital states of women are taken into account.

**Ethnicity.** Ninety-seven percent of non-Hispanic blacks voted for Obama, compared to 64 percent of Hispanics and 45 percent of non-Hispanic whites. When Obama announced his campaign, many black political and civil rights leaders were initially skeptical that white voters would support a black candidate. Before the caucuses concluded in predominately white Iowa, many of these leaders either withheld their endorsements or publicly endorsed Hillary Rodham Clinton. After Obama's victory over Clinton in Iowa, most shifted to vocal and proud support, and black voters around the nation shifted as well.

Obama's race was a net positive for his candidacy. The white vote remained steadily supportive of Obama throughout the perturbations of the nomination and general election campaigns. According to the national exit polls since 1972, only 40 percent of whites have on average voted for the Democratic candidate in the general election. Overall (i.e., the bivariate relationship of race to the vote),

43 percent of whites voted for Obama, a percentage matched only by President Clinton in his easy re-election victory in 1996 since national exit polls were introduced in 1972. Obama won a greater share of the white vote in 2008 than did Kerry in 2004 or Gore in 2000. As Paul Sniderman and Edward Stiglitz (2008) argue in their post-election analysis, the number of genuinely prejudiced whites is more than matched by whites who hold blacks in esteem. This positive racial view increased support for Obama, particularly among otherwise moderate and conservative Democrats, who often disagree with their national party on policy grounds.

To be sure, Obama did not win a majority of the white vote, but no Democratic candidate has done so since Lyndon Johnson's landslide victory in 1964. My interpretation of Obama's support among white voters is that they viewed Obama's candidacy as a way to express to themselves and others that they considered themselves to be racially tolerant. They were pleased to interpret Obama's victory as evidence that they were ready to put America's stained legacy of race relations to rest. Obama's multi-racial background and his success in positioning himself as a leader of all Americans had the consequence of making racial considerations no more important in 2008 than in any other elections of the post–civil rights era.

The exceptionally large sample size of the CCES permits good estimates of the votes of smaller ethnic groups. Fifty-four percent of Asian Americans voted for Obama, or about the same rate as Americans overall. Most interestingly, only 32 percent of Native Americans voted for Obama, which is the lowest of any of the ethnic groups in this study. This low vote level is controlled for the Southwestern residence of most Native Americans, which was second only to the Southeast as the most pro-McCain of any of the five regions.

**Religion and Religious Observance.** Although the Democratic advantage among Catholics that dates to the New Deal coalition continues to erode, Obama still enjoyed a seven percentage point advantage among Catholics, compared to Protestants, with all other social and economic variables controlled. The large sample size of the CCES permits us to estimate vote probabilities for Jews and Mormons, each of which comprise about two percent of all voters. At 68 percent, the Jewish vote was 31 percentage points more Democratic than Mormons, the most pro-McCain of the religious groups.

More important than denominational differences, however, are voters' habits of religious observance. I created a standardized factor score from two items: "How important is religion in your life?" and "Aside from weddings and funerals, how often do you attend religious services?" I include Religious Observance among the first-stage demographic variables because it is closely joined to the acquisition of religious identity itself. I define a more religiously observant voter as one who is one standard deviation more observant than the mean and a less observant voter as a person who is one standard deviation less observant than the mean. Only 37 percent of the more religiously observant voted for Obama. Seventy percent of the less observant voted for Obama, a 33 percentage point difference. The importance of religious observance in contemporary American politics is striking, as we shall see in the later discussion of its impact on moral traditionalism and the vote.

**Material Interests.** The political effects of material interests (family income, employment status, union membership, home ownership, and marital status) are all important, even when each is controlled for the influence of the others. Obama's vote share was 10 percentage points higher among the poorest income quintile than among the richest. The unemployed were nine percentage points more likely to vote for Obama than the employed. A person in a household with at least one member in a union was also about nine percentage points more likely to vote for Obama than someone in a household without a union member. Renters were nine percentage points more likely to vote for Obama than people who owned their homes or apartments. Single (never married) respondents were nine percentage points more likely to vote for Obama than married ones. The cumulative importance of all of these factors that influence material well-being on the vote is quite striking.

**Age and Education.** When their socioeconomic and demographic attributes are statistically controlled for each other, voters' material interests, identities, and affiliations mattered much more than their age and education. The difference in support for Obama between voters with a grade school education and those with some college was only two percentage points. Obama support was distinctively higher only for those with a four-year college or a post-graduate degree.

The effects of age matters least of all. Voters under 30 scarcely differed in their votes from those over 60, once the other social and economic variables are taken into account. Much has been made of the potential significance of the mobilization of young voters in the 2008 election.[10] Similarly, older voters are currently seen as the recruiting pool for the Tea Partiers united in opposition to Obama. To be sure, 67 percent of the respondents under 30 did vote for Obama, while 53 percent of voters in their 60s and 61 percent of voters over 70 voted for McCain. But age differences mattered little in the full vote model. Age is politically relevant only to the extent that it is associated with the politically more important elements of one's economic and social life circumstances, such as income, employment, marital status, and religious observance.

## Partisan and Ideological Identifications

Voters' long-term partisan and ideological identifications are always strongly related to their vote decisions, even controlled for their socioeconomic and demographic attributes.

First, we present the 2008 vote probabilities for each category of party identifiers (controlled for all other socioeconomic variables and ideological identification) and their share of the 2008 electorate:

*Percent 2008 Obama Vote*
93%      Strong Democrats (30% of the 2008 voters)
82%      Weak Democrats (20%)
51%      Pure Independents (8%)
17%      Weak Republicans (18%)
3%       Strong Republicans (22%)

And the same breakdown for ideological identification:

*Percent 2008 Obama Vote*
83%      Very Liberal (9% of the 2008 voters)
79%      Liberal (18%)
60%      Moderate (30%)
32%      Conservative (21%)
19%      Very Conservative (14%)

Two elements of the 2008 vote bear emphasis: First, Obama won a surprising percentage of the center-right in 2008. Majorities of pure independents and ideological moderates voted for Obama. Even those who viewed themselves as conservative or very conservative gave healthy shares of their votes to Obama. Conservatives were more likely to vote for Obama than liberals to vote for McCain. As we shall shortly see, these independents and moderates switched strongly to the Republicans in 2010, creating the national GOP surge in Congressional and state races.

Second, a corollary to Cantril and Free's dictum that many Americans are ideological conservatives but hold liberal policy views is that many more Americans identify themselves as Democrats than think of themselves as liberals. In 2008, 50 percent of the voters identified themselves as Strong or Weak Democrats, but only 27 percent identified as liberals. Ideological moderates outnumber partisan independents by more than 4 to 1, which explains much of this disparity. Little wonder that Democratic candidates proudly declare their partisan affiliation, but typically describe themselves as "progressives" rather than "liberals." Who doesn't believe in progress, after all?

## POLITICAL AND MORAL POLICY PREFERENCES IN 2008

The 2008 CCES survey includes many questions measuring people's policy preferences. I have reduced these items to a set of four underlying policy dimensions: views on the proper federal role in social welfare, moral traditionalism, preferences on means of reducing budget deficits, and conditions justifying the deployment of US troops abroad.

**Social Welfare and Moral Traditionalism.** The social welfare and moral traditionalism dimensions are standardized factor scores, with means of 0 and standard deviations of 1. Respondents' social welfare factor scores derive primarily from questions on affirmative action, increasing the minimum wage, health insurance for children, federal assistance in housing, guaranteed health care, and withdrawing troops from Iraq (the last being viewed by most respondents presumably as a desire to focus economic resources on domestic social welfare needs rather than on military deployments abroad). Scores on the moral traditionalism factor derive primarily from survey items on abortion, stem cell research, and support for a proposed amendment to ban gay marriage.

Figure 3-1 displays the exceptionally strong relationships of social welfare and moral traditionalism to the 2008 vote. For example, even controlled for voters' socioeconomic position and their partisan and ideological identification, moderate social welfare liberals (defined as voters one standard deviation more liberal than the mean) voted 88 percent for Obama. Comparably moderate social welfare conservatives voted only 16 percent for him. Moral traditionalism was as strongly related to voters' support for Obama as their views on social welfare policy, as Figure 3-1 clearly shows.

**Budget Policy.** The CCES survey gauged people's views on balancing the federal budget by asking them to choose their most preferred and least preferred of three options: cutting defense, cutting domestic spending, and raising taxes. Conservative budget policy preferences are defined as support for cutting domestic spending and as opposition either to raising taxes or to cutting defense. Liberal budget preferences are defined as opposition to cuts in domestic spending and as support for either cutting defense or raising taxes. Only 38 percent of fiscal policy conservatives voted for Obama, compared to 77 percent of fiscal policy

**Figure 3-1: Social Welfare, Moral Traditionalism, and the Obama Vote**

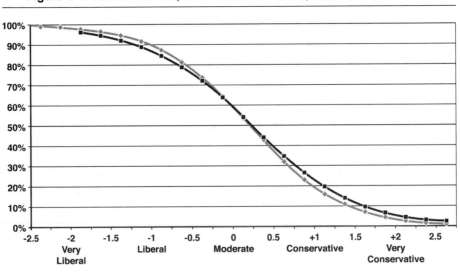

liberals, a difference of almost 40 percentage points. It is worth noting that 52 percent of the CCES respondents were fiscal conservatives by this measure, and only 24 percent were fiscal liberals, a conservative advantage on budget and fiscal issues of more than two to one.

**US Troops Abroad.** The CCES survey included several questions on conditions justifying the use of US troops abroad. I formed a standardized factor score from responses to four such conditions: "to destroy terrorist camps," "to intervene in a region where there is genocide or a civil war," "to protect American allies under attack by foreign nations," and "to help the United Nations uphold international law." As before, moderate supporters and moderate opponents are defined as voters whose policy views are one standard deviation above or below the mean. Moderate opponents of committing US troops under the listed conditions voted 62 percent for Obama, compared to only 45 percent among those who were moderate supporters of committing US troops in these circumstances. Although the relationship of opinion on committing US troops abroad was not as strongly related to the Obama vote as opinions on social welfare, moral traditionalism, and fiscal issues, people's policy views on the deployment of US troops in foreign conflicts influenced the 2008 vote substantially.

PERFORMANCE JUDGMENTS AND ECONOMIC EXPECTATIONS: THE ECONOMY, THE IRAQ WAR, AND THE BANK BAILOUT

This set of policy issues includes voters' judgments about the performance of the Bush administration in the context of their expectations about an Obama or a McCain presidency. These retrospective and prospective judgments are activated as the general election campaigns move into full swing. Our model includes four performance judgments from the 2008 CCES: consumer confidence in the current economy, consumer confidence in the economy's near future, opinion on US commitment to the Iraq War, and opinion on the 2008 bank bailout.

**The Economy.** Confidence in the current economy was measured by three items: the performance of the national economy "over the past year," people's ratings of "the present general business conditions" in their area, and their perceptions of the number of "available jobs" in their area.

Confidence in the economy's future prospects was measured by people's expectations about business conditions "six months from now." These expectations focused on "general business conditions," "jobs," and "total family income."

People's confidence in the current economy was neither substantively important nor statistically significant in explaining their vote decisions. Instead, it was their degree of optimism about the state of the economy six months into the future that moved vote decisions. Voters who lacked confidence that the economy would improve (i.e., those one standard deviation or more below the mean) voted 59 percent for Obama. Voters with higher confidence in the future economy voted only 48 percent for Obama. This 11 percentage point difference is important, especially when we remember that an absolute majority of all voters in the CCES survey rated the economy as the most important problem facing the country.

**The Bank Bailout.** From September 7 to 19, 2008, the public was shocked by the gravity of the crises in the housing and financial markets (Campbell 2008). The Bush administration determined to seize ownership of the government sponsored mortgage institutions, Fannie Mae and Freddie Mac. Lehman Brothers, the large bond firm, declared bankruptcy. At the federal government's urging, Bank of America absorbed Merrill Lynch as major banks came under great financial pressure. A reluctant President Bush proposed a $700 billion financial bailout program, which Congress convened to consider.

During this crisis, Senator McCain suspended his presidential campaign in order to participate in his party's consideration of President Bush's bailout initiative. He unsuccessfully proposed postponing the first presidential debate to free time for his involvement. However, he offered no alternative to Bush's proposal and played no leadership role in his colleague's deliberations.

Fifty-three percent of voters in the CCES survey opposed the bank bailout legislation compared to only 21 percent who supported it. One would have expected that many of the voters who opposed the president's bailout proposal would have shifted to Obama. However, people's views on the bank bailout at the time were not statistically related to their votes. Both opponents and supporters of the bailout voted for Obama at about the same rate. Thus, we are left with the puzzle that people's retrospective judgments on the bank bailout did not contribute more importantly to Obama's victory in 2008, given the fact that in the 2010 campaign the Tea Party activists made Bush's bank bailout and Obama's stimulus package primary examples of federal overreaching.

**The Iraq War.** In contrast, the Iraq War was much more influential for the 2008 vote than the bank bailout. The CCES survey tried to capture people's contingent and ambivalent feelings. Many people wished to support the troops and to justify their sacrifices, even while doubting the official justifications for the war. Others believed that the decision to go to war was right, even if the decision had been informed by faulty intelligence about Iraq's capacity to produce weapons of mass destruction or about the presence of al-Qaeda in Iraq. The survey asked respondents to choose between five competing statements on positions on the war.

The plurality of CCES voters (43 percent) agreed with the unqualified statement, "The Iraq War was a mistake from the beginning; it never should have been started, and the U.S. should withdraw now." These voters supported Obama at a rate of 77 percent. Only among this group did Obama win a majority of the vote.

Two other statements were endorsed by more ambivalent voters. Eleven percent agreed "The Iraq War was a mistake, but since the U.S. did invade Iraq, it has been worth the cost in American lives and money to avoid a failure that would be even worse for the U.S." Another 15 percent believed that "The U.S.

was right in going to war in Iraq, but mistakes made following the invasion made the results too costly in American lives and money to be worth it." These two groups voted 44 percent and 48 percent for Obama, respectively.

Thirty percent of the voters gave more unqualified endorsement of America's war aims. Of these, 23 percent agreed "The U.S. was right in going to war in Iraq, and despite mistakes following the invasion, the results have been worth the cost in American lives and money." Seven percent more agreed that the US was right in going to war and "made no serious mistakes following the invasion." These two groups of war supporters voted only 25 percent and 26 percent for Obama, respectively. In sum, people's retrospective judgments on the merits of President Bush's commitment to the Iraq War had a striking impact on their final votes, even controlled for all other variables influencing the vote.

### PARTISAN POLARIZATION, POLITICAL CHANGE, AND TRUST IN GOVERNMENT

Almost certainly, the shift in voter sentiment in 2008 that led to Obama's victory depended importantly on the high disapproval ratings of the Bush administration. In this sense, 2008 was similar to Reagan's first election victory over President Jimmy Carter in 1980. By the end of President Carter's first term in 1980, voter anger was at a boiling point over the combination of high unemployment and high inflation. His Republican challenger, Ronald Reagan, needed only to persuade an uncertain public that he was a competent alternative to Carter. This Reagan accomplished in the presidential debates. Similarly, voters saw Obama as winning all three of the 2008 presidential debates (Pomper 2010). Reagan's 1980 victory reflected in part the voters' conclusion that Carter's economic policies had failed and that a qualified challenger from the opposition party could be trusted to govern. In this interpretation, Reagan's victory did not necessarily imply that most voters endorsed his conservative policy principles.

Initial examinations of the 2008 exit surveys led some analysts to conclude that Obama's victory mirrored Reagan's win in 1980. That is, Obama owed his victory primarily to voter dissatisfaction with the economy and with Bush's performance as president, not to Obama's proposals on health care and other policies. For example, Gerald Pomper (2010, 68) argues,

> The fundamental causes were set months before the party conventions, the debates, and the campaign maneuvers. The voters' verdict was a retrospective negative judgment of the Republican administration. It resembled similar past elections, grounded in the public's economic discontents (as in 1932), its wish for a change in political parties (as in 1952), and the unpopularity of the president (as in 1980).

Yet, the 1980 and 2008 elections were not simply retrospective judgments about the failures of the Carter and Bush presidencies. James Stimson (1999) has established that voters' views on domestic issues track a long cycle of conservative and liberal "policy moods." As we see in Stimson's graph (Figure 3-2), Reagan's victory in 1980 came at the conclusion of a shift from 1968 onward toward more conservative policy views.[11] Similarly, the public's growing policy liberalism since 2000 contributed to Obama's election in 2008. Obama's victory reflected voters' policy hopes, and not just their negative appraisals of the Bush presidency.

Stimson's chart is suggestive of a broad pattern in postwar American elections. Voters do not typically elect the party out of power to the presidency until the policy mood that supports this change has almost run its course. Although Stimson's time series does not extend back into the 1940s, one imagines that a comparable graph for the policy mood then would show a growing conservative policy trend all during the 1940s, after a liberal trend in the 1930s. Eisenhower's victory in 1952 likely came just as the conservative policy mood of the 1940s had reached its maximum and shifted in a liberal direction. Kennedy in 1960 was elected only at the conclusion of the 1950s liberal trend, which remained predominantly liberal until Nixon's election in 1968. Reagan in 1980 began his administration just as the 1968–1980 conservative policy trend shifted back in a liberal direction. Clinton's victory over George H. W. Bush in 1992 came just as the 1980–1992 liberal trend reached its peak and a shift to conservatism ensued. George W. Bush's victory in 2000 coincided with a shift toward policy liberalism. An immediate shift to conservatism in 2009 followed Obama's election in 2008. It is as though Captain Obama, like his predecessors, called for the spinnaker just as the favoring wind stalled.

The recurrent pattern is so regular that it invites competing explanations of cause and effect. Are elections a "lagging indicator," with a change in the

**Figure 3-2: James Stimson's Cycle of Policy Moods, 1952–2009**

presidential party coming only when the supporting shift in policy mood has fully matured? Or, do incoming administrations wrongly interpret their policy mandates and, by the unpopular policies they initiate, actually cause the policy mood to shift against them? Secondly, what set of voters initiate the shift in mood? Are they those on the policy extremes, such as the liberal Vietnam dissidents in the late 1960s and the current conservative Tea Party activists? Or, do partisan independents and policy moderates shift the balance of liberal and conservative policy sentiment?

To the second question, Stimson argues that policy moderates are the key to shifts in the policy mood cycle (p. 123).

> The moderate electorate alternately experiences "too left" policies from one party and "too right" policies from the other.... As the parties constantly miss the center in their policies, the electorate constantly pulls back in that direction. The moderate electorate as a result produces a negative feedback, always moving left when the government moves right and moving right when the government moves left.... In the long run the counter-movement of public opinion enhances the likelihood of cyclical change of government, with parties alternating in power, neither ever able to hold on to it for lengthy periods.

If Stimson is correct on the second question, then he has presumably answered the first question as well. Presidents cause the policy mood to shift against them by governing against the grain of the moderate policy center.

Yeats wrote, "Things fall apart; the centre cannot hold." Yet, in US electoral politics, the left and right prevail only temporarily. Newly elected administrations champion the policy preferences of the coalition that supported them, which are typically more extreme than the policy views of independents and policy moderates.

Consider, for example, the social welfare policy views of Republicans and Democrats in Figures 3-3 through 3-6. As Figure 3-3 shows, the great majority of Democrats are social welfare liberals, just as the large majority of Republicans are social welfare conservatives. On social welfare provision, the modal Democrat and the modal Republican stand more than two standard deviations apart. When the party bases differ so markedly, each is prepared to hold their party's presidential and congressional candidates accountable for any deviation away from their liberal or conservative policy preferences on the federal role in social welfare provision.

Although abortion, stem cell research, and gay rights have not been politically contested for as long as social welfare policy, partisan division on these religious and cultural issues has been a feature of presidential contests since 1980. On the moral traditionalism dimension in Figure 3-4, the modal Democrat and the modal Republican are again more than two standards deviations apart in their policy views.

Compare the political views of independents in Figures 3-5 and 3-6 to those of Democrats and Republicans in Figures 3-3 and 3-4.

The social welfare policy preferences of independents are substantially more centrist than those of Democrats or Republicans. Though independents appear

## Figure 3-3: Federal Role in Social Welfare Policy
## by Party Identification

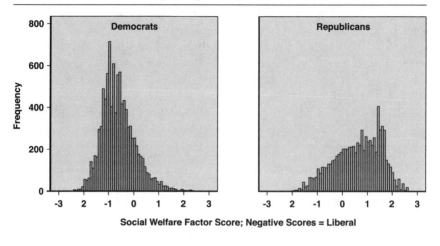

Social Welfare Factor Score; Negative Scores = Liberal

## Figure 3-4: Moral Traditionalism by Party Identification

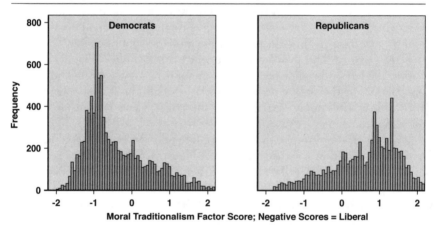

Moral Traditionalism Factor Score; Negative Scores = Liberal

in Figure 3-5 to be more liberal than conservative, the median independent is located at −.03 on the social welfare factor score, or very close to the overall mean social welfare policy view.

On the moral traditionalism dimension in Figure 3-6, the policy preferences of independents are closer to those of Democrats than to Republicans, but independents are again more centrist on abortion, gay rights, and stem cell research than Democrats or Republicans.

Similarly, independents stand midway between Democrats and Republicans on approaches to a balanced federal budget. Nearly nine of 10 Republicans have a conservative fiscal view. That is, if balancing the federal budget is a priority,

**Figure 3-5: Independents' Views on Social Welfare**

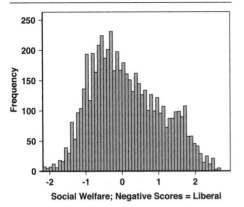

Social Welfare; Negative Scores = Liberal

**Figure 3-6: Independents' Views on Moral Traditionalism**

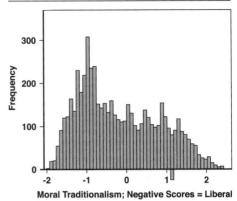

Moral Traditionalism; Negative Scores = Liberal

Republicans would rather do so by cutting domestic expenditures than by raising taxes or cutting the defense budget. Only a quarter of Democrats hold this view. Independents are again more centrist. Half of independents share the conservative budget preferences of Republicans. Half have liberal or mixed policy preferences.

The partisan polarization of both voters and their elected representatives in Congress creates a dynamic in which there is little electoral incentive for either party to cooperate with the other on legislation. In the House of Representatives and the Senate, members vote the policy views of their electoral bases, rather than court more centrist independents and policy moderates. Policy moderates in the electorate grow increasingly dissatisfied, and their confidence in both the president and the parties in Congress erodes. The policy mood reverses course against newly elected presidents, and mistrust of the institutions of governance hardens.

The journalists John F. Harris and Jim VandeHei describe this dynamic in these terms:[12]

The Flight of the Independents

Obama sees himself as a different kind of Democrat, one who transcends ideology but is basically a centrist. By some measures, his self-image fits. His war and anti-terrorism policies are remarkably similar to those advocated by the man he blames for most of the country's problems: George W. Bush. He's butting heads with the teachers unions by enticing states to quit rewarding teachers on tenure instead of merit. On immigration, he stresses border security instead of amnesty for illegal immigrants.

But on the issues voters care most about—the economy, jobs and spending—Obama has shown himself to be a big-government liberal. This reality is killing him with independent-minded voters—a trend that started one year ago and has gotten much worse of late. On the eve of his inaugural address, nearly six in 10 independents approved of his job performance. By late July of 2009—right around the time Obama was talking up health care and pressuring Democrats on cap-and-trade legislation—Independents started to take flight.

Many never returned. For the first time in his presidency, Obama's approval among Independents dropped below 40 percent in the past two weeks, according to the widely respected Gallup surveys.

This "flight of the independents" accounts for both the Democratic wave in the 2006 congressional elections and the Republican wave in 2010, according to the national exit polls (Pew 2010). The proportions of Democrats and Republicans voting in the two congressional elections held steady from 2006 to 2010. Republican voters supported Republican House candidates at rates of 91 percent in 2006 and 95 percent in 2010. Similarly, 93 percent of Democratic voters in 2006 and 92 percent in 2010 supported Democratic candidates. But in 2006, independents preferred Democratic House candidates 57 percent to 39 percent. In 2010 independents reversed this division almost exactly: 55 percent voted for Republican House candidates; only 39 percent for Democratic candidates.[13]

## REVOLT OF THE MODERATES OR OF THE POLICY EXTREMISTS?

This emphasis on the pivotal role of independents and policy moderates is not in tension with the earlier argument that political disaffection is particularly characteristic of voters on the policy extremes—i.e., very liberal Democrats and very conservative Republicans. If Stimson is correct, independents and policy moderates tend to react negatively to the policy agenda advanced by newly elected presidents, causing a shift in the aggregate policy mood, the alternation of party control of the presidency, and electoral losses for the president's party in Congress in midterm elections. The movement of independents and policy moderates affects the balance of party control of the presidency and the Congress.

In contrast, the policy disaffection of very liberal Democratic voters and very conservative Republican voters manifests itself in ideological fights in the primaries, rather than in the general elections. The Tea Party insurgency is a prime example. The Gallup poll (2010) headlined its July 2, 2010, report on Tea Party adherents thus: "Tea Party Supporters Overlap Republican Base: Eight of 10 Tea Party Supporters are Republicans." Based on a September 2010 YouGov poll, the *Economist* reported (2010) that "the [Tea Party] movement's supporters are older, whiter, richer and far more likely to be Republican than Democrat." The Tea Party is the conservative wing of the Republican Party rebranded for enhanced market appeal. National Tea Party leaders such as 2008 Republican Vice Presidential candidate Sarah Palin and Republican Senator Jim DeMint (SC), among other movement leaders, endorsed conservative challengers to incumbent Republican Senators Lisa Murkowski of Alaska and Bob Bennett of Utah. Murkowski lost in the Republican primary (though she prevailed in the general election as a write-in candidate) and Bennett lost in a pre-primary Republican state convention vote. With Tea Party backing, Sharron Angle in Nevada, Ken Buck in Colorado, and Christine O'Donnell in Delaware won

Republican Senate primaries, but all three lost in the general elections, running behind other state-wide Republican candidates and perhaps costing Republicans the opportunity in 2010 to control the Senate. The influence of the Tea Party thus far has been to pressure more mainstream Republican office holders to move to the right to protect themselves from future primary challenges by more conservative Republicans. The Tea Party, like the liberal Democratic dissidents of the Vietnam era, will push the policy centers of gravity of the congressional parties further apart, but it is not clear that the movement will affect the electoral balance between the parties or the overall public policy mood as much as independents and policy moderates do.

A large body of scholarship now addresses the causes and consequences of increasing issue polarization among voters and members of Congress on major policy issues (Abramowitz 2010; Hetherington 2009; Hetherington and Weiler 2009; Jacobson 2008; Kamarck 2009; Nivola and Brady 2006, 2008; Pildes Forthcoming).

We should expect partisan issue polarization to continue to typify campaigning and governing. The United States is a mature party system. The policy views of members of Congress are closely aligned with those of the party bases in the electorate. This feature of our party system is not new. It is the contemporary form of a politics that took root in the late 1960s and continued to develop over the ensuing half century.

## Effects on Trust in Government

When ideologies, partisanship, and policy views are so tightly linked and consequential, polarization and mistrust in elected leaders are mutually reinforcing. Galston (2010) has recently asked, "Can a Polarized American Party System Be 'Healthy'?" It is a question worth pondering. A virtue of this party system is that it can deliver policy change, particularly when a party has united control of Congress and the presidency. During Obama's first regular congressional session, with minimal support from congressional Republicans, the Obama administration succeeded in passing his major legislative priorities, including health care, the stimulus package, and financial regulation. In the Lame Duck session following the 2010, Obama added even more legislative successes: a compromise package extending the Bush tax cuts and unemployment insurance, the repeal of the Defense Department's "Don't Ask, Don't Tell" policy; a food safety bill, the 9/11 First Responders bill providing free medical treatment and compensation; and the Senate ratification of the New START nuclear arms reduction treaty.

Yet, legislative victories have not sustained the public's confidence in Obama, in Congress, or in the congressional parties. So it has been since the late 1960s, long before today's talk radio and politicized television. Through shifts in partisan control of national institutions and through liberal and conservative policy moods alike, voters have remained mistrustful and disaffected. Political discourse takes on a hard, mean-spirited edge. Suspicion is not reserved only for the political opposition. The party bases are also quick to turn on their own parties' representatives in Congress if they appear to stray from the party line or to cooperate legislatively with the opposition party. Obama hoped he could raise the quality of political discourse and increase trust in leaders and institutions. This aspiration will likely prove elusive, both for his administration and for his successors.

## NOTES

1. *The New York Times,* November 3, 2009, p. 1.
2. Weekly Gallup ratings. http://www.gallup.com/poll/124922/Presidential-Approval -Center.aspx. The presidential job approval ratings quoted here are measured at three points: the first poll after inauguration, the last poll in December of the first year in office, and the last poll in October before the November midterm election.
3. See Figure 3-2 later in this chapter, with Stimson's updates to his trends on the cycles of liberal and conservative domestic policy moods through 2009. In spite of the fact that the policy mood cycles into conservative as well as liberal periods, Stimson still thinks it is sensible to describe Americans as operational policy liberals. Even during increasingly conservative policy moods, the trend line typically stays above the 50 percent liberal level. This was true in the 1960s. The trend in policy mood was conservative beginning in 1968, but the overall policy mood was on balance still liberal. In contrast to the cyclical character of policy mood, the proportion of people who identify themselves as conservatives or liberals is remarkably constant over time and therefore does not vary in concert with the policy mood cycle. See, for example, Michael J. Robinson, "Static America: Myths about Political Change in the U.S.," Pew Research Center, September 27, 2010. The fact that self-identified conservatives have consistently outnumbered self-identified liberals since at least 1972 is the basis for the claim that Americans are ideological conservatives and that the US is a "center-right" nation.
4. http://www.electionstudies.org/nesguide/graphs/g5a_5_1.htm.
5. "Growing Opposition to Increased Offshore Drilling: Obama's Rating Little Affected by Recent Turmoil," Pew Research Center for the People & the Press, June 24, 2010. http:// people-press.org/report/?pageid=1744.
6. I am indebted to Professors James Thurber of the Center for Congressional and Presidential Studies at American University and Brian Schaffner of the University of Massachusetts for providing access to the common content of the 2008 election study and to Stephen Ansolabehere of Harvard University for assistance with the final codebook.
7. A full description of the project is available at http://web.mit.edu/polisci/portl/cces/ index.html. Ansolabehere, Stephen, Cooperative Congressional Election Study, 2008: Common Content. [Computer File] Release 1: February 2, 2009. Cambridge, MA: M.I.T. [producer]."
8. http://rboyd.web.wesleyan.edu/profile/boyd.htm.
9. This is verbal shorthand. What this really means is the probability of women voting for Obama is .60, controlled for all of the other socioeconomic variables introduced previously or at the same stage in this multistage vote model. This formulation should not be confused with the actual bivariate vote of men and women for Obama. In the simple bivariate cross-tabulation of gender and vote, 58% of women in the 2008 CCES survey voted for Obama, compared to 50% of men. I will use this verbal shorthand throughout this discussion. When I specify a vote division for Obama, I always mean the probability of an Obama vote controlled for all other variables in the model introduced by that point.
10. In "Save Us Millennials," Op-Ed column, *The New York Times,* June 3, 2010, Timothy Egan rhapsodizes, "The young were Barack Obama's strongest supporters, and still are...."

They were wise beyond their years and ahead of every other generation on the major issues—from offshore oil drilling (not so fast), to gays in the military (duh), to tolerance of the new ethnic stew (you mean that's still a problem).... You would never know, with the nightly images of jowly Tea Partiers and their inchoate discontents, that people ages 18 to 29 years old made up a larger percentage of the 2008 electorate than those over 65." Similarly, Andrew Kohut of the Pew Research Center writes, "The third important element of this election was the age gap—the divergence between the candidate preferences of the youngest and oldest voters was the widest in decades, perhaps ever. More young voters, those 18–29, have now moved into the Democratic column in three consecutive national elections—2004, 2006, and 2008—than in the three previous comparable elections." See Pew Research Center Publications, "Post-Election Perspectives," November 13, 2008.

11. See Stimson's updated chart from 1952 to 2009 in Figure 3-2 at http://www.unc .edu/~jstimson/. I gratefully acknowledge his permission to reprint this chart. The vertical bars in the chart are standard errors. Stimson regards 1964, 1980, and 1994 as three mandate elections. "The 1964 and 1980 cases represent the high points, liberal and conservative, respectively of policy mood (p. 114)."

12. In Politico.com, July 15, 2010. http://dyn.politico.com/printstory.cfm?uuid=D58D428A -18FE-70B2-A80D4E80D221BD8A.

13. The summary of the 2010 national exit poll is from an early November 3, 2010 release. The final poll figures may differ marginally.

# Chapter 4

# Obama's Personality and Performance

## Stephen J. Wayne

Character matters. It is the foundation upon which personal beliefs are built and an operating style developed. Beliefs and style, in turn, shape decisions and actions. They are not the only factors that affect how presidents decide and what they do, but they are always omnipresent and rarely irrelevant.

Character is relatively stable. For politicians, particularly elective officials, positions on policies shift with the political environment and the public mood. Not so with character. It is more difficult to change even when trying to do so. That is why it is necessary to study character and its cognitive and behavioral derivatives to understand how a particular president operates in the presidency.

Take a look at Obama's decisions and actions. Why did he take so long to make a policy decision to commit 30,000 more troops in Afghanistan? Bush did so instinctively. Why did Obama, who believes vision to be his key policy-making role, delegate the details of his key policy initiatives in health care, energy independence, and environmental improvement first to White House aides and then to members of Congress? Why would a president who advocates major change be so preoccupied with finding common ground? Why would a transformational leader adopt a transactional style of doing business?

The answers to these questions have to do with tensions and contradictions within Obama himself. They also have to do with the constitutional system in which an American president has to operate, the political climate in which

Obama found himself, and continuities and shifts in public opinion within a democratic society. This chapter discusses those character, environmental, and situational issues and their impact on President Obama's decisions and actions during his first two years in office.

## CHARACTER FORMATION

When Obama was 10 years old, his biological father visited him for the first time during the Christmas holidays. In *Dreams From My Father,* Obama describes an incident during that visit in which his father demanded that he stop watching television and do school work. "I tell you Barry, you do not work as hard as you should. Go now, before I get angry at you." (Obama 1995, 68). Unable to reply, Obama later wrote, "I felt as if something had cracked open between all of us.... I began to count the days until my father would leave and things would return to normal" (Obama 1995, 67–68).

The experience was traumatic for the young boy. It punctured the myths he had created about his father and reinforced the comfort and security of established familial relationships with his mother and maternal grandparents. The experience also heightened the resentment he felt toward his father's self-interested and self-promoting behavior, his dad's refusal to take his marital and parenting responsibilities seriously, and the senior Obama's overly opinionated, non-compromising attitude.

Genes are powerful. Obama displays the intellect of his parents: his father was one of the first young Africans to study in the United States, attending the University of Hawaii and Harvard, and his mother received a PhD in anthropology from the University of Hawaii. Obama possesses the ambition, articulateness, and self-confidence of his father and the social consciousness and humanistic inclinations of his mother. However, Obama's style of interacting with others is very different from that of his parents, particularly his father.

- Obama is a listener; his father was a talker who rarely listened.
- Obama is a conciliator; his father was a bossy man who had to have things his own way.
- Obama adapts easily and effortlessly to new environments and situations in which he finds himself, much more like his mother than his father. In fact, his adaptive skills have contributed substantially to his political successes.
- Obama is an idealist and a pragmatist who seeks policy change through a search for common ground; he is willing to compromise, whereas his father dominated discussions and held strong and, for the most part, uncompromising beliefs and opinions.

Obama's conciliatory manner, cool temperament, and laid-back manner also differentiate him from his biological father. That style, however, has not always produced the desired result. On occasion, it has made Obama look weak and distant as president. The perception of weakness, obviously not a desirable one for an ambitious politician and government leader, such as Obama, has forced him to compensate with harsh rhetoric. If pushed to the limit, he resists and fights back, although he prefers others around him to flex their muscles on his behalf.

In situations in which his political ambitions were directly challenged, however, as they were by former Illinois representative Alice Palmer, Rev. Jeremiah Wright, and indirectly by his pledge to accept government funds for the general election if his Republican opponent did the same, Obama responded forcefully and unequivocally. When Illinois State Legislator Alice Palmer, whose seat he was seeking in 1996, asked him to step aside after she was defeated in the Democratic primary for Congress, he refused to do so and went so far as to challenge the signatures on her petition to get on the ballot, a challenge that was successful.

When the Rev. Jeremiah Wright defended what Obama described as incendiary remarks at a speech at the National Press Club, Obama repudiated the Reverend and cut his ties with a man he considered a personal and family friend, who had presided over his marriage to Michelle, baptized him and his children, and with whom he had socialized on occasions.

Although as a presidential candidate he had indicated that he would accept federal funds for the general election if the Republican nominee did the same, he opted out of this pledge when he realized that he would have a significant fund-raising advantage with private funding.

Similarly, in situations in which his legislative priorities were threatened, he used both the carrot and the stick to get his way. He gave three Republican senators, Susan Collins, Olympia Snowe, and Arlen Specter, the specifics they wanted in return for their support of his massive economic stimulus bill known as the Recovery and Reinvestment Act (2009). When Senate Democrats lost their 20 vote advantage after a special election in Massachusetts to fill the seat of the late Edward Kennedy, he invited Republican and Democratic leaders to a public health care summit. When no agreements were reached at the summit, he met with Democratic leaders to fashion a legislative strategy, supported the use of parliamentary tactics to avoid a Senate filibuster, and compromised as many of the details as necessary to gain sufficient support for the legislation.

In general, Obama evidences less pugnacity on the details—they are always subject to negotiation—than on the priorities themselves, such as his economic recovery program, health care reform, and increased regulation of banking and investment firms, credit card companies, and the health insurance industry, priorities which were, for the most part, non-negotiable.

The reasons for Obama's flexibility on policy specifics stems from three factors: a generalist, Obama defers to the expertise of others in substantive areas in which he is not as knowledgeable; a visionary leader, he wants to set the goals and contours of policy without being responsible for or burdened with all the details; and a consensus builder, he is open to compromise, but as a president who wants to leave a legacy, Obama cannot compromise the goals themselves. Being flexible allows him to define victory.

## Basic Beliefs

Obama's beliefs are a product of his identity quest in his teen and pre-adult years. In his search for roots, he encountered different cultures (Indonesia, Hawaii, and the continental US), races (black and white), and ethnicities. He interacted with many of them, found roots in some of them, but only in one of them, the United States of America, did he find acceptance, opportunity, and ultimately contentment and success.

What Obama likes about America is its relatively peaceful heterogeneity. How to bridge the diversity gap on the basis of a common historic, philosophic, and political tradition is the lesson he took from his understanding of the American experiment and experience, the country's successful integration of diverse peoples into a vibrant, democratic society.

Obama points to common values and beliefs as the glue that holds the country's social fabric together. Those values and beliefs provide opportunities for its citizenry to live their American Dream. However, Obama is painfully aware that those opportunities have not been equal for everyone, as he indicated in his initial public response to the arrest of Harvard Professor Henry Louis Gates by Cambridge police in the summer of 2009:

> I think it's fair to say, No. 1, any of us would be pretty angry; No. 2, that the Cambridge police acted stupidly in arresting somebody when there was already proof that they were in their own home; and No. 3, what I think we know separate and apart from this incident is there is a long history in this country of African Americans and Latinos being stopped by police disproportionately. That's just a fact (Obama 2009a).

Despite the negative stereotyping and discrimination he has studied, witnessed, and personally experienced, Obama still has faith in the evolving fairness of the American system.

Obama's faith in the system is congruent with his operating style and his personal skills of conciliation and compromise. Conciliation accords with his belief in an ordered society governed by the rule of law, his psychological need to overcome his own rooted diversity by discerning common values and beliefs in the communities in which he has lived and worked, and his political goal of unifying a divided nation by building and maintaining dominant electoral and governing coalitions.

Compromise holds another virtue for Obama. It makes him seem level-headed, practical, flexible, and reasonable, unlike his predecessor, George W. Bush, who was viewed as ideological, stubborn, and uncompromising.

But compromise also has its limits. It has adversely affected Obama's leadership image as president and the capital that flows from that image. To some, compromise suggests weakness, not strength; pliancy, not firmness. It can also convey a lack of confidence in one's own judgment. Why compromise a sound decision unless compromise is the only way to achieve the desired result?

Despite Obama's goal of transforming public policy, the means he uses to achieve that goal are transactional, one transaction at a time. Compromise is a major inducement for buying into the final product. In this sense, he has maintained his legislative orientation of how to build and maintain a governing majority.

Despite the president's orientation to achieve major policy change, he seems to be in a perpetual search for common ground. In fact, consensus building often takes on as much importance as the policy objective itself. For Obama, reasoning together and arriving at a collective judgment is valuable because it bonds participants in a deliberative process and builds support for the policy because of the collective manner in which it was formulated.

Leading a public consensus also contributes to public approval. Together, consensus and policy approval demonstrate the underlying values and beliefs of American democracy. In his book, *The Audacity of Hope,* Obama writes that democracy is "not ... a house to be built ... but a conversation to be had" (Obama 2006, 92). That conversation is ongoing with public policy decisions continually adjusted as new information becomes available, new conditions emerge, and new ideas begin to take hold.

### *Role of Government*

In contrast to his Republican predecessors, especially Ronald Reagan and George W. Bush, Obama has an expansive view of government. He is not a socialist as some Republicans claim, but he does support a greater use of government to solve the nation's problems than they did and do.

Obama sees three principal roles for government:

- Government is necessary during crises, such as the economic downturn that began in the fall of 2008. He saw it as the only force with the power to "jolt the economy back to life" (Obama 2009c).
- Government has an obligation to constrain and hopefully prevent economic, environmental, social, and political abuses from occurring and undermining a system based on individual initiative, private enterprise, and self interest, hence his support of increased regulatory activity, new climate standards, and expanded medical (stem cell) and scientific research.
- Finally, and most controversially, government has a responsibility to reduce the differential in wealth and opportunity that have persisted over the years. Progressive taxes and credits, expanded health insurance coverage, and increased support for veterans reentering civilian society are ways in which the social resources can be distributed more fairly. In *The Audacity of Hope,* he writes:

> I am angry about policies that consistently favor the wealthy and powerful over average Americans, and insist that *government has an important role in opening up opportunity to all* [Italics mine] (Obama 2006, 10).

In discussing America's culture and values, he noted:

Like many conservatives, I believe in the power of culture to determine both individual success and social cohesion, and I believe we ignore cultural factors at our peril. But I also believe that *our government can play a role in shaping that culture for the better—or for the worse* [Italics mine] (Obama 2006, 63).

Obama's critics perceive government-initiated redistribution as unwise, unfair, and unamerican; Obama sees it as fair play, as an important foundational component of American democracy.

## Progressive Pragmatism

Obama is progressive. He desires policy change, campaigned on that theme, produced a large policy agenda, and achieved the enactment of much of it. He also wanted to transform partisan politics but has been unable to do so. He is not a revolutionary. He values history, traditions, and communities too much to be one. He has liberal policy inclinations and a conciliator operating style; he needs to get along and wants to bring people together.

Obama is a pragmatist and sees himself as a commonsense decision maker. He keeps his eye on reality, on the doable, not necessarily the optimal. Pragmatism conforms to his belief in how and why the American experiment succeeded. It is also consistent with his personal success in adapting to new conditions and environments and with his personal achievements within the political sphere.

Obama has little tolerance for absolutists (such as his father), "true believers" (such as Alan Keyes, his Illinois Senate opponent in 2004), and ideologues (such as George W. Bush and Dick Cheney) because of the difficulties of reasoning with them. They know "truth" and use it to stifle and end debate. In *The Audacity of Hope,* he notes, "it's precisely the pursuit of ideological purity, the rigid orthodoxy, and the sheer predictability of our current debate that keeps us from finding new ways to meet the challenges we face as a country. It's what keeps us locked in 'either/or' thinking" (Obama 2006, 40).

## Resilient Optimism

Obama's own achievements, particularly in school, law, and politics, have led to his optimistic outlook. He sees himself as successful, the embodiment of the American Dream, a model for others, particularly those who emigrated to the United States for a freer, better, and more fulfilling life. Obama writes, with characteristic immodesty, "what I have come to understand is that my mere presence before these newly minted Americans serves notice that they matter, that they are voters critical to my success and full-fledged citizens deserving of respect" (Obama 2006, 261).

Being optimistic is important for Obama. It confirms that his personal achievements were the results of making the most out of opportunities, not simply luck. Secondly, optimism imbues people with enthusiasm, which is a motivation for greater involvement in civic responsibilities and political activities. That involvement is central to Obama's belief in the merits of participatory democracy; the activism fueled his presidential campaign and justifies his political pursuits.

Optimism is also good politics, as Ronald Reagan found out. It contributes to positive performance evaluations so long as it is consistent with perceived reality. In 2009 and 2010, however, it was not. The weak economy muted Obama's optimism and produced a perceptions gap between the president's words and actions on one hand and the consequences of those actions on the other. The electorate reacted angrily to unrealized expectations in the 2010 midterm elections by voting a relatively large number of incumbents out of office. From the perspective of the voters, the president's vision had not been achieved.

## OPERATING STYLE

### *Cognition*

Obama's legal training influences how he thinks. Rigor, logic, and rationality structure his thought process. He tries not to let emotions affect his policy judgments or his reactions to people and events. In fact, he usually keeps his emotions well buried and out of public view. When he ran for national office, he seemed a bit embarrassed by his own revelations of teen and pre-adult behavior in *Dreams From My Father,* attributing those youthful actions to "his mixed racial background and an excess of youthful hormones."

Obama enjoys and thrives on the challenge of problem solving. He has considerable synthetic and analytic capabilities. He reads voraciously books, briefing papers, newspapers, and letters, usually until the late hours of the night. He describes himself as "a practical person, somebody who, I think can cut through some very complicated problems and figure out the right course of action" (Kroft 2008).

Making good policy judgments on complex issues requires a lot of information from a variety of sources with multiple perspectives and ideas. It also requires considerable time, a flexible mindset, and the ability to cut to the chase. When asked at a presidential news conference why he took several days to react publicly to the bonuses given to top executives by AIG, a company that had to borrow $173 billion from the federal government just to survive, Obama snapped: "It took us a couple of days because I like to know what I'm talking about before I speak" (Obama 2009b).

Although he is not afraid of making difficult decisions, he is afraid of making mistakes. Most of his decisions are risk averse. He plays it safe. His desire for consensus removes the most controversial items from his wish list and contributes to his penchant for compromise.

### *Decision Making*

Obama adheres to an elaborate and time-consuming decision-making process in which he identifies and assembles policy experts, listens as they debate the issues, asks tough questions, and requests the opinions and recommendations of everyone in the room. He casts a wide and deep net for information and advice.

The decision to send 30,000 additional troops to Afghanistan illustrates the process and product. It took Obama three months and 10 meetings with his national security and foreign policy advisers before he arrived at a final decision. And when he did, he required unanimity among his senior advisers before he was willing to issue a public policy statement. According to Bob Woodward, Obama needed to push back against recommendations and manipulative actions of senior military officers by reasserting civilian control and preventing the military leadership from undercutting the president's decisions later on (Woodward 2010, 326–327).

Similarly, the president's dismissal of General Stanley McChrystal because of remarks that he and his senior staff made that were critical of the vice president and civilian authorities prosecuting the war was another instance in which Obama had to impose his authority in order to maintain the unity of the United States' war effort in Afghanistan.

Once Obama makes a decision, he usually sticks with it; he is careful not to let peripheral changes in the political environment overturn previously considered political, policy, or even personal judgments, except, of course, when he has no other alternative, such as with his nomination of former Senate Majority Leader Tom Daschle to be secretary of the Department of Health and Human Services as well as his chief health reform adviser.

*Communication*

Obama is his administration's chief spokesman. He enjoys communicating and is good at it. For Obama, words have power and have given him power. They allow him to show off his "smarts," which is part of his mystique. The knowledge he displays reinforces the confidence he projects in his judgments; that knowledge and confidence contributes to the confidence people have in his intellectual abilities.

As a communicator, Obama is extremely disciplined. He is cautious with his words, although a few ad lib remarks and failed jokes have hurt him and taught him to keep to his script. He can talk without a teleprompter but rarely does so in public. He seems spontaneous but is usually well scripted and well rehearsed.

Once a professor, always a professor; Obama likes to teach and seeks teaching moments for the American people, such as his speech on race or his West Point address on Afghanistan. He believes that presidents have an obligation to explain the reasons for their actions and to educate the public. George W. Bush did not share that belief. Bush believed that actions speak louder than words. To *Newsweek*'s Jon Meacham, Obama stated:

> ... one of the things I've actually been encouraged by and I learned during the campaign was the American people, I think, not only have a toleration but also a hunger for explanation and complexity, and a willingness to acknowledge hard

problems. I think one of the biggest mistakes that is made in Washington is this notion you have to dumb things down for the public (Meacham 2009).

Information is also a critical component in a deliberative democracy. A proponent of participatory politics, Obama believes that informed debate not only results in better judgments, but it also generates a more civil tone. Civility, in turn, contributes to compromise, which is consistent with Obama's conciliator style and his desire to maximize support for his policy.

Finally, and most importantly, words allow Obama to shine, to demonstrate his intelligence, his thoughtfulness, and occasionally, his wit. Obama loves the adulation he receives from the crowds. "My time with them is like a dip in a cool stream. I feel cleansed afterward, glad for the work I have chosen" (Obama 2006, 104).

The time Obama spends communicating also helps explain his admiration for the communicative skills of Ronald Reagan and the priority his campaign gave to developing new communication technologies on the Internet.

Despite the president's rhetorical skills, his explanations of his policy decisions have not contributed to public approval of his presidency. The American public evaluates results more than it does words and actions. And the results in the first two years did not improve the most important problem in 2008 that contributed to Obama's election, the weak economy.

*Temperament*

Although Obama has occasionally shown impatience, he rarely explodes in anger. He does not demonize his opponents (as Richard Nixon and Bill Clinton did) or do anything publicly that would jeopardize his conciliator approach and his common-ground goals unless he is pushed to the brink. Even then, he prefers his aides to run cover for him, talking tough, using threats, and implying negative consequences that may flow from opposition to him and his policies. As candidate and president, Obama uses populist rhetoric to convey his "deep" feelings on social issues, targeting his accusations toward special interests.

Other than occasional outbursts he directs at self-interested group behavior, and some shortness he shows when he is tired or frustrated, Obama remains on an even keel. He rarely shows emotion in public. He gets rid of excess energy by exercising regularly early in the morning and playing basketball and golf, and he used to burn off excess anxiety by smoking a cigarette. He works long hours, travels extensively, and meets regularly with political and policy advisers and a cadre of personal aides and longtime friends.

The absence of perceived emotion has led some to conclude that the president lacks empathy, that he does not understand, much less feel, the pain that ordinary folks are suffering during the extended economic downturn. Obama has tried to counter this perception with references to people he has met or letters and e-mails he has received, but with only modest success. His cool manner and analytic approach undercut the impact of his stories.

## Presidential Performance

Obama promised to change policy and politics. He believed that such change was possible, and with the active support of his electoral base, achievable. He wanted to lead such change, but obviously could not achieve it on his own.

Obama's initial policy agenda came primarily from his presidential campaign, although it had to be reprioritized in the light of the economic recession that began in the fall of 2008. With the decrease in violence in Iraq, the number-one problem for most of 2007 became less important in 2008 (Gallup 2009a). As president-elect, Obama urged Congress to appropriate the second portion of funds from the Troubled Asset Relief Program (TARP) that it enacted in 2008. He also urged the Democratically controlled legislature to pass a large stimulus and investment package after his economic advisers warned him during the transition that the economic crisis would only get worse, deepen and extend, if the federal government did not act quickly and forcibly.

Despite making a bipartisan appeal for this legislation, Obama received only minimal Republican support. His desire to end strident partisan politics, a popular idea, met with Republican defiance and little Democratic support after he became president.

The rigid partisan divide increased the president's dependence on Democratic members of Congress, even as he made bipartisan appeals. Bipartisanship turned out to be good politics, however, even if it did not result in Republican votes. It fostered the impression, at least for a time, that the president was trying to reach out, be even-handed, and promote a public rather than partisan good (Jones 2009).

With a strong Democratic majority, the president achieved many of his initial legislative goals even without Republican support. The costs of these achievements, however, were high in terms of both their overall price tag and their partisan orientation.

The Recovery and Reinvestment Act totaled $787 billion on top of the $700 billion of TARP funds. With a drop in revenues due to the recession and tax cuts enacted during the Bush administration, the country faced huge budget deficits in the trillions of dollars for the foreseeable future.

In addition to the red ink, the president also paid a price for his dependence on the Democratic Congress. Knowing their votes were critical to Obama's policy success, many of his own partisans "rolled him," demanding constituency-related benefits in return for their support, a problem that Clinton also encountered during his first two years in office.

Obama and Clinton contributed to their dependency on fellow Democrats by announcing their willingness to compromise policy details. In addition, Obama further undercut his leadership image and political capital by delegating the legislative drafting of his key legislative priorities to Congress. Why would a president who wanted to transform policy and politics do so?

He may have done so on the belief that his White House staff, heavy with congressional experience, could influence congressional deliberations; he also overestimated his own persuasive skills and his administration's ability to convert his technologically sophisticated campaign organization into an effective instrument of governing. He thought he could control the news media's agenda, frame the policy debate, and impose a timeframe for decisions. But he was unable to do so.

## EVALUATION: WHY WERE THE FIRST TWO YEARS SO DIFFICULT?

The story of Barack Obama's first two years in office is a story of high hopes, great expectations, major policy problems, and disappointment in resolving them. Part of the problem Obama faced was the constitutional and political systems themselves, which divided power and deepened the partisan divide. Despite his pledge to end politics as usual, Obama was unable to change the highly charged partisan environment in which even he, with his bipartisan approach, was suspect.

Part of Obama's problem was the magnitude of the problems, the relatively short time frame in which Americans want to see results, and continued cynicism and mistrust of government. The economic downturn was deeper than most people expected and required more costly and comprehensive government spending than in the past. These expenditures, combined with the economic recession, substantially increased budget deficits and a growing national debt, a development bound to upset citizens already leery of big government programs and continuing budget deficits. Moreover, the persistence of high unemployment, mortgage foreclosures, and lower property values through 2010 raised questions about the merits of the legislation that had been enacted and its impact on the economy.

Had Obama delayed his other major policy initiatives, reduced their scope and cost, or modified his campaign promises because of the magnitude of the economic crisis, he might not have encountered the fierce partisan and public criticism that greeted his proposals to reform health care, regulate Wall Street, and create monetary incentives to decrease air and water pollution. But he did not. Rather, he took the advice of his first chief of staff, Rahm Emanuel, to use the economic situation and his large partisan Democratic majorities in Congress as rationale for moving ahead with policies that had clear economic implications and also as vehicles for rallying support behind the president. In times of crisis, Congress is more apt to follow the president's lead.

In proposing policies in which government was a major player and financier, Obama moved out of sync with the public mood. During his first two years, the public disapproved of most of his major domestic and economic policies even though his personal qualities were rated considerably higher (Gallup 2010c and d).

But Obama has also been out of sync with himself. His presidency has witnessed a bundle of personal contradictions: a transformational leader with a down-to-earth operating style; a man with lofty visions but a pragmatic outlook; a president who refuses to compromise his major priorities but who is extremely flexible on their policy details; an inspiring public speaker who often appears distant, stoic, and a person with whom it is difficult to identify; a candidate who advocates change; and a politician who is preoccupied with finding common ground.

At times, Obama has faced public institutions, such as Congress, the Supreme Court, and other governments that have impeded his policy goals; at times he has been confronted by various individuals and groups; but all of the times he has had to face himself, and unfortunately for Obama, has been against himself some of that time.

CHAPTER 5

# Organizing the Obama
# White House

*James P. Pfiffner*

Each new president faces the challenge of organizing the White House and structuring its relations with the rest of the executive branch. Enduring institutional tensions carry forward in the presidency, regardless of partisan control or the changing personnel in the presidency and appointed positions. The sources of these tensions are structural; just as the US economy and government have expanded, the modern presidency has grown tremendously since the creation of the Executive Office of the President (EOP) in 1939. A White House staff of a few generalist, personal advisers to the president has been transformed into a complex collection of bureaucracies, with 2,000 personnel in the EOP and 400 in the White House office (which is part of the EOP). The presidency is, in important ways, a separate "branch" from the rest of the executive branch (Polsby 1983; Hart 1995).

This chapter will consider how President Obama's administration illustrates the enduring tensions between centralized control and the necessary delegation of policy implementation to departments and agencies. After examining White House domination of policy making in the Obama presidency, the chapter will analyze the friction with the cabinet and Congress caused by Obama's appointment of many White House "czars." The linchpin in Obama's White House for its first two years was Chief of Staff Rahm Emanuel, and his abrasive but effective actions on the part of the president will be examined. After the 2010 congressional elections, President Obama admitted that the Democrats took a "shellacking." Several significant changes in the White House staff had been underway before the elections, and more would be announced before the 112th Congress convened on January 3, 2011. Personnel changes would be significant, but whether the changes signaled a sharp change in policy was not clear at the end of 2010.

## WHITE HOUSE STAFF VERSUS THE CABINET

As in most administrations since the 1960s, the Obama administration ran its policy priorities out of the White House rather than through executive branch departments and agencies. The Nixon administration was the turning point during which the modern presidency developed staff capacities in the White House that allowed presidents to bypass departments in formulating policy (Hult and Walcott 2004; Pfiffner 1999). In national security, Henry Kissinger recruited staffers from across the government to serve on the National Security Council (NSC) staff and marginalized the State Department in foreign policy making (Burke 2009). On the domestic policy side, John Ehrlichman recruited and headed up the domestic policy staff, which freed the president from needing department and agency analysis for his major domestic policy priorities. Once these capacities were created in the White House, no succeeding president successfully delegated policy advice to the departmental level (though Ford, Carter, and Reagan began their presidencies trying to) (Hart 1995; Pfiffner 2010b). Each subsequent president reinforced the structural trend of centralization, and President Obama was no exception.

Immediately after the 2008 election, President-elect Obama designated Rahm Emanuel to be his chief of staff, an indicator that his transition operation was well organized and that he realized the importance of establishing his White House staff early. Obama had learned from the mistake of President-elect Clinton, who spent much of his transition time recruiting his cabinet, which slowed his transition into office. In the third week of his transition, Obama publicly introduced his "economic team" of White House staffers and his Treasury Secretary, Timothy Geithner. In the fourth week he named his national security team, including National Security Adviser James Jones, Secretary of State Hillary Rodham Clinton, and Defense Secretary Robert Gates. These actions early in his transition demonstrated that careful planning had been done before the election, and the pace of his designations surpassed those of his recent predecessors. His designation of the "teams" indicated that he intended his White House staff and his cabinet secretaries to work together in advising him and formulating policy. He recruited strong and professionally impressive cabinet secretaries, but he also set up many White House "czars" who were supposed to "coordinate" administration policy. His designation of these "czars" signaled that he would continue the trend of centralizing policy making and advice to the president in the White House. Cabinet secretaries would be important, but they would likely be overshadowed by White House staffers.

In every administration of the modern presidency, the relationship between cabinet secretaries and the White House staff has been fraught with rivalry and tension. Charles Dawes, the first director of the Bureau of the Budget and later vice president, once remarked that "Cabinet secretaries are vice presidents in charge of spending and as such are the natural enemies of the president" (Richardson 1996, 146). The tension stems from the inevitable role of cabinet secretaries as advocates for their departmental programs and the necessary role of White House staffers as central controllers who must harness departments and agencies to the central purposes of the president (Hess 2002; Hart 1995). That central controlling function has been enhanced by the increased capacity of the White House staff to perform many of the advising functions that used to exist only in cabinet departments (Burke 1992; Warshaw 1996; Patterson 2000; Pfiffner 1999).

The exception that proved the rule of centralized White House control was Obama's initial intention to delegate the legal aspects of detainee policy to his attorney general, Eric Holder. Holder accepted the position with the understanding that he would make legal decisions independently of the White House, though of course the president would have the final say. Chafing from charges that he had been too accommodating to President Clinton and not having challenged the pardon of Marc Rich, when he served in Clinton's Justice Department, Holder wanted to demonstrate his legal autonomy and independence of political influence. He also wanted to distinguish clearly his relationship to the president from that of Alberto Gonzales, who was very close to President Bush and whom critics accused of compromising his legal judgment in order to accomplish the president's policy goals.

In addition, President Obama wanted to be seen as not letting politics interfere with legal principles. Thus he delegated some of the key legal decisions regarding detainee policy to Attorney General Holder. Obama told Holder to make the decisions on the merits of the law rather than on political grounds. Exercising his delegated authority, Holder decided to try the 9/11 terrorist suspects in criminal court rather than military tribunals and chose New York City as the venue. The decision caused a political uproar, with congressional leaders threatening legislation to mandate military commission trials and New York Mayor Blumberg backing off of his initial support of Holder's venue decision. Thus Obama faced the dilemma of backing the initial decision of Holder about the best legal strategy for handling detainees or bowing to political pressure.

Holder's decisions reinforced White House staffers' suspicion that he was not sufficiently sensitive to the president's political fortunes. Holder was aware of the conflict and tried to maintain a balance. "I hope that whatever decision I make would not have a negative impact on the president's agenda. But that can't be a part of my decision" (Klaidman 2009). White House staffers, however, considered Holder to be more concerned with his own legal reputation than the political success of the president. According to a lawyer close to the Obama White House, White House staffers "think he wants to protect his own image, and to make himself untouchable politically, the way Reno did, by doing the righteous thing" (Mayer 2010). Political aides in the White House were so concerned about what they considered Holder's tin ear for politics that they suggested appointing a "minder" in the Justice Department who had more sensitive "political antennae" than Holder (Kantor and Savage 2010).

Ultimately, the White House staff, particularly the chief of staff, convinced Obama that the political repercussions of Holder's decisions were more important than Holder's legal judgments and his independence from the White House. Obama in the spring of 2009 decided that some detainees would be tried in civil courts, but many would be tried by military commissions or detained indefinitely without trial. Thus ended Obama's experiment with delegation of policy making to cabinet secretaries. The centralization of control of high-visibility legal policy in the White House illustrates pressures faced by all contemporary presidents to ensure that departmental perspectives do not undercut broader presidential interests.

In contrast to Obama's initial attempt to allow legal decisions to be formulated at the department level, the administration intended from the very beginning to handle its signature policy priority, health care financing reform, in the White House. During the transition, when Obama asked former Senate Majority Leader Tom Daschle to be secretary of Health and Human Services (HHS), Daschle insisted that he also be designated as the White House czar of health care reform. The request for this unique designation reflected Daschle's understanding that the real action in policy making would take place in the White House rather than in cabinet departments. When Daschle withdrew his nomination because of tax problems, Obama appointed Nancy-Ann DeParle to be White House health czar, and former governor of Kansas Kathleen Sebelius to head HHS. In testimony before Congress in early February 2010, Sebelius admitted her secondary role in health care reform. "I am not a principal in the negotiations, nor is my staff." She said that they would provide "technical support" to Congress but they did not play a role in negotiating over the shape of the health care legislation (Pear 2010). In contrast, Treasury Secretary Timothy Geithner took the lead on administration financial policy and worked closely with the White House staff, though he was closely overseen by Emanuel.

To lead the NSC staff, Obama appointed former Marine General James Jones, who had a broad background working at high levels of the executive branch on military and national security issues, particularly the Middle East. Jones saw his role in the classic "honest broker" mold: "We're not always going to agree on everything, so it's my job to make sure that minority opinion is represented" (DeYoung 2009; Burke 2009). He emphasized the importance of avoiding the "back channels" of information and authority that characterized some of the Bush administration's national security policy process. But during policy making on Afghanistan, Jones's deputy, Thomas Donilon, came to play a major role in advising the president. Frustrated by being overshadowed by others in the White House, Jones decided to leave the administration in the fall of 2010 (Woodward 2010).

In carrying out his duties, Jones directed a staff of about 240 people, but the NSC coordinating mission would be complicated by special envoys for particular trouble spots around the globe, such as George Mitchell for Middle East problems,

Richard Holbrooke for Afghanistan and Pakistan, Dennis Ross for Iran, and Robert Burns for Iran nuclear issues. Hillary Clinton also played a major role in these policy areas in addition to her other duties as secretary of state.

Hillary Clinton, as a condition of accepting the position of secretary of state, demanded full authority to designate all political appointments (about 200) in the State Department (Romano 2010; Woodward 2010, 30). In demanding this autonomy in personnel selection, she echoed the independence that Melvin Laird and Casper Weinberger had sought as secretaries of defense in the Nixon and Reagan administrations. But since the Reagan administration, presidents have insisted that high level, Senate-confirmed political appointees be chosen in the White House and that lower-level executives (even though technically agency head appointments) be cleared through the president's personnel office (Patterson and Pfiffner 2001; Lewis 2009). Although Obama did grant Clinton significant leeway in choosing political appointees, by the summer of 2009 she was expressing frustration with the White House personnel office (Cohen 2010, 4).

Clinton did, however, play an important role in the Obama administration's foreign policy, in contrast to Secretary of State Colin Powell's role in the Bush administration. Clinton exerted her influence in the administration's internal policy making as well as playing the traditional secretary of state role of primary spokesperson for the United States abroad. She and Defense Secretary Robert Gates got along well, which greatly eased the traditional friction between the Departments of State and Defense (Luce and Dombey 2010). Importantly, they both favored the troop build-up in Afghanistan.

During his first year, Obama wanted tight, personal control over national security policy making. According to one senior aide, "President Obama is his own Henry Kissinger—no one else plays that role.... This president wants all the trains routed through the Oval Office" (Luce and Dombey 2010). Obama most often chaired the weekly "principals meeting" of the National Security Council, rather than National Security Adviser James Jones. By the end of Obama's first year in office, the Obama White House had established a "regular order" for the national security policy process. There was a systematic set of procedures for paper flow, consultation, and sign-off; the process was managed and enforced by Deputy NSC Adviser Tom Donilon and Rahm Emanuel (Ignatius 2010). The daily 9:30 a.m. national security briefings were conducted by Donilon, who also ran the "deputies meetings" of the NSC, the heart of the interagency process. In 2009 there were 270 deputies meetings, a very intense schedule, indicating the centrality of Donilon to the national security process (Luce and Dombey 2010). Obama went so far as to assert his control of the details of Afghanistan policy by personally dictating the November 2009 policy memorandum that specified the 30,000 troop buildup in Afghanistan (Woodward 2010, 325).

## OBAMA'S MANY POLICY "CZARS"

The term "czar" has no generally accepted definition within the context of American government. It is a term loosely used by journalists to refer to members of a president's administration who seem to be in charge of a particular policy area. For purposes of consistency, the term "czar" can be used to refer to members of the White House staff who have been designated by the president to coordinate specific policies that involve more than one department or agency in the executive branch; they do not hold Senate-confirmed positions, nor are they officers of the United States (Pfiffner 2009b). Within several months of his inauguration, President Obama had appointed a number of White House czars to oversee policy development of his major priorities. For instance, Carol Browner (head of EPA in the Clinton administration) would oversee administration agencies concerned with energy and climate change, including the WH Council on Environmental Quality, the EPA, and the departments of Energy, Defense, and the Interior. In announcing his choice of Browner, Obama described the role that he expected White House czars to play; she would provide "coordination across the government" and ensure "my personal engagement as president" in environmental policy. He said that she would have authority to "demand integration among different agencies; cooperation between federal, state and local governments; and partnership with the private sector" (Shear and Connolly 2009). Lawrence Summers (treasury secretary in the Clinton administration) would guide the administration's economic policy team, which included Treasury Secretary Timothy Geithner, Office of Management and Budget (OMB) Director Peter Orszag, Council of Economic Advisers Chair Christina Romer, and Senior Economic Adviser Paul Volcker. Nancy-Ann DeParle was designated to be White House health czar; she would lead policy development rather than HHS Secretary Kathleen Sebelius. In addition, the White House staff included czars for urban affairs, auto industry restructuring, financial bailouts, terrorism, drug control, and Native American affairs.

In contrast to officers of the United States, such as cabinet secretaries, members of the White House staff are appointed by the president without Senate confirmation (PA). They are legally authorized only to advise the president; they cannot make authoritative decisions for the government of the United States.[1] For practical purposes, however, staff personnel may have considerable "power" or influence, as opposed to authority. But this power is derivative from the line officer for whom they work. Thus White House staffers may communicate orders from the president, but they cannot legally give those orders under their own authority. In the real world, of course, White House staffers often make important decisions, but the weight of their decisions depends entirely on the willingness of the president to back them up. In February 2009, Senator Robert Byrd wrote a letter to President Obama, complaining that the designation of all of the czars undermined accountability to Congress under the Constitution. "The rapid and easy accumulation of power by White House staff can threaten the Constitutional system of checks and balances. At the worst, White House staff have taken direction and control of programmatic areas that are the statutory responsibility of Senate confirmed officials" (Bresnahan 2009). But constitutional issues were not the main problem with the multiplying czars. The president is accountable for administration policy, and cabinet secretaries can testify about programs. As Villalobos and Vaughn argue, czars "are not constitutionally problematic so long as they refrain from usurping authority or making policy decisions that Congress has explicitly set aside for their respective Senate confirmed principal officers, which include actions such as rule-making, issuing regulations, approving expenditures, or otherwise authoritatively interpreting laws" (Villalobos and Vaughn 2010, 13).

The real problem with White House czars (and sometimes even the national security adviser) is that they confuse the chain of command and leave open the question of who is in charge of administration policy. Czars are often frustrated because they lack the authority to carry out their responsibilities. That is, they do not control budgets or appointments, and they cannot order cabinet secretaries to do their bidding. For example, past drug czars expressed frustration because they could not authoritatively coordinate the FBI, Drug Enforcement Administration, Coast Guard, HUD, and other agencies that implement drug-control policies. Similar problems faced the first several directors of national intelligence. They were charged with leading the intelligence community of 15 separate agencies, but did not have budget or personnel control of most of them.

White House czars can act authoritatively when they directly represent the president's wishes, but presidents do not have the time to continually back up individual czars on a regular basis.The other problem with czars is that cabinet secretaries often resent the dilution of their policy-advising authority. In every administration, cabinet secretaries jealously guard their authority and seek access to the president. This is where policy czars have the advantage of proximity; they have the opportunity to see the president much more often than can cabinet secretaries, who have many departmental and implementation duties they must carry out. So the biggest problem with so many czars in the White House is the question of who is in charge of a given policy area. Who has the lead in developing policy alternatives for the president's consideration?

## CHIEF OF STAFF "RAHMBO"

Obama, who self-consciously sought to imitate some of President Lincoln's characteristics, seemed to seek a "team of rivals" in his White House and cabinet appointments (Goodwin 2005). That is, he welcomed diverse opinions and disagreement from equally forceful White House staffers and cabinet secretaries in order to be fully informed before making final decisions. When Obama was assembling his cabinet, he said that he sought "strong personalities and strong opinions" in order to foster robust debate on important policy issues. "One of the dangers in the White House, based on my reading of history, is that you get wrapped up in groupthink and everybody agrees with everything and there's not discussion and there are no dissenting views. So I'm going to be welcoming a vigorous debate inside the White House." But he concluded "As Harry Truman said, the buck will stop with me" (Baker 2008). The key to making Obama's complicated White House staff structure work was Chief of Staff Rahm Emanuel. With so many czars and competing power centers, someone short of the president had to be in charge to act as traffic cop and enforcer (Pfiffner 1993). David Axelrod, Valerie Jarrett, and Peter Rouse did not report to Obama through Emanuel; they were senior counselors who played important roles in his campaign for the presidency. Press Secretary Robert Gibbs, who had been with Obama since his campaign for the Senate, was also very close to the president; he sat in on virtually all policy meetings and was one of the few people who was comfortable giving Obama bad news (Horowitz 2010b). But Emanuel was the linchpin; he was a close adviser of Obama and came to the White House with six years of experience in the Clinton White House, four years as a member of Congress, and a background in Chicago politics.

The chief of staff in any presidency faces formidable challenges, and they were particularly daunting in Obama's high-maintenance White House staff structure. Emanuel would have to ride herd on the many policy czars, smooth ruffled feathers, corral large egos, guard access to the president, make the trains run on time, negotiate between White House staffers and cabinet secretaries, and get all of the separate political and policy threads to go through the eye of the needle at the same time.

By all accounts, Emanuel was up to the job. In addition to his impressive political experience, Emanuel was known for his abrasive personality, vulgar language, volatile temperament, and tactical brilliance. From Emanuel's perspective, he specialized in what he called "the art of the possible," and he was a master of "transactional politics," i.e., making deals and compromises, in contrast to ideological politics (Lizza 2009). To assist him in his job, Emanuel had two deputies, Mona Sutphen and Jim Messina, and a personal GPS system that was able to track the location of the president and senior White House staffers (think Harry Potter's Marauder's Map).

As the key to White House organization, Emanuel provided a complement to Obama in terms of temperament, personality, and style. Where Obama was idealistic, Emanuel was practical; where Obama was restrained, Emanuel was outspoken; where Obama was smooth, Emanuel was brash ("Rahmbo"); where Obama was given to policy analysis, Emanuel was a master of political calculation; where Obama was "no drama," Emanuel was histrionic (Baker 2010a). As policy adviser to the president Emanuel represented the pragmatic rather than the idealistic side of Obama's mind. On Afghanistan, he was against escalation; on detainee issues, he wanted to compromise with conservatives; and on health care reform, he favored incremental change rather than comprehensive reform. Obama did not always follow his advice, but took his counsel seriously. Obama was the idealistic leader; Emanuel played the heavy and knocked heads together to enforce the president's decisions.

Stories of Emanuel's political tactics emphasized his colorful language and his toughness. In one negotiating session, he reportedly made his point by standing on a table and screaming (Tumulty and Scherer 2009). Even President Obama kidded Emanuel about his volatile personality. On one occasion Obama recalled that in a recent trip to Egypt, Emanuel rode a camel, which made the president nervous because "this is a wild animal known to bite, kick and spit [pause] and who knows what the camel could do?" (Newhall 2009). Obama also said that when Emanuel lost half of his middle finger in an accident, it "rendered him practically mute" (Lizza 2009a). In his early career, Emanuel had worked as an aide on a congressional campaign, and the polling expert they hired made a serious mistake. After his candidate lost the race, Emanuel sent the pollster a box with a dead fish in it to indicate his displeasure. In his White House office, there was a plaque stating Emanuel's position as "Undersecretary for Go F*** Yourself" (Lizza 2009). Regarding his own hardball tactics, Emanuel admitted: "I wake up some mornings hating me too" (Kurtz 2009). When Emanuel left the administration in October 2010, *Saturday Night Live* announced, "On Friday, the White House released Rahm Emanuel back into the wild (Brooks 2010a).

Emanuel's office was the nerve center of the White House, with all paperwork and policy advice required to run the gauntlet of Emanuel's scrutiny before going to the president (Horowitz 2010a; Sullivan 2004). Emanuel was central to all of Obama's major policy decisions and negotiations with Congress. He was not a "neutral" broker in his advice to Obama, but his preferred policy positions tended to be tactical judgments rather than ideological convictions, in contrast to Vice President Cheney in the Bush administration (Scheiber 2010).

Emanuel was seen by Obama critics as a combination of Svengali and Rasputin. Critics on the right saw him as an advocate of big government and partisanship; critics on the left saw him as being too willing to betray Obama's campaign promises and compromise with Republicans (Baker 2010b; Scheiber 2010). He was attacked for being one of the Chicago insiders who supposedly insulated Obama from broader sources of advice. He was also defended for being a realist who tried to save Obama from idealistic policies (such as the closing of Guantánamo, the civil trial of Khalid Sheikh Mohammed, and comprehensive health care reform) favored by his supporters on the left, (Milbank 2010; Luce 2010; Gelb 2010; Alexander 2010; Horowitz 2010a).

Cabinet secretaries in the Obama administration often resented their treatment by Chief of Staff Emanuel, who they felt treated them as his "minions" rather than as major administration officials (Luce 2010). They were required to send weekly reports to Emanuel, who returned them with specific comments and instructions (Baker and Zeleny 2010). As in other administrations, cabinet secretaries often felt that the president paid too much attention to his inner circle of campaigners (in this case the Chicagoans Jarrett, Axelrod, and Gibbs) and did not grant enough access to old Washington hands and cabinet officials (Luce 2010).

During his first two years in office, Emanuel was the first to see the president in the morning to plan out the day's priorities, prior to Emanuel's staff meeting at 7:30 a.m. Emanuel was also the last person to see Obama in the evening, when the president received a briefing book on policy issues and the next day's events (Kornblut and Wilson 2010). In addition to Emanuel, the only other White House staffers to get copies of the briefing were Biden, Jarrett, Axelrod, and Gibbs (Kornblut and Wilson 2010).

Emanuel's style as chief of staff can perhaps be best illustrated by contrasting him with his successor, Pete Rouse. A month before the midterm elections in 2010, Emanuel announced that he was leaving the White House to return to Chicago to run for mayor, a long-time goal of his. At the same time, President Obama appointed Rouse, his former Senate chief of staff, as Emanuel's successor. Rouse had also previously served as chief of staff to Senator Thomas Daschle;

he was so skilled in his job that he was known as the "101st Senator." Rouse had been with the White House from the beginning of the administration as a "senior adviser" to the president. His duties were not fixed, but ranged across White House trouble spots, particularly personnel friction.

In temperament Rouse was much more similar to Obama than to Emanuel; one might even consider Rouse to be the "anti-Emanuel" (Stolberg 2010). He was low-key rather than histrionic; in contrast to Emanuel, he seldom or never used foul language. Perhaps the president summed it up best when he praised Rouse as "completely ego-free" (Kornblut 2010). Rouse was thus much more of an honest broker, internal manager, and behind-the-scenes actor than was Emanuel, who had strong views on policy issues and how they related to political realities.

## STAFF CHANGES FOR 2011

As the two-year mark in his presidency approached, President Obama began to make a number of changes to the top levels of his White House staff in addition to replacing Rahm Emanuel with Pete Rouse. The president's economic team underwent significant changes. National Economic Council Chair Larry Summers as well as OMB Director Peter Orszag would be gone. Obama appointed Jack Lew, who had previously served as President Clinton's OMB director, to replace Orszag. Austan Goolsbee, who had been on the Council of Economic Advisers, took over as chair when Christina Romer left the administration. National Security Adviser James Jones was replaced by his deputy, Thomas Donilon, and it was likely that Secretary of Defense Robert Gates would retire early in 2011. Obama adviser David Axelrod and Deputy Chief of Staff Jim Messina left to work on the reelection campaign, and David Plouffe, who had run Obama's 2008 campaign, came into the White House to replace Axelrod. Other senior staff changes were expected to be made as the Obama administration shifted gears from its initial agenda facilitated by a Democratic House to its second two years facing a Republican House and a more narrowly split Democratic Senate.

President Obama's first two years in office illustrated the verity that all presidents since Eisenhower centralized policy advice in the White House at the expense of cabinet secretaries. Obama's experiment with delegation of legal policy to Attorney General Holder was soon derailed when political backlash led Obama to adopt a more conservative approach to the prosecution of the 9/11 and other detainees. Obama did not initiate the extensive use of White House "czars," but he continued the trend and probably deputized more White House coordinators of administration policies than other presidents. As in all other modern presidencies, cabinet secretaries chafed under the direction of White House aides, particularly Rahm Emanuel. As chief of staff, Emanuel played the traditional role of strong director of White House process and policy. Since the Ford and Carter attempts to run the White House without a chief of staff, no other president has tried to do without a director. Nevertheless, Obama himself became deeply involved in the details of all of his major policy priorities, particularly economic recovery, health care reform, and Afghanistan strategy. The congressional elections of

2010, however, ensured that President Obama would not undertake major new domestic initiatives in his second two years in office.

## Note

1. There is a parallel between the concepts of "line" and "staff" in the US military. Staff personnel can advise line officers, but only line officers can make authoritative decisions, such as hiring and firing personnel or committing budgetary resources. Cabinet secretaries are in line positions and White House personnel are staff.

# PART II

## ON THE HILL AND OFF

CHAPTER 6

# Congressional Leadership in Obama's First Two Years

## Barbara Sinclair

For Democrats, election night 2008 was a resounding triumph. Barack Obama was elected president with 53 percent of the vote, an 8 percentage point margin over his Republican opponent; Democrats picked up 21 seats in the House on top of the 33 seats they had netted in 2006 and in three subsequent special elections and added at least 7 in the Senate. However, the magnitude and the nature of the victory posed daunting challenges to Obama himself and to the congressional majority party leaders who would be expected to help him succeed.

What were those challenges and how did Democratic congressional leaders meet them in the first two years of the Obama presidency? These are the questions I address in this chapter.

Obama ran on a highly ambitious policy agenda, and the Democrats' big win raised his supporters' expectations sky high. His voters expected him to deliver the significant policy change he promised, and the activists who played such a big role in the victory demanded swift and uncompromising action. Furthermore, many voters expected Democrats to deliver policy change through a more bipartisan and less fractious process, as Obama had promised he would. The financial system was in crisis, and the economy was sinking into an ever-deeper recession, if not a depression. Crises offer opportunities; still, although the problems dated back to the Bush administration, Democrats as the party in power would be held accountable if recovery lagged too long. Furthermore, the problems presented by the economy and the issues central to Obama's agenda, especially health care reform, were highly complex and did not lend themselves to simple solutions easily understood by the public.

## THE PARTY LEADERSHIP'S ROLE AND RESOURCES

Major policy change in the United States requires the enactment of legislation, and that requires leadership; Congress is, after all, composed of two chambers and a total of 535 voting members. Some of the necessary leadership can and must come from the president, but internal leadership is also needed, and in the contemporary era that responsibility falls heavily on the party leaders in each chamber.

In both houses of the US Congress, the central leaders are party leaders and are effectively chosen by their co-partisans in their chamber. In the 111th Congress, sworn in in January 2009, the House Democratic leadership consisted of Speaker Nancy Pelosi (CA), Majority Leader Steny Hoyer (MD), Majority Whip James Clyburn (SC), and a number of other members holding lesser offices. The three top members of the Senate Democratic leadership were Majority Leader Harry Reid (NV), Majority Whip Dick Durbin (IL), and Charles Schumer (NY), vice chair of the Democratic Conference. These were the members who would bear primary responsibility within Congress for the enactment of the Democratic agenda.

When the president is of their party, congressional majority party leaders define promoting the president's agenda as an important component of their job. In part, this is because the president's agenda is often their own and their members' agenda as well; presidential candidates frequently derive a good part of their agenda from issues and proposals incubated by their co-partisans in Congress. In addition, congressional leaders see their president's success as essential to their own success—to satisfying their members' policy and electoral goals and to maintaining their majorities. Leaders and their members are aware that the president's success or failure will shape the party's reputation and so affect their own electoral fates. Congressional leaders particularly are judged by whether they deliver on the president's agenda.

For the leaders of the 111th Congress, the incentives to make passing Obama's agenda a central objective were especially great. Democrats had been in the minority in both chambers for most of the 1995–2006 period, and during that time, their policy preferences had been largely rebuffed; pent-up demand for policy change among Democrats was immense. Speaker Pelosi is a strongly policy-oriented leader for whom passing major policy change is a priority. When the Democrats took back the majority in the 110th Congress, Pelosi and Senate Majority Leader Harry Reid often found their attempts to legislate frustrated by a president who profoundly disagreed with them and their membership on most major policy disputes. Now they had a president with whom they and their members mostly agreed. Furthermore, the public's high expectations and the dire economic situation made the likely cost of not delivering exceedingly high. Most of the senior Democratic leaders had served in Congress during the early Clinton presidency and were determined to avoid the mistakes they believed had led to the loss of the Democratic majority.

The leaders began the task of enacting the Democratic agenda with considerable—but far from unlimited—resources. The 2008 elections had increased their majorities significantly. House Democrats began the 111th Congress with a 257–178 margin. Senate Democrats, who had struggled through the 110th with a 51–49 majority, boosted their numbers to 58 with one seat undecided.

Further to the benefit of the congressional leadership, this Democratic membership was relatively ideologically homogeneous, at least by American standards. In the 110th Congress (2007–08), on recorded votes that pitted a majority of Democrats against a majority of Republicans, House Democrats on average voted with their party 92 percent of the time and Senate Democrats did 87 percent of the time (cq.com 2008, 3332–3342).

Obama and congressional Democrats ran on quite similar issues, as one would expect when the political parties are relatively ideologically homogeneous; thus they began with considerable agreement on a policy agenda broadly defined. The economic crisis fueled a sense of urgency in the public and among policy makers alike, further focusing the attention of the new president and his congressional partisans on the same agenda.

Congressional leaders command organizational and institutional resources useful for putting together and holding together the support needed to pass their party's agenda. In both chambers, party organization has become quite elaborate, consisting of a number of party committees and subordinate leadership positions; these provide assistance to the top leadership but also give other members an opportunity to participate in party efforts and thereby increase their stake in their success. Leadership staffs have grown significantly over the years and serve as the eyes and ears—and sometimes negotiating surrogates—for the leaders.

The contemporary House majority party leadership commands formidable institutional resources. The increasing ideological homogeneity of the parties over the last several decades made possible the development of a stronger and more activist party leadership (Rohde 1991; Sinclair 1995). The majority party leadership oversees the referral of bills to committee, determines the floor schedule, and controls the drafting of special rules that govern how bills are considered on the floor. The leaders can bypass committees when they consider it necessary or orchestrate post-committee adjustments to legislation. They can work with (and, if necessary, lean on) committees to report out the party's program in an acceptable form and in a timely manner, deploy the extensive whip system to rally the votes needed to pass the legislation, and bring the bills to the floor at the most favorable time and under floor procedures that give them the best possible chance for success. The House is a majority-rule institution; decisions are made by simple majorities, and opportunities for minorities to delay action are exceedingly limited. Thus a party leadership that commands a reliable majority can produce legislation.

Senate rules are a great deal more permissive than House rules and give individual members much greater prerogatives; a minority of 41 or more can block passage if it uses its prerogative of extended debate. Because Senate rules do not require amendments to most bills to be germane, senators can force to the floor issues the majority leader might prefer to avoid. Consequently the Senate majority leader lacks many of the institutional tools the speaker possesses. Still the majority leader does command the initiative in floor scheduling and is the elected leader of the majority party in the chamber (Smith 1993; Sinclair 2007b).

The congressional leadership's own experience was a resource as well. Pelosi had served as her party's top leader since 2002 and Reid since 2004, and both were party whips before that. Most of the rest of the leadership teams in both chambers were battle-tested veterans as well.

Although the Democratic congressional leaders began the 111th Congress with some important advantages and considerable resources, they also faced significant constraints. Even when the president and his party in Congress have run and won on similar agendas, there will always be differences about particulars and sometimes also about priorities. Different constituencies ensure that. Furthermore, although the congressional Democratic party was ideologically homogeneous by historical standards, it nevertheless was far from monolithic and less homogeneous than the Republican party it had replaced in the majority. To win majorities, Democrats in both chambers had recruited moderates in many states and districts that would have been unlikely to elect liberals. The 111th House majority included 49 members from districts that John McCain carried in the 2008 election; 13 Democratic senators represented states that McCain won.

In the 110th Congress, when Bush was still president, many of Democrats' fondest legislative goals were beyond reach. The leaders could concentrate on protecting their vulnerable members from "red" constituencies by avoiding votes on issues politically difficult for them. In the 111th, the leaders had to produce legislation to deliver on the promises they and Obama had made and were also under considerable pressure to avoid excessive compromises from the liberal mainstream of their membership, which had waited so long for the opportunity to enact their preferences into law.

One might expect such a severe economic crisis to produce a willingness among elected officials to work together across party lines. However, the high level of partisan polarization meant that the Democratic leaders certainly could not count on support from Republicans even for crisis-related legislation and less so for core agenda items such as health care. As the Republican party had shrunk as a consequence of the 2006 and 2008 elections, it became more ideologically homogeneous and moved further right. Especially in the House, Republicans' and Democrats' sincere beliefs of what constituted good public policy were very far apart. At the beginning of 2009, however, it was not yet clear what strategy the minority party would decide was in its best electoral interests; would limited cooperation or all-out confrontation serve the party best?

## EARLY TESTS: LEADERSHIP STRATEGIES
## AND REAL-LIFE CONSTRAINTS

What then did the congressional leadership make of the opportunities and the challenges they faced in 2009? Obama and the Democrats had promised change, so the leaders believed racking up some early legislative achievements was essential. The House Democratic leadership engineered quick passage of the children's health insurance program (SCHIP) reauthorization and the Lilly Ledbetter Fair Pay Act, bills the House had passed in the previous Congress but that had then been blocked before enactment. To speed the process, the House leadership bypassed committee and brought the bills directly to the floor; there they were considered under closed rules allowing no amendments. Lacking the high control over the process their House party leadership colleagues had, the Senate leaders took longer. SCHIP had passed the Senate by substantial margins in the 110th Congress, only to be vetoed by President Bush, so its passage in 2009 was relatively straightforward. However, the minority Republicans had blocked the Fair Pay Act in the Senate in the 110th and, to pass it in 2009, Reid was forced to muster a supermajority to impose cloture on the motion to proceed to consider the bill and then to pass it. His much bigger Senate majority made that possible. Thus President Obama was presented with popular legislation to sign soon after his swearing in, and Democrats achieved some long-sought policy successes.

The stimulus bill and the war supplemental appropriations bill were key early tests for the new administration and the Democratic congressional leaderships. An examination of the efforts to pass these bills illustrates the strategies Obama and the leaders employed and makes clear the nature and magnitude of the challenges they would face going forward.

## ADVANCING THE AGENDA BY PASSING THE STIMULUS BILL

By early 2009, a consensus had emerged among experts that, to meet the worst economic crisis since the Great Depression, a very substantial stimulus package was essential. Partly out of necessity because he was not yet president, Obama relied heavily on congressional Democrats to craft the stimulus package. To be sure, Obama team members begin meeting and discussing a potential stimulus bill with the congressional leadership before the November elections and, by mid-December, Obama transition team members and relevant Democratic congressional staffers were meeting almost daily. Nevertheless, as would become a standard Obama strategy, he gave congressional Democrats great leeway, calculating that members who had a major role in shaping legislation would have a much greater stake in its enactment.

Pelosi tapped Appropriations Chairman David Obey as the head negotiator for House Democrats; a considerable proportion of a stimulus bill would be within his committee's jurisdiction, and Obey was a political savvy and tough legislator. On this and the other major agenda items, Pelosi would delegate to her trusted committee leaders but would continuously oversee the process and involve herself deeply when she saw the necessity.

During his campaign, Obama had promised to transform Washington policy debate, replacing partisan hostility with bipartisan cooperation. In an attempt to do so, he reached out to Republicans on the stimulus bill, sending high-ranking appointees to consult with them and visiting with both House and Senate Republicans on their own turf himself. Furthering the president's bipartisanship outreach strategy, Pelosi sent the stimulus bill to the three committees of jurisdiction for mark-up as Republicans demanded, rather than bypassing committee consideration. Of course, by doing so she also assured rank-and-file Democrats on those committees a much-coveted role in the legislative process on this major piece of legislation.

Despite the outreach and the inclusion of a large tax cut component in the stimulus bill, Republicans opposed the majority's bill. When the parties are highly polarized, genuine and severe policy disagreement impedes bipartisanship. Furthermore, when the minority party faces unified government, they may perceive bipartisanship to conflict with their electoral interests. Their likely rationale: Obama and the congressional Democrats will get credit for any successes, but, if they support the bills, Republicans will share the blame for any failures.

Conservatives in Congress and on the airwaves launched an all-out attack on the Democratic plan. At one point in the stimulus battle, opponents seized the initiative in defining the bill, claiming it was not a stimulus at all but just a lot of useless and expensive pork. Urged on by the Democratic congressional leadership, Obama personally took over the job of selling the stimulus bill and did so aggressively, but some ground had been lost.

Demonstrating the control the House majority leadership commands as well as the extent to which Democrats saw passage of the stimulus as essential, the House committees marked up the stimulus bill during the first week of the Obama presidency, and the House passed it in the second. The bill was considered under a rule that "self executed" (meaning no vote was necessary) an amendment making several last-minute changes to the bill; these post-committee adjustments included provisions striking money for resodding the Mall and family planning funds. Democratic leaders had decided that these provisions had become lightning rods that were not worth the pain they were causing their members. Better to remove them than to try to explain in the face of the conservative onslaught. Of the amendments made in order by the rule, three were sponsored by freshmen Democrats, including one benefiting the textile industry by North Carolinian Larry Kissel. In constructing the rule, the leadership's first concern was facilitating passage of this key agenda item, but the leaders were also looking out for their more vulnerable members.

HR1, the stimulus bill, passed the House by 244 to 188; 11 Democrats, mostly more conservative Blue Dogs, voted against the bill; not a single Republican supported it. The Republican whip system was aggressively employed to keep any Republican members from straying; even Joseph Cao, newly elected from a poor, majority-black district, was pressured into opposing the stimulus bill (The Hill 12/13/09). The Republican House leadership seemingly had decided that the party's electoral interest lay in unequivocally and vigorously opposing Obama's and the congressional Democrats' policy agenda.

Because a simple majority can prevail in the House, even unanimous Republican opposition is irrelevant to passage. In the Senate, a minority of 41 or more can block passage. Thus Majority Leader Harry Reid's problem was how to get to 60 votes; with 58 Democrats, he would need several Republican votes, and the Republican Senate leadership had made its opposition to the Democratic approach clear. Thus when Senate moderates Ben Nelson, Democrat of Nebraska, and Susan Collins, Republican of Maine, began talks about possible revisions to the committee-reported bill, Reid encouraged their effort. Intense negotiations among these and a larger group of moderates and with Reid and White House officials finally yielded an agreement that could garner 60 votes. It cut the size of the stimulus; at Senator Susan Collins's (R-ME) insistence, aid to the states was significantly cut back and school construction funds were deleted. Yet, the many Senate Democrats who supported a bigger package had no real choice but to go along.

After cloture was invoked on the compromise bill with the essential help of three Republicans—Susan Collins and Olympia Snowe, both of Maine, and Arlen Specter of Pennsylvania—and the bill passed the Senate, a compromise between the House and Senate bills was necessary. That would require some serious bargaining, which, as is often the case, took place behind closed doors before a formal meeting of the conference committee. Although the Obama administration had left much of the detailed drafting to Congress, at this point the administration was deeply involved with Chief of Staff Rahm Emanuel and Office of Management and Budget (OMB) Director Peter Orszag acting as point men. Pelosi too was a key negotiator. And the Senate moderates had to be consulted and kept on board. When talks seemed to hit a wall over funding for school construction, the president phoned Pelosi and House Majority Whip Jim Clyburn to make sure that negotiations moved ahead.

The agreement reached by House and Senate negotiators was for a stimulus plan costing about $789 billion. As the leaders had promised, both chambers passed the conference report before the President's Day recess. Obama signed the bill on February 17, less than a month after his inauguration.

## Unified Control's Bitter Fruit: War Funding

Passing the supplemental appropriations bill to fund the wars in Iraq and Afghanistan presented another and somewhat different test. Because President Bush had not included war funding in his regular budget requests, one more supplemental appropriations bill was necessary. Many Democrats strongly opposed the Iraq War and had long refused to vote for funding, and they were developing increasing doubts about the war in Afghanistan, yet the Democrats as the new governing party could not fail to pass a bill providing for the troops. And the bill included other emergency funds such as money for swine flu preparedness.

Because Republicans supported the war funds as they had in the past, initial passage in the House was not a problem; 51 anti-war Democrats voted against the bill, but it passed 368 to 60. The issue of what to do with the Guantánamo detainees had required some adept leadership to manage. Obama had promised to close the prison at Guantánamo within a year, but Republicans claimed that bringing any of the detainees onto US soil endangered Americans. Congressional Democrats, especially junior and electorally vulnerable ones, feared votes on the issue as potential reelection killers, and the leaders knew they would lose a significant number of their members if they were forced to take such a vote; furthermore, the party leaders wanted to protect their members from such really tough votes if at all possible. Appropriations Chair David Obey had amended the bill in committee with a compromise Guantánamo amendment, but whip checks revealed it was not enough. A stronger amendment that still did not repudiate the president's policy was negotiated; the rule for floor consideration self executed that amendment and precluded any other amendments, so when the rule passed—on a largely party-line vote—the bill's passage was assured.

The Senate passed its bill 86–3. Because the Senate majority party cannot bar amendments as its House counterpart can, Democrats employed a strategy of preemption. The chairman of the Appropriations Committee himself offered a floor amendment deleting funds from the bill for transferring detainees or closing the prison, while also arguing that Guantánamo would have to be closed within a reasonable period of time. When the amendment passed overwhelmingly, the biggest potential problem in resolving differences between the chambers seemed to have been removed.

Two other issues would prove to be major problems in final passage of the bill. The Senate but not the House bill included $5 billion for the International Monetary Fund (IMF), a provision the administration argued was essential but that House Republicans vehemently opposed. The Senate had adopted an amendment by Lindsey Graham (R-SC) and Joe Lieberman (I-CT) that exempted photos showing prisoner abuse by US soldiers from being accessible through the Freedom of Information Act (FOIA). House liberals strongly opposed that amendment, believing that FOIA should not be thus weakened and, in many cases, that the photos should be made public.

The conundrum the House and Senate leaderships faced was that what it would take to pass the bill in the House might well make it impossible to pass in the Senate and vice versa. Pelosi decided that the IMF money had to be in the final bill, but that meant she would have to pass the conference report with Democratic votes alone. She would have to persuade a number of fervently anti-war Democrats to vote for a bill that included provisions she herself found hard to stomach; doing so would be impossible if the Graham-Lieberman language were included. Yet, Graham and Lieberman—backed up by most Senate Republicans—vowed to filibuster the bill in the Senate if their language was stripped.

Once the House leadership's insistence on dropping Graham-Lieberman was accepted by the negotiators, the task on the House side was persuasion. The administration deployed top Cabinet members—Treasury Secretary Timothy Geithner, Defense Secretary Robert Gates, and Secretary of State Hillary Rodham Clinton—as well as Obama himself to make calls. The Democratic whip system worked to get an accurate count and to persuade. However, because it was anti-war liberals who needed to be flipped, Pelosi, as an anti-war liberal herself, had to assume the central role. For days she stalked the floor, talking, listening, and persuading. As wrenching as voting for more war funding might be, as difficult as it might be to stand up to pressure from liberals bloggers, as hard as it might be to explain the vote to one's constituents, Democrats had to pass the bill to clean up after the Bush administration; Republicans were trying to defeat the bill to give Obama a black eye. Pelosi again made those argument in an impassioned speech to her caucus before the vote. Still, Democratic leaders were nervous enough about the outcome that they called Caucus Chairman John Larson (CT), out sick with food poisoning, to the Capitol to cast a vote in support (*Roll Call* 6/18/09). The conference report passed 226–202. Even though the speaker usually does not vote, Pelosi voted for the bill. Passing the supplemental was "the hardest thing we did," Pelosi would say at the end of the year (Pelosi speech 2009).

President Obama broke the impasse preventing Senate passage of the bill. Before the Graham-Lieberman amendment was even offered, Obama had announced that he opposed making the pictures public. Now he stated that he would use every "legal and administrative remedy" available to prevent the disclosure of the pictures (*Roll Call* 6/12/09). He made the promise first in a phone call to senators—heard over the speaker of White House Chief of Staff Rahm Emanuel's cell phone—and then in a letter addressed to the Senate and House Appropriations chairs.

## LEADERSHIP STYLES AND STRATEGIES

These and other tests—passing an omnibus appropriations bill and the budget resolution, especially—in the first half of 2009 illustrate the strategies developed and employed by the Democratic leadership and the Obama administration and the challenges they face in attempting to enact their ambitious agenda. The Obama administration's preferred strategy was to lay out broad objectives but rely on Congress to actually write the legislation and do the initial deals. It stepped in toward the end of the legislative process to shape the final product. A White House peopled by savvy operators with extensive congressional experience—Chief of Staff Rahm Emanuel, a former House member who had served as chair of the Democratic Congressional Campaign Committee and chair of the Democratic Caucus; OMB Director Peter Orszag, who has served as director of the Congressional Budget Office; head of congressional liaison Phil Schiliro, formerly chief of staff for senior House Democrat Henry Waxman; Chairman of the Energy and Commerce Committee, Senior Advisor Pete Rouse, a 30-year veteran of the Hill who had served as chief of staff to Senate Majority Leader Tom Daschle; and Obama himself—believed that members who have participated in crafting legislation have a greater stake in and thus will work harder for its success and, by not drawing lines in the sand early, the president retains more maneuvering room. These experienced Hill hands also know that members of Congress need a lot of "care and feeding," so top White House aides were often on the Hill and more often on the phone with members; Obama himself invited groups of members to the White House regularly. On a tough vote, everyone, including top Cabinet members, was expected to take part in persuasion efforts, and Obama himself made multiple calls.

Obama's strategy of outreach to the Hill very emphatically included Republicans, as illustrated by the stimulus campaign. Despite the limited payoff in terms of votes and considerable grumbling from liberal Democrats, he continued to reach across the aisle. However, sometimes under prodding from congressional Democrats, Obama was willing to "go public" defending his proposals and calling out obstructionist Republicans.

The Democratic leadership in the House was Obama's most valuable ally. Contact, usually by phone, between top leadership staffers and the White House was constant, and Pelosi and Obama spoke frequently. Both agreed on the necessity of close coordination of internal efforts and of message, though sometimes actually accomplishing that was difficult. Pelosi's leadership style combined toughness, discipline, and attention to detail with inclusiveness, a willingness to listen, and attention to members' individual needs. Her experience as a mother of five, Pelosi jokes, taught her to combine the roles of "disciplinarian and diplomat" (Pelosi speech 2009). An effort to pass major and controversial legislation typically involved multiple "listening sessions" with groups of members, often as organized in the various caucuses—the Blue Dogs, the Progressive Caucus, the Black Caucus, etc. Pelosi met weekly with the freshmen, and the entire leadership attended the weekly whip and caucus meetings. Majority Leader Steny Hoyer met regularly with the committee chairmen; as a moderate, he has close ties to the Blue Dogs and the New Democrats. Whip Jim Clyburn is a member of the Black Caucus himself and also kept in touch with the various elements of the party through his whips as well as multiple meetings.

Through early involvement on major legislation and listening to all segments of the Democratic membership, the leadership hoped to put together a bill that could pass on the floor without any last-minute drama. Seldom did the Democratic leaders count on any Republican votes. Pelosi, in fact, had little contact with her minority counterpart. Constructing a majority may take adjustments to legislation reported from committee, and that may require hands-on leadership deal making. The speaker's control over the Rules Committee, which sets the terms of floor debate, enables the leadership to protect the bill from attempts to unravel the compromises made.

Aggressive use of the institutional powers of the speakership is a central leadership strategy, and rules are central to that strategy. Of the 108 rules for initial consideration of legislation in 2009–10, 35 were closed, allowing no amendments, and only 1 rule allowed all germane amendments; the rest (72) were structured rules that allow only specific amendments to be offered. Twenty-nine of the rules had self-executing provisions, which incorporate provisions into the bill without a vote on the provisions.[1] Structured rules can be used to give members an opportunity to rack up a visible accomplishment. The huge number of noncontroversial bills the House considers under the suspension of the rules procedure provides the same opportunity, and the speaker controls what gets considered under the suspension procedure.

Persuasion is, of course, always a central element of leadership strategy in a body where the leaders are elected by their members. Pelosi is known as a persistent and tough persuader. Some observers even claim that Clyburn, conciliatory and low key, and Pelosi engaged in a "good cop, bad cop" routine (*Roll Call* 3/20/09). During the first Congress of the Obama presidency, the House leadership asked their members to take some very tough votes. Many participants believe that Pelosi made a major mistake in making her members vote on a highly controversial climate change bill when the prospects for it passing in the Senate seemed bleak; that vote will be an albatross in "red"-district Democrats' 2010 reelection bids and made getting the votes for other important legislation—health care, preeminently—harder, they argued. Pelosi's insistence that the House move on the climate change bill does illustrate the extent to which Pelosi is policy-oriented and a risk taker. This vote aside, the political context dictated that Democrats attempt to pass the ambitious agenda they had promised, and that made tough votes for House members inevitable. Because of the Senate's supermajoritarian requirements, the House would have to be "the assault force ... the first marines on the beach," as one long-time observer expressed it. High partisan polarization has increasingly forced that role on the House (Sinclair 2007a). In persuading their members to take the tough votes, the House Democratic leaders repeatedly stressed the extent to which Obama's success was essential to congressional Democrats' success. "Our political fortunes are tied to Barack Obama's. It's impossible to overstate that," declared Chris Van Hollen, a Pelosi lieutenant and chair of the Democratic Congressional Campaign Committee (Thrush 2009).

The early battles also made clear that Senate obstructionism and individualism would pose the greatest barriers to enacting the Democrats' agenda. When the contested Minnesota race was finally decided in favor of Democrat Al Franken, and Republican Arlen Specter switched to the Democratic party, Senate Democrats held 60 seats, nominally enough to cut off a filibuster at will. However, imposing cloture is a time-consuming process, and to run at all smoothly, the Senate depends on unanimous consent; that requires cooperation between the majority and the minority leader. Furthermore, the Democratic membership includes 13 members from states McCain won in 2008 and senators inclined to go their own way, such as Joe Lieberman. In fact, even though the Senate, like the House, has became more polarized along party lines, the prerogatives Senate rules give individuals tempt senators to pursue their own interests even when they conflict with those of their party; Senate individualism is far from dead.

The Senate majority leadership consequently has a considerably harder task in passing major policy change. Reid usually needs 60 votes. His institutional powers for facilitating passage are much less than the speaker's and, largely as a result, so are his carrots and sticks. Reid's leadership strategies consequently rested heavily on eliciting cooperation through negotiation and persuasion, especially from his fellow Democrats. Reid generally deferred to his committee chairmen. Through innumerable meetings with Democratic senators in small groups, one-on-one and in weekly caucus lunches, Reid kept members informed and elicited feedback. He tried to reach decisions that all members of the caucus could live with and cleared important ones with the caucus before they were finalized. The process could be maddeningly slow, and Reid was often subject to harsh media criticism for being ineffectual.

Most Senate Republicans sincerely opposed most of the Democrats' agenda, and many also believed that Democrats' failure to enact their agenda would benefit the Republican party electorally. Consequently Reid could expect little help from the Republican leadership. Democrats believed that Republicans were "slow walking" business in the Senate. Although not forcing Democrats to impose cloture on the motion to proceed just to bring measures to the floor as frequently as they did in the 110th, Republicans used that time-wasting device on eight important bills in 2009 alone. They placed "holds" not just on legislation but on many Obama executive branch and judicial nominations, delaying the process of staffing those branches to a crawl. Republicans were even slow to respond to unanimous consent agreement offers from Democrats, thus slowing the process of reaching agreements, Democrats contended. On the floor, they insist on offering multitudes of amendments. Thus bills that had in the past been noncontroversial, such as the transportation appropriations bill, took days on the Senate floor.

Still, Reid had no choice but to deal with Minority Leader Mitch McConnell on a continuous basis, nor did McConnell have a choice about dealing with Reid. McConnell could make Senate Democrats' lives considerably harder by not agreeing to unanimous consent agreements at all. Even now, the Senate does a large part of its business through unanimous consent and, while reaching agreements takes more time than it used to and may be tortuous on major legislation, the lack of agreement would bring the Senate to a halt. McConnell needed to protect his party's reputation, so he did not want to chance its being seen as responsible for a complete breakdown, though that became less of a concern as Obama's popularity fell. Still, his members have legislative goals quite apart from the big issues that separate the parties, and accomplishing them requires that the Senate be able to function.

Because the majority party sets the floor schedule with legislation it wants to pass, and especially when, as in the 111th Congress, the majority party has a big agenda, a minority leader has considerable bargaining power. Increasingly in the last few years, majority leaders have agreed to 60 vote requirements in unanimous consent agreements (UCA); that is, the UCA will specify that, for passage of the bill or of an amendment, 60 votes rather than a simple majority are required. The majority agrees because doing so saves time. For example, the UCA negotiated by Reid on the Lilly Ledbetter Fair Pay Act specified that passage would require 59 votes (three-fifths of the total number of senators sworn, which, at that time, was 98). After all, the Republicans could have forced Reid to go through the time-consuming process of imposing cloture. After a bill has been on the floor for a time, the majority leader often attempts to reach a unanimous consent agreement for finishing it off, and that usually includes agreement on the additional amendments that each side can offer. Again, McConnell could drive a hard bargain for his members because Democrats wanted to move the legislation. Reid had to convince his own members that they had to take hard votes in order to enact their agenda.

In sum, contemporary Senate majority leaders usually need to muster 60 votes to pass legislation—and often to get approval of nominations as well. When they are expected, as Reid and his leadership team were, to pass an ambitious agenda, they confront a situation in which individual senators and the minority party can exercise enormous bargaining power. When the minority, for policy or electoral reasons, is unwilling to negotiate and fully uses its prerogatives under Senate rules, it can often block action altogether or at least make action extraordinarily costly in time and effort for the majority.

## Passing Legacy Legislation: Health Care Reform, Climate Change Mitigation, and Financial Services Regulation

As important as passing the stimulus bill was, the legacy of the Obama administration and of the 111th Congress would depend on the enactment of legislation that fulfilled the marquee promises made in the campaign to reform health care, attack climate change, and reform financial regulations so as to lessen the chance of a repeat of the sort of crisis that had devastated the economy in 2008. Pelosi and the House of Representatives delivered on all three major agenda items; the Senate was unable to pass a climate change bill. It did, however, pass a stronger financial regulatory reform bill than the House had.

The strategies employed by the Democratic congressional leaders were largely the same as those used to pass the stimulus bill, and the problems and barriers were similar too, though in exaggerated form. The policy issues were more complex, they divided Democrats to a greater extent, and thus made putting together winning coalitions a trickier and more delicate enterprise, and they confronted even more adamant GOP opposition.

Passing health care reform proved to be a marathon. Obama again did not submit a detailed plan to Congress; he laid out general principles and depended on congressional Democrats to fill in the details. To get a bill to the floor that could command the necessary majority took intense leadership negotiations at a number of stages of the process and some painful compromises in both chambers. To avoid turf fights, Speaker Pelosi asked the chairmen of the three committees with jurisdiction to negotiate a single bill that then could be introduced in all their committees. Pelosi and her leadership team undertook a months-long campaign of consulting, educating, and negotiating with their members. The leaders knew they could expect no Republican votes at all, so they could lose at most 39 Democrats. That meant they would have to get a considerable number of moderate to conservative Democrats on board without losing their liberal members. In the end, Pelosi was forced to delete the "robust" public option, a government-run health insurance plan that would pay providers at the Medicare care rate plus 5 percent, and to allow a stringent anti-abortion amendment to be offered on the floor. Both were decisions House liberals opposed and that Pelosi herself disliked, but they were essential to the 220–215 victory on November 7, 2009; 39 Democrats voted against the bill (Hulse and Palmer 2009). A former Clinton staffer involved in the failed 1993–94 health reform effort said admiringly, "On the final vote, the whipping process was intense and impressive. Democratic leaders I have known in the past have rarely played this kind of hardball, but some kneecaps were broken Saturday night to get these votes, and the speaker did a masterful job of doing every little thing that needed to be done. She gave no passes to people, and she was very clear there would have been consequences to all who voted no. She got the job done." ( Lux 2009).

With fewer procedural powers and less leeway in terms of votes he could lose, Senate Majority Leader Reid had a still more difficult task. The Finance Committee whose chairman had tried for months to forge a bipartisan deal finally reported out a bill in September with one Republican vote; HELP, the other committee with jurisdiction, had reported a very different bill months earlier. As on the House side, putting together a bill that could pass required consulting broadly, a task that was directed by the leadership as was the case in the House. Reid, however, knew that he would need 60 votes just to get the bill to the floor and then 60 again to get a vote on final passage; he also knew that getting any Republican votes would be exceedingly difficult.

In the end, Reid would be required to make a number of compromises unpalatable to his more liberal members. Hardest to take was Joe Lieberman's demand that any form of the public option be dropped and then that the compromise of letting some 55- to 64-year-olds buy into Medicare also be scrapped. Reid, knowing he had to have the vote, acceded. The last holdout, Ben Nelson, was brought on board with compromise abortion language and some special provisions for his state

At 7 a.m. on Christmas Eve morning, the bill passed the Senate on a straight party line vote of 60 to 39. The Senate had debated the bill for 25 days, without breaks for weekends since early December, and Democrats had had to win five cloture votes; provisions that a large majority of the Democratic membership strongly supported had been dropped to get the requisite 60 votes. But Reid had gotten a major health reform bill though the Senate before the end of Obama's first year. He had done so, in Senator Tom Harkin's words, by "exhibit[ing] the patience of Job, the wisdom of Solomon and the endurance of Samson" (*Roll Call* 12/23/09).

The process of forging one bill from the two chambers' different versions was well under way when Republican Scott Brown won a special election to replace Ted Kennedy in the Senate. Brown's victory on an anti–health care platform in strongly Democratic Massachusetts shocked and scared congressional Democrats. It also deprived Senate Democrats of that crucial 60th vote.

In the first days after the January 20 special election, Speaker Pelosi was the strongest voice for finishing the job of enacting major reform. Despite advice to settle for smaller changes in health care policy, Obama too decided fairly quickly to plow ahead.

Over the course of the months-long battle, the White House had played a significant behind-the-scenes role, and Obama himself had sometimes used the bully pulpit as well. Senior White House aides had assisted the congressional leaders in their negotiations; they and Obama had met with innumerable members, attempting to keep the process moving and then to persuade them to vote for the bills. Although never doing as much to frame the debate favorably as congressional Democrats wanted him to do, Obama had made an extremely important health care speech to a joint session of Congress in September. Coming after a brutal August during which many Democrats had been attacked vociferously by Tea Party activists at home, Obama's well-received speech stemmed the panic. Obama had always intended to take a more prominent role in shaping the final language after both chambers had passed a bill. Even before the Brown victory, Obama had chaired lengthy negotiating sessions at the White House. Now a still more prominent role became necessary. Obama convened a health care summit to which he invited Republican and Democratic congressional leaders; over seven hours of civil and substantive discussion, Obama made the case for thoroughgoing reform and showed that the Republicans lacked a plan.

Obama's PR offensive gave the congressional leadership the time and the cover to implement a plan for finishing health care reform legislation. The loss of the 60th vote in the Senate made the normal ways of resolving differences between the chambers politically impossible because any compromise product would be filibusterable in the Senate. The House could have simply accepted the Senate bill, but, because it included some provisions that were extremely unpopular with House Democrats—the "Cornhusker Kickback" to get Nelson's vote and a stiff tax on the "Cadillac Health Care Plan," for example—Pelosi insisted she could not get the votes to do so. Fortunately, at the insistence of House Democrats and the White House, the budget resolution passed in spring of 2009 had allowed for a reconciliation bill with health care provisions. The Budget Act provides that such reconciliation bills are not subject to filibusters (Thurber and Durst 1993; Oleszek 2007). Because Budget Act rules restrict what can be included in reconciliation bills, enacting health care reform entirely through a reconciliation bill was not feasible; however, the main changes House Democrats needed to support the bill could be included in a reconciliation bill.

A full court press involving the White House, other members of the administration, and Obama himself, as well as the House Democratic leadership and its entire apparatus of persuasion, was required to pass the bills in the House. On March 21 the chamber passed first the Senate bill by 219–212 and then the reconciliation bill that fixed the Senate bill on a 220–211 vote. Obama signed the Senate bill on March 23. On March 25, the Senate passed the reconciliation bill 56–43, and the president signed it on March 30. No Republican supported health care reform on any of these votes.

During 2009, the effort to reform financial regulations was overshadowed by the health care battle. Financial Services Committee Chair Barney Frank took the lead role in the House and, after a lengthy series of mark-up sessions, negotiations with the leaders of other committees that shared some jurisdiction, and a carefully calculated set of post-committee adjustments, got a bill to the House floor in December. During a lengthy amending process, Frank and the Democratic leadership managed to keep the core tenets of the bill intact (*CQ Weekly* 2010). On December 11, it passed 223–202 with no Republican voting in favor.

Knowing he would eventually need 60 votes, Senate Banking Committee Chair Chris Dodd negotiated with Richard Shelby, his Republican counterpart, for months; when no deal seemed possible, he tried negotiation with Bob Corker, another committee Republican. Again no agreement was reached, and on March 22, the Banking Committee reported out a bill Dodd had negotiated with his fellow Democrats on a party-line vote. With health care now finished, the White House pressing for action, and continuing talks making no progress, Reid decided to force action. He moved to consider the bill on April 22 and filed for cloture. Cloture motions failed on April 26, 27, and 28; but after the third failed vote, Republicans called off their filibuster. The Democrats had agreed to drop a provision the Republicans opposed, but the GOP's decision seems to have been influenced more by the change in visibility of the battle. With health care no longer the big story, the media began to cover the financial regulation fight in earnest, and Republicans found themselves looking like the defenders of Wall Street. The Republican leadership's attempt to paint the bill as a bail out protection act seemed to gain little traction. After 35 recorded votes, 28 on attempts to amend the bill and 2 on cloture, on May 20 the Senate passed the bill. In the glare of media attention now focused on the Senate battle, the bill actually got stronger on the floor.

Taking advantage of this publicity effect, Barney Frank and Chris Dodd, with the agreement of their leaderships, decided to resolve their differences through a conference committee and a truly open one. The financial services industry lobbyists who had forced Frank to weaken his initial bill in the House and who had counted on further weakening at the resolution stage were largely disappointed. After two weeks of negotiations, the conference committee reached a compromise that it approved early in the morning of June 25. On June 30, the House approved the conference report on a 237–192 vote with 3 Republicans joining all but 19 of the Democrats in support.

Again the final steps were more complicated in the Senate, and getting to 60 was the problem. On July 28, Democrat Robert Byrd died, depriving Reid of a vote he was counting on to impose cloture on the conference report. The four Senate Republicans who had voted for the bill announced they would oppose the conference report because of a provision taxing big banks to pay some of the costs. Dodd and Frank reconvened the conference committee and removed that provision, but that only resulted in one of the four committing to support. Two Democrats had voted against the bill, arguing that it was too weak; one had been won over, but the other, Russ Feingold, was adamant, so Reid needed two more Republicans. Democrats were unable to get the needed votes before the July 4th recess, but two more Republicans committed afterward, and on July 15, the Senate imposed cloture and then passed the conference report and sent another major piece of legislation to Obama for his signature.

Passing climate change mitigation, the third big agenda item, proved to be impossible in the Senate. Energy issues split member of Congress along regional and agricultural versus urban lines as well as ideological lines. Putting a price on carbon emissions as a serious climate change bill amplifies the stakes and expands the interests usually involved in energy battles. Speaker Pelosi and Energy and Commerce Chair Henry Waxman, with a significant assist from Obama, managed to pass a bill in the House, but doing so was tough and required major concessions to a variety of interests. The bill passed on June 26, 2009, by a tight vote of 219–212; 44 Democrats voted against the bill, but 8 Republicans voted for it.

Western and agricultural interests are more heavily represented in the Senate and, of course, a supermajority would be needed. Despite Democratic attempts to negotiate a bipartisan bill, Republican opposition just hardened over the course of 2010. Environmentalists hoped the huge BP oil spill might spur agreement. By the summer of 2010, however, partisanship had brought the Senate to a near standstill. Bipartisan and largely noncontroversial bills such as legislation strengthening food safety were being blocked by GOP obstructionism; even the highly publicized case of widespread salmonella contamination of eggs did not lead hardliners to relent. Such circumstances made even a more modest energy bill—a "down payment"—impossible. No bill was ever considered on the Senate floor.

## MANAGING EXPECTATIONS, EXPLOITING OPPORTUNITIES, AND LIVING WITH CONSTRAINTS: THE BOTTOM LINE

The Democratic congressional leaders of the 111th Congress were highly successful in passing legislation; of course, not everything on the agenda was enacted, but a large number of important items were, including several truly nonincremental programs. Health care reform, if successfully implemented, will represent the sort of legacy few leaders can claim. So certainly the leaders and Obama exploited legislative opportunities effectively.

Yet by defeating scores of Democrats at the polls and giving control of the House to Republicans, voters delivered a stinging verdict on the 111th Congress in the 2010 elections. To the extent party leaders are judged by their success in protecting their members and maintaining their majorities, the Democratic leaders failed. To be sure, Pelosi and Obama did what they could in terms of campaigning and raising money for Democratic members, but clearly it was not enough. If they had made different choices, could they have averted the electoral debacle, or were the constraints too great to overcome?

The most formidable legislative constraint Democrats confronted was the combination of Senate supermajority rules and high partisan polarization. The necessity of getting 60 votes for almost everything in the Senate killed major legislation—climate change mitigation, immigration reform, and a host of less high profile bills—and it forced significant concessions on legislation that did pass. Furthermore, this legislative constraint and the process of overcoming it sufficiently to pass major legislation appears to have engendered political constraints. To a public with limited understanding of how legislatures normally work, the drawn-out, contentious, and deal-infused process of getting to 60 appeared shady at best and cast a pall of illegitimacy on the resulting legislation and the body itself.

The real failure of the congressional leaders and of Obama himself, one might argue, was in managing expectations. The Obama presidency and the 111th Congress began with extraordinarily high expectations. Given that, they should have done a much better job of explaining the problems confronting the country, of framing the choices Democrats faced, and of persuading the public of the rightness of the policy choices pursued. Obama, who as president has the bully pulpit, has come in for most of the criticism, including from Democratic members of Congress and sometimes from the leaders themselves. If Obama had just been a more effective communicator, the public would have understood and so liked the stimulus bill and health care reform better, and congressional Democrats would not have suffered such a big defeat in the 2010 elections, the strongest form of the argument goes.

Undoubtedly Obama could have done a more effective job communicating, as could members of Congress in their own districts. Congressional leaders could probably have done more to make the process appear less messy. In both cases, however, how much more is open to question. The "golden age" of presidential domination of electronic communication is over. From Franklin Roosevelt to Ronald Reagan, presidents could command a broad radio and then television audience in a way no other figure could; now presidents face many more competitors for people's attention. Democratic congressional leaders confronted a minority party adamantly opposed to their agenda and willing to use every tool available to make the majority party look as bad as possible. Orchestrating a legislative process that looks neat and pretty is difficult under those circumstances.

Some argue that, if Democrats had put off health care reform and "focused on jobs" instead, they would have done much better in the midterm elections. What that argument misses is, first, the impact of the dashed expectations among the Democratic base if the clear promise of tackling health care had been abandoned. Second, exactly what "focusing on jobs" would have entailed either is not specified or required politically unfeasible policies (a much bigger stimulus program). The bottom line is that, most likely, the congressional Democrats' fate was determined by the state of the economy and that, given the abysmal state of the economy in January 2009 at the beginning of the 111th Congress, there was not much within the realm of the politically feasible that Democrats could have done to improve it enough to have avoided big losses in time for the 2010 elections.

## NOTE

1. Rules data were compiled by Don Wolfensberger, Woodrow Wilson Center, and the author.

CHAPTER 7

# A "Post-Partisan" President
# in a Partisan Context

*John E. Owens*

Barack Obama ran for the presidency promising a new style of "post-partisan" politics and appealed to Democrats and Republicans to find "common ground." Following an unlikely journey from obscure state senator to president, Obama became the first senator since John Kennedy elected directly from the Senate. With Democrats gaining their largest House and Senate majorities since 1994 and 1978 and the strength of a president's party being a strong predictor of legislative success (Edwards 1989, 172–3; Binder 1999, 2003; Bond and Fleischer 1990, ch. 4), the new president could expect to win strong congressional support for his legislative priorities. In this chapter, we ask: was the strategic context that Obama encountered as favorable to the new president as the return of unified party government suggested? With what strategies did he pursue his legislative priorities over the first two years of his presidency with the 111th Congress, and with what success?

## OBAMA'S STRATEGIC CONTEXT

From the outset, it was evident that the strategic context that Obama encountered, and which would help or hinder his efforts to influence the Congress after the 2008 elections, included both positive and negative elements.

*The Positives*

As an elected—as distinct from a re-elected or nonelected president or an elected vice president or elected heir apparent[1]—Obama's credentials were strong. His attractive, relaxed personality and optimistic, well managed "change we can believe in" campaign enthused Democrats and independents and reaped a strong popular vote and a handsome Electoral College victory, which included nine more states than John Kerry in 2004, including three in the South. Claiming a 68 percent approval rating when he entered the White House, his political standing was high—just behind Lyndon Johnson, Dwight Eisenhower, and Ronald Reagan and at the same level as George H. W. Bush among the 10 post–World War II newly elected presidents.[2]

Obama's legislative standing[3] was also superior to almost all newly elected presidents over the same period—slightly ahead of Bill Clinton, just behind Eisenhower, although not in Johnson's or even Jimmy Carter's league. Building on their gains in 2006, congressional Democrats doubled their House majority to 78 and eventually gained a 60-vote majority in the Senate.[4] The highest level of synchronized House-presidential voting since 1972 also meant that popular majorities in 81 percent of House districts voted for the same party in both elections; just 83 districts (19 percent) split their votes between the parties. The same dynamic prevailed in Senate elections so that three-fourths of the new Senate belonged to the same party that won their state in the 2008 presidential election. Combining Obama's legislative and political standing scores, the new president ranked the third strongest of all newly elected post-1952 presidents (behind Johnson and Eisenhower). In addition, Obama could expect to benefit from the increased ideological homogenization of his party's core constituencies (Gelman 2008; Abramowitz 2010; and Abramowitz and Saunders 2008), by increased party voting and strong party leaderships in both chambers and by increasingly centralized party fund-raising (Sinclair 2006). In consequence, Obama would not have to contend with the committee barons and the solid bloc of conservative southerners that had blocked Kennedy's New Frontier legislation in the 87th Congress (Sundquist 1968, 471–81). The dominant norms and expectations of House members and senators, moreover, are now much more strongly infused by party loyalty, including loyalty to the party's president (Eilperin 2006; Mann and Ornstein 2008 122–40, 146–9; Lee 2009, 87–102), with increased possibilities for winning partisan legislation with bare majorities (Beckmann and McGann 2008, 202).

Obama would also find skilled and experienced central leaders and committee chairs of his own party at the other end of Pennsylvania Avenue. After eight years of a Republican president, they would be keen to help a Democratic president enact many of the proposals his predecessor had resisted. Indeed, immediately after the elections, House Speaker Nancy Pelosi (D-CA) firmly rejected demands that Democrats push a bold non-centrist agenda on the basis of a supposed sea change in US politics. Senate Majority Leader Harry Reid was similarly cautious, while Senator Charles Schumer (D-NY) pointedly recalled congressional Democrats' failure to cooperate with the Clinton administration after the 1992 elections (Herszenhorn and Hulse 2008).

*The Negatives*

Against these positive elements, there were several significant negatives, which would constrain or deny the new president opportunities to win approval of his legislative priorities, particularly if they entailed major changes in public policy (Neustadt 1990, 265), as Obama's campaign rhetoric promised.

The US faced the worst banking crisis and the most severe recession since the 1930s at the same time that the country was fighting two wars. In December 2008 alone, the US economy had lost 524,000 jobs, pushing the unemployment rate to 7.2 percent (11.1 million people), a 16-year record and almost 50 percent higher than a year ago. Not since 1980 had the US work force shrunk so much in just three months. More jobs were forecast to be lost in the forthcoming months with unemployment expected to rise to 9 or 10 percent and jobless growth continuing thereafter. At the same time, home values were falling, as many as 20 million families were facing foreclosures, the federal budget was fast heading toward a record $1 trillion deficit, and the banking system was dysfunctional.

While public and party expectations were great that the new Democratic president would solve these problems, the 2008 presidential results hardly gave Obama a strong mandate for a "change" agenda. The new president and his party were primarily the beneficiaries of a referendum on Bush and Republican rule, especially the decision to invade Iraq (Jacobson 2009a, 2010a, 24). But for the financial meltdown in September 2008, Obama may not have been elected (Campbell 2010, 225). Neither his nor congressional Democrats' victories were by a landslide, and his coattails were modest, with popular vote majorities in only 242 of the 257 districts won by House Democrats and him running ahead of only 5 of the 20 victorious Democratic senators, 4 of whom were newly elected. Forty-nine House Democrats (presumed to be centrists) were elected from districts that John McCain won. Even after the delayed result in Minnesota and Senator Arlen Specter's switch in Pennsylvania gave them a 60-seat majority, there would be only 44 Democrats (and two sympathetic independents) from the states he won and 13 from states won by McCain, including five elected in 2008 (two with less than 55 percent of the vote)[5] and three up for re-election in 2010. At least three of the eight new Democratic senators were thought to be centrists.

There would likely be a third negative element. Obama would seek congressional support for his "post-partisan" and bipartisan agenda in the context of highly polarized congressional parties (Aldrich and Rohde 2000, 2001; Theriault 2008). The previous 110th Congress was the most polarized since Reconstruction (McCarty, Poole, and Rosenthal 2006, 2010). Obama would likely encounter a new Congress that was at least as polarized as its predecessor. This polarization would likely be boosted, moreover, by an increasingly entrenched confrontational and oppositional ethos according to which the out-party feels duty-bound to perpetuate inter-party disagreements and differences with the in-party and make its life as difficult as possible, as part of a longer term strategy to wrest control of the White House and Capitol Hill. In this context, presidential interventions actually strengthen this confrontational ethos (Lee 2009, 22), reinforcing Skowronek's observation that presidents are nothing less than the "lightning rod" of national politics (1993, 20), especially if they are active agenda setters.

At the same time that ideological polarization and the contemporary confrontational ethos heighten inter-party conflict, presidents—regardless of any post- or bi-partisan inclinations to the contrary—are now obliged to govern from their party's base, which in turn further strengthens the out-party's resolve to oppose the president's agenda and portray him/her as out of touch. Add the increased use of the Senate filibuster, the sharp rise in partisan cloture votes, and the need to hold together 60 Democratic votes (Binder and Smith 1997; Binder 2003), and it becomes easy to reach the conclusion that, regardless of the return of single-party Democratic government, the strategic context that the Obama White House faced was unlikely to produce the kind of legislative cooperation and record that Franklin Roosevelt or Lyndon Johnson enjoyed when they first entered the White House.

## Obama's Legislative Agency

While hugely important, the strategic context that presidents face does not determine absolutely the extent to which presidents are able to achieve their legislative goals. Presidential agency is also important (Edwards 2009; Greenstein 2009; Hargrove 2003, 2008; Neustadt 1990; Rockman 2009, 791), although the degree to which scholars "count" presidential agency and how they "count" it varies greatly. How then might Obama's personal style influence his approach to the Congress? What perceptions, energy, skills, and other personal characteristics would he bring to the table? How would he organize his legislative presidency (Wayne 1978), and what strategies would he deploy to win congressional approval for his legislative priorities?

### Congress-centric Transition and White House Teams

New presidents must show respect for the governing institution that is their coequal (Pfiffner 1996, 118), as Ronald Reagan did and Bill Clinton and Jimmy Carter did not, at least to the same extent (Edwards 1998; Jones 1988, 43, 72–73, 142; 1999b, 135ff; 2005, 350; Peabody 1977, 150). From the outset, Obama's approach to the Congress was respectful, emollient, even deferential, especially with House and Senate Democratic leaders. "Congress exercises all sorts of prerogatives," he told a television interviewer just before he took office. "They've got all sorts of procedures. Everybody wants to be heard. And I'm respectful of that. I'm coming from the United States Senate. I understand why that is important … You know, one of the things that *we're trying to set a tone* of is that, you know, Congress is a coequal branch of government. We're not trying to jam anything down people's throats" (2009a).

Even before he was elected, Obama appointed Phil Schiliro, former House Oversight and Government Reform Committee chief of staff and staffer for former Senate Majority Leader Tom Daschle (D-SD) as his campaign's congressional liaison. Following his election victory, congressional relations became an intrinsic part of his transition team. His first appointment was an experienced Washington insider, Rahm Emanuel, at a stroke recognizing the centrality of the chief of staff in cultivating and maintaining strong relations with the Congress (Walcott, Warshaw, and Wayne 2001, 483). Emanuel came directly from the heart of the House Democratic leadership and was previously a senior strategist in the Clinton White House. "Rahm understands how to get things done in Washington," the president-elect told journalists. A whole swath of Washington insiders accompanied Schiliro and Emanuel.[6] Pete Rouse, known as the "101st Senator" when he was chief of staff to Daschle, later Obama's chief of staff in the Senate, became co-chair of his transition team with Valerie Jarrett and John Podesta, Clinton's former chief of staff. Early on, the transition team set up a series of well-publicized meetings with congressional Democratic leaders to consult and agree on a common legislative agenda and plot strategy and timing for its implementation (Weisman and Bendavid 2009; Burke 2009, 577, 585–6). The transition team also reached out to "Blue Dog" Democratic centrists (Murray 2008, A1) and Republicans (Hook and Parsons 2008, A1; Hulse 2009, A1).

Once installed in the White House, Schiliro was located "upstream" in the presidential decision-making process (Klein 2009), as head of congressional liaison, thereby sending out a strong signal to members of Congress that the president's chief congressional lobbyist enjoyed sufficient status and access to obviate them talking also with Emanuel or a Cabinet member. All 14 congressional liaison staff members were recruited straight off the Hill and known for their pragmatic approaches (Palmer 2009). Trusted and experienced assistant secretaries for legislative affairs were also appointed to the various executive departments and agencies to help ensure a coordinated congressional liaison effort and shepherd Cabinet members and other political appointees through the Senate confirmation process.[7] No administration since Nixon's in 1968 "had made swifter progress in filling out Cabinet positions" (Burke 2009b, 584), although some mistakes were made.[8]

*Obama's Pragmatic Conciliatory Style*

Obama's respectful approach to the Congress reflected a pragmatic conciliatory style (Toner 2008). "He really wants to get things done. He won't just stake out a position," one of his most trusted advisers told *USA Today* late in 2008 (Wickham 2008, A11). His involvement in Chicago politics had followed a similar pattern: "For all their differences in style and speech, Obama and [Chicago Mayor Richard M.] Daley shared a basic approach to politics as a constant negotiation of interests and ideals—Chicago's brand of *Realpolitik*. Both had advanced by capitalizing on the prevailing power structure, not by dismantling it, and they were united, above all, not by ideology but by pragmatism" (Osnos 2010, 38). Despite his liberal reputation, Obama was actually a relatively orthodox Democrat in the US Senate. He was careful to avoid being perceived as "ideological," "partisan," or ready to adopt hard and fast liberal positions (MacFarquhar 2007; Remnick 2010a, 427, 430, 433, 437). He cultivated a reputation as a deliberative, fair-minded, intellectual, and willing to consult and consider competing points of view. So, although he frequently articulated liberal Democratic policy preferences—on a firm date for the withdrawal of troops from Iraq, the Guantánamo detainees, NSA electronic surveillance, DC's handgun ban, caps on class action suits, and executive powers—ultimately, he voted pragmatic conciliatory positions that many liberals opposed. He was also willing to work with Senate Republicans and Democratic centrists on immigration reform, tighter control of former Soviet arms caches, and greater transparency in government contracting.

As a newly elected president and putative legislative leader, however, he was an unknown quantity. Although he had run a well-managed presidential campaign, he had experience neither as an executive nor in interacting with executives. Once account is taken of the last two years, when he was already running for the White House, his experience as a junior senator was short and never extended to him playing a significant role in writing major legislation. Moreover, experienced and skilled congressional leaders of his own party, who had been exclusively responsible for developing and processing his party's legislative priorities over the previous eight years, would likely not welcome an inexperienced newcomer demanding that they relinquish those responsibilities completely. Indeed, former Clinton White House aides counseled that the new administration should avoid "our overreaching, our arrogance, our lack of involvement at the front end of our efforts, our not letting Congress work their will, and our ignoring of the need to check our egos" (Clinton staffer 2009).

Still, Obama's inexperience and deliberative and conciliatory style raised as many questions as these characteristics inspired confidence and reassurance. His restrained reaction to unexpected political events, such as the financial meltdown, his professed faith in objective policy analysis and expertise, and his calls for people to come together, develop new ideas, and find common ground might otherwise be interpreted as arrogance, *hauteur,* and emotional detachment (e.g., Remnick 2010a, 433–35, 457). Although an inspirational speaker on the stump, his motivating passions were often difficult to detect (Alter 2010, 138–58; Renshon 2008, 409; Woodward 2010, 321). Clinton staffers warned of the dangers of overreaching, but with Obama there might be the opposite problem: underreaching, an inability to identify opportunities for political advantage and to bargain hard, insufficient political will and perseverance, a tendency to compromise too quickly, and a failure to establish a strong political reputation. As a state senator and a US senator, Obama had been easily bored and distracted (Remnick 2010a, 433, 444). In Springfield, he chafed at the limitations of legislating (Mundy 2007), and after just 18 months in the US Senate it was already clear to Majority Leader Reid that Obama was not "cut out to be a Senate lifer" (Heilemann and Halperin 2010). Apparently frustrated with his personal lack of influence and the chamber's "glacial pace" (Zernike and Zeleny 2008), Obama "hated being a senator," according to his political advisor, David Axelrod (Remnick 2010a, 444).[9] Years later, after one year in the White House, he would tell a television interviewer that he would "rather be a really good president than a mediocre two-term president."

How well Obama's uncertain passion, detached conciliatory style, and penchant for objective analysis would translate into effective legislative influence in the context of the highly partisan, polarized, and confrontational politics of Washington remained to be seen. If anything, Obama's professed desire to "move beyond the divisive politics of Washington and bring Democrats, independents and Republicans together to get things done" (Toner 2008) added to the uncertainty. If it meant anything beyond rhetoric, Obama's "post-partisanship" might be interpreted at best as arrogant overconfidence and wishful thinking born of inexperience and a desire to remain a Washington outsider above the legislative fray, and at worst as a dangerous pathological weakness for avoiding institutional and partisan conflict and the hard bargaining and time-consuming but obligatory schlepping and unsavory deal-making necessary to win congressional support.

## LEGISLATIVE PRIORITIES AND ACCOMPLISHMENTS

Obama's campaign promises to "turn the page" and effect the "change we need" (2008b, 2008c) were unquestionably ambitious, although hardly out of place among the declarations of previous presidents. The new president wanted to be "event-making" or "transformational" rather than "eventful" (Burns 1978, 344–45, 36; Hargrove 2008, 258–59; Hook 1943). "I really want to be a president who makes a difference," he told presidential biographer Doris Kearns Goodwin (Remnick 2010a, 476).

If presidents with ambitious policy goals are going to stand a chance of leading the Congress successfully, they need to designate their legislative priorities, communicate them clearly, act quickly and decisively, and husband their political capital. Opting for Reagan's and George W. Bush's "rifle" over Carter's "shotgun" approach (Pfiffner 1996, 116), the new president moved quickly to limit the size of his legislative agenda. In his second presidential debate with McCain in Nashville in October 2008, Obama had articulated three legislative priorities: 1) energy, climate change, and reducing reliance on foreign oil; 2) health care reform; and 3) education. Weeks later, he added the financial crisis and its consequences, including financial regulatory reform, at the same time reiterating energy independence as his second priority, health care third, followed by economic stimulus including middle class tax cuts (Hornick 2008). Of these policy objectives, only financial regulatory reform looked relatively easy, given popular hostility to the industries' irresponsibility, although here too staunch industry opposition could be expected (Alter 2010, 244–46; Stolberg 2009a, A1; Jacobs and Skocpol 2010, 43).

With the election won, Obama and congressional Democratic leaders agreed to move quickly on the president's legislative priorities before the 2010 midterm elections (Nather 2008). Priorities would be also be sequenced. "Instead of hoarding their political capital, Rahm said, they would leverage the capital earned on early wins to build more for the tough struggles down the road ... The concept of leveraging political capital was central to the president's mission" (Alter 2010, 79).

Two years after his election, Obama had presided over one of the most productive periods since the 89th Congress (1965–66). Table 7-1 lists the action taken or not taken by the House and Senate on 21 "major" proposals considered by the 111th Congress.[10] As the table shows, Obama was able to sign 15 and win ratification for the Strategic Arms Reduction Treaty (START). In keeping with the recent trend (Binder and Smith 1997; Binder 2003), all 5 of the 20 measures (30 percent) that required House approval[11] died in the Senate. Of these five, four did not receive Senate floor consideration, one failed to reach cloture, and two did not even receive committee consideration. [12]

The fifth column in the table provides a sense of these measures' significance by giving them weightings roughly comparable to those used by David Mayhew in his dataset of presidential proposals (2008). Only two (climate change and health care) warrant the maximum values of 4, and two (the Dodd-Frank Wall Street Reform and Consumer Protection Act and the Strategic Arms Reduction Treaty) a value of 3. On these most significant measures, Obama did well, with health care (the 2010 Patient Protection and Affordable Care Act), the Dodd-Frank Act, and START being the most significant achievements. The most significant failure was climate change. The remaining legislation is very much second order material, including the 2009 American Recovery and Reinvestment Act (won), tobacco regulation (won), and immigration overhaul (lost).

Table 7-2 puts Obama's record of major legislative achievements into historical perspective using Mayhew's data for presidents' first two years for comparison. As the table shows, notwithstanding different methodologies for identifying major legislation, Obama's "win rate" of 76 percent is above that of all his nine predecessors except Johnson. Focusing specifically on the most significant legislation (measures coded 3 and 4), Obama also scores well, winning the same number as Johnson but also including an elusive 4 against none for the 36th president. Winning passage of health care, financial reform, and the arms limitation treaty (but losing climate change), Obama achieved a 75 percent win rate.[13]

What difference, if any, did Obama's interventions make in influencing congressional outcomes on major legislation during the 111th Congress? In short, how significant was presidential agency and how effective was Obama's legislative leadership?

## CAUTIOUS LEADERSHIP: BETWEEN STANDING OFF AND LATE INVOLVEMENT

Over the first two years, the strategies employed by Obama's White House for winning congressional approval of his ambitious legislative agenda varied, but some common elements may be identified. First, in order to maximize the president's leverage over the legislative process, the White House rather than executive departments directed efforts. Second, the new president typically declined to send congressional leaders legislative blueprints and only set out broad policy parameters late in the game. By this strategy, the administration could avoid any suggestion that they were trying to ram legislation down congressional throats

## Table 7-1: Congressional Action on Obama's Legislative Proposals

| Legislation | House | Senate | Obama's Position | Significance Weighting |
|---|---|---|---|---|
| Extend Child Health Insurance Program (CHIP) | Passed | Passed | Signed | 1 |
| Economic stimulus | Passed | Passed | Signed | 2 |
| Foreclosure assistance | Passed | Passed | Signed | 1 |
| Lilly Ledbetter Fair Pay Act | Passed | Passed | Signed | 1 |
| Credit card regulation | Passed | Passed | Signed | 1 |
| Tobacco regulation | Passed | Passed | Signed | 2 |
| Climate change mitigation/cap and trade | Passed | No floor action | For | 1 |
| Defense acquisition overhaul | Passed | Passed | Signed | 1 |
| Health care overhaul | Passed | Passed | Signed | 4 |
| Food safety overhaul | Passed | Passed | Signed | 1 |
| Dodd-Frank financial services regulation | Passed | Passed | Signed | 3 |
| Student loan overhaul; education reform (part of health care overhaul) | Passed | Passed | Signed | 1 |
| Hate crimes expansion | Passed | Passed | Signed | 1 |
| Extend unemployment benefits & homebuyer credits | Passed | Passed | Signed | 1 |
| Tax Relief, Unemployment Insurance Reauthorization, and Job Creation Act, 2010 (Extend Bush tax cuts) | Passed | Passed | Signed | 1 |
| Immigration overhaul | Passed | No floor or committee action | For | 2 |
| Campaign finance regulation overhaul | Passed | Rejected cloture | For | 1 |
| Home energy rebate | Passed | No floor or committee action | For | 1 |
| Offshore Oil and Gas Worker Whistleblower Protection Act of 2010 | Passed | No floor action | For | 1 |
| Assistance to states for education and Medicaid | Passed | Passed | Signed | 1 |
| Strategic Arms Reduction Treaty | NA | Passed | For | 3 |

Source: Thomas.loc.gov; CQ Weekly.
Note: Shaded rows indicate measures not enacted into law.

while depriving opponents of a single target for their fire. Third, in the initial stages of congressional consideration of legislation on Obama's priorities, the president expressed a preference for bipartisan legislation and took steps to reach out to congressional Republicans. As the subsequent discussion shows, such efforts typically failed as Republican leaders resolved that bipartisan cooperation was not in their party's interests. The effect was to ensure that legislation on

### Table 7-2: Obama's Legislative Success in Historical Perspective, First Two Years

| President | Wins | Losses | % Wins | N Wins Weighted 3 | Unified/ N Wins Weighted 4 | Split Party Government |
|-----------|------|--------|--------|-------------------|----------------------------|------------------------|
| Eisenhower | 9 | 6 | 60% | 0 | 0 | Unified |
| Kennedy | 10 | 5 | 67% | 0 | 0 | Unified |
| Johnson | 17 | 3 | 85% | 3 | 0 | Unified |
| Nixon | 3 | 4 | 43% | 0 | 0 | Split |
| Carter | 8 | 8 | 50% | 0 | 1 | Unified |
| Reagan | 4 | 7 | 36% | 1 | 1 | Split |
| Bush 1 | 5 | 3 | 63% | 1 | 0 | Split |
| Clinton | 10 | 5 | 67% | 0 | 2 | Unified |
| Bush 2 | 8 | 3 | 73% | 1 | 0 | Split |
| Obama | 16 | 5 | 76% | 2 | 1 | Unified |

*Sources:* Table 7-1 and Mayhew 2008.
*Notes:* In Reagan's first two years, only the Senate was controlled by the president's party. After six months of Bush 2's first two years, the Senate was controlled by Democrats.

Obama's priorities was almost invariably approved with only Democratic support. Fourth, White House strategy was to let Democratic congressional leaders lead in writing legislation, help facilitate deals and shape proposals to give bills a more centrist hue, and then co-opt the products as its own. Beyond an ambitious list of legislative priorities, the approach was cautious.

### *Economic Crisis, Caution, and Compromise*

The first evidence of the new president's cautious approach was provided by his pragmatic and conciliatory response to the tricky question of the second $350 billion *tranche* of the Troubled Asset Relief Program (TARP) bailout of the banks orchestrated by the Bush administration. Despite severe personal misgivings, strong public hostility to the program, and considerable opposition from within his own congressional party,[14] Obama chose not to pick a fight and asked President Bush to request release of the TARP funds instead of insisting on new conditions requiring the banks to release more credit to homeowners and businesses and limiting executive bonuses. In characteristic fashion, Obama declared himself "an eternal optimist" who "over time [believed that] people respond to civility and rational argument." Many in his own congressional party wondered, however, whether he had been sufficiently forceful and an opportunity had been lost. Still, Obama had made his top priority passing a two-year stimulus bill that would address the worst economy facing any new president since Franklin Roosevelt in 1933.

In the first real test of his relationship with the new Congress, Obama's transition team agreed with congressional leaders that they would only publish a 15-page outline for an economic stimulus plan rather than a detailed legislative blueprint. Precise language and some policy details would be left to the Congress. With White House agreement, the initial bill would be written in House Speaker

Pelosi's office with significant input from the House Appropriations Committee (Alter 2010, 84) in the expectation that final action would be heavily influenced by the Senate, where Democrats lacked a 60-vote supermajority, and ready for signature by mid-February. By giving the Congress responsibility for writing legislation on such a vital political issue right at the beginning of his administration, of course, the White House risked signaling early on that it would not be a forceful legislative leader. Still, the Democratic Congress had been working for several weeks, if not months, on a stimulus package and the White House and Treasury did not yet have sufficient staff in place.

"You never want a serious crisis to go to waste," Emanuel had told a conference of corporate executives (2008). However, after agreeing on a $1 trillion ceiling with congressional Democratic leaders (Alter 2010, 83)—which it was claimed would "create or save" between three and four million jobs over two years—this total was revised down in response to concerns expressed by Emanuel, Axelrod, Schiliro, and his legislative affairs team (Lizza 2009a). Leaving aside Republican complaints that any increase in spending was unnecessary, many mainstream economists viewed the reduced total as too timid, particularly as almost 40 percent of the total cost was accounted for by $300 billion in tax cuts.

Apart from tax cuts not being an efficient way to generate jobs in the short term compared with direct spending, and their inclusion raising congressional Democrats' hackles (Parsons and Nicholas 2010), doubts were raised about the efficacy of Obama's strategy of seeking to entice Republican support by unilaterally proposing tax cuts even larger over two years than either of President George W. Bush's (Weisman and Bendavid 2009). While faithful to the president's conciliatory style and post-partisan definition of good public policy, as a first move in what would likely become a bargaining game, it suggested overconfidence and naïveté. Effectively, it deprived the White House of a powerful bargaining chip with congressional Republicans, as Obama later acknowledged (Alter 2010, 117, 130). Indeed, it soon became clear that congressional Republicans would not engage in a bargaining process over *any* stimulus deal, with or without these huge tax cuts. Congressional Republican leaders in both chambers instructed committee chairs and other members not to cooperate with Democrats in shaping the package (Davis 2010; Alter 2010, 129). Apparently, they had calculated already that if the economy recovered and unemployment fell, Obama—not Republicans—would receive the credit, whereas if the economy failed to recover, they would share the blame. Conversely, if they refused to play any part, Republicans would have gained tax cuts at no cost and would be free to lay the blame for a weak economy squarely on Democrats in the 2010 elections.

Nonetheless, Obama was determined to display his post-partisan *bona fides,* at one point speaking before the House Republican Conference, even though Minority Leader John Boehner (R-OH) had already instructed his colleagues not to vote for the stimulus package regardless of what Obama said. The White House also sought to limit liberal Democrats' influence and encouraged House Democrat centrists to criticize Pelosi's package as a means of molding it more to White House liking (Alter 2010, 118). Subsequently, Obama insisted that the overall cost of both House and Senate bills be cut and negotiated various deals with centrist

Democrats and Republicans to win their support, including new spending for the elderly (largely left out of Obama and the House's plans) and new tax cuts for higher income taxpayers. Whether as a result of White House intervention or effective deal-making and vote counting by Pelosi and Reid, Democratic defections on the final House and Senate votes were minimized: just seven Democrats voted against the House package, six of them "Blue Dogs," and none in the Senate. No Republican voted for the House version, which closely followed Obama's plan, and only three Senate Republicans were prepared to ignore their leader's instruction and work with the administration on a significantly pared back measure—and one of those subsequently switched to the Democratic Party.

The stimulus legislation gave Obama his first major congressional victory— four weeks into his administration. Whether a more forceful and skillful president could have won a larger package, as demanded by many economists—with or without the large tax cuts—must remain an open question. Whether the package would fulfill its objectives, significantly reduce unemployment, and enhance the new president's political reputation was for the future. For the present, poll results from Gallup showed a drop of nine points in Obama's approval rating at the same time public support for the package had increased to 59 percent (Steinhauser 2009). Indeed, it was congressional Democrats rather than Republicans who won the public's plaudits: a net 6 percent of Gallup's sample approved of their efforts compared with net disapproval of 29 percent for Republicans (Newport 2009b; Saad 2009). One year after the legislation's approval, however, the package had yielded few political or economic benefits for the president, despite the historic magnitude of stimulus spending and tax cuts. US unemployment had increased a further 1.5 points, while Obama's approval rating had fallen to just 46 percent at the same time that 56 percent said that the president did not have a clear plan for creating jobs and only 12 percent knew that the stimulus package had decreased taxes for 95 percent of Americans (Condon 2010).

*Climate Change Legislation—Leaving It to Congress,*
*Equivocation, and Failure*

The administration's strategy for winning approval of climate change legislation was even more cautious. In his campaign, Obama had made energy his first legislative priority and promised significant reductions in emissions by 2020, a 100 percent auction of pollution permits with $15 billion a year from the proceeds to be used to promote nonpolluting energy sources and cut energy waste (2008c). Barely a week before his inauguration, however, Obama's advisors were undecided on whether to push climate change or health care first. Carol Browner, Obama's assistant for energy and climate change, wanted cap-and-trade legislation to be the new administration's top legislative priority, but Emanuel was opposed to expending effort on legislation that did not enjoy the support of 60 senators. According to a senior administration official, "[t]he plan was to throw two things against the wall, and see which one looks more promising" (Lizza 2010). Ultimately, climate change was relegated. "We've got a lot of fights before we even get to cap and trade," Obama told Democratic senators. Besides, Obama told Henry Waxman

(D-CA), the new chair of the House Energy and Commerce Committee, "I care about health care more" (Alter 2010, 254–5). Health care would be easier and follow the stimulus package (Alter 2010, 94). Emanuel's skepticism and Obama's stronger preference for health care (shared by voters) pervaded the White House's reticent approach from start to finish, constrained White House engagement with the issue, and helped ensure a major legislative failure.

Unsurprisingly, the White House demurred from providing the Congress with any kind of White House blueprint. Congress would be left to build on its previous legislative efforts. Still, the administration included in its stimulus proposals and won congressional approval for $40 billion for energy efficiency and renewable energy programs. Then, in his budget speech in February 2009, Obama committed his administration to legislation that placed "a market-based cap on carbon pollution." The commitment was apparently a key part of an ambitious "Grand Bargain" strategy articulated by the White House, whereby Democrats would make concessions to Republicans on natural gas production, nuclear energy, and offshore oil in exchange for a cap on carbon emissions. If Republicans did not agree to the deal, the White House would threaten to use the Environmental Protection Agency's recently acquired power to regulate carbon like other air pollutants (Lizza 2010).[15]

The Congress had worked on cap-and-trade legislation for many years, most recently in the 110th Congress, led by a bipartisan group of senators including centrist Joseph Lieberman (I-CT). Lieberman was determined to take the lead in the new Congress and by late January had drafted legislation that evidently enjoyed some bipartisan support, as well as that of some major environmental groups and polluters, as an alternative to more restrictive legislation. Indeed, Browner privately assured Lieberman that he would be "absolutely central" to passing a climate bill but told him that the administration would not "go public" in support of cap-and-trade legislation, opting instead for a messaging strategy that placed heavy emphasis on green jobs and clean energy. To the apparent dismay of the White House (Alter 2010, 260), however, through deft negotiating by Waxman, the House Energy and Commerce Committee approved the first ever measure to cap emissions within five months of the new Congress convening. Although the bill's emissions targets were lower than those proposed by Obama in his election campaign and excluded auctioning all emission allowances and using the proceeds for tax cuts, the White House belatedly supported the legislation and helped win floor approval (Davenport and Palmer 2009, 1516–1517; Lizza 2010). While most congressional Republicans labeled the bill "a jobs killer" and "an energy tax," eight supported the bill on final passage; 44 Democrats (mostly from conservative and rural districts) voted against (33 more than on the stimulus bill). Obama claimed the bill as "historic" even though the main legislative drivers were Waxman, committee colleague Ed Markey (D-MA), and Pelosi (Dennis and Newmyer 2009, A1; Soraghan 2009, A1).

Despite Majority Leader Reid publicly expressing the hope that the Senate would pass a bill "this fall," the White House did not give the legislation high priority or provide meaningful leadership. Indeed, echoing Emanuel's earlier reservations, "the White House political operation thought passing the bill through the House was one of the biggest mistakes of the year" (Alter 2010, 260) because it had forced House members to take tough votes without much prospect of enactment and at a time when health care was the administration's top legislative priority. Obama continually reiterated his support for the House bill's 17 percent emissions cuts from 2005 levels by 2020, notably at the UN climate talks in Copenhagen, and for green jobs and clean energy, but the White House's "strategy" would wait for senators to work their will and certainly did not involve recommending any outline proposal or making much legislative effort. Nor did it offer any great encouragement or assistance to the Lieberman group's efforts (Lizza 2010), despite its centrist approach linking caps on emissions to incentives to expand natural gas usage, nuclear energy, and offshore drilling, the group's bipartisan composition (now including Democrat John Kerry and Republican Lindsey Graham), and its success in negotiating major concessions from the polluting industries.[16]

To Lieberman's consternation, Browner had only three aides working directly with her in the White House (Lizza 2010). Equally seriously, as detailed negotiations ensued with various industry interests on health care reform legislation, Obama's chief political advisor, David Axelrod, became increasingly concerned that the president was "losing his brand" as a Washington outsider and becoming too closely identified as the leader of the Congress (Lizza 2010). Worse still, several actions suggested that the White House really wanted to sink the Lieberman group's efforts. In late March 2010, without consulting Lieberman's group, Obama suddenly announced the end of a moratorium on gas and oil drilling in US waters in the Gulf of Mexico, the Arctic Ocean, and off the East Coast, at a stroke undermining a deal that the group had proposed whereby the energy industries would exchange new drilling rights in the Gulf and the Atlantic coast in return for new emissions caps (Lizza 2010). The previous month, again without consulting Lieberman's group, Obama included $54.5 billion in new loan guarantees for the nuclear industry in his FY2011 budget at the same time that Graham and other Republicans had proposed using the promise of loan guarantees and tax incentives to attract Republican support for a cap-and-trade deal. The Environmental Protection Agency also announced proposals to weaken and delay the introduction of its proposed standards for emissions from stationary sources in response to complaints from Republican and Democratic senators with strong ties to coal, oil, and industrial polluters. Again, the administration did not consult with Lieberman's group, which had wanted to use the promise of relaxing EPA standards as a bargaining chip in negotiations with Senate colleagues. The White House also erroneously informed the conservative Fox News that Graham supported a proposal to tax polluters (the so-called "linked fee" proposal) when the group had already discarded the idea (Garrett 2010), causing Graham huge embarrassment with his conservative constituency.

Ultimately, the White House's tenuous involvement became abandonment. Emanuel called Reid and asked him to push instead for a more modest bill requiring utility companies to generate more electricity from "clean" sources. Weeks later, Axelrod refused to commit the White House to Lieberman's bill, citing the pressures already placed on congressional Democrats to pass other legislation

(Lizza 2010), and shortly after Reid succumbed to party pressures to advance immigration legislation instead, effectively ending the Lieberman group's efforts.

Whether the White House's equivocal approach determined the failure of cap-and-trade legislation, given the extent of bipartisan opposition from senators representing states containing heavy energy using and producing businesses, cannot be known. Nonetheless, strong suspicions must remain as to whether the Obama White House took full advantage of its opportunities and showed sufficient political will, perseverance, and energy, specifically by not providing greater support for the efforts of Lieberman, Kerry, and Graham in negotiating often unsavory deals with the polluting industries, who now see carbon emissions controls as inevitable and would prefer the regulatory certainty that would come with new legislation (Talley and Power 2009, A6). There may have been a better legislative opportunity than the Obama administration imagined. Ultimately, the White House did not want to risk failing, but its own tenuous strategy helped make failure certain.

*Health Care: Leaving It to Congress,*
*Broad Principles, and Success*

Making health care the top legislative priority after the stimulus was very much Obama's personal decision. Even as US health costs have risen inexorably, and the numbers of uninsured and those filing for bankruptcy as a result of medical bills increased sharply as the economy declined, health care reform did not become the defining issue in the 2008 election. Once in office, Obama's closest advisors were characteristically cautious in promoting reform legislation. Previous presidents had failed. Yet, under pressure from congressional Democrats as well as a perceived personal obligation to the ailing Senator Edward Kennedy (D-MA), Obama came to believe that enacting well-designed health care legislation would reduce costs and significantly extend coverage. Obama was also persuaded by a sequencing rationale articulated by Emanuel, which echoed Neustadt's argument (1990) that the higher a president's reputation, the easier it will be to facilitate further successful negotiations with the Congress: major legislative "victories [on health care] would beget victories" on other high priority issues, including energy and financial regulatory reform (Alter 2010, 247; Baker 2010e, 6).

Led by Daschle as head of its health policy team, the transition team instituted a strategy that was altogether different from that pursued on the stimulus package and climate change. A grassroots effort was launched to tap the president's huge base of supporters in support of health care reform and to air concerns and generate proposals. Again, the new administration's legislative strategy did not entail sending Congress a detailed blueprint.[17] In 1993–94, Hillary Rodham Clinton's plan had been crafted entirely within the White House, effectively denying the Congress opportunities for influence while providing powerful interests with a single target that they sought to dismember, with unfavorable consequences for the Clinton administration's political reputation. Obama would let the Congress take the lead, leaving opportunities for the White House (and the Congress) to negotiate with industry lobby groups as the process unfolded. Indeed, throughout 2008, Senate Democrats Max Baucus (D-MT) and Kennedy, chairs respectively of the Finance and Health, Education, Labor, and Pensions committees, had worked on drafting a policy to fulfill a long-held legislative goal for congressional Democrats. Immediately after the 2008 elections, with the support of a bipartisan group of senators, Baucus announced that he wanted to "hit the ground running in January" (Herszenhorn 2008). Days later, he published an 89-page "white paper" that proposed a mandate requiring all Americans to have health insurance, a national marketplace to purchase it, and a government-run option for individuals to buy insurance in competition with private insurance plans.

Barely a month into his presidency, Obama nailed his administration's colors to the health reform mast. In the same speech that he committed his presidency to a cap on carbon emissions, he made "a historic commitment to comprehensive health care reform" and backed it up with a proposal for a 10-year, $634 billion reserve fund as a down payment to help pay for reform. The speech also set out the broad outline of the kind of centrist legislation he wanted: "affordable health care ... paid for in part by efficiencies in our system." A reformed system must build on the existing market-based health system of employer-based policies,[18] and contrary to liberal Democrats' wishes (and unlike the Baucus proposal), it should not include an individual mandate or create a government-run program similar to Medicare. Crucially, it must "pay for itself" without increasing the budget deficit. Half the reserve fund would be paid for with new revenues from tax increases for the better off, but the other half had to be achieved through efficiency gains from Medicare and Medicaid.

As congressional negotiations prolonged past a summer deadline set by Obama, and with the president touring the country drumming up support and negotiating deals with important industry groups out of the public eye while steering clear of congressional fights (Alter 2010, 253–54, 417; Jacobs and Skocpol 2010, 57, 66–75), it became clear that Obama was failing to articulate a clear case for reform in accessible language. Between May and early September, his approval ratings had dropped 15 points. Just over 43 percent approved of his handling of health care, according to Gallup. During this period, most attention focused on the Senate Finance Committee, where Committee Chair Baucus pursued an "Everything on the table" approach. By September, as congressional Democrats pressed Obama to set out more precisely the kind of package that he wanted, it was evident that the White House had tolerated Baucus's negotiations for too long. Decisive presidential action was needed for the process to move forward. Ignoring Emanuel's renewed doubts (Alter 2010, 395–6),[19] Obama showed determination and insisted on getting "big things done," even if that meant his party losing the 2010 elections (Alter 2010, 262, 399). In another speech to a joint session of Congress, he outlined legislation that largely embraced Baucus's outline bill and again reached out to Republicans. Evidently, his strong intervention boosted support for his plan by 14 points among those who watched the speech (CNN/Opinion Research 2009a) and prompted the Finance Committee to pass Baucus's bill (including a public option) with the support of a single Republican senator.

Any lingering White House hopes that Obama's proposals would attract substantial Republican support were soon dashed, however. Republican congressional leaders had already perceived greater political advantage in refusing to cooperate or compromise. Republican Scott Brown's win in Massachusetts on a platform opposing Democrats' health reforms and the sharpest fall in approval ratings for any president in his first year for 50 years cemented Republican opposition. The White House now saw its bipartisan outreach strategy as a mistake (Alter 2010, 257, 265). Apart from Olympia Snowe in the Senate Finance Committee, no Republican offered any support. Meanwhile, the delay caused by seeking Republican support had thrown out the White House's timetable for completing and selling the legislation to the public.

At this point, the White House switched to a strictly partisan strategy that relied on Pelosi and Reid writing the floor bills in their offices and maximizing House and Senate Democratic support. Predictably, the House and Senate floor debates in November and December 2009 were vitriolic and partisan, but both chambers approved legislation on very tight party-line votes with the help of some heavy White House lobbying and concessions (Hulse and Pear 2009, A1). No Republican supported either measure (Herszenhorn 2009, A1), and in the House, 33 centrist Democrats voted against. In the inter-chamber negotiations that followed, the White House pressed Pelosi and Reid to find a workable set of modifications—and a clever parliamentary maneuver—to win final passage but also renewed its bipartisan pleas and even hinted at scaling back the proposed reforms (Connolly 2010; Drew 2010, 50–52; Stolberg and Herszenhorn 2010, A1; Stolberg, Zeleny, and Hulse 2010, A1). Finally, Obama unambiguously claimed ownership of and responsibility for finalizing a (partisan) product that focused much more on cost controls rather than coverage. He proposed "his own" plan, which was essentially a summary of the provisions already agreed by both chambers, and encouraged congressional Democrats to maneuver around the Republican minority. Following House agreement to the Senate version and some clever procedural maneuvering, Obama signed the bill.

Undoubtedly, the passage of health reform legislation was a major victory on what became the White House's signature issue. Obama's bet was substantial. Repeatedly rejecting advice to accept a small bill, he insisted on major legislation and won it. Previous presidents' bills had failed. His success also provided a vindication of his cautious yet resolute approach and a fairly accurate reading of his strategic context. Obama's political and legislative standing was not the same as Lyndon Johnson's in 1965. There was no way that he could bombard the Congress with his proposals and win, as Johnson did, and Clinton's experience in 1993–94 taught that he should not try. Instead, the White House let the Congress develop proposals while tracking developments, providing technical assistance in testing and designing specific policies, and intervening at crucial points to establish broad parameters, for example, on deficit-neutrality and cost reduction. Certainly, Obama's over-long obeisance to Baucus's bipartisan efforts was a mistake, but the ideas developed and the deals made by Baucus's group (with White House help) ultimately gave the administration an outline plan, which was within Obama's centrist comfort zone and actually very similar to congressional Republicans' counter proposals to Hillary Clinton's 1994 plan, with its series of mandates, subsidies, and a version of a public insurance option that supplemented the existing private system. In order to win congressional approval for this package, however, Obama was obliged to ditch his post-partisan or bipartisan aspirations and acknowledge the quintessentially partisan and oppositional character of his strategic context. As David Axelrod conceded, "There's a constant tension between the need to get things done within the system as it is and the commitment to change the system. Finding that line at any given moment is really, really difficult" (Baker 2010e, 1).

The hand that contemporary US politics dealt Obama—the strategic context that he encountered—was not that favorable to his ambitious legislative agenda or his post-partisan aspirations, notwithstanding the enthusiasm accompanying his election and the return to single-party government. Yet, because there was a Democratic Congress with effective leaders, and Obama worked closely with these leaders, the list of legislative accomplishments of his administration and the 111th Congress was considerable. Most notable was health care reform, the Dodd-Frank Act, and the ratification of START. But, as the analysis has shown, the record is not as strong as Lyndon Johnson's and the 89th Congress. Unlike Johnson, however, Obama was not elected in the wake of a presidential assassination, and he did not win election by a landslide. There were also some glaring failures, notably climate change. In no sense, moreover, could Obama claim either to have changed the basic parameters of the strategic context that he encountered or to be a transformational president, as he had hoped. Indeed, it is difficult to resist the conclusion that the legislative products that were finally approved—particularly the stimulus and the health care legislation—remained essentially congressional Democratic products facilitated partly by White House interventions. Within those broad parameters and most significantly on health reform, Obama demonstrated skill, tenacity, and some good political judgment, identified opportunities for influence, and took them, thereby helping the legislative process move forward. He was also persuasive in helping win over some of the necessary House and Senate votes. When, moreover, he did not choose to engage with the Congress—as over climate change—he helped facilitate failure. Both scenarios, then, illustrate the importance of presidential agency at crucial points in the legislative process as well as its variability across different legislative issues and time.

While the Obama White House established clear legislative priorities and carefully limited its interventions, its strategies for winning congressional approval were hardly flawless if the objective was to win bipartisan support. The best opportunities were surely in the first year. If it wanted Republican support for the stimulus package, it played a good hand poorly. On climate change, it seemed to be caught unawares by swift congressional action and then lost its nerve during Senate negotiations. On health care, it tarried too long in seeking bipartisan support and ultimately settled for a product that won no Republican support. For all his post-partisan aspirations, then, Obama was obliged to rely on his own party and its congressional leaders. Why this was so first and foremost has to do with the strategic context that Obama faced, but it also has to do with a flawed post-partisan strategy, Obama's conciliatory style, and perhaps also the president's basic lack of enthusiasm for dealing with the Congress and its members "with room-temperature IQ's" (Alter 2010, 326). With his party's "shellacking" in the 2010 midterms and his personal political capital further reduced, it remains to be seen how Obama will approach a Congress divided between the parties and led by Republican congressional leaders publicly opposed to compromise and committed to Obama being a one-term president. While Obama's political instincts will remain pragmatic, conciliatory, and bipartisan, he will continue to face a strategic environment whose defining characteristics are not.

## NOTES

I am grateful to numerous anonymous congressional staffers and journalists for their generosity in granting interview time and other data. I would also like to thank Jim Thurber of the Center for Congressional and Presidential Studies in the School of Public Policy at the American University, Washington, DC, for providing me with a congenial research base. An earlier version of this chapter was presented at the conference on the Early Obama Presidency sponsored by the Centre for the Study of Democracy at the University of Westminster, the Eccles Centre at the British Library, and the Cultural Office of the US Embassy in London held at the University of Westminster in May 2010.

1. The categories are Jones's (2005, 37).

2. The computation is calculated simply by adding the percentages of the popular and Electoral College vote to job approval on entering office. Obama's score was 189 (Jones 2005, 52).

3. Calculated by adding the percentage of House seats held by the president's party, plus bonuses of five each for majority status. Using the same calculation (Jones 2005, 52), Obama's score was 129.

4. Including independents Joseph Lieberman of Connecticut and Bernie Saunders of Vermont, who caucus with Senate Democrats, the majority eventually numbered 60 following Arlen Specter (PA) switching parties in April 2009 and Al Franken being declared the winner in the disputed election in Minnesota in June.

5. McCain also lost North Carolina by just fewer than 14,000 votes, while Democratic Senator Kay Hagan beat Republican incumbent Elizabeth Dole with just 52.7 percent of the vote.

6. Other transition and administration officials with extensive congressional experience included Vice President Joe Biden, Hillary Rodham Clinton (State), Ken Salazar (Interior), Ray LaHood (Transportation), and Hilda Solis (Labor), Leon Panetta (CIA), Melody Barnes (Domestic Policy Council), Greg Craig (White House Counsel), Chris Lu (Cabinet secretary), Dan Pfeiffer (deputy communications director), Carol Browner (White House Office of Energy and Climate Change), Robert Gibbs (press secretary), Jim Messina (deputy chief of staff), and Cassandra Butts (deputy legal counsel).

7. For example, Assistant Secretary for Legislative Affairs Rich Verma was previously a member of the Obama/Biden Defense Department Transition Team, senior national security advisor to Senate Majority Leader Harry Reid (D-NV) between 2002 and 2007, and before that staff assistant to Congressman John Murtha (D-PA), chairman of the House Defense Appropriations Subcommittee.

8. Obama ruffled congressional feathers when he apparently did not consult over Leon Panetta's nomination as CIA Director. Senator Diane Feinstein (D-CA), putative chair of the Senate Select Intelligence Committee and an Obama campaign supporter, told the *Los Angeles Times* that she had not been consulted and was considering opposing the nomination.

9. During a long-winded speech by Chairman and Future Vice President Joe Biden before the Senate Foreign Relations at the nomination hearings for future Secretary of State

Condoleezza Rice in 2007, Obama passed a note to a Senate aide saying "Shoot. Me. Now" (Wallace-Wells 2008).

10. This list includes only legislation on which the president took a public position and/or signed a measure, according to *CQ Weekly*'s regular Bills to Watch listings up to December 12, 2010.

11. The House is not required to act on the Strategic Arms Reduction Treaty.

12. *CQ*'s more general measure, which does not differentiate the political significance of different measures, gave Obama an "historic" 96.7 percent for 2009, beating Lyndon Johnson's success rate by 3.6 percent, and 85.8 percent in 2010. However, in 2009 Obama took a position on fewer House and Senate votes than most of his predecessors. Obama's levels of support from his own party (91 percent for both years in the Senate and 91 and 89 percent among House Democrats) also rank well above those of other presidents with congressional majorities of their own party: Eisenhower (71 percent/73 percent), LBJ (74 percent/61 percent), Clinton (77 percent/87 percent), and Bush 2 (86 percent/94 percent). (The first figure in each set is for the House, the second for the Senate.) *CQ* reports that in 2010, House Democrats were only slightly less supportive (83 percent); House Republican support actually increased on these votes from 26 to 30 percent. (Cranford 2010a: 2327)

13. Reagan, Bush 1 and Bush 2 also achieved 100 percent win rates on the most significant legislation but, respectively, with only 2, 1, and 2 measures in this category.

14. A Gallup Poll taken in mid-January 2009 showed that 62 percent of respondents wanted the Congress to block Obama's request to release the remaining funds until more details were provided about how the funds would be spent. The rest of the sample was split between those wanting the funds to be released immediately and those who did not want any funds released.

15. In *Massachusetts et al vs. EPA et al*, 549 US 497 (2007), the Supreme Court had declared constitutional the EPA's statutory authority to regulate greenhouse gases as pollutants.

16. For example, in return for a lobbying/ad campaign ceasefire, Kerry, Lieberman, and Graham included a provision in their bill that would allow the oil companies (responsible for something like one third of all US carbon emissions) to pay a "linked fee" based on how much gasoline they sold linked to the average price of carbon over the previous months, instead of having to buy government permissions or allowances to cover all emissions by vehicles on the carbon market, as provided for in the House bill (Samuelsohn 2010).

17. On a third Obama priority, financial regulatory reform (on which lack of space precludes discussion), the Treasury Department rather than the White House took the lead. Initially, the Treasury provided Congress with a plan that was too vague, incoherent, and unsupported (Cho and Montgomery 2009, A1) but, subsequently, submitted a more detailed legislative blueprint, which the Congress substantially endorsed when it enacted the Dodd-Frank Act (Cho 2010, A1).

18. Throughout the decade, Gallup Polls show a plurality of Americans consistently favored maintaining the current private system, although support fluctuated. In November 2008, Gallup reported that 49 percent favored the current system, while 41 percent favored "a new government run health care system." While almost 9 out of 10 Republicans and Republican leaners favor maintaining the current system, support among Democrats and Democratic leaners for a government-run system is less monolithic; more than a third of Democrats would favor maintaining the current system (Newport 2009c).

19. Evidently, over the summer, Emanuel had instructed White House staff to prepare an 800-page secret health care bill covering every contingency with a view to offering it directly on the Senate floor should Baucus's bill not be voted out of committee. "If it failed there, they'd come up with another compromise. If that deal didn't work, they'd move to [using the budget] reconciliation [procedure]," which prevented filibusters (Alter 2010, 266).

CHAPTER 8

# Obama's Battle with Lobbyists

## James A. Thurber

Widespread scandal and public opinion helped to fuel Senator Barack Obama's nonstop attack on the role of lobbyists in American politics, starting as the Democrat's ethics and lobbying reform leader in the US Senate in 2006, continuing in his 2008 election campaign, and repeated in 2009 and 2010 with his sustained attempts as president to change the culture of lobbying and influence in Washington. Lobbying is a profession that has been deeply sullied in the last five years by the illegal actions and conviction of Jack Abramoff, the criminal convictions of Representatives "Duke" Cunningham (bribes for earmarks) and Bob Ney (accepting illegal gifts from lobbyists), the resignation and conviction of Representative Tom DeLay (illegal use of corporate campaign funds from lobbyists), the conviction (later overturned) of Senator Ted Stevens (illegal gifts from lobbyists), as well as the criminal conviction of 21 lobbyists, former congressional aides, and executive branch officials (illegal gifts to members of Congress). More recently in 2009 and 2010, Congressman Charles Rangel (D-NY) was asked to step down as chair of the powerful House Ways and Means Committee, and after a lengthy investigation and trial before the House Ethics Committee, he was convicted on 11 counts related to breaking House Ethics gift ban and travel rules associated with lobbyists. In 2009, the House Ethics Committee investigated Representatives Todd Tiahrt (R-KS), Peter Visclosky (D-ID), John Murtha (D-PA), Norm Dicks (D-WA), and Jim Moran (D-VA), all on the House Appropriations Committee, for the reciprocal exchange of campaign contributions for earmarks from corporations through PMA, a now defunct lobbying firm owed by a former House Appropriations subcommittee committee staff director (Milbank 2010b).

Are lobbyists distorting what is in the public interest and undermining pubic trust in government and ultimately the integrity of American democracy, as argued by Senator/candidate/President Obama? Has President Obama changed the murky world of the revolving door of lobbyists/advocates in campaigns and government? Has he changed the way Washington works? These are not new questions for Washington; they echo James Madison's lament in *Federalist Paper Number 10* (1962, 79).

> Complaints are everywhere heard from our most considerate and virtuous citizens, equally the friends of public and private faith, and of public and personal liberty, that our governments are too unstable, that the public good is disregarded in the conflicts of rival parties, and that measures are too often decided, not according to the rules of justice and the rights of the minor party, but by the superior force of an interested and overbearing majority. However anxiously we may wish that these complaints had no foundation, the evidence, of known facts will not permit us to deny that they are in some degree true.

President Obama has often prominently paraphrased James Madison's argument in *Federalist No. 10* that factions or narrow interests undermine the rights of other citizens and that it is the duty of government to regulate the factions so that they do not do harm to others (Madison 1962, 79). Obama also used Madisonian arguments when he stated that factions (interest groups and lobbyists) are "adverse to the rights of other citizens or the permanent and aggregate interests of the community" (Madison 1962, 83).

The overwhelming public perception of lobbyists, whether convicted or investigated for malfeasance, is that they are bad, a corrupting influence on government and the way Washington works. This negative public perception of lobbyists was a major cause of Obama's attacks on them. Fifty-eight percent of the respondents in the 2008 Cooperative Congressional Election Study (CCES) national poll felt Obama would be very likely or somewhat likely to change the way Washington works. (See the appendix for CCES public opinion survey results.) After the economic crisis, government corruption was the second-most important issue mentioned by voters in national surveys in 2008 and the most important issue among the electorate in the midterm election of 2006. (See the appendix for 2008 CCPS/CCES public opinion about Obama and lobbying reform.) Anger against Washington politics continued to be a major issue in the 2010 midterm elections. The irate public had high expectations for the president to change politics by reforming lobbying and the "political influence culture" that permeates Washington (Jacobson 2011). President Obama used that strong public anger with Washington in his attempts to garner support for his policies in Congress.

This chapter explores the causes, characteristics, and consequences of President Obama's attacks on lobbyists and his attempt to change the way Washington works. It concludes with a discussion of the barriers President Obama has faced in reforming pluralist democracy in Washington and assesses his successes and failures during his first two years in office.

## OBAMA'S LOBBYING AND ETHICS REFORMS

Lobbying and ethics reform started for President Obama when he was a senator. With Obama's leadership and the bipartisan help of Senator McCain, discussion of ethics and lobbying reform in Congress in 2006 resulted in the passage of the most significant reform since 1995, the Honest Leadership and Open Government Act (HLOGA) of 2007. HLOGA attempts to slow or stop the "revolving door" between public service and lobbying, to curb excesses in privately funded travel and gifts, and to enhance disclosure and transparency of lobbying activities. The 1995 Lobbying Disclosure Act (LDA) and HLOGA define lobbying and lobbyists and require those who register under the acts to disclose the identities of people attempting to influence government, the subject matters of their attempts, and the amounts of money they spend to accomplish their goals on a quarterly basis.[1] Senator Obama's goal in HLOGA was supposed to make it easier for the public to know about campaign contributions from lobbyists to lawmakers and to make it easier for the public to be aware of lobbyist advocacy topics, targets, and expenditures. HLOGA prohibits senior Senate staff and Senate officers from lobbying contacts with the entire Senate for two years (changing the one year "cooling off" rule), instead of just their former employing office. The act also continues to prohibit senior House staff from lobbying their former office or committee for one year after they leave House employment.

Obama continued his pointed criticism of lobbyist power brokers and the role of big money in Washington in his 2008 election campaign. He began by banning federal registered lobbyists from his campaign organization, but ultimately made many exceptions to his rule.[2] He then made this promise to the public:

> I intend to tell the corporate lobbyists that their days of setting the agenda in Washington are over, that they had not funded my campaigns, and from my first day as president, I will launch the most sweeping ethics reform in U.S. history. We will make government more open, more accountable and more responsive to the problems of the American people (Thurber 2010).

Obama also addressed the destructive power of lobbyists in a town hall meeting in Bristol, Virginia: "We are going to change how Washington works. They will not run our party. They will not run our White House. They will not drown out the views of the American people (Applewood 2008; Thurber 2010). He continued his tough attack on lobbyists and special interest money on August 8, 2008: "I suffer from the same original sin of all politicians, which is we've got to raise money. But my argument has been and will continue to be that the disproportionate influence of lobbyists and special interest is a problem in Washington and in state capitals" (Obama 2007).

Rhetoric, executive orders, regulations, and law aside, what has been the reality of the congressional and White House "revolving door" in the first two years of the Obama administration? Has President Obama achieved his promise to restrict the role of lobbyists and change the culture of big money fund-raising. Once elected, Obama restricted participation by federal registered lobbyists on his transition team and later in his administration. He instituted a strong code of ethics for all executive branch appointees, implemented a tough gift ban, ordered more transparency rules for decision making, and on his first day in office he issued an executive order restricting the "revolving door" of lobbyists both in and out of government (Obama 2009a). He also banned direct lobbying for funds and tax breaks from the Troubled Assets Relief Program (TARP) (Public Law 110-343) and the 2009 American Recovery and Reinvestment Act of 2009 (ARRA) economic stimulus package bill.

After taking office, Obama employed his executive power to restrict lobbyists from service in government and limit their access to policy making in the executive branch. Immediately after he was sworn into office, he also directed his departments and agencies to avoid even the appearance of conflicts of interest (Executive Order No. 13490). The president centralized White House control over government ethics and lobbying by hiring lobbying reformer Norm Eisen to head this topic in the transition and later as Special Counsel to the President for Ethics and Government (the Ethics czar).

The president has also used attacks on lobbyists as a way to build support for his policy agenda, especially in the battle over health care and financial regulation. During his first two years office, President Obama attacked lobbyists dozens of times for hindering or even stopping (e.g., cap-and-trade legislation) his policy agenda, stating that they undermined democracy and the public interest. However, he used them, when needed, to help push through historic reforms. He used criticisms about the role of lobbyists and money in politics to his advantage in building support for health care reform and financial regulation reforms, but was later criticized for "selling out" to the special interests when compromises were necessary and when their support was essential for passage of these historic acts. For example, in a speech on the need for health care reform on March 19, 2010, he attacked health insurance lobbyists for stopping what he felt was in the public interest:

> At the heart of this debate is the question of whether we're going to accept a system that works better for the insurance companies than it does for the American people because if this vote fails, the insurance industry will continue to run amok. They will continue to deny people coverage. They will continue to deny people care. They will continue to jack up premiums 40 or 50 or 60 percent as they have in the last few weeks without any accountability whatsoever. They know this. And that's why their lobbyists are stalking the halls of Congress as we speak, and pouring millions of dollars into negative ads. And that's why they are doing everything they can to kill this bill (Obama 2010b).

The president reiterated his criticisms of lobbyists in his State of the Union message on January 27, 2010, and pledged again to lead the effort to change the way they work in Washington.

> It's time to require lobbyists to disclose each contact they make on behalf of a client with my administration or with Congress. It's time to put strict limits on the contributions that lobbyists give to candidates for federal office. Each time

lobbyists game the system or politicians tear each other down instead of lifting this country up, we lose faith. The more those TV pundits reduce serious debates to silly arguments, big issues into sound bites, our citizens turn away. No wonder there's so much cynicism (Obama 2010c).

Obama has continued his passion to reform lobbying and the way Washington works by instituting more regulations to reduce conflicts of interest and to increase transparency about the lobbying industry, by issuing two historic Executive Orders and several presidential memos on lobbying and ethics, as listed in Table 8-1. In general, the president has tried to change the political culture of Washington by attempting to increase transparency and public participation in decision making and by stopping conflicts of interest in his administration.

President Obama is fighting an integral part of pluralist representative democracy in the United States. Lobbyists, interest groups, and advocates of all kinds are increasingly influential and controversial both in American elections and governing, impacting the quality of campaigns and elections and later governing and policy making. Lobbyists influence the way issues and problems are framed and ultimately the way policy is made in Washington. They promote candidates and policies, raise money, sway voters, and continue their influence through major lobbying campaigns after an election. They provide services such as general strategic advice, issue-advocacy advertising, and polling; offer advice about media strategy; organize get-out-the-vote (GOTV) strategies; and provide volunteers, and general tactical guidance for many candidates (Thurber and Nelson 2000; Medvic 2001). Ultimately Obama is trying to limit the continuation of these identical tools and tactics after elections for major policy battles.

## HAVE OBAMA'S LOBBYING REFORMS MADE A DIFFERENCE?

Although candidate Obama promised to change the way lobbyists influence Washington politics, as president he has found changing the lobbying industry

---

**Table 8-1: President Obama's Ethics and Lobbying Reforms, 2009–2010**

- Ethics Commitments by Executive Branch Personnel, Executive Order 13490, January 21, 2009.
- Memorandum for the Heads of Executive Departments and Agencies on Transparency and Open Government, January 21, 2009.
- Memorandum for the Heads of Executive Departments and Agencies on Ensuring Responsible Spending of Recovery Act Funds, March 20, 2009.
- Reducing Improper Payments and Eliminating Waste in Federal Programs, Executive Order 13520, November 23, 2009.
- Memorandum for the Heads of Executive Departments and Agencies on Freedom of Information Act, December 18, 2009.
- President Obama's Weekly Address: President Obama Vows to Continue Standing Up to the Special Interests on Behalf of the American People, January 23, 2010.

---

*Source:* WhiteHouse.gov, Briefing Room, May 2010.

difficult because of its size and adaptability and because it is an integral part of pluralist democracy. By official estimates, the lobbying industry is the third-largest enterprise in our nation's capital, after government and tourism (Thurber 2009). The statutory definition of "lobbyist" under the Lobbying Disclosure Act is narrow and does not recognize every person in Washington's advocacy industry. A broader definition of advocacy includes all methods of influencing public policy decisions, including traditional lobbying, such as personal contacts with policy makers, but also grassroots lobbying, testimony at public hearings, submissions to administrative rulemakings, legal and strategic advice on political and policy matters, coalition building, public relations operations, and political strategy development, all with the ultimate goal of shaping policy. As of January 1, 2009, there were more than 13,664 federal-registered lobbyists representing virtually every type of interest in America (Center for Responsive Politics 2010a; Thurber 2009). The number of registered lobbyists dropped slightly in the first two years of the Obama administration. However, the number of persons employed in Washington who either are lobbyists or are associated with all dimensions of the advocacy industry (registered and unregistered advocates and supporting institutions) has been estimated to be well over 100,000. Spending by registered lobbyists has more than doubled in the last 10 years, from $1.56 billion to $3.49 billion in 2009, and that is just for the visible, registered activities (see Table 8-2).

The $3.49 billion is just the tip of the lobbying expenditures iceberg, because it includes only what is recorded by registered lobbyists in public records. These expenditures average to more than $20 million in lobbying expenditures each day Congress was in session in 2009, or over $65 million per member of Congress. Moreover, the total does not include money spent for other forms of lobbying such as grassroots organizing, coalition building, issue advertising on television, radio,

### Table 8-2: Lobbying Expenditures, 1998–2009

|  | Total Lobbying Spending | Number of Lobbyists |
|---|---|---|
| 1998 | $1.44b. | 10,404 |
| 1999 | $1.44b. | 12,943 |
| 2000 | $1.56b. | 12,541 |
| 2001 | $1.64b. | 11,845 |
| 2002 | $1.82b. | 12,131 |
| 2003 | $2.04b. | 12,923 |
| 2004 | $2.17b. | 13,158 |
| 2005 | $2.43b. | 14,070 |
| 2006 | $2.62b. | 14,516 |
| 2007 | $2.85b. | 14,869 |
| 2008 | $3.30b. | 14,216 |
| 2009 | $3.49b. | 13,664 |
| 2010 | $2.61b.* | 12,488 |
| *Estimate as of 7/26/10 | | |

*Source:* Total spending and number of unique, registered lobbyists who have actively lobbied from Senate Office of Public Records data downloaded on July 26, 2010.

and in the print media, support of think tanks, issue-related survey research, and advocacy on the Internet. There are estimates that the total spent on lobbying is closer to $9 billion per year in Washington—or about three times the officially reported amount (Thurber 2009). None of these figures include the additional $4 billion spent for the 2010 congressional campaigns.

## Lobbyists, Advocates, and the White House

A major dilemma for the president is that sometimes he likes and needs lobbyists and other times he attacks them and uses his criticism to build support for his policies. Sometimes he tries to stop them and other times they have become essential to his legislative strategy. He has publicly praised his "stakeholders" (often federal registered lobbyists) from organizations such as the AARP, the pharmaceutical industry, the American Hospital Association, and the American Medical Association in the health care battle, who supported his policies, while generally criticizing lobbyists as part of the corrupt political culture of Washington. Part of Obama's inconsistent rhetoric with his policy needs may stem from the dual roles of campaign consultants and lobbyists in Washington. The capital's integrated culture of big money fund-raising and K Street power brokers is difficult to change.

Campaign-consultants-turned-lobbyists/advocates who build strong reciprocal relationships with candidates-turned-elected-office-holders (presidents) or appointees are part of the Washington political culture that President Obama is finding almost impossible to reform. One of the reasons may be his own inconsistency. It is hard to reform them when you need them. He is using these relationships to help move his policy agenda as revealed by his public statements and by the log of White House visitors from a variety of special interests. He did not stop the prominent role of lobbyists and unregistered "advocate strategists" like former senator Tom Daschle in campaigning and fund-raising, and ultimately lobbying, in 2008 and 2010.

President Obama's Executive Order prohibits the lobbyist–White House revolving door in and out of government, but it has proven difficult to break old habits in the way Washington works, as shown by the extent and strength of the revolving door of lobbyists in and out of the White House in recent years (Baumgartner, LaPira, Thomas 2008). Individuals who do not meet the narrow statutory definition of "lobbyist" but are engaged in all methods of influencing policy decisions have heavily populated the Obama White House, and departments and appointment exceptions have been made (CRP 2010a). Advocates, such as former Senator Tom Daschle, President of the Center for American Progress John Podesta, and many other non-federal registered lobbyists have had easy access to the White House in the first two years of the Obama administration, as shown on the White House log of visitors.[3]

What is the difference between lobbyists and nonregistered stakeholder advocates (e.g., former Senator Tom Daschle), who are both public advocates for his policies? Advocates and lobbyists cite the same source of legitimacy; that is, a fundamental right of free speech, of assembly to petition government for grievances, all guaranteed under the First Amendment. A federal registered lobbyist, defined in law, must report quarterly the details of their lobbying activities, clients, and money spent. Fines and jail are possible for those who do not comply. Nonregistered "stakeholders," as President Obama calls some of his supporters, are not held to that standard; their activities and spending are not reported publicly, and generally their advocacy activities are nontransparent. They are not under the threat of fines and jail if they keep their activities secret. They also can escape the revolving-door restrictions and can be appointed to executive branch positions.

The campaigning and later advocacy activities of Daschle, Podesta, and hundreds of others who both played key roles in the Obama campaign and his transition are examples of people with outside interests who have inside access to power in the White House (CRP 2010a). Because of the new transparency rules about White House visitors, there is a public record of dozens of meetings between Daschle, Podesta, and White House staff (including the president) during health care battles in 2009 and 2010. The Sunlight Foundation and the Center for Responsive Politics (2010b) analyzed the White House visitor logs and found, for example, that within a few months of being sworn in, President Obama and his top White House aides also met dozens of times with leaders from the pharmaceutical industry, unions, AARP, the American Medical Association, the American Hospital Association, American automobile companies, bankers, Wall Street executives, and other "special interests" to develop health care and Wall Street reforms that eventually passed in Congress.

The Center for Responsive Politics (2010a) analyzed Federal Election Commission (FEC) records and lobbying disclosure records by these organizations and showed sharp increases in campaign contributions and lobbying expenditures for health care issues from these organizations during 2009 and 2010. The CRP found that the pharmaceutical industry spent more than $28 million on lobbyists, $8 million on campaign contributions to both Democrats and Republicans on the Hill, and more than $100 million on issue advertising that went to White House Senior Advisor David Axelrod's former firm AKPD (which owed Axelrod $2 million). The role of lobbyists and campaign fund raisers has not abated; it has increased during President Obama's first two years in office, as shown by the historic levels of raising and spending money in the 2010 midterm election cycle.

## CAMPAIGN CONTRIBUTIONS AND LOBBYING EXPENDITURES

The most prominent problem raised by Obama is that the enormous amount of campaign money raised and spent by interest groups for candidates and political parties raises serious ethical questions about corruption in financing elections. The president has argued that the amount of issue advertising, independent expenditures, and campaign services raised from interest groups can dwarf the input from voters, political parties, and other groups with fewer resources, thereby almost ensuring narrow and possibly exclusive interest-group influence on public policy making.

The cost of all presidential and congressional campaigns, including soft money and issue advertising by interest groups, has increased dramatically in the 2008 and 2010 election cycles. It reached approximately $5 billion in the 2008 presidential election and $4 billion in the 2010 midterm elections, more than doubling the campaign expenditures of four and six years earlier. The president had little impact on reducing the amount of interest-group money raised and spent in 2010. In fact, he helped the Democrats raise large amounts of money from lobbyists and interest groups for the 2010 election.

The amount of campaign money spent in the 2010 election was partially as a result of the *Citizens United vs. FEC* Supreme Court case. Obama criticized the *Citizens United* decision and argued that the decision makes it more difficult to change the way money and politics work in Washington.[4] This massive increase in the 2010 election campaign money from special interest groups, often nontransparent, confirms President Obama's fears. Washington has not changed.

An unintended consequence of President Obama's expansive policy agenda has been a new spending frenzy by lobbyists and interest groups for and against his reforms. The increase in the amount of money spent by federal registered lobbyists and others in the advocacy business involved in battles over the stimulus legislation, health care reform, financial regulation, and climate change (cap and trade) alone was massive in 2009–2010 (see Table 8-2). Moreover, not included is the money spent on other nonregulated related lobbying activities (e.g., paid media, grassroots, grass tops, coalition building and maintenance, use of the Internet, survey research, and research at think tanks). Many think including such activities in the totals of expenditures on lobbying would triple the actual amount of advocacy spending in Washington (Thurber 2009). President Obama has not been able to stop or slow down this flow of money and influence either.

## INTEREST GROUPS AND THE PERMANENT CAMPAIGN

Another issue identified by Obama (and scholars) is that interest groups feed the negative effects of the "permanent campaign," defined by Hugh Heclo as, "the combination of image making and strategic calculation that turns governing into a perpetual campaign and remakes government into an instrument designed to sustain an elected official's popularity" (Heclo 2000, 3). This campaigning results in an unrelenting demand from incumbents for campaign funds that are more easily collected from particular interest groups than broad-based networks. In an era of seeming endless partisan parity, the permanent campaign creates the need for advice from campaign consultants-lobbyists that is broadened beyond the strategy of conducting a winning campaign to include which issues and policies to embrace in order to win the next election (Heclo 2000; Blumenthal 1982).

National politics has thus gone past the stage of campaigning to govern and has reached the "more truly corrupted condition of governing to campaign," with campaign consultants and lobbyists playing a central role in the phenomenon (Heclo 2000, 34).

Although President Obama has tried to be the post-partisan president and to stop the negative effects of the permanent campaign, the partisan war, he has not succeeded. Although he tried to break the lock of extreme partisanship, wedge issues, and the constant campaigning, he has failed. The more competitive the elections, the more heated the permanent campaign. Neither party has stopped the mean-spirited permanent campaign (Thurber and Nelson 2000). Divided party government in the 112th Congress and the seemingly partisan parity exacerbates the problem.

## CAMPAIGNING, LOBBYING, AND GOVERNING

A third problem is when interest groups participate in election campaigns and then lobby the same people they helped to get elected. Serious questions of conflict of interest arise, particularly with respect to the question of who is paying for what in the campaign and later for lobbying the newly elected public officials. These are serious consequences for what is in the public interest. For example, on May 8, 2010, White House Counsel Bob Bauer was granted a waiver from ethics rules President Barack Obama established for his administration to allow him to deal in an official capacity with his former law firm, Perkins Coie, on Obama's personal matters and on issues of campaign finance. Bauer played a key role in the Obama campaign and transition as well as an advocate-lobbyist for Perkins Coie before moving to the White House. Norm Eisen said that Executive Order 13490, which Obama signed upon taking office to establish ethics rules for his administrations, never conceived of a circumstance like Bauer's, and allowed for an exception. However, at least eight other exceptions to the revolving-door rules were granted for White House and executive branch appointees within the first two months of the Obama administration. More exceptions are likely to be made.

Obama's campaign consultants were often lobbyists before the election (such as Bauer and 23 other top campaign advisors), and some became lobbyists or advocate fund-raisers after the election (such as Daschle and Podesta). He did not stop the practice of these dual political identities. He seemed to encourage it, to need it, during the 2010 midterm election campaign when the congressional Democrats needed help. Are the lobbyist-campaign consultants loyal to their private clients or to the candidate and later elected public official? President Obama has not blocked the growth of people with dual political identities (lobbyist/advocate-campaign consultants) in the last two years, another measure of his inability to change the political culture of Washington. The Center for Responsive Politics Revolving Door project has identified more than 3,500 people whose careers have taken them from Capitol Hill, the White House, and

Cabinet offices to the lobbying profession and vice versa (CRP 2010b). It reveals the strong reciprocal relationships between those who represent special interests and those in government who regulate those interests.

## RECIPROCITY AND THE ETHOS OF POLITICAL POWER

Reciprocity is a major norm of political life. It is defined in Webster's dictionary as: "To return in kind or degree; the mutual or equivalent exchange or paying back of what one has received; a mutual exchange; mutual dependence, action or influence; a mutual exchange of privileges." Has President Obama weakened the norm of reciprocity from American politics? It is unlikely. Reciprocity is one of the strongest embedded customs in public life. It is directly related to the problems and ethical scandals that created the environment of reform. It is part of the linkage among consultants, lobbyists, and elected public officials. The "iron law of reciprocity" is like gravity. That it exists is beyond dispute. That it has been changed by President Obama is questionable.

Reciprocity helps build political power in Washington. It can certainly be the basis of the movement of people through the political and government "revolving door." Reciprocal campaign contributions and the drive for political self-preservation (re-election) is something President Obama has not stopped or even slowed. Candidates with the most campaign resources are able to hire the best campaign professionals, thus improving their probability of winning elections. Most of the campaign contributions (money, volunteers, and services) come from powerful businesses, unions, associations, and interest groups (Makinson 2002). Well-known campaign consultants also help generate campaign funds, thus helping to build incumbency advantage for the next election (Thurber and Nelson 2000). Successful campaign consultants are often financially successful in nonelection years because their business is both campaigning for candidates and lobbying for and against public policies. Electoral success for top campaign consultants breeds lobbying success or even service in government (e.g., President Bush's Karl Rove and President Obama's David Axelrod). More than 3,000 individuals have been identified from public records by the Center for Responsive Politics (2010b) as moving from campaigns to public service to lobbying and back. President Obama has not broken these strong political relationships through his rhetorical attacks on lobbyists or through his executive order. Reciprocity is at the heart of contemporary politics in the United States. It may undermine civic responsibility and reduce public trust in the policy-making process, but it is hard to stop. The public's strong negative reaction, especially in the 2010 election, to spending earmarks and the way Washington works is partially about this problem of reciprocity ("I will help you, if you will help me"). Although Obama promised to stop earmarks and change the cozy influence networks in Washington, he failed to do so in the first two years of office.

President Obama has far from smashed the reciprocal nexus of campaign consultants and lobbyists in policy-making networks, as shown by who served in his own White House. His governing style in his first two years in office used advocates from outside government to build coalitions of support and to do direct lobbying of members of Congress. Some of his supporters were federal registered lobbyists and many are not; they all represent special interests in America. Campaign consultants and lobbyists or advocates build relationships to bring money to candidate campaigns to help them win and to influence elected public officials. President Obama has tried to break those ties, rhetorically and legally, but with limited success. He has proven that he needs those relationships to govern, thus doing little to change the political culture of reciprocity in Washington.

## Lobbying and Declining Public Trust in Government

Increasing public complaints about politics and the decreasing trust in governmental institutions is a fifth problem that President Obama has said stems directly from interest-group activity in elections (Mayer and Canon 1999; Mann and Ornstein 2008; Jacobson 2009a, 2009b). The strong networks of campaign consultants and those trying to influence policy were factors fostering voter cynicism toward government in 2008 (see appendix) and again in 2010 (Jacobson 2011a). However, President Obama's attacks on lobbyists may have increased unrealistic expectations for reform and had the unintended effect of reinforcing distrust in their role American politics (Thurber 2009). Obama's promised change did not happen before the 2010 election, and it hurt congressional Democrats. The level of trust in President Obama, Congress, Democratic leadership, and other governmental institutions has declined significantly in the last two years (Jacobson 2009a, 2009b, 2011a). Political trust has been declining over the last three decades for a variety of reasons, but one major factor is certainly the public perception about the way money and lobbyists work in Washington (Johnson and Broder 1996; Jacobson 2001; Thurber 2009). Obama has not stopped this continued decline in public trust of governmental institutions and public officials, as shown by Jacobson and Boyd earlier in this book, although his speeches have continued to identify this as a major challenge to US democracy.

## Summing Up Obama's Lobbying Reforms

In the first two years of his administration, President Obama's lobbying reforms and his effort to change the way Washington works boil down to three basic principles of sound government: transparency, accountability, and enforcement.

President Obama has brought some new transparency, but generally his transparency initiatives have had limited effect. He tried to bring an unprecedented amount of transparency to the deliberations in the White House, in the executive branch agencies, and with the Congress (e.g., televised health care reform summit at the Blair House). However, with his attacks on lobbyists has come less transparency as a consequence of deregistrations of federal registered lobbyists and the increase in people using other legal but nonregistered means to influence government (see Table 8-2). This has led to reduced transparency about who is lobbying, for whom and for what, and how much money is being spent on those advocacy activities (Thurber 2009).

President Obama has called for more accountability and enforcement of the law and rules related to lobbying and ethics. He has made it clear who is responsible for monitoring and maintaining ethical behavior for the White House and the agencies, the Office of Government Ethics in the White House, and other executive branch departmental ethics offices. President Obama's new rules have brought more accountability for lobbyists and executive branch officials, but ultimately it is the responsibility of the US Department of Justice (DOJ) to investigate and prosecute illegal lobbying behavior. The congressional ethics committees must ensure accountability of members of Congress and staff through its investigative function. Congress also has the oversight function over the implementation of lobbying laws. There have been more than 4,000 referrals from Congress to DOJ under LDA and HOGLA since 2007, but there have been no investigations.[5] Partially because of the new independent House Office of Congressional Ethics, the House Ethics Committee has had several high-profile investigations and convictions (Representatives Rangel and Maxine Waters in 2009–2010), but the Ethics Committee seems to be lapsing into their old habits of overlooking transgressions when it comes to most allegations of member and staff malfeasance. There have been no congressional oversight hearings of HOGLA since its passage in 2007.

President Obama's rhetorical reform goals and ethics and lobbying regulations fall far short of fulfilling these three basic principles. Lobbying disclosure, especially with the decline of federal registered lobbyists since 2007 and the growth on non-registered advocates, has had limited impact on changing the influence industry in Washington. Increased deregistration of lobbyists and growth of advocates giving strategic advise but not registering have resulted in a lack of transparency. An unintended consequence of President Obama's attempt to reduce conflicts of interest has seriously limited those with expertise from serving as appointees and on government advisory panels. President Obama has changed the rhetoric, but not the way Washington's political culture works.

President Obama's executive orders have set a new high standard of transparency, accountability, enforcement, and public participation, but with imperfect implementation and weak enforcement, his reforms are not yet transforming Washington. He has limited those who can be appointed to executive positions, but it has had little impact on those who actually influence the decision-making process. Moreover, President Obama has worked closely, often in a nontransparent way, with networks of "special interests" (lobbyists/advocates) in crafting the economic stimulus funding, health care reform, financial regulatory reforms, climate change legislation, education reform, immigration policy, and a wide array of other issues on his public policy agenda in 2009–2010. He has also met with many campaign contributors who have a vested interest in the policy battles. President Obama's populist rhetoric of greater transparency, more accountability, increased enforcement, and wider participation by the American public was a popular theme in the 2008 election and early in his administration. His failure to reach these goals helped to create high expectations and an angry electoral backlash against Democrats in the historic 2010 midterm election (Jacobson 2011a). The constitutional and political reality of Washington has so far hobbled President Obama's ability to bring major change to the way decisions are made and in the negative public attitudes about how Washington works. Obama promised change, to be the reform post-partisan president, but he has failed to meet the expectations of the American public.

## Appendix

CCPS/Cooperative Congressional Election Study (CES) Candidate Lobbying and Ethics Questions—Pre- and Post-Election Surveys, October and November 2008

*CCPS/CCES Lobbying and Ethics Questions—Pre-Election Survey*

1. If elected President, how likely is it that Barack Obama will be influenced heavily by lobbyists and special interest groups? [*Percent listed is percent of those answering the question. Number in parentheses is actual number of respondents selecting that answer.*]

   | | |
   |---|---|
   | Very likely | 41.05% (408) |
   | Somewhat likely | 19.22% (191) |
   | Not very likely | 20.82% (207) |
   | Not at all likely | 9.46% (94) |
   | Not sure | 9.46% (94) |

2. If elected President, how likely is it that John McCain will be influenced heavily by lobbyists and special interest groups?

   | | |
   |---|---|
   | Very likely | 34.44% (343) |
   | Somewhat likely | 23.69% (236) |
   | Not very likely | 22.99% (229) |
   | Not at all likely | 9.34% (93) |
   | Not sure | 9.54% (95) |

3. Is it possible to run for President in today's world without having ties to any lobbyists and special interest groups?

   | | |
   |---|---|
   | Yes | 24.80% (248) |
   | No | 48.60% (486) |
   | Not sure | 26.60% (266) |

4. Is Barack Obama more ethical, less ethical, or about as ethical as most politicians?

   | | |
   |---|---|
   | More ethical | 36.67% (366) |
   | Less ethical | 32.57% (325) |
   | About as ethical as most | 25.15% (251) |
   | Not sure | 5.61% (56) |

5. Is John McCain more ethical, less ethical, or about as ethical as most politicians?

| | |
|---|---|
| More ethical | 35.87% (358) |
| Less ethical | 21.64% (216) |
| About as ethical as most | 35.97% (359) |
| Not sure | 6.51% (65) |

6. If elected President, how likely is it that Barack Obama will change the way Washington works?

| | |
|---|---|
| Very likely | 30.39% (303) |
| Somewhat likely | 27.68% (276) |
| Not very likely | 14.64% (146) |
| Not at all likely | 20.66% (206) |
| Not sure | 6.62% (66) |

7. If elected President, how likely is it that John McCain will change the way Washington works?

| | |
|---|---|
| Very likely | 13.04% (130) |
| Somewhat likely | 23.67% (236) |
| Not very likely | 27.88% (278) |
| Not at all likely | 30.29% (302) |
| Not sure | 5.12% (51) |

*CCPS/CCES Lobbying and Ethics Questions—Post-Election Survey*

1. How likely is it that President-Elect Obama will be influenced heavily by lobbyists and special-interest groups?

| | |
|---|---|
| Very likely | 37.82% (306) |
| Somewhat likely | 19.65% (159) |
| Not very likely | 24.35% (197) |
| Not at all likely | 9.77% (79) |
| Not sure | 8.41% (68) |

2. Is President-Elect Obama more ethical, less ethical, or about as ethical as most politicians?

| | |
|---|---|
| More ethical | 37.79% (305) |
| Less ethical | 24.41% (197) |
| About as ethical as most | 29.12% (235) |
| Not sure 8.67% (70) | |

3. How likely will President-Elect Obama change the way Washington works?

| | |
|---|---|
| Very likely | 24.41% (197) |
| Somewhat likely | 31.60% (255) |
| Not very likely | 18.71% (151) |
| Not at all likely | 19.21% (155) |
| Not sure | 6.07% (49) |

# NOTES

1. A person who must register as a federal lobbyist is one: (1) who is employed or retained by a client for compensation; (2) who has made more than one lobbying contact on behalf of such client; and (3) who spends at least 20 percent of his/her time working for that client during a three-month quarter on "lobbying activities" (defined in the LDA).

2. Both candidates publicly banned federal registered lobbyists from serving on their campaign staffs, but 42 top campaign staffers for McCain were recently lobbyists, and 23 top campaign staffers for Obama were recently lobbyists.

3. See WhiteHouse.gov Visitor's log for 2009–2010.

4. On January 21, 2010, President Obama stated: "With its ruling today, the Supreme Court has given a green light to a new stampede of special interest money in our politics. It is a major victory for big oil, Wall Street banks, health insurance companies, and the other powerful interests that marshal their power every day in Washington to drown out the voices of everyday Americans. This ruling gives the special interests and their lobbyists even more power in Washington—while undermining the influence of average Americans who make small contributions to support their preferred candidates. That's why I am instructing my Administration to get to work immediately with Congress on this issue. We are going to talk with bipartisan Congressional leaders to develop a forceful response to this decision. The public interest requires nothing less."

5. This was reported by a legislative assistant on the Senate Rules Committee to the author in May 2010.

# PART III
## OBAMA AND THE MEDIA

# CHAPTER 9

# Fall of the Favorite

## *Ron Elving*

Theodore Sorensen, counsel to President John F. Kennedy, was struck by how very different the world looked from inside the White House. He might have added that a newly installed president and White House staff also suddenly look quite different to the world. One might expect them to seem larger than life in their newly elevated authority, and in certain moments they may. But more often, in the media mix of actuality and artifice through which most people experience them, the president and entourage soon lose the Inauguration Day aura and appear decidedly mortal (Kernell and Popkin 1986).

No politician's rise to the White House has been such a fulfillment of a fantasy—for that individual, for the movement behind him, or for many in the media watching and participating—as the election of Barack Obama in 2008. But even for this, the first African American president, the campaign magic that won voters and observers to his side did not work in the same way after his election. He and his supporting cast continued to follow much the same discipline and inner dicta they had for two years of campaigning, but the reaction of the public and the media was distinctly different.

The vital link with the electorate, the essence of a successful campaign, became less of a priority than the burdens and opportunities of office. And the consequences of this dynamic, visible from the earliest days of the transition, culminated in a crushing defeat for the president's party in the midterm elections of 2010.

Perhaps the sheer magnitude of Obama's goals made it impossible to pursue them and stay in tune with the average American's reactions at the same time.

But after nearly two years in office, the progress he had made was not return-ing political dividends, and where progress had not been made, there was little forgiveness. In some respects, his successes were responsible for his political predicament. The saving of the banking and credit systems, the bailout of the auto industry, the enactment of an economic stimulus program, the overhaul of the health care insurance system, and the revised regulation of the financial system—all came at enormous fiscal and political cost. And even as the new White House won the legislative battles it chose to fight, it was losing the war for public approval—to some degree by forfeit.

The irony was that a campaign portrayed by the media as masterful in exploiting the zeitgeist of 2008 was regarded by the media as insensitive to the electorate of 2010—even though so much of the campaign team had come with Obama to the White House. Their message, clear and consistent during the campaign, had become muddled and confused. They focused on the substantive program as the mission, the pre-eminent priority. And they neglected the prior-ity that makes all others possible: maintaining connection with the electorate. Late in their second year in power, it would be tempting for many at the top of the Obama administration to blame this loss of connection on uncoopera-tive intermediaries—the media. Yet many were prepared to blame themselves, including the president himself.

In September 2010, Obama told Peter Baker of *The New York Times* that any president "has to remember that success is determined by an intersection in policy and politics, and that you can't be neglecting marketing and P.R. and public opinion" (Baker 2010). The president sounded all the more resigned to this realization after the disastrous midterms of November, telling Steve Kroft of CBS *60 Minutes*: "Making an argument that people can understand, I think we haven't always been successful at that. And I take personal responsibility for that" (Kroft 2010).

In our time, presidencies usually begin as a romance between a hopeful candidate and media people—reporters, editors, producers, bookers, hosts, and anchors—in search of a new story and a new star. As the candidate rises to the nomination, the media take notice, and the courtship begins in earnest. As the nominee concludes a winning campaign, the media write the success story, and the courtship progresses. Then the media write additional stories (some book length) about the brilliance of the candidate and the campaign. As the candidate takes office, the media celebrate his achievements: His needs and those of the media are fully wed. There is often a honeymoon, however brief, followed by a marriage that is rarely happy.

This is a universal context for leaders of democracies and the media through which they are perceived. But Barack Obama was a special case. The circum-stances of his life and political success provided a narrative so powerful that they ultimately overrode all other plot lines in a presidential cycle unusually rich in human drama. Obama was, in a real sense, a legend before he even took office, drawing immense crowds in Berlin when he was only the Democratic nominee and being awarded a Nobel Peace Prize, in essence, just for being elected (Nobel Prize Committee 2009).[1]

Ultimately, the power of that narrative became a problem for Obama's presidency, because it instilled expectations that could not be fulfilled. Political media scholar Kathleen Hall Jamieson saw Obama's difficulties in office as inevitable, in part because the campaign itself made them so—with a big assist from the media. What she called the campaign's "apparent mastery of the media and, through the media, the national political conversation," was impossible to sustain.

"Unrealistic expectations were being created from the very beginning—an appetite for change that implied the change would be immediate. 'The fierce urgency of now' means just that. Do you take that literally? Not if you've been around politics you don't, but if you're a 'surge voter' maybe you do. The first time things fall short you are setting yourself up to fail" (Jamieson 2010).

As falling short was inevitable, so was the falling out between the candidate and the media, who must mark the inescapable contrast between the mountaintop of Election Day and the valleys that follow. And, by their nature, the media must move on to the next compelling and competing narrative—whatever it might be.

## CANDIDATE OBAMA: THE ULTIMATE MEDIA FAVORITE

Attending his first White House Correspondents Association dinner as president, Obama introduced himself by saying: "I am Barack Obama. Most of you covered me. All of you voted for me" (White House Transcripts 2009). Obama may have been mocking his audience, or himself, or the popular perception of their relationship—or all of the above. But for many who heard him, Obama's tone also carried a hint of wistfulness. He smilingly referred to it being the "tenth day anniversary" of his 100th day in office, satirizing the media obsession with that milestone. But in truth, just four months into his term, Obama already had a sense of how coming to office transforms a successful candidate's relationship to the media.

The observation that candidate Obama benefited from a friendly news report was a common refrain not only among his rivals but also within the media. "During the 2008 elections, Obama was the object of near-veneration, possessed of a persona and a campaign narrative that were irresistibly compelling to all but his rivals and the right wing press," wrote Ken Auletta, media critic for *The New Yorker* (Auletta 2010). "The media's extreme pro-Obama coverage [was] the most disgusting failure of people in our business since the Iraq war," wrote Mark Halperin of *Time* (Leibovich 2008). Halperin saw it up close: His own publication put Obama on its cover 15 times between October 2006 ("Why Barack Obama Could Be the Next President") and January 2009 ("Great Expectations").

But no political story, however captivating, is ever the last. And the power of a given story is often matched by the counter-force of the next. The pushback becomes the new narrative, and it begins before the principals in the preceding narrative even realize it is happening. Susan Page, Washington bureau chief for *USA Today* and a veteran of more than two decades in the White House briefing room, has noted that this process typically takes each new administration unaware. Every president since Ronald Reagan "had much sweeter coverage in the campaign than in office," she said, yet each new regime "is a little surprised the positive press they used to get just isn't there anymore" (Page 2010).

## Transition: Immediate Portents

One month after Election Day, Illinois Democratic Governor Rod Blagojevich was arrested and accused of seeking to profit from his power to appoint Obama's successor in the Senate, looking to trade the seat for fund-raising help or other favors (Cohen, Pearson, Chase, Kidwell 2008). Among the miraculous aspects of Obama's rise was his relatively unsullied passage through the political mud pits of Chicago and Springfield. He and his Chicago-based team were loath to get involved in the Blagojevich story and simply declined comment. Blagojevich was impeached and removed from office early in 2009, but not before he had made an appointment to the vacant seat and exposed himself, his party, and the president-elect to further embarrassment.[2]

This new image of the Obama team hamstrung by circumstances beyond its control would recur as problems developed in the naming of the new cabinet. Most of Obama's top personnel choices won praise in the mainstream media. His choice of Hillary Clinton as Secretary of State was widely applauded. Obama also got credit for bipartisanship by asking Robert Gates to remain as Secretary of Defense and for continuity in making Wall Street expert Timothy Geithner Secretary of the Treasury.

But Geithner also proved embarrassing for Obama when it became known he had not paid $43,000 in taxes on some of his income—an issue that would dominate coverage of his confirmation (Weisman 2009). Two weeks after the inauguration, a similar taint would prove fatal to the nomination of Tom Daschle as Secretary of Health and Human Services and "health care czar." Daschle, the former Senate Democratic leader from South Dakota, had befriended Obama the senator-elect from Illinois in 2005 even after losing his own re-election bid the previous November. But Daschle was found to have accepted free car service without declaring it as income. The amount of back tax involved was more than $128,000, and stories about it cast Daschle, once known as a prairie populist, quite literally as a limousine liberal. Moreover, it was impossible to say that the choice of such an influential and well-connected lawyer-about-town did not violate at least the spirit of Obama's ban on lobbyists in top White House jobs. Obama would later tell aides he was amazed to learn "how many people in Washington did not pay their taxes" (Weisman, Meckler, Bendavid 2009; Zeleny and Stout 2009; Baker 2010a).

In addition, miscommunications with two prospective nominees for Commerce secretary (Bill Richardson, the governor of New Mexico and former candidate for the Democratic presidential nomination, and Judd Gregg, Republican senator from New Hampshire), further demonstrated the pitfalls of the personnel process in an era of maximum media exposure (Shear and Leonning 2009).

So the last litter on the Mall from Inauguration Day had scarcely been cleared before the media (and consequently much of the public) began to wake from their Obama dream. To borrow a phrase from Mario Cuomo, the poetry of campaigning had become the prose of governing. Obama and his aides were pivoting from their intense involvement with voters to a concentration on changing federal laws and policies and policymakers. The voters would notice the difference.

## STRATEGIES FOR EXPOSURE AND CONTROL

The challenge to every White House includes communicating the chief executive's views and program to all interested parties. This includes policy elites who eagerly await each utterance of the president (especially on the issues of primary concern to each). But it also includes average citizens who only occasionally pay attention to White House pronouncements (Jones 1998; Kumar and Sullivan 2003).

Obama had a large communications team from the beginning: 69 by the reckoning of Marcia Joynt Kumar of Towson State University in Maryland, compared to 52 for George W. Bush and 47 for Bill Clinton (Auletta 2010). The team, defined to include the Office of Communications as well as the press secretary and the speech writers, is expected to maintain the president's standing with the public, promulgate his views, and facilitate action on his legislative and political agenda. They are also expected to promote the election and re-election of supportive officeholders at the federal, state, and even local levels. Ultimately, they must prepare for the president's re-election campaign (in a first term) and his place in history (in a second).

Like John F. Kennedy half a century earlier, Obama had a clear political interest (and personal satisfaction) in continuing to deploy his personal charisma and that of his wife and young family. Like Kennedy, he needed to address perceptions of excessive youth and inexperience. Obama also had to deal with the "otherness" of his race, much as Kennedy had to do with his Catholicism. To all these ends, both were well served by showing themselves often in public and in the media—smiling in the role of husband and father, stern in the role of national leader amidst trying times.

Obama followed his inauguration address with a February speech to a joint session of Congress and in his first six months held four formal news conferences, easily exceeding his predecessors. Overall, the president would "meet the press" in varying formats 42 times during his first year, double the number of his immediate predecessor, according to Mark Knoller, CBS radio correspondent. Most of these were joint appearances with foreign leaders at which only one or two questions were allowed. But even these events made news, contributing to the sense that the new president was taking on the world and the nation's problems—at times, seemingly, all at once[3] (Knoller 2010).

Obama continued his early visibility but reduced his reliance on the traditional prime-time news conference. After the initial flurry of four in six months,

Obama held just one formal news conference in the second six months—and that one not in prime time. In 2010 he held just two such news conferences, one in February (after a hiatus of nearly seven months) and another in September (Knoller 2010). The formal news conferences were curtailed because the president and his aides were displeased with the unpredictable directions these events tended to take and the distracting issues that arose—such as the arrest of Henry Louis Gates, a black Harvard history professor—and dominated subsequent coverage (Seelye 2009b).

In place of the news conference, the Obama team emphasized one-on-one interviews with TV anchors, radio hosts, commentators, and reporters for all media—including Spanish language media, foreign media, and media organizations delivering their report exclusively online. Over the course of the first year, by Knoller's count, the president sat for 158 such interviews, far more than any predecessor in the first 12 months in office. Of these, 90 were for TV and 11 for radio, the rest for print and online organizations. "This is a striking number of interviews and far more than any of his recent predecessors in their first year," wrote Knoller. "The number reflects the White House media strategy: that Mr. Obama can best respond to questions in an interview setting" (Knoller 2010).

It served their purposes better than the unscripted news conference, noted ABC's Ann W. Compton, a White House regular who had covered presidential administrations since Gerald Ford came to office in the fall of 1975: "What they like are the one-on-ones on the president's turf, the Green Room, the State Dining Room. It's a highly controllable situation, and control is the key to the strategy of every president" (Compton 2010). The Obama White House also pursued less conventional venues. Margaret Talev of McClatchy Newspapers noted that in the span of a week, "President Barack Obama spoke via video to Iranians and separately to viewers of a Latin music awards show, appeared on Jay Leno's *Tonight Show* and on *60 Minutes*, held a prime time news conference at which he called on several special-audience publications, and wrote an opinion column that ran in newspapers around the world" (Talev 2009).

The Leno appearance included a joke by the president about how his bowling skills qualified him for the Special Olympics. This gaffe and subsequent apology were widely noted, prompting the first round of musings about the president being overexposed (Linkins 2009). Jennifer Senior of *New York* magazine wrote that "It's gotten to the point where one expects to see and hear from him every day" (Senior 2009).

In the course of his first year, Obama would also appear multiple times on the *Late Show with David Letterman*, turn up on Monday Night Football, present his own predictive "bracket" for the NCAA college basketball tournament on ESPN, and precede an interview on MSNBC by killing a fly with his bare hand. In his second year, a similar blitz would include a visit to the daytime talk show *The View*—the first such appearance by a sitting president. He also got out of town 46 times to 58 cities and towns in 30 states. That was more than the 22 states Bill Clinton visited in his first year in office (1993) but slightly fewer than the 39 George W. Bush got to in his (2001). While on the road, Obama held 28 town hall meetings in his first year (Knoller 2010).

One reason for all this effort was the difficulty of reaching the public via the major mainstream media alone, as previous presidents had done. A news conference or an Oval Office speech no longer commanded near-universal attention from the public, even if the main broadcast networks and cable channels carried it in full. The State of the Union address delivered on January 27, 2010, earned a combined rating of only 11 across the three commercial broadcast networks—meaning only one television set in nine was tuned in on these channels (Baum 2010).

The viewing public simply has too many other programming options to guarantee a large audience, so the president had to pursue his audience where he could find it. "There is no such thing as a truly mass audience," according to Robert Thompson, director of the Bleier Center for Television and Popular Culture at Syracuse University. "You collect a mass audience by piecing together a patchwork of niche audiences" (Memoli 2010).

Even a speech to a joint session of Congress, such as the president gave on health care (September 9, 2009), could not be counted on to convey a clear message to the nation. On that occasion, the president was upstaged by Republican Rep. Joe Wilson of South Carolina shouting "You lie!" when the president said his bill would not provide insurance to illegal immigrants. Slightly distracting in the moment, the outburst became a major theme of much of the post-speech coverage and analysis—in part because former President Carter and others attributed it to racist disrespect (Caliendo and McIlwain 2009).

That same September, the president sat for live interviews with Sunday television programs on ABC, CBS, NBC, CNN, and Univision. The idea was to push the health care bill in a concerted way at a critical juncture in the House's floor consideration. But the decision not to include Fox News, the top-rated cable news channel, became a distraction in itself—especially on Fox. Over the course of the fall of 2009, the contretemps became known as Obama's "war on Fox"—excellent grist for the Fox mill as well as for countless bloggers of all stripes (Fox News 2009).

## RESISTANCE ON THE RIGHT

In the early months of the Obama administration, official Washington and much of the media were increasingly sensitized to Fox News, the brainchild of former Nixon campaign aide Roger Ailes and conservative media mogul Rupert Murdoch. Fox News helped promote the early stirrings of the anti-tax Tea Party in the spring of 2009 and give saturation coverage to conservative protestors who jammed the town hall meetings held by members of Congress during the August recess. The protestors were incensed by the bank and auto bailouts and by what they had heard about the health care bill. Many members of Congress who had experienced the town hall phenomenon firsthand returned to Washington shaken and discouraged (Chaddock 2009).

The protests came to dominate TV news over the month, and not just on Fox. The Pew Research Center's Project for Excellence in Journalism found that the town halls were the most-watched story for three weeks running across all television news channels. Even news of the economic crisis was eclipsed, especially on the cable news channels, which devoted more than one third of their total air time to the story (Pew Research Center Project for Excellence in Journalism 2009).

In fact, the most spirited opposition to the Obama presidency from its inception came not from elected Republicans but from the conservative media. Here the attitude was not traditional loyal opposition but fundamental defiance. "I hope he fails," said talk radio icon Rush Limbaugh four days before the inauguration. "What is unfair about my saying I hope liberalism fails?" For a time, some Republicans expressed embarrassment at this attitude, including Republican National Chairman Michael Steele, who dismissed Limbaugh as "an entertainer." Almost immediately, however, reaction from other Republicans forced Steele to recant and apologize (Limbaugh 2009; Preston 2009).

Not long after Inauguration Day, cable television personalities Lou Dobbs and Glenn Beck used part of their programs to question Obama's birth certificate, suggesting erroneously that the 44th president might be foreign born (and thus ineligible for the office). That notion continued to occupy media time and space for months thereafter.[4]

In subsequent months, similar stories arose in partisan media—blogs, talk radio, Fox News, various newspapers and magazines—and often made the leap to the mainstream. Some, such as claims that Obama was a Muslim, had been aired and answered in the campaign. Others, such as the video tapes shot secretly at offices of the ACORN community organization, offered tales of dubious provenance and marginal importance that nonetheless had powerful visual impact. The ACORN story migrated from Fox News to talk radio to other cable channels and then to the legacy media, with the ombudsman for *The New York Times* saying his paper had been too slow to respond to it. ACORN saw its multifaceted programs cut off from federal funding as a consequence. The time devoted to battling assaults at this level was keenly felt within the White House, where veteran aides recalled how previous Democratic presidents had struggled against political headwinds[5] (Isenstadt 2009).

Fox remained on the offensive, pursuing not only the large issues of the day but also emotional stories such as the "Ground Zero mosque" controversy in the summer of 2010. Fox News continued to dominate ratings for cable television news (Carter 2010). While cable audiences remain small by the standards of broadcast television in its heyday, the influence of Fox News is manifest in surveys that ask the public where it gets its news. Here, too, Fox overshadows its cable competition, with more "votes" from media consumers than any other news brand.[6]

Thus the attempt by the Obama administration to freeze out the Fox reporters and producers in late 2009 was at best a calculated risk and at worst a clumsy mistake. Although Obama has never become as friendly to Fox as he has to the broadcast television networks, the White House stopped the "war on Fox" not long after that phrase gained currency in the media. But the effort to isolate Fox was part of a larger struggle to break out of the frustration common to every White House, the sense that the president and the presidency are at the mercy of a handful of news organizations.

## "GOING OVER THE HEADS": OLD SCHOOL

Presidents have long aspired to an alternative way to reach the public, circumventing the usual media coverage. Finding this imagined "Northwest Passage" has in recent decades been the responsibility of the White House Office of Communications. President Nixon made this a formal separate entity to encourage each executive agency to promote itself—and to direct unfavorable attention away from the White House (Hess 2010). President Carter was fond of reaching out directly via his own televised version of FDR's fireside chats. President Reagan and his team were famed for their use of visuals to establish their message, subtly or not so subtly, using symbolic locations and props.[7]

President Clinton attempted to "go over the heads" of the White House correspondents, reaching out to local television anchors and other opinion makers and making political announcements on CNN's *Larry King: Live*. White House reporters seethed for years over what they considered the high-handed treatment they received from Clinton in the early days of his first term, particularly the attempts at circumvention (Jones 1998; Walsh 1996). To some degree, the White House of George W. Bush under Karen Hughes reprised the experiment, staying away from Washington as much as possible and seeking friendlier climes. Part of the idea was to bypass the conduits anxiously making themselves available in the briefing room (Cook 2002).

Obama's regime arrived with a new take on the familiar Office of Communications dedicated largely to direct contact with constituency groups and other forms of non-mediated outreach. But its place in the hierarchy was unclear at first in relation to Press Secretary Robert Gibbs, a confidante who had accompanied Obama from the Senate to the campaign to the White House. The first communications director, Ellen Moran, was not an Obama veteran but a former director of EMILY's List, a fund-raising operation for women candidates who support abortion rights. She left within the first 100 days to become chief of staff to Commerce Secretary Gary Locke.

Next up was Anita Dunn, familiar to Washington reporters as a Democratic campaign contact since the 1980s and a contractor with the Obama campaign in 2008. Dunn had gained some notoriety with remarks about "controlling" the news toward the end of the 2008 campaign. At a South American development conference in January 2009, she referred to "making reporters report on what Obama was actually saying," rather than on a secondhand report of what he had said. "By the general election, very rarely did we communicate through the press anything that we did not absolutely control" (Melber 2010). Dunn weathered this but was soon targeted by Fox News and others after tape surfaced of her listing both Mother Theresa and Mao among her favorite political philosophers. Although she dismissed this as an ironic reference, she left the White House not long after (Elliott 2009).

The third communications director, Dan Pfeiffer, was a youthful campaign veteran who had been involved in such projects as the White House outreach offices: a dozen or more specific functions sending the president's messages to Hispanics, Asians, African Americans, younger voters, and older voters. Pfeiffer had worked closely with Gibbs and Deputy Press Secretary Bill Burton. He soon expanded the portfolio of the office to become a more frequent source of quotes in all media. Pfeiffer was also an early advocate of the "flood the zone" strategy that brought his boss onto voters' multi-sized screens in unusual ways, including the non-news television option and the new media and social media the campaign had used to great advantage.

## "Going Over the Heads": The New Media Imperative

One measure of the pace and impact of technological change on American media and politics can be glimpsed in the changing meaning of the phrase "new media" itself. As Tom Rosenstiel of the Pew Center for Excellence in Journalism has observed, "we have lived through what amounts to two generations of technological revolution" (Talev 2009). The process of replacing—or at least supplementing—one mode of communication with another has so accelerated that "generations" are now measured in fractions of a decade rather than fractions of a century. Not so long ago, "new media" meant CNN in the 1980s and Bloomberg News terminals and crude uses for the Internet in the 1990s. In current usage, "new media" usually refers to Internet communications via the World Wide Web, which also entails the personal involvement of tens of millions of individuals in web-based "social networking" through MySpace, LinkedIn, Facebook, and Twitter.

As the Project for Excellence in Journalism reported in March 2010, the proliferation of these Internet offerings has put an end to the era in which news consumers relied on one or two news sources and demonstrated brand loyalty much as they did in buying cars or cigarettes.[8]

The new entities penetrate the national consciousness from a technological base that costs far less to start and sustain than the machinery of traditional mass media. Thus they need not attract and hold the mass audience that major newspapers and commercial broadcast networks must have to survive. Niche media need only mark a far smaller territory and defend it, and they have proven increasingly able to attract advertising dollars away from legacy media in the process[9] (Downie and Schudson 2010).

These economics are attractive to smaller business entities, nonprofits, and individuals who may accept minimal profits (or even losses) in order to be part of the national conversation on public affairs. Thus a new media player such as *Politico,* launched in January 2007 by Allbritton Communications, can become a major player in political journalism almost overnight. Allbritton, once the publisher of the now defunct *The Washington Star* and still the owner of several broadcast stations, hired editors and reporters from his old nemesis, *The Washington Post,* and other frontline news organizations. Some of these were well-known reporting stars (Mike Allen) and columnists (Roger Simon), but the news operation depended on a shop filled with ambitious young people slinging out stories around the clock and throughout the week.

*Politico* readers were numbered in tens of thousands, not hundreds of thousands like those of *The Washington Post.* But the goal was not to lure away the *Post*'s circulation so much as to pre-empt its reportorial edge and prestige—and make off with a lot of its targeted advertising (Chainon 2007).

The journalism of *Politico* has had a telling effect on political news gathering and delivery, and it has changed life for other news organizations and other media. Traffic hit 11 million unique visitors at the height of the 2008 cycle. Its degree of profitability may be an open question, but its constant outpouring of quick-trigger reporting affects the perceptions and judgments of others throughout the media and political communities (Leibovich 2010; Wolff 2009).

This influence factor—irrespective of the potential for profit on the scale of the national television broadcast networks—has been enough to prompt major investments in online journalism by other wealthy media figures interested in influencing the national political conversation. These include Arianna Huffington *(The Huffington Post),* Michael Bloomberg (Bloomberg News Service), and David Bradley *(Atlantic Media).*

During the campaign, the Obama forces often regarded themselves as beneficiaries of these new media trends, regarding them as a link to younger news consumers just entering the electorate (and favoring Obama by more than two to one). When Obama came to office, he called on a reporter from *The Huffington Post* among the baker's dozen he singled out at his first news conference (White House Transcript 2009).

But the White House has also been critical of the intensely competitive, hair-trigger reporting these websites offer as they compete for unique visitors and other measures of market share. "Make no mistake, many on the White House senior staff dislike *Politico*'s brand of journalism, and they do not like the effect that *Politico*'s metabolism has on the rest of the press corps," wrote Marc Ambinder on his blog on *The Atlantic* website (Ambinder 2009).

The same is true of the journalism practiced on cable television, where politics in general and the Obama administration in particular have become the prime source of daily fodder. Quite apart from political biases for and against a candidate or party, the overall approach to the news in the new media emphasized conflict and the personal aspects of public affairs. That was not a media trend likely to facilitate White House efforts to sell the country on complex plans for health care, financial regulation, and climate change—let alone Iraq and Afghanistan

Even in the early CNN era, of course, cable news changed what the rest of the media did. Well before the entire country was wired for cable, newsrooms were. Editors and producers watched compulsively throughout their workdays, coming to believe, if subconsciously, that others were watching it too. The stories they ordered up from their own reporters had to go beyond what had been on CNN or risk being boring. Writing in the mid-1990s, when "new media" was yet to be a widely used term, veteran White House reporter Ken Walsh observed that CNN-watching in newsrooms led to "coverage that is too often dominated by analysis of political maneuvering and policy esoterica with a strong dose of edge or 'voice' by the reporter" (Walsh 1996).

But 15 years later, Walsh's earlier observation seemed both prescient and quaint. By the time Obama became president, CNN had been surrounded by Fox News, MSNBC, CNBC, Fox Business, and Bloomberg News. And all of the above were scrambling to stay abreast of online reporting that could stream live video along with still pictures, text, and tabular material. The effect of all this immediacy and competition is a dazzling array of options for the instant gratification of the news consumer. But it is also a dizzying world of both factual and dubious reporting, delivered with frantic and often faux urgency. The challenge for other media is to constantly assess the content and validity of these reports, and the challenge for a White House media team is to track and respond to them.

Beyond the realm of news organizations, old and new, is another dimension of political communication even less tethered to traditional journalistic values. This is the world of the blog, the cybernetic descendant of the old penny-sheet newspapers cranked out on crude presses by proto-journalists in colonial America. While some are sponsored by well-known media entities, scores are produced by individuals—a new generation of self-selected and self-produced pundits. Wildly divergent in ideology, these independent blogs often have a populist air, if only because they are a kind of personal journalism in competition with corporate media. They also tend to extremes in analysis, theory, and prescription, driven at least in part by the need to stand out in an enormous crowd.

Many are known simply by the names of their authors, who may be previously well-known journalists (Andrew Sullivan, Hendrik Hertzberg) or who may have built an online audience without a career in legacy media. Some of these command enough of a following to be interesting or irritating to the White House, and in this new cacophony, the voices that have most rankled the Obama team have come from the left (Hagey 2010).

For example, the president and his team were nettled by bloggers at *Salon* and *Firedoglake* and elsewhere who dwelt on the scaling back of the stimulus package, the dropping of the public option in the health care law, the failure to close the Guantánamo prison for terror suspects, and the continuation of Bush-era policies on other civil liberties.

The eagerness of these bloggers not only to critique but to excoriate wore thin quickly. The Obama team was especially exasperated with comparisons that equated their policies with those of George W. Bush, such as this one from movie producer and *Firedoglake* co-founder Jane Hamsher: "The frightening unconstitutional excesses of the Bush administration have been enshrined and reinforced by a Democratic White House, ensuring that they will become precedent and practice" (Daou 2010).

## The Social Media: All the World's a Watercooler

By 2008, the phrase "new media" was no longer limited to alternative means of delivering news and comment via the Internet. Just as often, the phrase referred to the use of the Internet for social networking. In the political world, that meant using websites as a pitch and receptacle for contributions as well as a space for campaign messaging, volunteer recruitment, and organizing. In 2004, Howard Dean's presidential campaign had raised as much as $4 million online in one day and $30 million online over the course of his truncated primary campaign (Frantzich 2009).

Obama's campaign quickly left all previous efforts at online organizing in the dust. College students began organizing through Facebook pages in mid-2006, months before Obama formally declared his candidacy. In the weeks before his official announcement, Obama toured a number of high-tech firms in California, demonstrating his web awareness and savvy. Some of the brightest young talents in the industry became apostles, moving in many cases to Chicago to work for the fledgling campaign (Siroker 2010).

The Obama campaign fulfilled the promise the Internet had long had as an alternative to traditional fund-raising focused on large events and personal pitches (Frantzich 2009). But the campaign also used the web to connect to people. Here again Dean had been the pathfinder, signing up 190,000 potential supporters using the Meetup.com site. Obama would soon dwarf these precedents: the campaign used mybarackobama.com to compile 13 million email addresses and record 150 million unique visitors. Obama videos prompted 100 million views on YouTube, and his campaign's Facebook page made 2.4 million "friends." The website visitors and YouTube views exceeded those of 2008 GOP nominee John McCain by five to one, and the Facebook friends by four to one (Vargas 2008).

And yet, almost as soon as the Election Night parties were over, the Obama party on the web began to fade as well. Superstars such as Chris Hughes, the Facebook co-founder who worked at Obama's Chicago headquarters in 2008, and Joe Rospars, who gave up his own BlueStates.com operation for Obama, did not stay for the governing phase. Some of their subordinates transferred to Washington for a season, trying to keep the web action going with a new website called change.gov that would solicit ideas on issues and policy. For a time, change.gov provided just the bridge to governing the Obama team had hoped. But then it was subsumed into whitehouse.gov, the official presidential site, which was handsome but staid (mybarackobama.com had been insurgent, infectious, and cool). The shift was emblematic of a larger mindset that came with occupying the White House.

Dan Siroker worked on change.gov as deputy director of new media for the transition and was proud of the aggregation of voter views and policy information. He had moved from Silicon Valley to Chicago to work on the campaign, then on to Washington. But he was soon on his way back to California: "Is it different [in government]? Totally. It's extremely difficult. You previously had this sports-like function: Get people really gung ho so they go out and tell everybody they've got to go vote for Obama. It's like: do this, do this, do this. But I don't know how we could tell people: 'Hey, please say you approve of the president if you get called by Gallup'" (Siroker 2010).

After Election Day, the fabled organization of campaign manager David Plouffe called Obama for America was reinvented as Organizing for America. The idea was to keep the troops mobilized on behalf of the candidate's program, even after he was in office and possessed of the powers of the presidency. "We'll see whether it works or not," Plouffe told *The New York Times.* "It's never been tried before" (Leibovich 2008). During the transition, social networking was used to organize meetings in support of a health care overhaul. But that effort was hard to sustain as that bill became subject to months of negotiation in Congress. The sense that campaign zeal could be transferred to the post-campaign reality was soon lost or abandoned (Pryzbyla 2009, Zeleny 2009).

Political scientist Tim Groeling studied the performance of the Obama new media efforts after inauguration and found a sharp drop-off. He wrote that Organizing for America "appears to be far less effective at mobilizing supporters than during the campaign." Moreover, Groeling noted, "the general public was also less responsive, tuning in less often to monitor [Obama's] communications via new media after the election." For example, in one study Groeling cited, the number of page views for Organizing for America in May 2009 was down 64 percent from that of Obama for America in October 2008 (Groeling 2010; Owens 2009).

Traffic on the official Obama YouTube channel also plummeted from a million daily viewers around the time of inauguration to about 42,000 eight months later. The president's September 10, 2009, speech to a joint session of Congress, a critical juncture for the health care bill, got just 4,123 weekly views (Sifry 2009). In March 2009, Jamieson had speculated about the connection of "newly involved individuals" in government—beyond the campaign (Vargas 2009). Remarking on the pace of the progress in October 2010, Jamieson said simply: "They've never figured out how to use the web. It's still a mystery" (Jamieson 2010).

It took several presidential cycles after the arrival of the Internet for a candidate to truly harness its power in a campaign. Perhaps it will take a similar gestation period before that power is brought to bear in the White House. At the same time, some of the web tools the Obama campaign found so effective in 2008 have proven effective again—for the president's opposition. In the spring of 2009, the early signs of the Tea Party movement, which began as a protest of taxes (the name was an abbreviation of "taxed enough already") was communicating with sympathizers largely through websites and email (Bai 2010).

## SPEAKING FOR THE PRESIDENT

Unable to match their campaign success in the new and social media, the White House found itself relying on media they could not control. And that meant the administration's message would be conveyed to the world by the mainstream media and largely delivered by an array of spokespersons ad surrogates—as in the past. The president was fortunate in a wife who was both an Ivy-educated lawyer and a candidate for a modeling contract. While she chose traditional "first lady" issues—fitness, childhood obesity, education—she pursued them with vigor and seriousness. And by the fall of 2010 she had become one of most sought after personalities in the party's arsenal. In many cases, a visit from her was adjudged more helpful to an embattled member's re-election prospects than one from her husband (Thomma 2010). The White House also deployed Vice President Joe Biden as a more multi-purpose source for journalists and all-purpose fund-raiser and campaigner (Hirsh 2010).

As symbols or as messengers, the vice president and the First Lady were surely preferable to the two Democratic leaders of the House and Senate. Both Speaker Nancy Pelosi of San Francisco and Senate Majority Leader Harry Reid of Nevada were inside players who had risen within their party organizations in their home states before coming to Washington and doing the same within their respective caucuses (Barone 2009; McCutcheon and Lyons 2009). Although both were consumed with the passage of Obama-backed bills in 2009 and 2010, neither could be said to have driven the national political conversation about those bills. Yet both would be vilified in the 2010 campaign as hyper-partisan and out of touch. In this, too, they were surrogates for Obama.[10]

Obama was more fortunate in his secretaries of State (Hillary Clinton), Defense (Robert Gates), and Energy (Steven Chu). All were highly visible and articulate advocates for the president's policies. Other Cabinet figures were caught in the media glare from time to time and did not always fare well.[11]

Within the White House itself, the primary spokesperson was Gibbs, who became one of the most familiar faces for the administration. As an aide to Daschle and to various campaigns, Gibbs had earned a reputation as a policy insider who could be authoritative in briefings without revealing too much. He was a guy who "had it all buttoned down," as Obama said of him, an adviser as well as a mouthpiece, and his office less than 10 yards from the Oval Office attested to that role.

But Gibbs did not make a discernible difference in what the average American wound up knowing or thinking about the president or the administration on any given day. He was not framing or formulating ways of thinking about the issues, or generating key words and phrases that might stick in the American psyche. A typical attitude among White House regulars was voiced by ABC's Compton: "Gibbs is a fascinating informational briefer in the sense of being well-informed; but he's a lousy spokesman in the sense of coming up with concise and explanatory sound bites you can take to people" (Compton 2010).

If Gibbs was not originating or conveying media messages that made a difference, there was little indication that the White House expected him to do so. In many ways, Gibbs embodied the mindset of the inner circle of the campaign that had survived into the White House. They had their own internal clock and timetable, an inner sense of meaning and a reliance on the long view. He was steeped in what was often called the "zen" of the campaign. And he was enmeshed in that complex weave of personalities that was "Team Obama" in 2007–2008 and which transferred itself, not unaltered but largely intact, into the White House (Horsley 2010; Leibovich 2008).

As such, Gibbs was arguably succeeding at information management, message discipline, and control. But as Stephen Hess of the Brookings Institution notes: "Staying connected is more important than staying in control." The problem of the president's attenuating connection to the electorate and evanescing ability to shape the national conversation was not, strictly speaking, Gibbs's problem. And it was not clear whose White House portfolio it belonged in. In a sense, the entire White House seemed to be waiting for Obama to do it himself. And that proved problematic. Jamieson addressed this point in the fall of 2010:

> Obama was great at the epideictic speech, like the keynote at the 2004 convention and the last night in Denver at the nominating convention of 2008. Inspiring. Soaring. But he had trouble making a case for policy, such as health care, or TARP or the stimulus.... And there's no confidence [in the White House] that he could deliver that kind of speech, the compelling speech for why we have to do something that's hard and why it's hard and sell it. I don't think Obama has that kind of speechwriting staff, they're too young and they lack life experience (Jamieson 2010).

Toward the end of the two years, David Axelrod, the president's main political strategist and a former reporter and columnist for *The Chicago Tribune,* shouldered more of the media burden. He reached out to reporters, especially those he had known from the campaign, both within and beyond the White House briefing room. Much of what he said amounted to a mea culpa. "I readily concede that it wasn't optimal from a messaging standpoint," said Axelrod in one such interview. "We didn't have time to unpack it and do a few months on tax cuts and a few months on clean energy" (Bendery 2010).

Beyond that, the Obama team often returned to the specter of global depression that loomed in late 2008 and early 2009. Everything that followed, in both policy and communication, stemmed from the crisis atmosphere of those weeks. The Obama team admitted they had not advertised the tax cuts in the stimulus package, for example, explaining that reducing payroll deductions was a better way to get people to spend the money rather than save it. Refund checks, as used by the previous administration, might be deposited in savings by workers worried about losing their jobs.

Of course, the paucity of deliberate and effective media messaging did not mean the media had gone entirely unfed. Many messages were being transmitted—often unintentionally. One of the most salient came from Christina Romer, chair of the Council of Economic Advisers, who said in February 2009 that, without the president's stimulus plan, unemployment would rise above eight percent. The media and much of the country heard in this an implicit promise that the stimulus would keep unemployment at eight percent or below (Montgomery 2010).

Another White House message with lasting impact was Rahm Emanuel's statement about health care legislation: "The only non-negotiable principle here is success, everything else is negotiable" (Bai 2009). This not only reinforced Emanuel's own reputation as a transactional (rather than transformational) politician, it underlined the degree to which this approach had become Obama's. Beyond that, Emanuel's open-for-business sign confirmed media perceptions that doctors and insurance companies and the pharmaceutical industry were cutting deals in exchange for their pledge not to torpedo the health care bill. That impression grew stronger when the Senate Democrats dropped the public option, a government health insurance plan for those who could get no other.

Dropping the public option dismayed liberal supporters of the bill, whose disaffection dovetailed in the polls with resistance from conservatives (who perceived a federal takeover of the health care system or "socialized medicine"). The headlines written on these polls made little distinction between these two protests, and the overall image of the legislation in the media suffered. This enabled Republicans and other critics to paint the administration and congressional Democrats as defying the will of the people, even when polls were far more mixed than decisive (Gallup 2009–2010).

The Obama team was convinced that getting a law enacted was better for Democrats politically than failing to do so (a lesson derived and perhaps overlearned from the Clinton experience in 1994). Given the lingering effects of the recession and growing alarm at the growth of government and deficit spending, public approval of the new health care law did not improve in time to forestall disaster in the midterm elections of 2010, when Republicans campaigned on promises to repeal the new law or cut off funds for its implementation (Garrett 2010).

## Pushback from the Left

Midway through 2010, as difficult midterm elections loomed, the political lobe of the White House brain seemed preoccupied with its media problem. Confronted with the most powerful wave of conservative populism in at least 16 years, many within the inner circle were fixed on the criticism they were hearing from elites on the left. Gibbs gave vent to his feelings in an August interview with *The Hill*, referring with evident distaste to what he called the "professional left." Gibbs said, among other things, that some of these critics who were equating Obama with George W. Bush needed to be "drug tested" (Youngman 2010). Thereafter, Axelrod scheduled a conference call with liberal bloggers in attempt at reconciliation. But the rift was deep with those who had given no quarter in criticizing every compromise the president had made and every agenda item that had been postponed or compromised.[12]

The president allowed his own annoyance with these critics to show in public. At a fund-raiser in Greenwich, CT, he spoke to the dissatisfaction on the left: "If we get an historic health care bill passed—'Oh, well, the public option wasn't there.' If you get the financial reform bill passed—then, 'Well, I don't know about this particular derivatives rule, I'm not sure I'm satisfied with that.' And, gosh, we haven't brought about world peace. 'I thought that was going to happen quicker'" (Keating 2010).

And in a widely read interview with Jann Wenner, the long supportive editor-publisher of *Rolling Stone,* the president sounded a similar note of resentment toward erstwhile supporters in his coalition and in the media as well: "I could have had a knock-down, drag-out fight on the public option that might have energized you and *The Huffington Post,* and we would not have health care legislation now. I could have taken certain positions on aspects of the financial regulatory bill, where we got 90 percent of what we set out to get, and I could have held out for that last 10 percent, and we wouldn't have a bill" (Wenner 2010).

The Wenner interview expressed Obama's own ambivalence toward the media, as well as a larger uncertainty on media strategy within his administration. In mid-year 2010, after the flurry of signing ceremonies, the Obama team had veered from upbeat messaging ("Recovery Summer") to bitter denunciations of business for hoarding cash rather than investing and hiring. Eager to enact R&D tax credits and a stimulus package for small business, the administration was also trying to respond to anger at BP and other energy companies that followed the Gulf oil spill of the spring (Freeland 2010). It was easy to conclude that the White House attitude toward the business sector was conflicted, and from there to extrapolate that its ideas for improving business conditions and creating jobs were confused. It was also noteworthy that no one in the White House would consent to calling the small business bill a stimulus. That term, though initially one of their own choosing, had by fall 2010 become an epithet and a bludgeon in the hands of their opponents.

## THE FALL OF 2010

In the second August of the Obama presidency, there were no boisterous town halls. The noise was coming instead from campaign rallies of Republicans and Tea Party activists preparing for the November elections. Back in Washington, enough Democrats were worried about re-election that important legislation could no longer move in the House. In the Senate, Republicans were able, by threatening filibusters, to block nearly every item of business the Democrats proposed for floor action, including nominations, appointments, and the usual bills of the annual appropriations process.

The first phase of the Obama administration had come to a close. The White House could tout a catalog of achievements, including the keeping of many promises large and small. But by the fall, the White House had so lost control of the national political narrative that even a recitation of its legislative work was more likely to damage than to bolster the electoral prospects of incumbent Democrats (Packer 2010a).

Even more striking was the public's lack of simple factual clarity regarding the administration's record. A Bloomberg News national poll released the week before the midterm election found that by two to one, likely voters thought the economy had shrunk (despite 15 consecutive months of growth), that taxes had risen (despite tax cuts), and that the hundreds of billions lent to banks under the TARP program had been lost (despite reports that nearly all the funds would be recovered and some elements of TARP would show a profit). The poll told an essential truth that would be devastating to Democrats in the November 2 midterms. Poll director J. Ann Selzer said: "It does not matter much if you make change, if you do not communicate change" (Przybyla and McCormick 2010).

In the November midterm elections, congressional Democrats lost 63 House seats, their worst loss in that chamber since 1938. In the Senate, Democrats lost a net of six seats but retained a slim majority. Republicans also raised their total of governorships to 29 and added nearly 700 seats in state legislatures (just in time for reapportionment and redistricting for the decade to come). The sluggish and "jobless" recovery could be called the mainspring of these outcomes, but many critics believed the losses had been more severe because Obama and his party had not focused sufficiently on jobs, foreclosures, and other economic issues. Somewhere, the connection with voters that had been locked in for the 2006 and 2008 cycles had been lost. Geoff Garin, a Democratic pollster, said some of the problem stemmed from failures of the White House. At first a "blank slate" for voters, even after his election, Obama's early moves defined him as something the voters did not want, in Garin's view: "[Obama] defined himself as different from them, as an old Democrat, a tax-and-spend Democrat. Trying to sell what you've done is fruitless after you've been defined. For the voters, health care fell in the category of 'not the economy,' so as far as they were concerned Washington took its eye off the ball" (Garin 2010).

When asked to respond to these points, the mantra of White House talkers, in public and in private, was that "no communications strategy covers 9.6 percent unemployment"—a line they had used for months, adjusting for each month's jobless rate (Pace 2010; Bendery 2010). But there was more to the Democrats' frustration than the jobless statistics. They were stunned at the lack of credit for things that had been done and for improvements that had taken place.

The sentiments of the voters were surely based in their own perceptions of their circumstances. But they also reflected the dominant impression of national conditions presented in the media generally. This was an impression the White House found itself powerless to change in the near term, especially in a media world in the midst of its own transformation. "How do you drive a national political conversation," asked Garin, "when there are 100 voices and sources of information instead of three?" (Garin 2010).

In the campaign weeks, Obama did a series of "backyard chats" with voters, some literally in backyards and all with a sense of closeness to real people. A woman at one such event in September, working mother Velma Hart, asked an eloquent and moving question that was featured in media accounts and quickly viral on YouTube and elsewhere. "Frankly I'm exhausted at defending you," she told the president. Fox Business labeled her "an American hero," and she became a household name overnight. In subsequent interviews, Hart expressed underlying support for Obama and said she had thought he would have a great answer for her. But nothing the president said to her that day or thereafter was as powerful as her challenge, or the way the middle-aged black woman looked in posing it (Singletary 2010).

The demands of the crises faced early on, the focus on a legislative agenda and the primacy given to the process problems of Congress, had left the White House fatally off the wavelength of the electorate. And while the White House had been disconnected, its adversaries had been on the march, increasingly confident they spoke for the people and increasingly able to make that case in the media.

On each of the issues on which the Bloomberg poll found the public unaware of crucial facts, the question arises: If there has been failure to communicate, who is responsible for it? The public, the media, or the White House? But that is a philosophical question rather a practical one: There was no question who would pay the price on Election Day. Wrote Peter Baker of *The New York Times* after interviewing the president in September 2010: "What's striking about Obama's self-diagnosis is that by his own rendering, the figure of inspiration from 2008 neglected the inspiration after his election. He didn't stay connected to the people who put him in office in the first place. Instead he simultaneously disappointed those who considered him the embodiment of a new progressive movement and those who expected him to reach across the aisle to usher in a post-partisan age" (Baker 2010a).

Much had been expected, and great expectations had been encouraged by the media as much as by Obama's own campaign. The motivations differed, but the pursuit of the narrative had driven them together. The change from campaign to governance broke this bond, especially as competing narratives of resistance and pushback gained currency and power. This change, interacting with ferment in media economics and culture, produced a reversal of fortune for the candidate who had been the ultimate media favorite. All of these are dynamic relationships that continue to change and may look quite different by the time the president himself faces voters again in 2012.

## NOTES

1. Raised by a single mother who sometimes relied on food stamps, Obama made his way through a series of prestigious private schools on scholarship, a meritocratic tour de force culminating in his election as the first black president of the Harvard Law Review (Obama 1995; Remnick 2010a). In 2006 most political observers considered Obama's 2008 scenario implausible. But over time, the magnetism of the story became hard to resist. An inflexion point occurred with the Jefferson-Jackson Day speech he gave in Des Moines, Iowa, on November 10, 2007. After thousands heard Obama speak that night (some on C-SPAN), hundreds of thousands saw the speech on YouTube. The entire campaign took on a different feel (Balz and Johnson 2009). Such events reset the calibrations of correspondents in the field and caused news managers to give Obama a fresh look. Soon, polls taken in Iowa showed Obama moving into a three-way tie in Iowa. Soon after, he was forging a lead (Nagourney and Zeleny 2007). Obama also had the media wind at his back in the fall campaign against Republican John McCain, a previous media favorite who had once referred to reporters as "my base." But McCain by late 2008 was no longer the self-styled rogue or maverick of those campaigns. McCain had to bear the burden of the incumbent President George W. Bush. McCain's choice of Alaska Governor Sarah Palin as his vice-presidential running mate also cost him with many in the media, who regarded her as poorly prepared (Heilemann and Halperin 2010).

2. Blagojevich would be impeached by the Illinois House in January, convicted and removed from office by the Illinois Senate on January 29, 2009. But by then he had appointed Roland Burris, 71, to serve in Obama's seat. Burris had been the first African American to win statewide office in Illinois, becoming state comptroller in 1979. But he had been out of office and four times an unsuccessful candidate since 1994. Initially, Senate Democratic leaders questioned the legality of the appointment. But after Burris held a news conference

outside the Capitol, surrounded by African American supporters in a freezing rain, the media sentiment shifted dramatically and he was sworn in on Jan. 15, 2009. Blagojevich was tried on two dozen counts in 2010 and found guilty of only one: obstructing justice by lying to the FBI. US Attorney Patrick Fitzgerald immediately vowed to try at least some of the other counts again in 2011. The Senate seat held by Burris was captured by Republican Mark Kirk in the election of November 2010.

3. Mark Knoller of CBS radio, a longtime veteran of the White House beat, has become the unofficial chronicler of all presidential movements in public, compiling statistics of this sort obsessively and becoming all but the official White House record of same (Knoller 2010).

4. The "birthers" argued that Obama had never proven his eligibility to be president because he had not produced a physical copy of his birth certificate. Officials in Hawaii, including the state's Republican governor, had long since and repeatedly attested to the validity of his birth documents, corroborated by hospital and newspaper records from 1961. But for months, the story made the rounds in the blogosphere, in conservative publications, and occasionally on television news programs. It was driven by a few entrepreneurial fringe figures but also by the refusal of many Republicans to renounce the issue or disavow the protestors. Some mainstream media figures also promoted the issue for a time, including Lou Dobbs and Glenn Beck, who still had programs on CNN at the time (Nather 2009b).

5. A similar dynamic had overtaken the last three Democrats who succeeded Republicans in the White House. In 1993 and 1994, despite a robust economic recovery already underway when he took office, Clinton was beset with congressional pushback and assailed by conservatives of every stripe—including a "militia movement" with a paramilitary edge. He lost both House and Senate in a crushing midterm in 1994 that saw Republicans win a majority of Southern congressional seats and governorships for the first time since Reconstruction. Similarly, Jimmy Carter in 1977–78 encountered resistance in a heavily Democratic Congress that his White House team (dominated by people from his home state) never mastered. Carter saw his margins in Senate and House greatly reduced in 1978 in a prelude to his own defeat (and still worse congressional losses) in 1980. Even John F. Kennedy in 1961–62 discovered how potent the combined forces of anti-communism and resistance to desegregation could be in the early months of his presidency. He escaped a punishing midterm thanks to public approval of his performance in the October 1962 Cuban Missile Crisis (and to the fact that his win in 1960 had brought few Democrats into Congress on his coattails).

6. Pew Research Center in September 2010 found 23 percent of the total public saying it watches Fox News regularly, while just 18 percent said the same of CNN and 11 percent of MSNBC. This has enabled Fox News to become a prime influence on the national news menu, following the pattern by which CNN did the same in earlier decades. Fox News prospers largely on its appeal to certain demographics, especially to older, white viewers and to those who self-identify as conservatives or as Republicans. In the September 2010 survey, Pew found 40 percent of Republicans said they regularly watched Fox News, while just 12 percent said they watched CNN and just 6 percent MSNBC. Of those who call themselves supporters of the Tea Party, 52 percent say they watch Fox News, while even higher percentages say they watch Fox News personalities such as Bill O'Reilly (68 percent), Sean Hannity (75 percent), or Glenn Beck (76 percent) (Pew Research Center for the People & the Press 2010b).

7. CBS News correspondent Lesley Stahl produced a piece for CBS in 1984 that she regarded as highly critical of the Reagan campaign's manipulation of emotional symbols. She then got a thank-you call from Dick Darman, a Reagan aide. He said he appreciated her airing highlights of the red-white-and-blue footage one more time, and told her to watch her own broadcast with the sound off if she wanted to understand what was getting through to the public. This particular anecdote has become part of the lore of the 1984 campaign and of the campaign media relationship to the candidates, so much so that its usual meaning has become a subject for debate (Rosen 2004; Schram 1987).

8. In its introduction, the PEJ report said: "The days of loyalty to a particular news organization on a particular piece of technology in a particular form are gone. The overwhelming majority of Americans (92%) use multiple platforms to get news on a typical day, including national TV, local TV, the internet, local newspapers, radio and national newspapers. Some 46% of Americans say they get news from four to six media platforms on a typical day. Just 7% get their news from a single media platform on a typical day. The internet is at the center of the story of how people's relationship to news is changing. Six in ten Americans (59%) get news from a combination of online and offline sources on a typical day, and the internet is now the third most popular news platform, behind local television news and national television news" (Pew Research Center Project for Excellence in Journalism 2010).

9. In the same four years it took Obama to go from the Illinois state Senate to the White House, the growth of Internet advertising (especially classified print advertising) savaged the business models of broadcast and print journalism. Amazingly, the mainstay delivery platforms of "serious news" had remained handsomely profitable as late as the middle of the first decade in the twenty-first century. But decline set in during the second term of the second President Bush, and with the market panic of 2008 the rout was on. Gannett, the nation's largest newspaper chain and operator of *USA Today*, saw its stock price fall from a peak of more than $90 in 2004 to a low of less than $5 in 2008. *The New York Times* and *The Washington Post* also experienced stock value declines of more than 70 percent over the same period before share prices began to recover. Even in the fall of 2010, the market capitalization for the *Post* was down 60 percent from its peak, and that of the *Times* and Gannett by more than 80 percent (MarketWatch.com 2010).

10. Both Pelosi and Reid were re-elected in the midst of their party's 2010 midterm election debacle and returned to their leadership roles shortly thereafter. Pelosi represented a safe Democratic district (San Francisco) and Reid outlasted a controversial Republican nominee backed by the Tea Party. In their respective party caucuses, despite widespread angst within their diminished ranks, Democrats could not muster a real challenge to their leader in either chamber (although a symbolic challenge was mounted to Pelosi in the House).

11. Attorney General Eric Holder had early scrapes with the media (notably after saying Americans were "cowards" when it came to talking about race) and thereafter tried to avoid most coverage. Agriculture Secretary Tom Vilsack had to apologize for firing Shirley Sherrod, an over-reaction to initial reports on Fox. Homeland Security Secretary Janet Napolitano did not help the administration's case responding to the "Christmas Day bomber" incident in Detroit in 2009 by saying "the system worked" (Baker and Shane 2009). Former Colorado senator Ken Salazar, who gave up his seat to be Secretary of Interior, was uninspiring at best as a surrogate spokesman for the federal regulatory system after the Massey mine disaster and again after the BP oil rig disaster in the Gulf of Mexico in April 2010 (Broder 2010; Dickinson 2010).

12. Peter Daou, blogging on his own site (peterdaou.com) on September 27, 2010, took the Obama White House to task, as he usually did, for several policy decisions with which Daou disagreed. Then he turned to the issues of support and betrayal raised by various White House voices. Daou believed that Glenn Greenwald was the chief irritant, perhaps because salon.com is a broader base from which to launch attacks on the White House, and also because the White House had previously been reported to be highly attentive to Greenwald (Ambinder 2009). Greenwald thought he saw something deliberate in the timing and orchestration of complaints about liberal critics: "As we head into a November election that looks more and more like Democrats are going to get slaughtered, I think they are trying to set up a villain, someone to blame other than Obama. And that villain will be the left" (Greenwald 2010).

CHAPTER 10

# Communication Is Destiny

## Scott Lilly

The morning after the 2010 midterm elections, President Obama told the assembled White House press corps, "I am not recommending to any future president that they take a shellacking like I did last night." As Obama pointed out, his first midterm election experience was not that dissimilar from those of Ronald Reagan and Bill Clinton, both of whom saw their party take major losses after their first two years in office (Branigin 2010). But Obama's losses were bigger, and the zealousness of his opponents made his loss of political capital all the more dramatic.

Both the accomplishments of Obama's first two years in the White House and the causes of the electoral losses suffered by his party will be more easily understood as time provides greater perspective and the smoke of the current battles have lifted. Yet there are certain facts that are already apparent.

The timing of Obama's election to the White House relative to the deteriorating state of the economy did not work in his favor. Obama also faced a complex array of problems that all seemed to demand immediate attention and made communication about the myriad of policy choices with which the White House was contending inordinately difficult. In addition, he faced an unusually determined, disciplined, and hard-hitting political opposition. Finally, he was hammered 24 hours a day by conservative talk radio, websites, and in particular, Fox News, which has emerged as a unique force in American politics over the course of the past decade.

But part of the huge electoral disaster suffered by Democrats is not attributable to the difficulty of the challenges faced by this White House. Rather, it was

167

a result of how the White House responded to those challenges. This chapter will examine each of these problems and how they contributed to a "shellacking" of truly historic proportions.

## BAD TIMING

First, the timing of his election to the White House did not work in his favor. The problems facing the country at the time Obama became president have often been compared to those confronting Franklin Roosevelt in 1933. There is an important difference, however, in the timing of the two presidencies: Franklin Roosevelt was sworn into office after the US economy had hit rock bottom, while Obama became president just as the economy was going over the edge.

The five-month hiatus between Roosevelt's election and his March inauguration was a period of great suffering, accompanied by tremendous frustration that the incoming president could not take the reins of power and begin to move the nation in a new direction. But it also positioned Roosevelt to take dramatic action once he was in office and sustain his policies over time. By the time Roosevelt was sworn in, it had been 3½ years since the stock market crash. Unemployment had risen from 3.2 percent in 1929 to 8.9 percent a year later, 16.3 percent the year after that and to 24.1 percent in 1932. By the time of Roosevelt's inauguration, unemployment was estimated at 25.2 percent (Bureau of the Census 1975). It was difficult to argue that Roosevelt or the New Deal was in any way culpable for the state in which the country found itself.

Obama inherited a smaller calamity but one that was still evolving. In December 2008, as Obama was negotiating with the new Congress about the makeup of a proposed economic recovery package, economic forecasters as a whole were still struggling to comprehend the magnitude of the emerging housing and financial crises and the consequences on the shrinking economy. Sentiment about the nation's economic prospects had deteriorated throughout 2008. The Blue Chip Forecast, a survey of 50 leading economic analysts, lowered its forecast for growth with each successive month in the second half of 2008 (Waitz 2008; Nutting 2008).

A few economists, such as Jan Hatzius at Goldman Sachs, recognized the magnitude of the economic collapse even before Election Day, but most forecasters did not grasp its severity until several months into the New Year (Willis 2010). In December, the Blue Chip Forecast for the average rate of unemployment for 2009 was only 7.8 percent (Waitz 2008). Three months later that forecast had risen to 8.6 percent (Waitz 2009). By early summer the Blue Chip was forecasting unemployment to be over 10 percent by the end of 2009 (Waitz 2009).

Like Roosevelt, Obama could not point to a major turnaround in economic activity at the close of his second year in office. He was instead stuck with trying to convince his critics that his policies had prevented things from being much worse, and that an economic crisis of this magnitude requires a longer recovery period. While most economists accepted that argument, the public either did not accept it or felt the president's efforts were less than the nation could have reasonably expected.

## Too Many Challenges

While the challenge faced by Obama on the economic front was huge, it paled in comparison to the economic challenge facing Roosevelt. On the other hand, Roosevelt did not inherit two costly foreign wars, face grave scientific concerns about the future of the global environment, or have decades of frustration within his own party about the cost, quality, and availability of health care, as well as conflicting demands for new policies on immigration and discrimination based on sexual orientation. Obama faced difficult choices at every turn in terms of maintaining a focus on the issue of greatest concern to the overall electorate and while attempting to address the issues of importance to key components of his electoral coalition.

## Virulent Opposition

Obama's first two years in the White House differed from Franklin Roosevelt's in other important respects. Throughout the twentieth century, opposing political parties have opted not to obstruct incoming presidents in the wake of decisive elections. They have chosen instead to cooperate on some issues and criticize the president's policy choices on others. The congressional Republicans of 1933 went beyond the normal level of cooperation extended to an incoming president with a large electoral majority. They were described by some contemporary critics as being supine. Historian George H. Mayer describes congressional Republicans after the 1932 election as follows:

> The magnitude of the disaster undermined morale and led to mutual recriminations between the victims. Congressional Republicans blamed Hoover for an inept campaign and he blamed them for dragging their feet. The agrarian element in the party denounced the wealthy industrialists, while the latter claimed that the unsound proposals of Western Republicans had deepened the depression and scared the voters. An ideological dispute about the viability of the free enterprise system was superimposed on older sectional animosities ... The sources of frustration were too diverse to receive expression in clear-cut fashion. Yet polarization of a sort expressed itself: the bulk of the congressional minority acquiesced in New Deal emergency legislation (Mayer 1966).

Congressional Republicans were so anxious to dissociate themselves from the executive branch of their party, still under the leadership of Herbert Hoover, that they separated congressional and senatorial campaign committees from the national committee. Henry Fletcher, Hoover's selection as chairman of the

Republican National Committee, countered that the 73rd Congress was "full of rubber stamps and feeble minds" (Mayer 1966).

This is in dramatic contrast to the approach Republicans of the 111th Congress took in dealing with Barack Obama. The incoming president had won with a margin of 9.5 million votes, 53 percent of the electorate, and a 7.5 percent margin over his opponent (Federal Election Commission 2009). That was short of the 57.4 percent share of the popular vote gathered by Roosevelt in 1932, but it was still the largest winning percentage in a presidential election in 20 years. It was a significantly larger electoral mandate than those enjoyed by Ronald Reagan, John Kennedy, Jimmy Carter, or George W. Bush as they entered the White House (The American Presidency Project).

The Republicans of the 111th Congress launched a bold strategy of confrontation. They fought the new president on every major initiative, their attacks were persistent, and their rhetoric was often extreme. Pressure was intense on every member of the conference to close ranks and maintain a united front of opposition. Within nine days of Obama's inauguration, House Republicans voted unanimously against his central economic proposal, the American Recovery and Reinvestment Act of 2009 (Calmes 2009).

House Republicans later tried explaining that their opposition was the result of having been shut out of deliberations on crafting the legislation. Democrats responded that Republicans had themselves refused invitations to participate. Committee Chair David Obey said, "The minority continually spouts the myth that the minority was not allowed to be involved in the development of this legislation ... if someone says, I'm sorry I was shut out, but it is they who turned the key in the lock that kept them on the outside, that certainly isn't our fault (Seabrook 2009).

Ultimately the final package was fashioned in the Senate with three Senate Republicans, Olympia Snowe and Susan Collins of Maine and Arlen Specter of Pennsylvania, providing the votes to block a filibuster supported by the other 39 Republican senators. They not only provided the necessary votes to limit debate on the legislation, but also dictated its final form to a remarkable degree. A total of $40 billion was cut from the package, which dramatically slashed fiscal relief to state and local governments. Tax cuts were boosted and targeted in larger proportion toward higher-income households (Espo 2009).

Republican leaders insisted that bipartisanship might come later in the Obama administration, but from the date of the inauguration to the date of the midterm elections, their assault was unrelenting. By early summer, House and Senate Republicans were in full assault on the administration's climate-change legislation and preparing their assault on health care reform (Woellert and Lomax 2009).

The worst was to come in late summer, when an army of grassroots activists with significant funding from major donors to Republican campaign committees began swarming and disrupting public forums held by members of Congress of both parties considered supporters of what they labeled "Obamacare" (Rucker and Eggen 2009).

## A HOSTILE PRESS

Another challenge facing Obama was a far more hostile press than had confronted Roosevelt during his first two years. University of Virginia's Larry Sabato, who described the philosophy of journalism in the Roosevelt era as the "lap dog" press, writes in his book, *Feeding Frenzy*:

> Whatever the precise combination of causes, Roosevelt was protected by the press in ways that would have amazed some of his harassed predecessors. Roosevelt, a polio victim, was wheelchair-bound, but of thirty-five thousands press photographs of FDR only two showed his wheelchair. When the President occasionally fell in public, photographers would take no pictures and live radio broadcasters would make no mention of the fact (Sabato 2000).

Roosevelt did eventually have detractors both on the radio and in print, people such as syndicated newspaper columnist Westbrook Pegler (Witwer 2005), magazine columnists Garet Garrett (Garrett 2002) and David Lawrence (Kingbury 2008), publishers William Randolph Hearst (Kennedy 2010) and H.L. Mencken (McCarthy 2003), and radio commentator Father Charles Coughlin (Social Security Administration). But many of these people actually supported Roosevelt in the early years of his presidency, and none had the constant presence of the 24-hour news networks or radio talk show hosts that have pummeled Obama since the day of his inauguration.

Sabato classifies three periods in modern American journalism, beginning with the "lap dog" period, which extended from the Roosevelt administration through the mid-1960s. It was followed by the "watch dog" period that evolved during the Vietnam War and was replaced by the "junk yard dog" period that began with Watergate and extends to the present. Sabato describes political reporting during the "junk yard dog" period as "often harsh, aggressive, and intrusive, where feeding frenzies flourish, and gossip reaches print. Every aspect of private life potentially becomes fair game for scrutiny" (Sabato 2000).

One might argue that in the course of the past decade we have passed into a fourth period of American journalism called the "trained attack dog" period. It has most of the attributes of Sabato's "junk yard dog" journalism, but it is more systematically organized to promote specific points of view and political agendas. Rather than avoiding bias, it uses bias to attract and hold audiences predisposed to that bias.

When Fox News opened its doors 14 years ago, it could be accessed by less than 20 percent of American households (Pew Research Center for the People & the Press 2010b). Since then, Fox has built viewership in periods when viewer attention focused on events such as 9/11, the Iraq War, and the 2008 elections, and it has held viewers better than its competitors when new viewer interest in world events was less intense. Despite the fact that the Fox News audience is rarely at any point in the day more than one third the size of the leading broadcast network evening newscast, it has become a dominant force in the information Americans receive because it has a huge audience that watches for at least some time in each 24-hour period (Pew Research Center for the People & the Press 2010b).

A recent George Washington University Battleground poll found that 81 percent of those interviewed got some news about the midterm elections from cable news, whereas only 71 percent got information on the elections from broadcast networks. Among those who got midterm election information from cable news channels, 42 percent said that Fox was their main source. That compared with 30 percent who said that CNN was their main source for such news, and only 12 percent stating that MSNBC was the main source (*Politico*/GWU 2010).

Fox's dominant position comes largely from the fact that in recent years the network has become the overwhelming choice of Republican voters. Polling of likely voters over the past two decades by the Pew Research Center for People & the Press shows that the portion of Republicans who regularly watch Fox News has increased dramatically over the past decade. In 2000 only 18 percent were regular watchers. In 2002 it had grown to 25 percent, but Fox still trailed CNN that year among Republican viewers by 3 percentage points. Today 40 percent of Republicans watch Fox News on a regular basis compared with only 12 percent watching CNN and just 6 percent watching CNBC (Pew Research Center for the People & the Press 2010b).

While political operatives normally focus on the attitudes and information sources of undecided and independent voters, the 2010 election was a case study on the impact that a constant drumbeat of negative information targeted at opponents of a political leader can have on the broader electorate. Not only does having such a large audience of partisan viewers provide a platform to reach beyond partisans (Fox is regularly listened to by 20 percent of independents, a larger independent viewership than CNN and twice the independent viewership of MSNBC), but it also creates an echo chamber in which the intensity of Republican perceptions about the policies and performance of the government reverberate and make it appear to Democrats and independents that they are more broadly held than is in fact the case (Pew Research Center for the People & the Press 2010b). One of the lessons of the past two years may be that building a high level of intensity among opponents of a political leader can have a powerful impact on independent voters—and even voters affiliated with that leader's own party. This is important in measuring the performance of the Obama White House when compared with its predecessors, because no previous president has ever faced such relentlessly harsh criticism broadcast to an audience anywhere the size of the audience now watching Fox News.

Further, the rapid growth of philosophically segmented audiences in the viewership of cable news outlets is just part of a larger phenomenon. The Pew survey indicates that the 2010 election was the first time in electoral history that Americans spent more time using news online than getting news from print newspapers. Average daily time spent getting news online has grown from 6 minutes in 2006 to 9 minutes in 2008 and 13 minutes in 2010. Time spent reading newspapers has declined from 15 minutes in 2006 to 9 minutes in 2010. While much of the news obtained online is from the sites operated by traditional print newspapers, a significant portion is coming from the increasing number of websites, blogs, and e-mail chains directed at philosophically segmented readerships and promoting an overt political agenda (Pew Research Center for the People & the Press 2010b).

When such resources are used by a committed opposition, they make the effective use of the White House bully pulpit significantly more difficult. The result is that the ability of any president to exert leadership is diminished.

## A FAILURE TO COMMUNICATE

Having catalogued the considerable challenges that confronted the Obama administration during its first two years in office, it must be said that these challenges, substantial as they may be, do not appear to fully explain the results of November 2, 2010. The president's party lost 63 of 258 seats held in the House of Representatives, or 25 percent; 6 of 19 seats held in the Senate (32 percent); 13 of 21 governorships held by Democrats prior to the election (62 percent) ("Election 2010," *New York Times* 2010), and about 680 state legislative seats, giving the GOP the most seats in the state legislatures than they have held at anytime since 1928 (National Conference of State Legislatures 2010).

For those who say such losses can be expected when the national unemployment rate remains above 9.5 percent, one need only point out the losses suffered by Ronald Reagan in November of 1982 when unemployment peaked at 10.8 percent. Republicans lost only 26 House seats or 14 percent on the seats they held, and they lost no seats in the Senate. Roosevelt, who, like Obama, had struggled to show real signs of economic growth during his first two years in the White House, saw voters go to the polls with an unemployment rate of 21.7 percent and still picked up 9 Republican seats in the House and 9 more in the Senate (Bureau of Labor Statistics 2010; Office of the Clerk, US House of Representatives 2010; US Senate 2010).

Perhaps the most telling statistics about the 2010 elections are those that compare the perceptions voters took to the polls with objective descriptions of administration policies and the actual state of the American economy. A poll conducted by *Bloomberg* the week prior to the election showed that likely voters believed:

- 52 percent to 19 percent that taxes on the middle class had gone up under the Obama administration
- 60 percent to 33 percent that *most* of the Troubled Asset Relief Program money will be lost.
- 61 percent to 33 percent that the economy had shrunk over the course of the past year (Pryzbyla and McCormick 2010).

The importance that each of these misperceptions had in the outcome of the election must be weighed in light of the fact that each would appear to significantly impact on voters' views about the economy as well as the efforts by the administration to restore growth and reduce the economic suffering of ordinary families. Exit polls found that the economy was the most important issue for an overwhelming portion of the electorate—62 percent of those who went to the polls. Health care finished a distant second, being chosen by only 19 percent (ABC News 2010). Yet these views were extraordinarily out of sync with reality.

The relentless charge by Obama detractors that he was a tax-and-spend politician trumped the reality that his policies to date have resulted in tax cuts. "He's all about raising taxes ... He's all about big government and big spending," a Minnesota resident told the Bloomberg pollster (Pryzbyla and McCormick 2010).

Despite the fact that 37 percent of the money taken from the Treasury in the $787 billion Recovery and Reinvestment Act went for tax cuts, only 19 percent of those surveyed disagreed with the assertion that taxes under Obama have gone up. Further, middle-income voters were significantly more likely than upper-income voters to believe that taxes had gone up (63 percent for households with incomes of $25,000–$50,000 and 45 percent for households with incomes above $100,000), despite the fact that the administration insisted and prevailed on the question of targeting most of the tax cuts to middle-income households (Pryzbyla and McCormick 2010).

There is no doubt the president's detractors contributed much to these misperceptions, but in many cases they were shared by Democrats. This indicates that the White House failed to communicate fundamental facts about its efforts to even its own supporters. On the question of "Do you think federal income taxes have gone up or down for the middle class in the past two years?" Democrats said up by a margin of 43 to 27 (Pryzbyla and McCormick 2010).

The creation and use of the Troubled Asset Relief Program, or TARP, has clearly been the most controversial and divisive issue of the entire economic recovery effort. An earlier poll also conducted for Bloomberg News in July of 2010 showed that a remarkable 58 percent of voters would be more likely to vote for a candidate who "supports spending government money to create jobs and stimulate the economy," while only 24 percent would oppose such a candidate. The same group of voters was asked whether they would support a candidate who "voted to give financial assistance to the banking industry when it was in crisis." Only 19 percent said that they would be more inclined to support such a candidate while 51 percent would be less likely to oppose such a candidate (Bloomberg News 2010).

The dramatic disconnect between support for "spending government money to create jobs and stimulate the economy" and opposition to the Recovery Act appears to be result of the misperception that it included the TARP funding. That misperception required a muddling of the Obama record, that he rather than his predecessor signed the legislation creating TARP. Carried further, that TARP was the result of the Obama administration's efforts to "expand the role of government."

Obama did not sign TARP into law, but he was in charge of administering it—and by all objective measures should receive credit rather than disdain for his efforts. Initial estimates of how much of the $700 billion available under TARP might be lost were slightly above 50 percent, or $300 billion, although some critics at the time it was enacted warned of much greater losses (United States Congress, Congressional Budget Office 2009a). The most recent estimate of TARP losses indicates losses of only about 4 percent—one tenth the original estimate (Puzzanghera 2010). Remarkably, the largest failure of the financial system since the bank failures of 1931 is now estimated to have cost the taxpayers only about a third as much as the costs of bailing out the Savings & Loan industry during the administration of George H.W. Bush (US General Accounting Office 1996).

There is no question that the misperception about the overall condition and direction of the economy was a major negative for the president and his party in the midterms. While 61 percent of likely voters believed the economy was still shrinking, all of the various methods of measuring the growth documented the opposite conclusion. The broadest measure of economic activity, Gross Domestic Product, was reported by the Bureau of Economic Analysis in October to have reached $14.7 trillion in the third quarter of 2010. Even allowing for inflation, the economy had grown by more than 3 percent, or $400 billion, over the previous 12 months. The October report indicated that the economy had expanded in five of the six full quarters of the Obama presidency with growth reported in all but the first full quarter (Bureau of Economic Analysis 2010).

Employment is generally viewed as a lagging indicator of economic growth, but over the past 12 months the number of private-sector jobs in the United States increased from 107.1 million to 108.1 million. The problem facing the Obama administration and unemployed workers is that as jobs return to the economy, the number of workers seeking those jobs also increases. As has been the pattern in previous recessions, strengthening employment numbers result in little if any change in unemployment percentages until well into a recovery. But the numbers are still starkly at odds with the perception. Not only has the number of private-sector jobs not declined—as the Bloomberg poll numbers indicate 61 percent of voters believed a month before the election—but they also have grown steadily, increasing every month since last December (Bureau of Labor Statistics 2010).

Another measure of economic growth is the performance of the stock market. The Standard and Poor's 500 index of leading corporations stood at 1225 points the day prior to the 2010 election, 9 percent above where it had been three months earlier, 15 percent above where it had been a year earlier, and 47 percent above where it had been at the time of the Obama inauguration (Standard & Poor's 500 Index).

While efforts to revive the economy were the most important issue to voters, they were not the only area where perception was badly out of sync with reality. The second biggest area of concern was health care. Most polls show that the American people are fairly evenly divided over whether the law signed by the president should be retained or repealed, but polling evidence shows that many of those who support repeal have a limited understanding of the legislation's contents. A *New York Times*/CBS poll conducted in mid-October found that 41 percent of respondents said they wanted to see health reform repealed. When asked if they would support repeal if that meant insurance companies would no longer be required to cover people with pre-existing conditions, support for repeal fell to 25 percent (Poll: October 21–26, 2010, *The New York Times*/CBS News Survey).

Polling by the Kaiser Foundation has in fact found large majorities of Americans supporting five of the six major provisions of the health care legislation with even majorities of Republicans supporting several of them. Nearly four-fifths (78 percent) favor provisions providing tax credits to small businesses. Nearly as many (72 percent) favor gradual closure of the so-called Medicare "doughnut hole" for private payments for prescription drugs, and 71 percent favor requiring insurance companies to cover those with pre-existing conditions; the same percentage favor providing financial help to lower-income Americans to help them purchase coverage. Even a majority (54 percent) favor the increases in the Medicare payroll tax. The one unpopular provision is the requirement that individuals have health insurance, which 68 percent of voters want repealed (Kaiser Health Tracking Poll 2010).

In every election, opposing parties attempt to "spin" the media and the voters with the most positive or negative interpretation of the facts depending on which interpretation best advances their political interests. This election was no different in that respect. It was different in terms of the outcome of those efforts at spin control. It's difficult to recall any previous election in which one party so fully dominated the other in spinning the facts to voters, as this survey data appears to indicate happened in the 2010 midyear elections.

Ann Selzer, president of the firm that conducted the survey for Bloomberg, told the publication:

> The public view of the economy is at odds with the facts, and the blame has to go to the Democrats, It does not matter much if you make change, if you do not communicate change (Pryzbyla and McCormick 2010).

The Republicans clearly had a disciplined and well-executed plan for convincing voters to adopt their view of the new president, his party, and the policies that party was bringing to Washington. They had unprecedented resources for executing their plan, and they stuck to it day in and day out regardless of the distractions. There is little doubt that they have set a new precedent for how incoming presidents will be greeted by the opposition party.

It is also true that the expansion of agenda-oriented or "trained attack dog" media worked to the benefit of the opposition. But future political strategists in both parties will look to this period and ask, "What could the White House have done differently?"

Was the agenda too broad? Almost any president has the capacity to develop new policy initiatives across the whole spectrum of possible government activity. But any president also has a much more limited capability to monitor the development of those policies, and even more limitations on how much he can effectively sell to the Congress and the American people. The Obama White House clearly believed that it should attempt to meet all of the major challenges facing the country: "we *can* walk and chew gum at the same time" (Montopoli 2010). But did their appetite for policy exceed their capacity for salesmanship?

It is probable that the Obama administration did not have to sell every policy initiative, but they did have to win the big confrontations with their political opposition on the policy issues that got the greatest measure of public attention. This they clearly failed to do. The polling data throughout the 21½ months between the inauguration and the midterm elections left no doubt that the public was interested in one issue to the exclusion of all others—the economy.

A review of presidential "speeches and remarks," weekly addresses," and "statements and releases" from the first six months of the Obama administration reveals an extraordinary array of policy activity. In addition to the president's weekly radio address, there were 362 separate sets of comments made by the president, vice president, or First Lady in the first 180 days, and an additional 870 statements and releases issued by the White House. This is on top of the three to five press briefings held each week and the weekly radio address (The White House Office of the Press Secretary 2009).

A review of the presidential addresses indicates that by far the largest number involved foreign policy, with a significant number delivered overseas or in the presence of a visiting head of state. Domestic topics included "cyber infrastructure," "hurricane preparedness," "weapons system acquisition reform," "fuel efficiency standards, "credit card reform," "high-speed rail," "investments in clean energy," "immigration," and "non discrimination in benefits provided to federal employees." The president and vice president did give speeches on the economy and job creation, but they did not make up a majority of the speeches delivered even among those speeches directed at domestic policy (The White House Office of the Press Secretary 2009).

## The Turning Point

Early July of 2009 was a critical turning point in the public's perception of the Recovery Act, the new president, and his party. The activity of the White House and its opposition in Congress provides some insight into how public perceptions may have evolved about the government's efforts to bring about economic recovery.

A July 1 tracking poll by the Gallup organization had measured his approval at 61 percent compared to a disapproval rating of 30 percent. That was roughly where he had been since the first weeks after the inauguration (Gallup 2009). July 2, 2009, was an important date because it was the day data on the nation's employment situation for the month of June was released by the Labor Department. During recessions such releases are always important, but this release was of particular importance (Bureau of Labor Statistics 2010).

April had been a terrible month for job losses as the economy had given up more than half a million jobs. May statistics gave considerable grounds for hope that worst might finally be behind us, with the rate of job loss being trimmed to 345,000. Forecasters were projecting that June would roughly fall in line with May, and that the economy might actually start generating job growth by fall. But contrary to the forecast, the Department of Labor reported on July 2 that the economy had given up 467,000 jobs. When the stock market opened an hour later, the Dow Jones Industrials dropped 240 points before ending the day down 223 (Thomasson 2009).

Minority Leader John Boehner issued a statement saying,

> Today's announcement is an acknowledgement that the Democrats' trillion-dollar stimulus is not working, and the American people know it. When they passed this spending plan, Democrats said it would immediately create jobs, yet nearly four months later unemployment has continued to climb and none of their rosy predictions have come true (CNN Politics 2009a).

Boehner also released a television ad he had already filmed for the occasion featuring two bloodhounds that were helping Boehner search for the jobs that had been created by the recovery package (Boehner 2010). As the House of Representatives was shutting down for a 10-day, July 4 District Work Period, congressional Republicans were sent home with a set of talking points to explain to their constituents and local media outlets the "huge amounts of money wasted on a failed recovery plan."

The White House had scheduled a meeting on July 2 between the president and "business leaders from both small and large companies to discuss job creation and ways to develop [a] long-term solution to strengthen our economy" (The White House Office of the Press Secretary 2009). It was decided that the president should add to the schedule a brief speech following that meeting, at which he stated:

> And obviously, this is a timely discussion, on a day of sobering news. The job figures released this morning show that we lost 467,000 jobs last month. And while the average loss of about 400,000 jobs per month this quarter is less devastating than the 700,000 per month that we lost in the previous quarter, and while there are continuing signs that the recession is slowing, obviously this is little comfort to all those Americans who've lost their jobs.
>
> We've taken some extraordinary measures to blunt the hard edges of the worst recession of our lifetime, and to offer assistance to those who've borne the brunt of this economic storm. But as I've said from the moment that I walked into the door of this White House, it took years for us to get into this mess, and it will take us more than a few months to turn it around (The White House Office of the Press Secretary 2009).

The bulk of activity at the White House that day centered on the president's departure the following Monday for Russia, Italy, and Ghana. Over the course of the next nine days, the White House issued the texts of 17 presidential addresses alongside 60 briefing papers and releases. It was not, however, until the weekly radio address the following Saturday that the administration returned to the topic of job losses and the economy (The White House Office of the Press Secretary 2009). The fact that his concern about lost jobs in the United States was being transmitted from Ghana probably provided little comfort to the skeptics.

By the time the president had returned to the States he was facing mounting criticism even from his allies. Paul Krugman wrote in *The New York Times* on July 9:

> The bad employment report for June made it clear that the stimulus was, indeed, too small. But it also damaged the credibility of the administration's economic stewardship. There's now a real risk that President Obama will find himself caught in a political-economic trap ... in which the very weakness of the economy undermines the administration's ability to respond effectively (Krugman 2009).

On July 30, Obama's approval rating in the Gallup daily tracking poll was 54 percent with disapproval at 40 percent. It has not risen above 55 percent since July of 2009 (Gallup 2009).

One of the favorite pieces of advice offered by Republican pollster Frank Luntz is "it's not what you say, it's what people hear" (Luntz 2006). That would seem to be good advice for the Obama White House. They clearly believed that when they were talking about "green jobs," "cyber infrastructure," "high-speed rail," and "investments in clean energy," they were providing credible and thoughtful solutions that would transform and revitalize the American economy. But the election leaves little doubt that unemployed factory workers in Ohio, unemployed construction workers in Florida, and struggling small businessmen coast to coast did not find those visions convincing.

There is also little room for doubt that when the president met with foreign leaders or talked about risks to the environment, the message was not what the White House had hoped: "he is not only doing everything he can to bring about economic recovery but he is working to ensure our security and the future of our environment." Instead, the message seems more along the lines of "he's spending time on things other than whether I, or my friends and family members, are going to get back to work."

## Lessons Learned?

It is puzzling why this level of miscommunication occurred in the first place, but it is even more difficult to understand why it was not recognized and corrected. Learning from the communications miscues of the first six months of the administration could have become a major asset in using the remaining 15 months before the midterm elections to win the public back on key issues. There is little evidence that such an effort occurred.

One possible explanation is that this White House has clung to the assumption that successful policy would automatically translate into successful governance. While good governance requires good policy, good policy is by itself insufficient. Good governance also requires an ongoing dialogue between those who govern and those who are governed. Further, the quality of that dialogue must be measured not by what is said but by what is understood.

Now the Obama White House is operating with a more visible and emboldened opposition. All prospects for funding of administration policies and priorities are dependent upon reaching compromise with that opposition. Success will depend not so much on the magnitude of the compromises offered, but on how well the administration is able to defend its vision of the future and denigrate the vision of its opposition in the court of public opinion. Success will require a very different approach in talking to the American people.

# PART IV

## OBAMA AND DOMESTIC POLICY

# Chapter 11

# From Ambition to Desperation on the Budget

## Joseph White

President Obama inherited a situation that appeared to offer both opportunities and dangers. The budget, and its effects on the economy, were at the center of both. His early choices were very ambitious, and the results included two significant successes: the stimulus bill and health care reform. Yet the administration faced a series of political and policy traps, and after the midterm election these traps appeared to have snapped shut with a vengeance.

## The Economic Terrain

The economy affects spending for some programs, such as unemployment insurance and Medicaid; interest rates on federal borrowing; and the profits and earnings that are available for taxes. Yet budget decisions about spending, taxes, and debt are also a major way that politicians seek to influence the economy. The Obama administration's budget decisions therefore were driven by the economic crisis it inherited, yet the economic and political results could be and were overwhelmed by the same economic risks that the budget sought to address.

The crisis was bad enough to help elect him, but, unlike Franklin Delano Roosevelt, President Obama took office when the consequences of the financial system breakdown had only begun to spread through the rest of the economy.

183

Avoiding a total meltdown required the kind of activism that was sadly lacking in 1930, but Republican responsibility for failure was nowhere near so deeply established as it had been in 1933.

Part of the administration's inheritance was the previous response to the crisis. The Bush administration obtained $700 billion from Congress for a Troubled Asset Relief Program (TARP). The Federal Reserve "undertook a series of extraordinary actions to stabilize financial markets and institutions." Between July of 2007 and the end of 2008, it increased its assets by nearly $1.4 trillion, mainly by issuing loans and other support to financial institutions (United States Congress, Congressional Budget Office 2010d, 1). These measures, in retrospect, helped prevent a total meltdown of the financial system, but could not prevent great damage from the collapse that had already occurred. When the incoming White House team met on December 16 to consider a response, incoming Chair of the Council of Economic Advisers Christina Romer shocked many of her colleagues by arguing for $1.2 trillion in new economic stimulus and "indicated that the minimum amount needed to prevent another depression was in the range of $800 billion" (Alter 2010, 88). As Barbara Sinclair reports in her chapter of this book, the incoming administration and Congressional leadership began work on the $800 billion stimulus before Obama took office. Even this urgent response, however, reflected an underestimation of the problem.

At the beginning of 2009, the Congressional Budget Office (CBO) predicted "a recession that will probably be the longest and deepest since World War II," but still expected unemployment to average only 9 percent in 2010, without any stimulus (United States Congress, Congressional Budget Office 2009b, 1). Looking at similar data at that time, the administration's economists projected that the stimulus would limit peak unemployment to 8 percent (Alter 2010). At the end of February, CBO was predicting only modestly worse results: unemployment at the end of 2009 between 7.8 percent and 8.5 percent, and at the end of 2010 between 6.8 and 8.1 percent (United States Congress, Congressional Budget Office 2009c). Within a few short weeks, however, CBO estimated that unemployment with the stimulus would average 9.0 percent in 2010, based on a judgment that, without the stimulus, "the unemployment rate probably would have exceeded 10.0 percent by the end of the year and peaked at around 10.5 percent in the first half of next year" (United States Congress, Congressional Budget Office 2009d). Even this estimate was too optimistic; instead, unemployment in the first half of 2010 averaged 9.5 percent (United States Congress, Congressional Budget Office 2010b).

The recession ended in 2009, but growth was much weaker than after previous deep recessions (United States Congress, Congressional Budget Office 2010b). The deficit in Fiscal Year 2010 would hit $1.3 trillion, or 9.1 percent of the Gross Domestic Product. Collapsing revenues (to 14.6 percent of GDP, compared to a norm of 18.0 percent) and a mix of automatic and stimulus spending (23.8 percent of GDP, compared to an average of 20.7 percent), created this gap. Thus the Obama administration ended up with the worst of both worlds: high and unpopular unemployment plus high and unpopular budget deficits. The stimulus did improve economic conditions (United States Congress, Congressional Budget Office 2010c), but not enough to help much, if at all, politically.

## BUDGETARY PREFERENCES

The challenge of budgeting is how to match preferences about totals to preferences about details (White 2009). This was particularly difficult given the Obama administration's preferences and the difficult economic circumstances. The bailouts at the end of the Bush administration, as columnist John Cranford of *CQ Weekly Report* wrote, "shattered any pretense that laissez-faire capitalism alone would continue to guide Washington policy-making" (Cranford 2009). Working off the seeming invalidation of laissez-faire approaches to the economy, President Obama called for active government so as to build an economy that would be solid as a rock rather than foundering on shifting sands. He wanted to reduce the role and risks of financial speculation, and create a health care system that would be more affordable for all Americans, a new energy economy that would create jobs for Americans and limit pollution while shipping far fewer dollars overseas, and a reformed education system that would make American workers far more competitive on the world market (Obama 2009g). He also had to budget for two wars: one of which (Iraq) President Obama had promised to wind down, but the other of which (Afghanistan) he had talked up as a crucial mission. He had also promised a middle-class tax cut during his campaign. A massive stimulus, even if acceptable in the short run, would yield larger debt and, eventually, larger interest payments.

All of these preferences would add to spending or reduce revenues, so they could make the budget situation significantly worse than it had been before the recession hit. But the administration rejected this result. The first wave of retirements by the "baby boomers" would begin in 2012, and, according to a powerful conventional wisdom, this constituted a major economic threat to the nation. The president and most of his advisers agreed and viewed deficit-reduction after the stimulus—in spite of all the planned new spending—as an essential part of the "new era of responsibility" he announced in his inaugural address (Obama 2009g; Alter 2010). Therefore he promised to "get serious about fiscal discipline," which meant to "get serious about entitlement reform" (Obama 2009g).[1] Making such a pledge might be popular; following up on it anything but. Entitlements meant Medicare and Social Security, the core achievements of the Democratic party, so such promises could panic the Democratic base. Yet in order to pass legislation to achieve any of the president's other goals, he would need support from more conservative Democrats for whom the budget was the primary issue, and whose legislators believed the conventional wisdom.

Divisions among the Democrats would be especially problematic because, in spite of the president's campaign rhetoric about moving beyond partisanship, there was little chance of doing so on budget issues. Not only did the minority have little interest in cooperation, as is discussed in other chapters, but the substantive gap was huge. At best, Democrats would worry about the deficit (if they did) because they thought the difference between spending and revenues would have some ill effect. During the Reagan and Bush administrations, it was possible to bargain about packages with more or less revenue or spending measures (White and Wildavsky 1991). When the new century began, however, Republican officeholders overwhelmingly held a different view: that "excess deficits" and "excess spending" were the same thing, and tax increases were virtually never a proper response to deficits.[2] Because "deficit" didn't even mean the same thing to the two parties, there was little basis for cooperation.


## BUDGET BASELINES

The Obama administration's budgeting task was made even more difficult by peculiarities of budget "scorekeeping." CBO is required to estimate how much legislation would increase the deficit over a 10-year period compared to existing law. In a series of cases, however, the *law* was not the actual *policy*. Thus even maintaining the status quo would be accused of increasing the deficit.

One case involved the Sustainable Growth Rate (SGR) formula for Medicare payments to physicians. Because total spending rose more quickly than the formula, physician fees were supposed to be cut each year. But the cuts had been postponed or reduced, "temporarily," each year for a number of years. The accumulated difference meant that if the SGR formula were allowed to go into effect in 2010, doctors' fees would have been slashed about 21 percent (United States Congress, Congressional Budget Office 2009b, 20). This clearly would not happen, but CBO had to assume it would.

A second involved the Alternative Minimum Tax (AMT), which was designed to ensure that very high income taxpayers could not reduce their payments too much by claiming deductions. The definition of "high income" has to be raised as average income rises. Since 2000, however, Congress had only enacted "patches" that raised the threshold temporarily. This made Congress and the administration look like they were raising the 10-year deficit less, but the accumulated difference between the patch level and what would happen when the patch ran out meant that, when Obama took office, a permanent fix would reduce estimated revenues by at least $600 billion over 10 years (United States Congress, Congressional Budget Office 2009b, 24–25). Failure to fix the AMT, however, would raise taxes on at least 20 million households (United States Congress, Congressional Budget Office 2010e).

A series of other tax provisions were generally popular with both parties but for various reasons had been enacted on a "temporary" basis at some time and thus were "extended" on some short-term cycle. Only some of them would come up in 2009, but the cost over 10 years of making them all permanent would be about another $700 billion (United States Congress, Congressional Budget Office 2009b, 22–23).

The greatest amount of money and controversy, however, was attached to the tax cuts enacted by Congress and the Bush administration in 2001 and 2003. Republican moderates had wanted a lower total for cuts, over 10 years, than would accommodate all the specific cuts preferred by the Bush administration. Republican leaders "solved" the problem by enacting larger cuts on an annual basis but legislating that they would "sunset" at the end of 2010. In the most extreme version of this approach, they cut the estate tax substantially, but postponed total repeal of the tax until 2010 and then had it return to the 2000 level in 2011! CBO therefore had to estimate that, if no legislation was passed, revenues over the period from 2011 through 2019 would be about $3 trillion higher than they would have been with the terms that existed in 2010 (United States Congress, Congressional Budget Office 2009b, 22–23).[3]

Obama campaigned on a platform of letting tax cuts that affected income over $200,000 for individuals and $250,000 for families expire, but continuing the "middle class" cuts and returning the estate tax, in 2011, to the level in 2009. Republicans could try to block this proposal. But if they filibustered, they might get blamed for denying tax cuts to most Americans, and without legislation they could not extend tax cuts for high incomes. In fighting to extend all of the Bush tax cuts, they would also be arguing for higher deficits. Each position seemed like something that could easily be criticized.

In order to pass either an SGR fix, an AMT fix, or a partial extension of the Bush tax cuts, however, the Democrats would have to officially "increase the deficit." Therefore budget-focused legislators might demand "offsets"—particularly cuts in spending programs—to pay for those measures. Any offsets would lose votes, and if Republicans were not cooperating, the Democrats couldn't afford to lose any votes in the Senate or many in the House. Moreover, at least a few Democrats would want to continue the Bush tax cuts for incomes somewhere above the $200,000/$250,000 thresholds, and a number from farm states thought the 2009 estate tax levels were too high. For the new president to benefit from the expiration of the Bush tax cuts, then, he would have to be more committed to a game of "chicken" than the Republicans were and be confident that conservative Democrats would back him.

## An Ambitious Beginning: Stimulus and the 2010 Budget Proposals

How would the new administration resolve the tension between its large policy agenda and the dangerous budgeting environment? With an ambitious set of proposals. President Obama believed that problems were linked and so had to be addressed together, that the results would be what mattered most politically, that short-term political pain had to be accepted for long-term policy and political gain, and that success led to success (Alter 2010; Baker 2010b; Bettelheim 2009a; Nather 2009a). Yet saying policies were linked did not eliminate the practical contradictions.

Obama's stimulus was 50 times larger than the $16 billion that President Clinton had failed to enact in 1993. Its passage testifies to both the level of economic fear at the time and the work done by the president and his party's leaders in Congress (see Barbara Sinclair's chapter in this volume). Yet it was hard to both win sufficient political credit and sufficiently stimulate the economy.

The bill included provisions to jump-start efforts to upgrade national infrastructure, begin creating a new energy economy (mostly through research), and begin transforming health care delivery (through electronic medical records). Yet many of these measures would take time to implement, so they delayed stimulus of the economy.

A tax cut passed earlier in the recession (February of 2008) had been sent as one-time checks to voters, so it would be more visible. Most of this noticeable lump sum, however, was used to increase savings or pay off debt, instead of increasing demand for goods and services. ("2008 Stimulus" 2009). Therefore the new tax cut was set up to increase paychecks by small amounts through the year, but that made it less visible and so contributed to the mis-perception of the administration's record on taxes that Scott Lilly reports in his chapter.

In addition to tax cuts that were not noticed and infrastructure investment that happened slowly, the third major component of the stimulus was aid to states to ease their budget crises. By definition this could only save jobs (by prevent-ing layoffs and benefit cuts), not add new ones. It was a good way to use money quickly, but unless governors spent lots of time publicly praising the president and Congress, it was also not likely to be noticed by voters.

Even before he took his oath of office, President Obama had felt com-pelled, even though the TARP was very unpopular, to lobby Congress to allow expenditure of the second half of the program's funds (Alter 2010, 79). In spite of the fact that mainstream budget hawks endorsed a major stimulus (Cranford 2009), Republicans calculated that they could afford to oppose it en masse. Part of their reasoning was that the stimulus could be tarred as a "bailout," and so it was associated by many voters with the highly unpopular TARP. This strategy worked. Even though CBO (2010c) reported that the stimulus had a substan-tial positive effect, most voters disagreed. By October of 2010, *CQ Weekly* was reporting that, "lawmakers lament that somehow the very word 'stimulus' seems to have been linked to the word 'bailout' and the two together, stimulus and bailout, to 'debt' and 'deficit.' . . . [O]pinion surveys show that a large segment of the public (two-thirds according to a *Washington Post*/ABC News poll) believes the stimulus was a waste of money" (Schatz 2010).

The stimulus passed because conservative Democrats who made deficit con-trol their defining issue thought, as one leader of the House Blue Dog Coalition explained, that "there clearly needs to be an injection of money. I don't like it at all, but I understand the necessity of it" (Baumann 2009). In principle, an even bigger stimulus could have had a large enough effect to win credit. Yet the fact that the bill was reduced a bit in the Senate, at the insistence of the Democrats' more conservative members, suggests that a larger bill was not in the cards. In order to get more, President Obama would have had to insist that the economy was in even worse shape than it seemed in January. But the president appeared to be walking a tightrope, trying to show he recognized voters' pain without further depressing consumer and investor confidence (Bettelheim 2009b). In retrospect, he may have been walking on thin air.

The president outlined his proposed budget for Fiscal Year 2010 (FY2010), which would begin on October 1, 2009, on February 24. He declared that the "day of reckoning has arrived, and the time to take charge of our future is here," promising to "invest in areas like energy, health care, and education that will grow our economy, even as we make hard choices to bring our deficit down" ("Big Plans" 2009). The proposal's ambition matched the rhetoric.

To begin, Obama used what was essentially a current policy baseline, rather than current law, to describe the effects of his policies on the deficit. For example, he assumed that the AMT would be continually adjusted over the next 10 years, that the Bush tax cuts would continue, and that the wars in Iraq and Afghanistan would be funded (Bush had left them out of the regular budget) and continue. This was somewhat more honest than assuming current law would be followed, but it also allowed him to call proposals deficit-reducing or neutral that otherwise would be called budget-busters.

The tax proposals in the budget outline were breathtaking in scope (for a summary, see Schatz 2009). Obama proposed that the Bush cuts for incomes under the $200,000/$250,000 income thresholds be extended, but not the higher-income cuts. He wanted to keep the estate tax at 2009 levels, and also proposed a permanent fix of the AMT. He then proposed to fund other priorities with taxes that he considered justified for other policy reasons as well. A new system to charge for carbon emissions and create a market to trade rights to pollute—"cap and trade" in the energy policy lingo—was projected to yield $646 billion over 10 years. This would give businesses very strong incentives to reduce pollution, preferably by finding alternative energy sources. He proposed to use $120 billion of the revenue to fund renewable energy programs. The rest would be used to make the "making work pay" tax credit in the stimulus bill permanent. The administration sought to fund a "middle-class" (and in fact progressive) tax cut with a tax increase that would have uncertain incidence, but could be justified as part of building a new economy (for discussion, see United States Congress, Congressional Budget Office 2009e).

Similarly, he proposed to create a $634 billion (over 10 years) "reserve fund" for health care reform. Half would be achieved with cuts in payments for Medicare and Medicaid, in ways that Democrats thought would have little effect on beneficiaries.[4] The rest would come from capping the value of deductions claimed by taxpayers in the top two brackets to the value those deductions would have in the 28 percent bracket. This could be viewed as addressing an inequity in the tax code, which gives larger "subsidies" from tax breaks to people who are paying higher rates. The president's budget outline also would have redistributed income by expanding a range of tax credits for mainly middle-class individuals and raising taxes for businesses (especially on income earned overseas and by private equity fund managers).

In addition, by first increasing the baseline for military spending and then "drawing down troops from Iraq responsibly" (Office of Management and Budget 2009, 53), the administration made room for some increases in spending, such as for education programs, beyond the underlying rate of inflation.[5] The administration projected that its policies would cut the deficit more than in half, reducing it to a stable level of about three percent of GDP by the end of Obama's term. Investments in health care, energy, and other priorities could still be funded by the new taxes and cuts in a number of small programs (Office of Management and Budget 2009).

The Budget Resolution agreed between the House and Senate in April included, or did not specifically exclude, many of the proposals. It allowed some increase in domestic spending (though not as much as the president requested). Most important for the future, the resolution allowed the Democrats to use the procedure called reconciliation to pass both health care reform legislation and reform of student loan programs—though not until after October 15. But the proposal did not eliminate the key constraints.

CBO's updated economic forecast just a few weeks later projected that the deficit would be cut in half from the extremely high 2010 level but, rather than stabilizing, would then grow as a share of the economy (United States Congress, Congressional Budget Office 2009b). Hence the administration could not claim to either its more reluctant allies or outside critics that, if its policies were enacted, the deficit would be controlled.

Second, the president declaring a different baseline didn't change how CBO would evaluate proposals. In principle, Congress could have instructed CBO to adjust its baseline to match the administration's; in practice they would have been accused of "rigging the numbers." In any event, doing nothing meant that budget-focused Democrats would hesitate to deal with the booby traps in the baseline.

Third, Congress did not include the changes to the AMT, Bush tax cuts, and other "tax extenders" in reconciliation instructions. There were logical reasons not to do so: Democrats had blasted the Republicans for using reconciliation to pass the tax cuts in the first place, and using reconciliation for health care reform was already controversial. But this meant that dealing with these issues would require 60 votes, which is a key reason why they were still unresolved when the midterm election occurred.

Fourth, some policies were not explicitly rejected in the budget resolution process, but the reactions at the time made them seem very unlikely to happen. Thus "cap and trade" would have been allowed and actually was passed by the House—but by April it was clear that it was unlikely to pass in the Senate. The proposed limits on itemized deductions were criticized by Senate Finance Committee Chair Max Baucus, and other Senate Democrats opposed other Obama tax proposals (Schatz 2009).

Last but not least, more conservative Democrats were very nervous about supporting the budget resolution. It passed in the House only after Speaker Pelosi and Majority Leader Hoyer promised, in writing, process reforms that Blue Dogs sought. Senate budget hawks, especially Budget Committee Chair Kent Conrad, made clear that they would also be demanding extraordinary measures to address long-term deficits.

## WISHFUL THINKING: HEALTH CARE REFORM

If 30 million Americans gain health insurance due to the Affordable Care Act, they could legitimately argue that these shortfalls in the budget resolution were dwarfed by the provision that allowed health care reform to finally pass. After the election of Scott Brown from Massachusetts to the Senate established that the Republicans could defeat any conference agreement with a filibuster, a last-minute reconciliation turned out to be the only way to change the Senate bill in a way that House Democrats could accept.

There are numerous sources about the health care reform battle (Alter 2010, 244–271; Hacker 2010; "House Vote Caps Long Legislative March" 2010; Jacobs and Skocpol 2010; Marmor and Oberlander 2010; Wayne and Epstein 2010). We only need to look at the budgetary dimension, which is central to understanding both the decision-making and results of the Obama presidency.

The budgetary politics of health care derive from the politics of the "entitlement crisis." Projections continually show massive increases in spending over the decades to come on Medicare, Medicaid, and Social Security. In reaction to the claim that "greedy geezers" would bankrupt the nation, analysts who believed these programs were central to a decent society argued that the growth in spending was to a great extent caused by projected increases in spending on health care, that these increases were due mainly to expected growth in spending per person rather than to the aging of the population, that the same projections suggested that health insurance for all Americans would become unaffordable, and that therefore the "entitlement crisis" was really a health care cost crisis. Moreover, for many reasons, if costs were out of control outside of the government programs, it would be harder to control the government's costs. From this perspective, "[f]undamental, systemwide reform of health care financing and delivery is the key to controlling Medicare and Medicaid expenditures—and reducing projected long-term deficits—without imposing draconian cuts that would harm the poor, the elderly, and people with serious disabilities" ("A Balanced Approach to Restoring Fiscal Responsibility" 2008, 2).

Aside from any policy merits, this argument provided a policy approach that in principle could unite the deficit-hawk and liberal wings of the Democratic party. Health care reform to expand coverage and control costs for everyone would also help the budget. The president took this position in his campaign (Alter 2010), and the administration continually linked health care reform to budget control in its statements about long-term budget issues after taking office (e.g. in Fiscal Responsibility Summit 2009, 2, 11).

The catch, however, was whether any particular systemic reform would actually control costs. Orszag fervently believed, and appears to have convinced the president, that the "cost curve" could be "shifted" by measures that addressed unnecessary use of care. Research showed that the volume of specific services and therefore costs varied substantially across communities or hospitals, that this variation was not clearly connected to need, and that medical results were no better in the more expensive communities and hospitals. If practice patterns could be reduced to the level in the less expensive communities and institutions, there could be massive savings with no effect on people's health (Clarke and Young 2009; Fiscal Responsibility Summit 2009; Alter 2010).

From this seed a forest of ideas for "delivery system reform" had grown. It emphasized ideas such as paying doctors "for performance" rather than per service, or creating "accountable care organizations" to integrate care. Unfortunately, all of these ideas were unproven, so CBO would not credit claims of meaningful savings from any of the delivery reform measures that the administration and its allies proposed (United States Congress, Congressional Budget Office 2008; Marmor, Oberlander, and White 2009).

Moreover, arguments that variations should be controlled, even ideas such as that the government should promote "cost-effectiveness research" or "evidence-based medicine," appeared to imply that the government would set standards for medical practice. This could be represented as the government interfering with the doctor/patient relationship, and so could arouse fears of "rationing" that had, for generations, been the main conservative argument against government expansions of health insurance. The administration, and President Obama himself, had no simple answer to this concern (Alter 2010, 261; Bettelheim 2009c; Nather 2009c).

There *was* an alternative cost control approach: to address the huge difference in prices and administrative overhead between the United States and any other country (Marmor, Oberlander, and White 2009; McGillis 2010). Regulation of prices was more popular with the voters than any hints of restricting care could be (Oberlander and White 2009). Medicare had a better cost control record than private insurance (which isn't saying much) because it had more market power to limit prices per service. Advocates of the "public option"—a major dividing line within the Democratic party—supported it because, if it were linked to Medicare's market power, it should be able to underprice private insurers, forcing them either to drive harder bargains with providers or find other ways to control costs (Hacker 2010; Oberlander and White 2009). If this argument were correct, the public plan would make insurance more affordable for the currently insured as well as the newly insured. CBO made clear that it would "score" savings from the public plan, though they would depend on the rates it could pay.

The Affordable Care Act rejected this approach. It included a wide variety of pilot programs and other versions of the delivery system reform agenda, for which CBO recognized virtually no savings. It included some cuts to Medicare spending, which might well be justified but could be attacked as paying for reform from benefits of the elderly. Moreover, using Medicare savings to pay for health insurance expansions meant that, at least for the next 10 years, they could not be used for deficit reduction—which contradicted one of the administration's signature claims (Clarke 2010a). Last, the law included a tax on supposedly excessive health insurance benefits. The merits of this "Cadillac tax" were dubious enough (for two sides, see Jost and White 2010 and Van de Water 2010), but the politics were awful. It was unpopular and certainly would not make care more affordable for the people it affected.

The conventional political wisdom among health care reformers said that the majority constituency for reform would not be based on expanding coverage but on relieving fears about losing coverage. Why, then, did the administration adopt cost control methods that either were not deemed effective by CBO, or were *actually designed to reduce coverage*? Four reasons stand out:

- Key administration advisers didn't like price regulation or passionately believed in the reduction-of-variation agenda (Cutler 2010; Emanuel 2008).

- Provider interests hated price regulation and would not support the law if it included a public plan that could extend anything close to Medicare rates beyond the Medicare population. In the words of a veteran congressional aide, "(e)very provider group would be 4-square against the bill. That's not an assumption, that's a known. That's Armageddon for them."
- More conservative Democrats, such as the Blue Dog Coalition, did not like the public plan and especially did not like it paying anything like Medicare fees (White 2011).
- If there was anything on which both conservative and liberal economists (with a few eminent exceptions) agreed, it was that allowing companies to provide insurance as an untaxed benefit was unfair and caused excess costs (Rampell 2009 and personal conversations). This consensus influenced the White House, press, and legislators such as Senator Baucus.

If implemented, the reform would be the most significant social policy initiative since passage of Medicare and Medicaid in 1965. But that does not change the facts: the savings achieved were too small, uncertain, or far in the future to reduce budget hawks' worries about long-term deficits or reassure currently insured voters. In short, both because his circle of advice was apparently united in one view and because of a political calculation about what was necessary to pass the bill, President Obama pushed through legislation that did not satisfy the political and budgetary goals of reform.

## WRIGGLING IN THE NET: THE POLITICS OF PROCESS

Unable to achieve the new revenues it sought or do much more than pay for insurance expansion from its health care cost initiatives, the administration was left with no good response to concerns about the deficit that intensified over time. The result was a bewildering and frustrating series of maneuvers in two dimensions.

One involved efforts to pass budget-related legislation, such as further economic stimulus, routine appropriations, or supplemental appropriations to fund military needs. These were continually caught up in arguments that they would increase the deficit too much, so either the proposed tax cuts or spending should be reduced or it should be "offset" with cuts to other programs (the Republican preference was to rescind funds from the first stimulus).

Bills that are in some sense "must-pass" have for years tended to get ensnared in the culture of hostage-taking and creative combinations that permeates Congress. One faction will attach an unrelated idea to a bill; others may oppose the bill because of the addition; still others offer amendments designed to embarrass the administration or opposite party. Thus, for example, a supplemental appropriation in the spring of 2009 for costs of the wars in Afghanistan and Iraq was caught up in disputes about adding extra funding for the IMF, extra funding to respond to a possible flu epidemic, and closing the Guantánamo Bay prison for alleged terrorists (Rogin 2009). At the end of 2009, efforts to pass a series of stimulus measures failed, and only short-term (to the end of February) extensions of unemployment benefits and other programs were attached to the defense appropriations bill. In the spring and summer of 2010, a bill to extend some of the more routine expiring tax cuts and unemployment insurance was caught in disputes about offsets and the length of the unemployment benefits extension (Rubin and Lesniewski 2010).

In general, Republicans opposed extensions of unemployment and other benefits; House Democratic leaders and sometimes the White House tried to stimulate the economy through both tax cuts and spending; Senate Democrats usually wanted to do less than the House because they needed 60 votes to do anything; House Blue Dogs sought to scale back or offset whatever was proposed by House leaders; most initiatives failed; and so many extensions that might have been expected to be routine still had not occurred when Congress recessed for the midterm election. Deficit concerns and posturing nearly paralyzed efforts to respond further to the economic crisis—much to the opposing party's benefit.

The other set of maneuvers in response to deficit concerns involved budget process arguments. One conflict involved posturing about earmarks: provisions in legislation or the accompanying reports, through which Congress directs spending to particular beneficiaries or projects, such as hospitals, cities, defense contracts, or dredging specific ports. Republicans blasted earmarks as a form of "corruption," which fit beautifully with their broader view of government spending, even though they had greatly increased the amount of earmarks after taking over Congress in 1995, and about 40 percent of the earmarks in the appropriations bills written for FY 2009 by a Democratic Congress were Republican requests (Clarke 2009). House Democrats and the administration proposed procedures (such as revealing all requests) that were meant to defuse claims of corruption. Senate Democratic leaders tended to think the issue was a challenge to Congress's legitimate responsibilities, so resisted the anti-earmark campaign (Clarke and Epstein 2010; Epstein 2010). The administration was either too weak to resist or too tempted to echo a criticism that, after all, was the position of all administrations (which always want more power vis à vis Congress) and a good way to posture for voter support. The politics of earmarking obstructed both routine appropriations and stimulus efforts, while it could never have had meaningful effect on deficits (Cranford 2010b; Epstein 2010).

Another conflict involved rules limiting congressional discretion. Blue Dog Democrats in the House sought procedural reforms so that they could say they were enabling future budget control even as they voted for larger deficits in the short run. They especially wanted to recreate a statutory "Paygo" provision that had been in effect from 1990 to 2003, and which provided for automatic cuts to some programs if, at the end of a year, Congress had enacted legislation that raised the deficit. The president and most Democrats supported this in principle, but did not want it to apply to the baseline problems discussed above. Republicans opposed Paygo because it would apply to tax cuts as well as spending increases.

Meanwhile, Senate Democratic budget hawks, such as Budget Committee Chair Kent Conrad, believed Paygo was insufficient because it would only stop deficit increases, rather than forcing spending cuts or tax hikes. Conrad allied with Committee Ranking Member Judd Gregg (R-NH) and others to demand a Deficit Reduction Commission that would propose legislation on which Congress would be forced to vote, yes or no. The Paygo legislation on which House Democrats had agreed in February of 2009 therefore was blocked until February of 2010. At that point it was attached to an increase in the limit on the federal government's debt, as part of a wider deal about such a commission (Clarke and Vadala 2010).

The third set of process controversies involved efforts to bypass normal congressional procedures. Advocates for a deficit-reduction commission believed the deficit would be reduced if only "politics" were taken out of the equation. They argued that a bipartisan commission meeting without special interest pressure could agree on a package, and that, if forced to vote up or down on doing the right thing, Congress would be far more likely to do so. This view was especially attractive to people who distrusted the political system and to politicians who identified themselves as "centrist." At a minimum, they hoped, it would heighten public awareness of the crisis and generate proposals and momentum for change (Clarke 2010a, b).

It was hard for President Obama, who had campaigned as a person who would clean up politics, to oppose this reasoning. But a commission was resisted by legislators who felt it violated Congress's constitutional position, such as Senate Finance Committee Chair Baucus; by Republicans who worried a commission would propose tax increases; and especially by liberals who believed it could only have bad results or none at all. They reasoned that there were too many moderate Democrats who had accepted the idea of an "entitlement crisis"; that Republicans on a commission would only accept a deal that heavily emphasized spending cuts over tax increases; and so that a commission would either not report, or would report large cuts to Social Security and Medicare.

In early 2010 this led to another stalemate: budget hawk Democratic senators held an increase in the debt limit hostage, insisting on creation of a statutory deficit reduction commission, but they did not have 60 votes to add the plan to the debt bill. Instead, President Obama promised to appoint a commission by executive order. He would appoint six members, half Democrats and half Republicans, and the House and Senate Democratic and Republican leadership would each appoint three. The House and Senate Democratic leadership pledged that if the commission reported a recommendation by December 1, and it was supported by 14 of the 18 commissioners (so majorities from each party), they would schedule the report for votes in the House and Senate during a Lame Duck session of Congress (Clarke and Vadala 2010).

This timing would minimize voters' influence on legislation, because the plan would not be debated in the election and would be voted on by Lame Duck legislators. It also typified budgeting in the Obama administration's second year: maneuvering to avoid unpopularity, while postponing decisions to a future in which the administration and its allies would be in an even weaker position, unless they got lucky in the midterm election.

## AFTER THE MIDTERMS

After the election, crucial decisions about issues such as the Bush tax cuts would be made under much worse circumstances for the Democrats. The Fiscal Responsibility Commission's results compounded the difficulty.

During the controversies about creating a commission, some analysts had told more liberal colleagues that it was not such a big deal: the president would not make appointments that would create a large majority for cutting Social Security. They (we) were wrong. He appointed co-chairs of the commission, former Senator Alan Simpson and former White House Chief of Staff Erskine Bowles, who clearly believed the Social Security was unaffordably generous. He also appointed Alice Rivlin, former Director of OMB for Clinton and founding Director of CBO, a fervent budget hawk who was on the right wing among Democratic budget experts.

After the election, Bowles and Simpson released a proposal that most Democratic activists and some legislative leaders termed, in Nancy Pelosi's words, "simply unacceptable" (Calmes 2010a). It called for large cuts in Social Security and Medicare, relied much more on spending cuts than tax increases to achieve balance, set an arbitrary limit of 21 percent of GDP on total revenues as a share of GDP (which had been a conservative constitutional amendment proposal in the 1980s), and would have imposed substantial cuts on annually appropriated programs (National Commission 2010; Horney 2010). This proposal did not receive the necessary 14 votes to force a vote in Congress, but at the final meeting of the commission on December 3, 11 of the 18 members and 5 of the president's 6 appointees expressed support for it (Calmes 2010b). The votes of President Obama's appointees, and his failure to criticize the plan's details, led liberal interest groups and advocates to fear that Obama, either from conviction or weakness, was on the way to selling out the most important legislative achievement of the New Deal.[6]

Meanwhile, the economy remained in parlous condition. Advocates for the high-end tax cuts could argue that any measure that reduced demand was risky. This emphasis on maintaining demand might have seemed a bit more sincere if congressional Republicans were not simultaneously resisting extension of unemployment benefits, continuation of subsidies to states to limit layoffs, and other measures that had been part of the stimulus package. Yet the economic dangers made letting all the tax cuts expire look particularly dangerous for an administration that had just suffered one of the worst midterm election defeats in history.

This is the context in which the president on December 6 announced a deal with Republican leaders. He agreed to extend all of the 2001 and 2003 Bush income tax cuts for two years. The estate tax would not be abolished, but was cut substantially below the 2009 level for 2011 and 2012. In return, the president received a 13-month extension of unemployment benefits, continuation of some of the Recovery Act's tax credits for two years, and a temporary tax cut for business investment. The proposal also included a major new temporary tax cut: the Social Security payroll tax paid by workers would be reduced, for one year, from 6.2 percent to 4.2 percent—a $120 billion reduction in federal revenues. The entire package, as *The New York Times* reported, "would cost $900 billion over the next two years, to be financed entirely by adding to the national debt, at a time when both parties are professing a desire to begin addressing long-term fiscal imbalances" (Herszenhorn and Calmes 2010).

The administration and some of its allies could argue that, with a Republican House arriving in January, Republicans in the Senate blocking unemployment benefits, and an economy that badly needed stimulus, this deal was better than could be expected. Robert Greenstein, executive director of the Center on Budget and Policy Priorities, declared that, "Congress should approve this package—its rejection will likely lead to a more problematic package that does less for middle- and low-income workers and less for the economy" (Greenstein 2010). Yet these were arguments based on weakness. This weakness was not simply a matter of the administration not being willing to fight. Senator Baucus wanted to challenge the Republicans to block middle-class tax cuts on behalf of wealthy constituents by bringing up legislation before the election, but "many Senate Democrats ... made it clear that with Republicans construing the White House plan as a historic tax hike, they would just as soon leave the issue until after the election" (Young, Friel, and Schatz 2010). Either way, however, the Democrats were conceding to Republican hostage-taking.

Democrats who shared the values Obama promoted so vigorously at the beginning of his administration were fearful about what could happen next. If he had caved on the upper-income tax cuts in 2010, how would he prevent further extensions before the 2012 election? Worse yet, the tax deal suggested it would be even harder than expected to address future deficits with tax increases, yet the administration was talking about the need to reduce future deficits. Even worse, in the context of a campaign against Social Security that claimed it was unaffordable and running out of money, the administration had accepted a reduction in the payroll tax, which was the program's main source of revenue. The proposal would credit the trust fund with the revenues that were not collected, but that would just add credibility to conservative claims that the trust fund was "fake," and Republicans might argue that the taxes should not be restored in 2012 (a good summary of these concerns and their sources is the National Committee to Preserve Social Security and Medicare 2010).

As this chapter was being completed, these worries about the future and disagreement with specific provisions of the deal had split the Democratic party. A closed-door caucus of House Democrats voted against bringing the package up for a vote. The president was criticizing liberals for being "purists," and liberals were saying someone with such a bad track record in bargaining should not be the one who claims to be the realist.

The compromise was enacted, as should be expected when both the president and the opposition offer the public large tax cuts. But this bipartisan compromise should not be confused with any sort of viable "move to the center," especially given the concern among both elites and independents about the deficit and debt, which the package increased. Instead, the administration had moved from attempting to create a bold Democratic party approach to the nation's problems, to using desperate short-term maneuvers and intrapartisan recriminations. It was a far cry from the promises to build a future economy on rock rather than on shifting sands.

## NOTES

1. For an account of the development and entrenchment of this view, see White (2003). For a good example of offhand acceptance of the conventional wisdom, see the reference to "entitlements (the deadweight sitting on the future of the economy)" in Alter 2010 (424).

2. For discussion of the origins of this view, see Savage 1990; for more on versions of anti-deficit arguments see White and Wildavsky 1991. On the George W. Bush administration's disinterest in deficits as the difference between revenues and spending, see White 2009.

3. The fiscal effects of different baselines were greater than this sounds, because fixing the AMT, if combined with extending all the Bush tax cuts, would cost another $700 billion.

4. I regret that there is no space for a discussion; much of these cuts were broadly supported by liberal and nonpartisan health policy experts.

5. This adjustment in the military spending baseline could well be criticized, but, as OMB sources told me in interviews during 2008, there is no good way to do defense baselines during a war.

6. I could not begin to summarize the anguished commentary among pro–Social Security experts and advocates at the time.

# CHAPTER 12

# The Politics of Regulation in the Obama Administration

*Claudia Hartley Thurber, Esq.*

Federal regulations that implement President Obama's policies will likely be the showcase achievements of the last two years of his term. This is not just because of the legislation passed in the first two years, including the stimulus package, the health care reform, and the financial reform legislation, all of which will require rulemaking in some form, but because with a divided government and low support scores, he will have to command the one sector of the government over which he has control—the federal bureaucracy. This president, who has vowed to implement his policies, may have to do so through federal agencies making rules and regulations pursuant to their enabling statutes.

United States Federal regulations affect everyone in almost everything they do. For example, the electricity that lights your home and business is regulated by the Federal Energy Regulatory Commission (FERC), your water quality is regulated by the Environmental Protection Agency (EPA), your coffee by the Food and Drug Administration (FDA) and the Department of Agriculture, and your car by the International Trade Commission (import restrictions), the Occupational Safety and Health Administration (OSHA), the National Highway Transportation Safety Administration (NHTSA), and the EPA, among others.

The costs of federal regulations are high. Rulemaking can move at glacial pace, with a particular rule taking more than a decade to promulgate and defend from legal challenges, meaning regulation frequently spans several presidential terms. Table 12-1 shows that costs for the 95 major rules promulgated from 1999 to 2009 by the federal rulemaking agencies were between $42,700 and $54,597 million (in 2001 dollars), while benefits ranged from $127,962 to $616,282 million (in 2001 dollars).

Often, particular agencies within a department or agency are responsible for the major rules. Table 12-2 shows the agencies that promulgated the most rules or the most significant of the rules.[1]

OMB compiles statistics for fiscal years, and the most recent data show that 66 major rules were reviewed, and although that represents only 20 percent of the final rules reviewed and 1 percent of the final rules published, the 66 rules account for the majority of the total benefits and costs. Table 12-3 shows the 16 rules where the agencies monetized costs and benefits.

While these data are useful to indicate rulemaking entities, costs and benefits, and trends, they may not accurately set forth an administration's accomplishments or even its policies, especially in the early years of a presidency. For example, the major rules promulgated between October 1, 2008, and September 30, 2009, include the midnight regulations from President Bush's last quarter. Moreover, the often-glacial pace of rulemaking means that final rules implementing President Obama's policy may not show up in OMB's analysis during his presidency. Still other rules are "court ordered" and may not have been within the policy of the administration at the time. As to rules that are not finalized within an administration, a succeeding administration has options about their finalization. Nevertheless, as discussed below, a new president has ways to deal with his predecessor's late rulemaking.

Federal agencies are part of the executive branch of government and administer the laws that the Congress passes. Because the laws are often broadly

### Table 12-1: Estimates of the Total Annual Benefits and Costs of Major Federal Rules by Agency, October 1, 1999–September 30, 2009 (Millions of 2001 Dollars)[i]

| Agency | Number of Rules | Benefits | Costs |
|--------|-----------------|----------|-------|
| Department of Agriculture | 6 | 906–1,315 | 1,014–1,353 |
| Department of Energy | 8 | 6,251–8500 | 3,328–3,856 |
| Department of Health and Human Services | 20 | 21,895–44,435 | 4,651–6,232 |
| Department of Homeland Security | 1 | 20–29 | 13–99 |
| Department of Housing and Urban Development | 1 | 2,303 | 884 |
| Department of Justice | 1 | 275 | 108–118 |
| Department of Labor | 5 | 252–1,375 | 301–327 |
| Department of Transportation | 23 | 14,158–24,983 | 6,603–12,502 |
| Environmental Protection Agency | 30 | 81,903–533,066 | 25,789–29,227 |
| **Total** | **95** | **127,962–616,282** | **42,700–54,597** |

[i] *2010 Report to Congress on Benefits and Costs of Federal Regulations and Unfunded Mandates on State, Local, and Tribal Entities*, pp. 11–12.

### Table 12-2: Major Rules by Agency[ii]

| Agency | Number of Rules | Benefits | Costs |
|---|---|---|---|
| Department of Agriculture Animal and Plant Health Inspection Service | 3 | 862–1,163 | 726–931 |
| Department of Energy Energy Efficiency and Renewable Energy | 8 | 6,251–8,250 | 3,328–3,856 |
| Department of Health and Human Services Food and Drug Administration | 10 | 2,551–22,287 | 893–1,256 |
| Center for Medicare and Medicaid Services | 8 | 18,075–20,811 | 3,377–4,561 |
| Department of Labor Occupational Safety and Health Administration | 3 | 242–1,365 | 342–369 |
| Department of Transportation National Highway Traffic Safety Administration | 11 | 11,758–21,504 | 5,202–10,772 |
| Environmental Protection Agency Office of Air | 19 | 77,383–518,941 | 20,581–23,706 |
| Office of Water | 7 | 1,975–5,593 | 2,044–2,313 |

[ii] *2010 Report to Congress on Benefits and Costs of Federal Regulations and Unfunded Mandates on State, Local, and Tribal Entities,* pp. 12–13.

### Table 12-3: Estimates by Agency of the Total Annual Benefits and Costs of Major Rules: October 1, 2008–September 30, 2009 (Millions of 2001 Dollars)[iii]

| Agency | Number of Rules | Benefits | Costs |
|---|---|---|---|
| Department of Energy | 2 | 1,297–3,109 | 261–738 |
| Department of Health and Human Services | 4 | 1,466–12,175 | 841–1,913 |
| Department of Housing and Urban Development | 1 | 2,303 | 884 |
| Department of Transportation | 8 | 3,081–6,150 | 113–2,241 |
| Environmental Protection Agency | 1 | 455–5,203 | 113–2,241 |
| **Total** | **16** | **8,602–28,940** | **3,685–9,512** |

[iii] *2010 Report to Congress on Benefits and Costs of Federal Regulations and Unfunded Mandates on State, Local, and Tribal Entities,* p. 20.

written and contain vague provisions, the federal agencies have to promulgate regulations that determine exactly what is required by the law. There are many reasons why the Congress passes laws that lack specificity, including the need to get support for passage from their colleagues who hold different views. The federal agency rules or regulations prescribe future conduct or action that must or may be taken by a person or persons. The rules promulgated by the agencies must be based on laws (statutory authority), and they are primarily concerned with policy considerations. For example, acting under its authority under the Clean Air Act, §114(a)(1)[2] EPA published, on July 12, 2010, Mandatory Reporting of Greenhouse Gases from Magnesium Production, Underground Coal Mines, Industrial Wastewater Treatment, and Industrial Waste Landfalls, which added four new source categories that must report Greenhouse Gases (GHGs).[3]

*Legal Requirements*

The legal basis for rulemaking is the Administrative Procedures Act (APA) of 1946.[4] The APA requires agencies to publish a notice of proposed rulemaking, provide an opportunity for public participation, and publish the final rule with its explanation. These basic requirements still provide a "floor" for agency actions, but agency rulemaking requirements have been greatly expanded by court decisions, specific legislation, executive orders, and agency practice.

In cases where a person or group of persons is dissatisfied with a rule that has been promulgated, several appeals processes are available. The first is an appeal to the agency, which is usually a letter pointing out where the writer believes the agency misinterpreted the evidence or failed to follow prescribed procedures. If satisfaction is not forthcoming from an appeal to the agency, the APA provides for judicial review.[5] Courts have defined the rights of persons aggrieved by agency action that was based on the administrative record. Judges must consider relevant factors for errors of judgment and whether the rule is based on the administrative record. The standard for judicial review is "arbitrary and capricious," which will be found if the agency failed to follow requirements in statutes (APA, and the agency's enabling statute), failed to consider important aspects of the issues, made decisions counter to the evidence, or made decisions too implausible for just a difference of views or particular agency expertise. Other statutes are stricter, requiring the rule be based on "substantial evidence in the record as a whole," and through statutes and court decisions more requirements, such as that the rule be technologically and economically feasible, have been added. Court challenges to the promulgation of a rule made by persons or groups that are affected by it generally must take place within 59 days of promulgation, and where there are multiple parties, the actions are combined and heard in one court. For example, in a challenge to OSHA's 2006 rule on Hexavalent Chromium, Public Citizen, United Steel, Paper and Forestry, Rubber, Manufacturing, Energy, Allied Industrial Service Workers International Union, and Edison Electric Institute, joined by the Aerospace Industries Association of America, Inc., Portland Cement Association, Surface Finishing Industry Council, Color Pigments Manufacturers Association, Inc., National Association of Manufacturers and Specialty Industry of North America, as intervenors, all sued the US Department of Labor. The Third Circuit Court of Appeals upheld all of the rule's provisions, save the exposure determination provisions, which were remanded to OSHA for further rulemaking.[6] Courts can uphold the agency action, uphold parts of the rule, or vacate the entire rule. Finally, judicial appeal can occur when an agency action is enforced against a person or entity. In this process, the appellant usually must present the case to an administrative law judge and a review commission prior to the federal courts.[7]

Since 1996, there has been another way to vacate an agency rule, and that is by a finding of disapproval by Congress under the Congressional Review Act (CRA).[8] Nearly all major rules (47,540 as of March 2008) are submitted to Congress for review, but only one rule, OSHA's Ergonomics Rule, has been disapproved in the 15-year history of the Act. Of the 49 rules where a joint resolution to disapprove was introduced, none has gone further. In the 111th Congress, a rule submitted by the National Mediation Board relating to election procedures and a rule relating to status as a grandfathered health plan pursuant to the Patient Protection and Affordable Care Act failed to get the Senate to agree to proceed. While these results suggest the law has not been effective, it is equally possible that the agencies have been writing their rules to avoid the application of the Act. Thus, the financial and health care reforms could be weakened or derailed even without the threat of outright disapproval under the CRA.

*The Regulatory Process*

The regulatory process begins with a catalyst, which could be a specific requirement in a new law or an action pursuant to an enabling statute that is the result of a petition, a catastrophe, or a policy decision to address an issue. The agency will generally collect information on such issues as costs and benefits, necessity, risks, affected persons or groups, and the quality of available data. The draft proposed rule, which will become the Notice of Proposed Rulemaking (NPRM), will be reviewed by the Office of Management and Budget's OIRA for compliance with Executive Order 12866[9], which has been supplemented and reaffirmed by the more detailed instructions on general principles, public participation, integration and innovation, flexible approaches, science, and retrospective analyses of existing rules in Executive Order 13563, issued January 18, 2011.[10] In addition, OIRA will review the draft for compliance with its guidelines on data quality and peer review, other laws, and the president's priorities. The NPRM is published in the *Federal Register,* and public comment periods are set and a public hearing is scheduled, if a request has been made or is anticipated. Along with research acquired by the agency, the comments and hearing testimony and exhibits become part of the administrative record upon which the rule will be based. Following the close of the comment periods, the agency, using the entire record, drafts the final rule, which then goes through all the administrative approval processes and is submitted to Congress for review under the Congressional Review Act.

## MIDNIGHT REGULATIONS

Midnight regulations are promulgated in the last part of an administration, typically within the last three months. Though recent presidents have had four or eight years to get these rules out, they fail to do so. Why they fail to do so is a mystery: Are they too busy doing other things to focus on specific regulatory issues? Are the issues to be tackled so controversial that promulgation can only be assured by speeding up the process? What is sure is that presidents from Jimmy Carter on have resorted to midnight regulations and that future presidents are likely to do the same. President Carter's regulations (with their explanations) took up 10,000 pages in the *Federal Register* and covered diverse topics such as standards for crash tests for cars and access to medical records. George H.W. Bush promulgated a greater proportion of rules in his last three months than any other president. President William J. Clinton's midnight regulations took up more than 26,000 pages in the *Federal Register* and included the Occupational Safety and Health Administration's Ergonomics rule, which has the distinction of being the only federal regulation overturned by Congress under the Congressional Review Act of 1996.

George W. Bush, known in regulatory circles for his deregulatory policy, was no slacker in midnight regulations. Some of his most controversial rules included removing a provision from the Endangered Species Act that required fish and wildlife scientists to make sure endangered species would not be harmed by federally approved logging, mining, and road building and allowing the reviews of species endangerment to be made by agencies such as the Federal Highway Administration and the Army Corps of Engineers, whose primary focus and expertise are not on species, endangered or otherwise. The Federal Motor Carrier Safety Act was modified to increase to 14 the number of consecutive hours per day that a truck driver could drive. The Clean Water Act forbids discharge of oil in "harmful quantities" into navigable waters, a term that was defined narrowly in 1973, but broadened by court decisions thereafter. In a rule that replaced current policy with the 1973 definition of navigable waters, formerly covered streams, marshes, and other smaller waters were no longer protected, angering environmentalists. A new Department of Health and Human Services regulation, Ensuring That Department of Health and Human Services Funds Do Not Support Coercive or Discriminatory Policies or Practices in Violation of Federal Law, requires federally funded health care facilities to certify that employees can refuse to provide services they find morally reprehensible or that are at odds with their religion, a rule that pro-choice advocates believed targeted abortions.

An incoming president's options in dealing with his predecessor's midnight regulations are limited by the stage of the rulemaking. Every incoming president puts a hold on agency activity, usually for the two to four months it takes for his political appointees to take office and be briefed. The exceptions are rare, usually limited to regulations ordered promulgated by a court. Thus if a regulation is not in effect when the new president takes office, it lies in wait for his review and decision on whether to continue. Far more difficult are the regulations that have taken effect, in whole or in part. Legally, the primary options for overturning these regulations are: a new rulemaking (a costly and time-consuming process), a court finding that the rule was illegally promulgated, or a congressional finding under the Congressional Review Act that disapproves the rule. While a new rulemaking is costly in every way, the direct final rule, in which an agency publishes an identical proposed rule and final rule simultaneously, with the final rule becoming effective if no significant comments are received, can be used to a new president's advantage, though only when there is little opposition to the rule. Because the Congressional Review Act, which requires agencies to submit rules to Congress prior to when they become effective, has only been used successfully one time in the more than two decades of its existence, it is probably not a good option for the incoming president. Courts overturn regulations all the time. For example, President George W. Bush's regulation allowing concealed guns in national parks, promulgated January 9, 2009, was blocked by a federal judge on March 19, 2009, who said the promulgation process with its inadequate environmental analysis was too flawed. (This was later overturned on appeal, and guns are now allowed.) In addition, the regulation to increase truckers' daily hours will be revised in a new round of rulemaking as part of the settlement of a lawsuit brought by Public Citizen. Nevertheless, not all rules go to court, and of those that do, many are upheld. Finally, no new president wants to spend all his resources fighting the last administration.

## President Obama's New Regulatory Initiatives

President Obama's regulatory initiatives address current problems and his priorities for change. They include major regulatory actions in the areas of the environment, occupational safety and health, mining, consumer protection, health care reforms, the economy (stimulus legislation), and financial reforms, along with numerous executive orders regulating the federal government through topics as large and small as, for example, ethics for government executives and cell phone use while driving.

President Obama's policies for the environment are significant and far-reaching. Despite his failure to get a new Cap and Trade Law, he has and can continue to make considerable and meaningful progress on climate issues through EPA rules addressing pollution, pursuant to the Clean Air Act (CAA). The National Ambient Air Quality Standards Program under the CAA has proposals to reduce ozone levels to between 0.060 and 0.070 ppm from 0.075 to protect the public health and to set a separate standard to protect the environment, especially trees and plants. Also proposed is a rule requiring monitors for lead to be placed near sources that emit .5 tons/year, up from 1 ton/year. Early work on requiring pesticide labels to list ingredients has started. In the important area of Greenhouse Gases (GHGs), EPA made a finding that GHGs pose a threat to public health and the environment. The agency has proposed to limit GHGs from passenger vehicles and power plants, factories, and other facilities. In a final rule, the agency has created a GHG Registry to collect emissions data and significantly increased the number of facilities that must report their emissions, by lowering the tonnage emitted for inclusion from 25,000 tons to 10,000 tons. The agency announced December 23, 2010, that it would be proposing GHS standards for fossil fuel power plants and petroleum refineries in July 2011 and December 2011 and final standards in May 2012 and November 2012, respectively, following listening sessions with the business community, states, and other stakeholders. According to World Resources Institute, this could result in one-third the carbon cuts the US pledged to make by 2020. Nevertheless, the president of the National Petrochemical & Refiners Association said "that the proposal was unrealistic and that his industry will urge lawmakers to block EPA's move."[11] EPA has set stricter exhaust emission standards and cleaner fuel standards for large marine diesel engines on large US-flagged ships, and harmonized those standards with international standards. EPA is also proposing to strengthen the national air quality standards for nitrogen dioxide and sulfur dioxide. On December 2, 2009, President Obama's EPA proposed to withdraw a rule that reclassified thousands of tons of hazardous waste as "fuel," a categorization that led to less government oversight and regulation.

Consistent with his commitment to make mines safer, President Obama has directed the Mine Safety and Health Administration (MSHA) to begin work on proximity detection systems for underground mines and safety and health management programs for mines, and to propose rules on lowering exposures to coal mine dust, patterns of violations, and preshift examination of work areas in underground coal mines for violation of health and safety standards. MSHA will also work with OSHA to set limits on exposures to silica. Rules completed in this administration include: Mine Rescue Teams[12], High-Voltage Continuous Mining Machine Standard for Underground Coal Mines[13], Coal Mine Dust Sampling Devices[14], and Criteria and Procedures for Procedures for Proposed Assessment of Civil Penalties/Recordkeeping and Reporting: Immediate Notification.[15]

Under President Obama, OSHA has an ambitious regulatory program that the Secretary of the US Department of Labor describes as a "renewed commitment to worker protection." Major projects include regulatory action on hazards of cranes and derricks; the chemicals crystalline silica, beryllium, and diacetyl; combustible dust; global harmonization of classification; and labeling of chemicals. The agency plans to publish a final rule updating its 1971 rule on cranes and derricks to address electrocution, crushing and struck-by, and overturning hazards along with weight load limits and operator training.[16] OSHA will propose a new standard for crystalline silica to reduce the incidence of lung disease, silicosis, and lung cancer that results from inhalation exposure to airborne silica dust in cutting, sawing, drilling, and crushing of concrete, brick, block, and stone, and operations using sand products, such as glass manufacturing and sand blasting. Beryllium, a lightweight metal used in aerospace, telecommunication, and defense, can cause chronic beryllium disease when its dust is inhaled, and is at the rulemaking stage of peer review of its sections on health effects and risk assessment. Diacetyl, a chemical in artificial butter, causes bronchiolitis obliterans (popcorn lung) in workers, and its health effects and risk assessments are scheduled to be peer reviewed. Combustible dust can cause catastrophic explosions in a variety of industries. A prime and tragic example is the 2008 explosion at Imperial Sugar, in which 14 workers lost their lives. Materials involved include wood, coal, plastics, spice, starch, flour, feed, grain, and fertilizer; and the agency will begin meetings to determine what can be done about this serious hazard. Global harmonization of classification and labeling of chemicals and safety data sheets has been a goal for some time, and following a hearing in the spring and completion of a final rule, chemicals produced in the United States will bear labels with information that is consistent with United Nations Directives and regulations in other countries throughout the world.[17]

In a secretarial order, President Obama's Secretary for the Department of the Interior directed the Bureau of Land Management to consult with the public and local communities to designate areas with wilderness characteristics as "Wild Lands" and to manage and protect their wilderness values. Unlike the "Wilderness Areas" that must be designated by Congress and can only be modified by legislation, the "Wild Lands," because they result from a public process, can be modified through a new public process as need arises.[18]

The Commodity Futures Trading Commission has flexed its regulatory muscle by investigating whether the Fuel Oil-180 Singapore Swap, traded on the Intercontinental Exchange, Inc., performs the required significant price discovery function. The commission found that it did not and issued an order to that effect.[19]

With considerable White House participation, Democrats in Congress passed the Financial Reform Act on July 21, 2010, a law so extensive it could require the promulgation of more than 500 rules. The legislation covers consumer protection by creating an independent watchdog at the Federal Reserve whose job it is to ensure clear, accurate information for consumers on mortgages, credit cards, and other financial products, and protect them from hidden fees, abusive terms, and deceptive practices. Financial firms can no longer look forward to bailouts, as rules will be written on safe ways to liquidate, on new capital and leverage requirements, on updating the Fed's authority to support the system, and on putting in rigorous standards and supervision to protect all sectors of the economy. A council is to be created to identify systemic risks from large companies, products, and activities. Loopholes that allowed risky practices in derivatives, asset-backed securities, hedge funds, mortgage brokers, and payday lenders will be closed, and transparency and accountability will be required. Bank supervision will be streamlined with emphasis on clarity and accountability. Shareholders will be able to address pay and corporate affairs with non-binding votes on executive compensation. Investors will be protected with new rules for credit rating agencies. Finally, regulators will be encouraged to enforce the rules already in effect on financial fraud, including conflicts of interest and manipulation of the system for the benefit of special interests.[20] This wide-ranging legislation provides regulatory authority for many regulatory agencies, such as the Federal Reserve, the Securities and Exchange Commission and their new Office of Credit Ratings, Department of Treasury and the new Office of National Insurance, and the Federal Deposit Insurance Corporation with its new Consumer Financial Protection Bureau. There will be extensive rulemaking, but because the legislation garnered little support from Republicans, who now hold the majority in the House, there is likely to be Congressional action to weaken or derail segments of the law as regulators take over the job of determining the particulars. However, President Obama will be able to steer the administrative agencies toward his policy goals through direction and appointments of key regulators.

The Affordable Care Act (health care reform), passed March 30, 2010, focuses on consumer protections, improving quality and lowering costs, increasing access to affordable care, and holding insurance companies accountable over its five-year implementation period. In 2010, consumer protection will be increased by putting health information online, prohibiting insurance coverage denials to children with pre-existing conditions, prohibiting insurance companies from rescinding coverage, eliminating lifetime limits on insurance coverage, providing for appeals on insurance company decisions, and establishing consumer assistance programs in the states. Quality will be improved and cost lowered by provisions to provide small-business health-insurance tax credits, provide relief from the Medicare prescription drug "doughnut hole," require policies to provide free preventive care, prevent disease and illness through a $15 billion fund to invest in proven prevention and public health programs, and provide new resources to crack down on health care fraud. Access to affordable care will be increased by providing access to insurance for uninsured Americans with pre-existing conditions, extending coverage for young adults on their parents' plans, expanding coverage for early retirees, rebuilding the primary care workforce, holding insurance companies accountable for unreasonable rate hikes, allowing more states to cover more people on Medicaid, increasing payment for rural health care providers, and strengthening community health centers. Other provisions become effective between 2011 and 2015.[21] The law is administered primarily by HHS, which has already indicated it will be issuing regulations and guidance to implement many of the provisions. Its Office of Consumer Information and Insurance Oversight will do regulations or guidance on medical loss ratios, amending the regulation on "grandfathered" health plans, Medicaid IT and federal funding for eligibility determination and enrollment, pre-existing condition insurance plans, health insurance exchanges, consumers' right to appeal health plan decisions, preventive services, patient's bill of rights, dependent coverage of children under 26, and insurance web portal requirements. The Centers for Medicare and Medicaid Services have begun work on COBRA continuation of coverage that might otherwise be terminated, health insurance reform for consumers, health insurance reform for employers, and self-funded nonfederal government plans. The Internal Revenue Service will deal with the tax provisions. All in all, there promises to be a plethora of rulemaking pursuant to the Affordable Care Act.

A final way a president implements his policies is through executive orders (EOs), which, though they apply only to the federal government, can effectively repeal the policies of his predecessor, can implement his policies, and may become voluntary standards of conduct for others. As of January 31, 2011, President Obama had signed 76 executive orders directing his administrative agencies on various topics large and small. Some of the most significant are EO 13490, Ethics Commitments by Executive Branch Personnel;[22] EO 13497, Revocation of Certain Executive Orders Concerning Regulatory Planning and Review;[23] EO 13492, Review and Disposition of Individuals Detained at the Guantánamo Bay Naval Base and Close of Detention Facilities;[24] EO 13501, Establishing the President's Economic Recovery Advisory Board;[25] EO 13513, Federal Leadership on Reducing Text Messaging While Driving;[26] EO 13514, Federal Leadership in Environment, Energy, and Economic Performance;[27] EO 13531, National

Commission on Fiscal Responsibility and Reform;[28] EO 13539, President's Council of Advisors on Science and Technology;[29] and recently, EO 13554, Establishing the Gulf Coast Ecosystem Restoration Task Force;[30] EO 13563, Improving Regulation and Regulatory Review;[31] and EO 13564, Establishment of the President's Council on Jobs and Competitiveness.[32] Through these orders, President Obama can address issues quickly and exert maximum control over his administration.

President Obama enjoyed stunning success in his first two years with his extensive legislation on stimulating the economy, reforming health care, and financial reform. The regulatory agencies have already begun, continued, or completed rulemaking projects reflecting his policies. Major new initiatives have been brought forth in all the agencies. The departments, agencies, and offices charged with promulgating regulations on the new legislation are starting to collect information and propose rules. With the divided party government and continued deadlock in Congress that President Obama faces in the next two years, regulations may be able to implement the most significant policies. The president now has ample statutes on the books to put his policies into practice. Let us pay close attention to rulemaking and see if he succeeds.

## NOTES

1. *2010 Report to Congress on Benefits and Costs of Federal Regulations and Unfunded Mandates on State, Local, and Tribal Entities,* pp. 12–13.

2. 42 U.S.C. § 7401.

3. Mandatory Reporting of Greenhouse Gases from Magnesium Production, Underground Coal Mines, Industrial Wastewater Treatment, and Industrial Waster Landfills, (75 FR 39736; July 12, 2010).

4. 5 U.S.C. §§ 551–559, 701–06, 1305, 3105, 3344, 5372, 7521.

5. 5 U.S.C §§ 701–706.

6. *Public Citizen and United Steelworkers v. OSHA, 2009,* 557 F.3rd 165 (3rd Cir. Court of Appeals).

7. Laws, too, can be challenged as is happening right now with the health care reform. In fact, 20 states are in the US District Court, Northern District of Florida, arguing whether it is constitutional to make citizens buy health insurance, a case that is sure to go to the Supreme Court.

8. 5 U.S.C. §§801–808.

9. E.O. 12866 was expected to be replaced by a new executive order. President Obama issued Memorandum of Regulatory Review on January 30, 2009 (74 FR 5677; Feb. 3, 2009). OMB published a request for comments: Federal Regulatory Review (74 FR 8819, Feb. 26, 2009), and a request for comments: Improving Implementation of the Paperwork Reduction Act (74 FR 55259; Oct. 27, 2009). In fact, E.O. was not replaced, but was affirmed and supplemented by E.O. 13563.

10. Obama, Barack, 2011 Improving Regulation and Regulatory Review, Executive Order 13563, Federal Register vol. 76 p. 3821, January 18, 2011.

11. Eilperin, Juliet, 2010 "White House presses for new climate, wilderness protections." *The Washington Post,* December 24, 2010.

12. 75 FR 286606; June 17, 2009.

13. 75 FR 17529; April 6, 2010.

14. 75 FR 17512; April 6, 2010.

15. 75 FR 21990; April 27, 2010.

16. 75 FR 47906; August 9, 2010.

17. Department of Labor, OSHA, Hazard Communication Proposed Rule (74 FR 50280; September 30, 2009).

18. Salazar, Ken, 2010 *Protecting Wilderness Characteristics on Lands Managed by the Bureau of Land Management, Order No. 3310,* December 22, 2010.

19. 75 FR 38487; July 2, 2010.

20. Summary: Restoring American Financial Stability, Create a Sound Economic Foundation to Grow Jobs, Protect Consumers, Rein in Wall Street, End Too Big to Fail, Prevent Another Financial Crisis, banking.senate.gov/public/_.../Financial ReformSummary231510FINAL.pdf.

21. About the Law, Provisions of the Affordable Care Act, By Year, HealthCare.gov.

22. Obama, Barack. 2009 Ethics Commitments by Executive Branch Personnel, Executive Order 13490, *Federal Register,* vol. 74, p. 4893, Jan. 26, 2009.

23. Obama, Barack, 2009 *Revocation of Certain Executive Orders Concerning Regulatory Planning and Review,* (revoking EO 13258, February 26, 2002 and EO 13422, January 18, 2007), Executive Order, *Federal Register,* vol. 74, p. 6113, Feb. 4, 2009.

24. Obama, Barack, 2009 *Review and Disposition of Individuals Detained at the Guantanamo Bay Naval Base and Close of Detention Facilities,* Executive Order 13492, *Federal Register,* vol. 74, p. 4897, Jan. 27, 2009.

25. Obama, Barack, 2009 *Establishing the President's Economic Recovery Advisory Board,* Executive Order 13501, Federal Register, vol. 74, p. 6893, Feb. 11, 2009.

26. Obama, Barack, 2009 *Federal Leadership on Reducing Text Messaging While Driving,* Executive Order 13513, Federal Register, vol. 74 p. 51225, Oct. 8, 2009.

27. Obama, Barack, 2009 *Federal Leadership in Environment, Energy, and Economic Performance,* Executive Order 13514, Federal Register vol. 75 p. 52117, Oct. 8, 2009.

28. Obama, Barack, 2010 *National Commission on Fiscal Responsibility and Reform,* Executive Order 13531, Federal Register vol. 75 p. 7927, Feb. 23, 2010.

29. Obama, Barack, 2010 *President's Council of Advisors on Science and Technology,* Executive Order 13539, Federal Register vol. 75 p. 21973, Apr. 27, 2010 (revoking EO 13226, Sept. 30, 2001).

30. Obama, Barack, 2010 *Establishing the Gulf Coast Ecosystem Restoration Task Force,* Executive Order 13554, Federal Register vol. 75 p. 62313, Oct. 8, 2010.

31. Obama, Barack, 2011 *Improving Regulation and Regulatory Review,* Executive Order 13563, *Federal Register* vol. 76 p. 3821, Jan. 21, 2011.

32. Obama, Barack, 2011 *Establishment of the President's Council on Jobs and Competitiveness,* Executive Order 13564, *Federal Register* vol. 76 p. 6309, Feb. 3, 2011.

# CHAPTER 13

# The Obama Administration and Internet Policy

*Douglas E. Van Houweling*

Barack Obama is the first president of the United States for whom the Internet has played an important personal and political role. His presidential campaign used the Internet to build the community that supported him in the primaries and carried him to a general election victory. As the administration turned to the business of developing its own Internet policy, however, it had to contend with the history of Internet development and policy in the United States that unfolded through the presidential administrations of Bill Clinton and George W. Bush.

The Clinton administration provided strong support for the rapidly developing Internet technology, recognizing its potential as key infrastructure for the nation's future. The Bush administration, in contrast, viewed private enterprise as the key to the Internet's continued development. The Obama administration has returned to a policy of providing more active federal support for Internet technology in pursuit of three goals: 1) global leadership in the development and deployment of Internet technology, 2) enabling American enterprises and citizens ubiquitous access to high-speed broadband Internet connections on par with other leading economies, and 3) ensuring that public serving institutions have adequate Internet connectivity. Throughout this brief history, the core question has been whether the Internet is a key element of societal infrastructure worthy of public investment or just another service best provided by private enterprise.

## An Overview of the Public and Political Dynamics of Internet Development

The Internet as we know it today had its beginnings in the United States and benefited greatly from key federal government programs at the Department of Defense and the National Science Foundation (NSF) (Hafner 1998; Abbate 1999). The key innovation funded by that research was the development of packet communications. Prior communications networks had all depended on providing an electrical circuit connecting the communicating parties. The advent of computers made it feasible to break communications into many short segments, or packets, and thereby enabled many separate interactions to be interspersed on one shared circuit. Research in packet networking was funded by the Defense Advanced Research Projects Agency beginning in the 1960s and resulted in the development of the Internet protocols at Stanford University in 1974 (Abbate 1999). The first large-scale deployment of the Internet was carried out by the NSF's NSFNET project, beginning in 1988 under a grant to MERIT, a statewide network organization hosted at the University of Michigan (NSFNET). The World Wide Web (WWW) protocols were developed by British scientist Tim Berners-Lee (Berners-Lee) at CERN, an international high-energy physics research facility funded partly by the United States. The first popular browser for the World Wide Web, Mosaic, was released in 1993 by the NSF National Center for Supercomputing Applications at the University of Illinois. The NSFNET grew at an average rate of 15 percent per month from 1988 on, and in the early 1990s a series of government decisions opened the NSFNET to other networks (NSFNET). In 1995, the NSFNET project ended through commercialization of all of its components and the launch of the commercial Internet Service Provider (ISP) industry. Public access to the Internet combined with commercial implementations of electronic mail and the WWW to spark an explosive growth industry. In light of this history, it is no surprise that federal policy toward the Internet has continued to be important to the development and functioning of the Internet and engendered a complex interaction between public and private interests in United States since the mid-1990s.

Because Internet technology allows all types of information to be packetized and transmitted over a highly efficient shared infrastructure, it has disrupted every sector of business that provides or uses communications. This new set of combined capabilities has given rise to whole new industries and some of the largest US companies, such as Google and Cisco. Traditional retailers such as Walmart and Sears have had to launch entirely new divisions focused on selling over the Internet rather than in stores. Amazon has driven countless bookstores out of existence and has now become one of the largest general retailers in the US. AT&T now provides a service, U-verse, which uses the Internet protocol to deliver television, telephone, and Internet access all together on one pair of wires into homes. Verizon has made a massive investment in installing fiber-optic connections directly to homes. Cable television companies have deployed technology that allows Internet connectivity to be provided via the infrastructure previously dedicated to delivery of television. As a result of these types of disruptions of existing industries, telecommunications policy has become a far more salient political and policy concern than it was in the pre-Internet era.

Internet policy in the United States is shaped by five principle groups: the telecommunications and Internet applications industry; public interest groups; federal regulatory agencies, in particular the Federal Communications Commission (FCC); the courts; and the executive branch through the National Telecommunications and Information Administration (NTIA) in the Department of Commerce and other Cabinet-level federal departments. Except for the passage of the Telecommunications Act of 1996 (Telecommunications Act of 1996), which itself barely mentioned the Internet, Congress has stayed mostly on the sidelines, both because the pace of change has been too rapid to be accommodated by the legislative process and because no clear consensus regarding Internet policy has emerged in an increasingly partisan environment. In any case, Congressional action on issues like peer-to-peer file sharing and child pornography traffic have not had a substantial impact on the evolution of the Internet in the United States.

Depending on the presidential administration's approach and the underlying political environment, initiative on Internet policy has shifted back and forth over the years as the administration, the courts, the regulatory agencies, and industry have all seized the lead from time to time. The telecommunications industry has attempted to limit the disruption generated by the Internet and regain control of its future, initially by restraining the development and deployment of Internet technology and now through attempts to become the dominant provider. Telecommunications companies take different stances on a number of policy issues than companies that provide Internet application services. Public interest groups such as Public Knowledge, Free Press, and the Open Internet Coalition have focused on the societal benefits that broad access to the Internet can provide. As Claudia Thurber pointed out in the previous chapter, regulatory agencies provide an additional avenue to achieve policy goals. In the arena of Internet policy, the Federal Communications Commission, an independent regulatory agency led by commissioners who are appointed by the president and confirmed by the Senate, has steered a course that reinforces the policies of the administration in power. And the cabinet departments have worked to implement the policies of the president. The courts have been drawn into the fray to resolve differences among key policy stakeholders in business and among public interest groups.

## INTERNET POLITICS UNDER PRESIDENTS CLINTON AND BUSH

There have been only three presidential administrations since the Internet came into being as a broadly available telecommunications service—those of Presidents Clinton, Bush, and Obama. As a result, a brief review of the policies in the previous two administrations provides a useful background to enable an understanding and assessment of President Obama's policies.

There are three policy stances available to an administration regarding a technology and industry such as the Internet:

1. Abdicate—let the market operate with minimal regulation or stimulus,
2. Regulate—depend on private sector activity but regulate it to achieve the desired objectives, or
3. Facilitate—invest government resources and implement policies designed to foster growth.

These alternatives are not mutually exclusive, and any administration seeks an appropriate combination for different segments of the Internet environment. It is useful to think of them as positions along a continuum ranging from a "hands-off" to an activist orientation. The ideal point on the continuum depends on whether the Internet is best viewed as a private good that will be adequately managed by the interplay of market forces or a public good that will be under-provisioned if the market operates without government intervention.

## The Clinton/Gore Administration

The Clinton/Gore administration tended toward the activist end of the continuum, focusing primarily on development and expansion of the Internet. Partly because Vice President Gore had played a major role during his service in the Senate in providing the federal funding that led to the creation and early implementation of the Internet,[1] the Clinton administration recognized it very early as an opportunity for major economic expansion. At the same time, Congress was enacting legislative changes that deregulated the telecommunications industry and set it looking for opportunities to grow in the new competitive environment.

The Internet itself was so new that the extent of its disruptive impact was not yet apparent, so very few forces were mobilized against it. The Federal Communications Commission took the stance that the Internet was still an experiment and exercised a restrained regulatory policy. Because Internet technology was largely the result of invention and implementation that the research and education community had made with support of federal funding, that community worked closely with public interest groups to encourage policies that supported broad access and the Internet's use for the public good. It seemed obvious that the Internet was valuable in both an economic and a social sense and that government funding had been key to its creation and early deployment, so it seemed natural to continue a facilitative federal involvement.

Furthermore, the government as a whole was preoccupied with policy making and regulations designed to further competitiveness in the traditional telecommunications industry by removing regulatory barriers to entry. The major focus was on drafting and passing the Telecommunications Act of 1996, which President Clinton signed into law on February 8 (Telecommunications Act of 1996). The conference report stated that the bill would "provide for a pro-competitive, de-regulatory national policy framework designed to accelerate rapidly private sector deployment of advanced services and information technologies and services to all Americans by opening all telecommunications markets to competition" (Conference Report 1996).

In this environment, the Clinton administration moved to put the full force of the federal government behind facilitating Internet innovation. The two most important initiatives were the Next Generation Internet Program (NGI) announced on October 10, 1996, and the founding of the Internet Corporation for Assigned Names and Numbers (ICANN) in September 1998. NGI was established to invest $100 million per year for three years[2] through empowering the National Coordination Office for Computing, Information, and Communications to coordinate federal agency efforts to develop advanced Internet technology in which the United States had a strategic leadership position.[3] In addition to funding advanced networks for mission agencies, such as the Department of Energy and the National Aeronautics and Space Administration, NGI funded the NSF's High Performance Connections Program that supported efforts by the research community to develop and deploy a more advanced version of the Internet (NGI). The community established a not-for-profit organization, Internet2, to realize these community goals. Internet2 became one of the world's first National Research and Education Network (NREN) organizations.[4] There are now more than 100 networks supported by similar organizations working to meet the advanced networking needs of research and education institutions in other countries around the world.[5]

ICANN is responsible for managing the Internet's addresses and the names associated with those addresses on a global scale.[6] Names such as www.google. com are all linked to specific numerical addresses that are used by the packet switches in the Internet to route traffic among communicating parties or devices. The association between those names and the corresponding numerical addresses was initially funded as part of the NSF's Internet research program, but as the Internet became a commercial service on a global scale, the Internet community worked with the federal government to establish a not-for-profit organization to provide that capability.

While the specific actions of the Clinton administration probably had only a small impact on the explosive growth of the public Internet that began in 1995, they combined with the hands-off stance of the FCC and the reduction in federal regulation of telecommunications in general to generate an enormous amount of economic growth that helped propel the United States and world economy for a decade. Indeed, the economic boom in the United States during the Clinton years, while it was certainly much more broadly based, has been referred to since as the "dot-com boom." In summary, the Clinton/Gore administration had the good fortune to reap the benefit of the Internet's launch and its stimulus of the national and global economy. A strongly facilitative approach came naturally to an administration that believed the federal government had to play a key role to "build a bridge to the twenty-first century"[7] and had a vice president who was an early supporter of the technology. Indeed, had it not been for the initiatives of the administration, the Internet might not have first taken root in the United States.

## *The Bush/Cheney Administration*

The Bush/Cheney administration abdicated federal government influence over the Internet. When George W. Bush defeated Vice President Gore in 2000, his supporters were largely critical of "industrial policy," that is, government support for any particular technology or industry. Indeed, Vice President Gore was ridiculed for his role in the development of the Internet and was sarcastically misquoted as claiming to have "invented the Internet." The traditional telecommunications carriers were hostile to the FCC's efforts to stimulate competition in the industry. The resulting policy minimized regulation of the Internet. The notion that a facilitative federal role was required to achieve overall societal goals was dismissed in favor of a set of policies that left the future of the Internet primarily in corporate hands. Further, the domestic terrorist attacks on September 11, 2001, resulted in a shift of focus to international and defense issues. As a result, funding for efforts such as the NGI, the National Telecommunications and Information Administration (NTIA) in the Department of Commerce, and other telecommunications infrastructure programs was either withdrawn or sharply reduced (McLoughlin 2006).

As a counterbalance, Internet2, working with other higher education and research organizations, such as the Computing Research Association (CRA), led efforts to generate increased federal funding for advanced network research and deployment. The National Science Foundation commissioned a Blue-Ribbon Advisory Panel on Cyberinfrastructure, led by Dan Atkins. The panel's report eventually led to the establishment of the NSF Office of Cyberinfrastructure (OCI 2003). However, even after several positive discussions with senior officials, the Bush administration was not supportive of the funding required to allow OCI to accomplish the broad vision outlined in the panel's report.

During the same period, the dominant corporations in the telecommunications industry welcomed this laissez-faire environment and were able to consolidate their hold on the provision of Internet services. The FCC, now under Republican leadership, interpreted the 1996 Telecommunications Act in such a way as to substantially increase the concentration of telecommunications activity under a smaller number of large corporations (Turner). The FCC did, however, recognize the need to substantially improve networking services to health care providers serving rural communities and decided in 2006 to make a major investment in the Rural Health Care Pilot Program. That program designated Internet2 and National LambdaRail (NLR) as the source of national connectivity for the participants. This was the first time an entity of the federal government recognized the potential of the nonprofit higher education–affiliated networking organizations to serve the broader community. In November 2007, the FCC selected 69 entities to receive $417 million of funding to improve connectivity to rural health care providers. Unfortunately, the very cumbersome process utilized by the Universal Service Administration Company meant that only a small portion of that funding was disbursed during the Bush administration. Toward the end of the administration, the economic downturn further diverted attention from Internet issues and development.

At the same time, other nations had concluded that the Internet was a key part of national infrastructure and were investing to "catch up" with the United States in Internet technology and deployment. Thus, while penetration of Internet technology in the United States was substantially ahead of most nations in the late '90s, by the end of the Bush years the United States had fallen well behind leading nations in Europe and the Far East in penetration and performance of Internet connectivity (FCC). In summary, the Bush administration policy of deregulation and lack of stimulus resulted in the United States surrendering its global leadership in the deployment of and broad access to Internet technology.

One exception to this general trend resulted from efforts by organizations such as Internet2 and NLR to provide advanced connectivity to universities and research laboratories, both public and commercial. Both organizations used carrier facilities and commercially available equipment to provide Internet performance a thousand times faster than that available in the consumer and small-business marketplace. They also enabled high-performance connections for schools, hospitals, libraries, and museums across the nation.[8] These resources subsequently provided an important foundation for the objectives of the Obama administration's efforts to rejuvenate Internet capabilities in the United States.

## Internet Politics Under President Obama

The Obama/Biden administration shifted quickly back to the investment and development policies seen in the Clinton/Gore era by appointments to the FCC and the Cabinet agencies to facilitate advancement of the Internet in the United States. The Internet policy environment, though, had in the meantime become much more complex. Very substantial financial interests were now involved in what had become a major industry, making Internet politics much more contentious.

Coming into office inheriting serious domestic economic and financial crises and two intractable wars abroad, President Obama undertook an aggressive set of investment efforts to stimulate economic growth—including further development of Internet infrastructure. Looking to the future, he worked with the Congress to secure passage of the American Recovery and Reinvestment Act of 2009 (ARRA), which both commissioned the FCC to develop a National Broadband Plan and included a $7.2 billion commitment to fund capital investment in broadband and wireless Internet access.[9] This combination of activities has resulted in the largest federal commitment to Internet technology in United States history.

The administration's policies toward the Internet were stimulated by a continuation of efforts by the research and education community working with public interest groups. As the presidential campaign took shape in 2007, a number of the organizations that had been advocating greater Internet investment to the Bush administration began looking forward to the next administration. In particular, the Computer Research Association, EDUCAUSE, NLR, and Internet2 began informal discussions regarding high-performance network capabilities for research and education. Those efforts were facilitated when the Subcommittee of the National Science and Technology Council's Committee on Technology on Networking and Information Technology Research and Development (NITRD) in August 2008 began work to develop a Five Year Strategic Plan.[10] That was followed up by a NITRD February 2009 Strategic Plan Forum at which many of the policy recommendations were discussed.

When President Obama was elected, organizations such as the Computer Research Association, the Information Technology and Innovation Foundation, the American Council on Education, EDUCAUSE, and Internet2 followed up by providing recommendations to the new administration's transition team. President Obama also asked members of the higher education and public interest community to join his team.[11]

Julius Genachowski played a key role as chair of the FCC. He worked with President Obama's staff to shape the study that resulted in the National Broadband Plan (National Broadband Plan). That planning effort, begun in April 2009, included very extensive public participation. As the plan stated:

> Thirty-six public workshops held at the FCC and streamed online, which drew more than 10,000 in-person or online attendees, provided the framework for the ideas contained within the plan. These ideas were then refined based on replies to 31 public notices, which generated some 23,000 comments totaling about 74,000 pages from more than 700 parties. The FCC also received about 1,100 ex parte filings totaling some 13,000 pages and nine public hearings were held throughout the country to further clarify the issues addressed in the plan (National Broadband Plan).

The plan set six goals:

> Goal No. 1: At least 100 million U.S. homes should have affordable access to actual download speeds of at least 100 megabits per second and actual upload speeds of at least 50 megabits per second.
> Goal No. 2: The United States should lead the world in mobile innovation, with the fastest and most extensive wireless networks of any nation.
> Goal No. 3: Every American should have affordable access to robust broadband service, and the means and skills to subscribe if they so choose.
> Goal No. 4: Every American community should have affordable access to at least 1 gigabit per second broadband service to anchor institutions such as schools, hospitals and government buildings.
> Goal No. 5: To ensure the safety of the American people, every first responder should have access to a nationwide, wireless, interoperable broadband public safety network.
> Goal No. 6: To ensure that America leads in the clean energy economy, every American should be able to use broadband to track and manage their real-time energy consumption (National Broadband Plan).

These very ambitious goals were outlined through detailed recommendations for their achievement, including a financing plan based on spectrum auctions. These recommendations highlight several policy currents:

1. The need for higher-performance consumer Internet connectivity, both fixed and mobile, than has until now been provided through the actions of the telecommunications industry;
2. The need for high-capacity connections for public-serving institutions;
3. The need for public investment to realize benefits to the general public good in safety, energy conservation, and Internet literacy.

The plan also lays out an extensive case for the broad public benefits to health care and education that would result from a more robust Internet infrastructure in the United States.

One of the most important impacts of these goals for the Obama administration's early initiatives is contained in the recommendation for high-speed access to "anchor institutions" (the fourth goal) because of the impact it had on the US Department of Commerce Broadband Technology Opportunities Program (BTOP) (see below). The FCC identified high-performance connections for anchor institutions to be a need that was least likely to be fulfilled by market forces. Anchor institutions are schools, universities, hospitals, health clinics, libraries, public safety organizations, and governmental entities. All have in common the need to simultaneously serve thousands and even millions of users from their respective communities. These needs are especially important in emergency or disaster response situations. In a world where each community member has access to at least 10 million bits per second (10 megabits) of Internet capacity, an anchor institution needs a large multiple of that capacity to enable prompt response. Furthermore, emergencies or disasters can generate large peaks of traffic. The National Broadband Plan therefore recommended that anchor institutions have at least one billion bits per second (1 gigabit) of Internet capacity.

The network services provided by the telecommunications carriers, such as the telephone and cable companies, are not designed to meet these needs, but to cost-effectively deliver services to millions of users, each of which consumes a small portion of the network's overall capacity. As a result, they can operate their networks without allocating much reserve capacity. Each anchor institution can from time to time require a very substantial portion of the network's overall capacity and often requires that capacity in situations with life-safety implications. As a result, a network capable of meeting the needs of anchor institutions has to be designed to deliver large amounts of traffic on demand. This requires that the provider reserve substantial excess capacity in the network. Large corporations with these requirements typically enter into a contract with a network provider to obtain a network dedicated to their needs, rather than attempting to use the public Internet. But the anchor institutions are widely dispersed geographically and organizationally fragmented across many jurisdictions, so they have not been able to aggregate their needs to stimulate a response from the marketplace to meet their unique needs.

The FCC Broadband Plan noted that the higher education and research community had addressed this problem through the creation of not-for-profit entities such as Internet2 and NLR and suggested that that model could be extended to the rest of the anchor institution community. In other words, the plan's Recommendation 8.22 was that "The federal government and state governments should develop an institutional framework that will help America's anchor institutions obtain broadband connectivity, training, applications, and services" (National Broadband Plan).

Through coordination by the White House staff, this recommendation was implemented through the Department of Commerce Broadband Technology Opportunities Program (BTOP). The American Recovery and Reinvestment Act contained two programs designed to expand and build Internet infrastructure: the $4.7 billion BTOP under the NTIA in the Department of Commerce and the $2.5 billion Broadband Initiatives Program (BIP) under the Department of Agriculture's Rural Utilities Service.[12] As of October, 2010, all of these funds were committed to projects (Broadband). Given the requirements for matching funds on these grants and loans, the total investment likely to ultimately result will be close to $10 billion. Further, because the funds were restricted to capital investment, and operating expenses were to be funded by the activities supported by this new capital infrastructure, another $2 billion per year is the minimum direct additional operational activity that these investments will stimulate.[13] In total, then, the ARRA will inject approximately $16 billion into United States Internet provisioning enterprises over the coming three years. The overall direct payments to Internet service providers in 2009 were estimated to be $70 billion (Quelch 2009), so this injection will potentially constitute more than a 20 percent expansion of those activities. While substantial, this is not sufficient to achieve either the first or the third of the FCC goals for high-performance and broadly accessible Internet service to the public. The administration had to find a strategic focus that would move the nation forward toward ubiquitous access.

Therefore, as the NTIA policy makers examined the priority for responding to grant requests, they increasingly concluded that the best use of their funds was to assist organizations that were focused on providing service to anchor institutions. As stated above, the FCC Broadband Plan also recommended expanding the role of the US higher education and research networking organizations to serve the needs of anchor institutions (National Broadband Plan). As a result, a very large proportion of the $3.5 billion granted by the NTIA BTOP infrastructure program went to provide network facilities in support of anchor institutions, and most of that went to not-for-profit higher education-related organizations, both at the national (Internet2) and state levels. This multibillion-dollar injection of funding to those organizations is likely to create a new category of organizations capable of providing Internet services, a business that has until now been dominated by "telephone" carriers, such as AT&T and Verizon, and the cable companies, such as Comcast and Time-Warner.

The established telephone and cable carriers have begun to react to this injection of a new set of players and new politics to the Internet service environment. Because the new not-for-profit organizations are not planning to serve the public or corporations, there is potential for a cooperative approach through which those customers continue to be served by the established carriers and then connected to anchor institutions through the lower-cost specialized capabilities provided by the not-for-profit sector. To date, the telephone carriers have made comments that appear to oppose the new entrants[14], while the cable carriers have engaged in discussions through the National Cable Telecommunication Association to find a more cooperative path forward.

All of these efforts by the FCC and the NTIA have been called into question by a court case between Comcast and the FCC in which the US Court of Appeals for the District of Columbia ruled in April 2010 that the FCC lacks authority to require Internet providers to give equal treatment to all Internet traffic flowing over their networks.[15] The Telecommunications Act of 1996 and subsequent FCC decisions under the Bush administration classified Internet service as an "information service" over which the court has declared the FCC has less regulatory authority than over "telecommunications service," which is required to treat all traffic equally (now popularly known as the principle of "network neutrality"). This ruling complicates achieving the larger agenda outlined in the National Broadband Plan. One avenue would be for the FCC to redefine Internet service as a "communications service" so it could exercise the required regulatory power to fully enforce network neutrality. The telephone and cable carriers have strenuously objected to such a redefinition, so the FCC instead chose the course of pursuing network neutrality through a compromise that is designed to survive amid the competing interests of the telecommunications industry, the Internet applications provider industry, and the public interest groups. As of this writing, that compromise has already been challenged through lawsuits filed by Comcast, a cable provider, and MetroPCS, a telephone carrier.

## The Future

All of which brings us to the present and looking into the future of Internet policy. The 2010 midterm election resulted in Republican capture of the House of Representatives and increased voting power in the Senate, which could seriously challenge some aspects of the Obama administration's continued effort to enhance Internet capabilities in the United States. Further efforts to stimulate Internet infrastructure through grant programs such as BTOP are unlikely to be funded because they are resisted by for-profit corporate interests and they require federal resources in a period when an ascendant Republican Party prioritizes tax reduction over government investment. Even though the Broadband Plan does not require substantial new federal funding, any legislation required to fund programs such as the public safety network will also be opposed by the more Republican Congress. Finally, if the FCC is unable to enforce network neutrality, the established carriers will be able to discriminate against traffic from the new not-for-profit providers of service to anchor institutions. Because the anchor institutions not only exchange traffic with one another, but also serve the broader public, it is crucial that traffic flow unimpeded from the traditional carriers through the new anchor institution networks to the institutions they serve. Success for the Obama administration's major initiative to serve communities through their anchor institutions would be endangered by a lack of cooperation, and the new anchor institution networks will have to establish collaboration with the traditional carriers.

The likely outcome is the continued dominance of the Internet in the United States by the established carriers. As Claudia Thurber suggested in the previous chapter, the administration may have to depend heavily on a regulatory agency, the FCC, to achieve its policy goals in the political environment of the second half of Obama's first term. Even so, the restraints on FCC action will probably limit its impact. Because carriers will be lightly regulated in their provision of Internet service, they will continue to pursue corporate policies designed to achieve maximum financial return, and the United States will probably fall further behind nations that treat the Internet as a public good. The bottom line in the short run is higher profitability for the telecommunications industry but lower growth for new Internet applications providers and a slower pace of overall Internet applications innovation. In the longer run, the public debate over the nation's stake in an advanced Internet infrastructure will become more urgent as the United States falls farther behind other nations. In the final analysis, American leadership in Internet technology will require recognition that the Internet is a public good and a key societal infrastructure.

Notwithstanding this uncertainty about the future, the Obama administration's first two years have resulted in a major step forward for Internet capabilities in the United States. A more active FCC, the investment and accompanying activity resulting from the ARRA stimulus program, and the increased investments in network capability for science and research have all reenergized America's Internet development community. While the competing political forces surrounding the Internet in the United States will continue to cloud the future, there is no question that the first two Obama years have provided substantial impetus to the development of Internet infrastructure—and have, perhaps more importantly, signaled a renewed recognition of the broad societal interest in the Internet as a public good.

## NOTES

1. On December 9, 1991, the Congress passed the High Performance Computing and Communication Act (Pub. L. 102–194). It was often referred to as the Gore Bill because it was created and introduced by Senator Albert Gore, Jr.

2. NGI Draft Implementation Plan, Executive Summary, http://web.archive.org/web/19990502011102/www.ccic.gov/ngi/implementation-Jul97/exec_summary.html.

3. Next Generation Internet (NGI) Home Page, http://web.archive.org/web/19971210184945/http://www.ngi.gov/.

4. Internet2 Timeline, http://www.internet2.edu/about/timeline/.

5. http://www.internet2.edu/international/reachable/.

6. http://www.icann.org/en/about./

7. William J. Clinton, Second Inaugural Address, January 20, 1997.

8. Internet2 K20 Connectivity Data, http://k20.internet2.edu/connectivity.

9. H. R. 1, Division A, Title I, pps 4, 5, 14 and Division B, Title VI, pps 398–402.

10. Networking and Information Technology Research and Development Request for Input, Invitation to Submit White Papers to Inform the Five-Year Strategic Plan for the

Federal Networking and Information Technology Research & Development Program, http://www.nitrd.gov/about/documents/NITRDStrategicPlanRFIv13.pdf.

11. Two key appointments were Tom Kalil, who had been Special Assistant to the Chancellor for Science and Technology at the University of California, Berkeley, and a member of the Clinton administration's National Economics Council, and Susan Crawford, a faculty member from the University of Michigan Law School who had long been a prominent figure in debates over Internet and communications policy. Both went on to occupy policy advisory positions in the Obama administration.

12. H. R. 1, op. cit.

13. Operational expenses for Internet infrastructure typically exceed the capital costs over the life of the investment, which is approximately five years.

14. Reply comments of AT&T Inc. to the Federal Communications Commission, WC Docket No. 02-60, September 23, 2010, pps. 14–17.

15. Comcast Corporation v. Federal Communications Commission, United States Court of Appeals for the District of Columbia Circuit, No 08-1291.

# PART V

## OBAMA AND FOREIGN POLICY

CHAPTER 14

# Structural Challenges for American Foreign Policy in the Obama Administration

*Jonathan Wilkenfeld*

President Barack Obama inherited a complex, dynamic, and dangerous world. As the Obama administration passes the midpoint of its first term in office, it appears to have settled on the broad outlines for dealing with some of the more vexing immediate foreign policy issues that it inherited from the previous administration. It now faces the development and implementation of broad policy on key global issues that will define its own unique foreign policy agenda. We know a lot about the headline issues—how the administration is dealing with the aggression and expanding nuclear programs in North Korea and Iran, resetting ties with Russia and reaching a new balance with China, a new START treaty with Russia, the war in Afghanistan, and the evolving crises over leadership and political reform in Tunisia, Egypt, and elsewhere in the Middle East. But an open question has to do with whether the Obama administration will recognize and address some of the longer-term critical underlying issues facing the international system—those factors that are likely to define the nature of the international system for our children and grandchildren, long after President Obama leaves office. What tools do we have to recognize such long-term threats to the stability and prosperity of the world, and what measures might be developed to help the administration begin to address these threats?

227

This chapter identifies the sources of several of these threats to world stability and prosperity facing President Obama: ethnic diversity, inconsistent governance, ineffective conflict resolution, and poor development strategies. The analysis addresses deceptive myths and uncomfortable realities in the international system, and will draw in part upon data and analyses presented originally in Hewitt, Wilkenfeld, and Gurr (2010). The chapter ends with some prescriptions for the Obama administration on how best to deal with the more dangerous consequences of these threats.

Members of the international system continue to attempt to address challenges facing the global community primarily from a nation-state perspective— old institutions facing new challenges, or fitting square pegs into round holes. Despite warnings about the demise of the nation state dating to the end of World War II, all signs point to its continued viability and even dominance of the international system. But this particular institutional form has endured while the issues facing the international system have evolved and become increasingly multi- and trans-national in character. We will examine some of these challenges in the context of the continued dominance of the nation-state as the current and foreseeable organizational structure of humans and society. The long-term challenges to the global community will require foresight, imagination, and creativity by the Obama administration, in collaboration with other nations and international, regional, and non-governmental organizations, if we hope to address them while clinging to an institutional arrangement that seems on the surface to be ill-equipped to address them on a global scale.

Complicating the task further are the results of the 2010 midterm elections in the US. The resurgence of the Republican Party and its majority in the House of Representatives has emboldened other nations to take tougher stands against administration policy. This has been apparent in a number of arenas, from pushback from the Israeli government against tough American demands for the limitation of housing construction in settlements on the West Bank and in East Jerusalem, to the inability of the administration to close a free trade agreement with South Korea during Obama's participation in the ASEAN meetings in November 2010, and to the significant criticism by China, Germany, and Brazil of the Federal Reserve's plan to inject $600 billion into the US economy. Thus, the administration's hand has been weakened internationally at precisely the moment at which decisive, forceful, and forward-looking leadership by the US is perhaps more critical than ever before.

## DIVERSITY AND THE STABILITY OF THE STATE

If we have any hope of addressing global challenges through the institution of the nation-state, we must first attend to the conditions conducive to its continued stability. Our first myth is that the international system as a whole thrives on the diversity of its societies. They are culturally dynamic, facilitating individual and collective identity, and fostering creativity, imagination, and invention. Ethnic, religious, cultural, and racial diversity are facts of life in most countries. Such identity for many is important to their self-concept, expressed both in the home and in community and political life.

But the reality is that one in every seven people worldwide is a citizen of a diverse society in which ethnic minorities suffer some form of discrimination—political, economic, social, or cultural (United Nations Human Development Report 2004; Minorities at Risk Project 2010). Although that in and of itself is disturbing enough, even more disturbing is that seven of the ten most lethal terrorist acts in the past decade have been perpetrated by organizations with strong ethnic links (Asal, Johnson, and Wilkenfeld 2008). What are the contributing factors in moving an ethnicity-based organization from the adoption of legitimate means of political and social mobilization and action to violence and in some cases terrorism? Current research shows that these factors include a non-democratic ideology, advocacy of self-determination, foreign and diaspora support, rhetoric justifying violence, and significant repression by the governments of the countries in which they reside. If all five factors are present, there is an 89 percent probability that the organization will engage in violence, often in the form of terrorism (Wilkenfeld, Pate, and Asal 2009). While President Obama has attempted to alter the tone of the war on terrorism and address its broader sources of ideology and support, there remains among the American public a widely held perception that Islam in and of itself is a major source of terrorism in the world (Gottlieb 2010).

Ethnic diversity itself is not particularly problematic, and as indicated can be a force for innovation and creativity in society. But when ethnicity is politically mobilized in a divisive manner—as it has been in the past in countries as far flung as Rwanda and the former Yugoslavia, or as it is today in Iraq, Afghanistan, Pakistan, and in many parts of Africa, it can become a very powerful means of organizing individuals for violence.

Figure 14-1 shows the countries in the world that, according to 2006 data from the Minorities at Risk Project (2010), have at least one militant, ethnically based minority organization. So the reality is that when the ethnic blend does not work, it does not work in spectacularly negative fashion.

## Conflict Management or Conflict Resolution

The second challenge for the international community in general, and the Obama administration in particular, has to do with achieving real and lasting resolution to seemingly intractable conflicts. The international community is playing an increasingly important role in the settlement of armed conflicts. With the end of World War II and the creation of the United Nations, the international community has done a better job of developing a vast array of institutions and mechanisms to deal with armed conflict. Since the end of the Cold War, there has been a further proliferation of international and regional institutions, as well as NGOs specifically charged with addressing aspects of conflict. In fact, in the post–Cold War era, almost 60 percent of all international and intra-state crises have been the subjects of mediation efforts on the part of third parties. Figure

## Figure 14-1: Global Ethnic Militancy

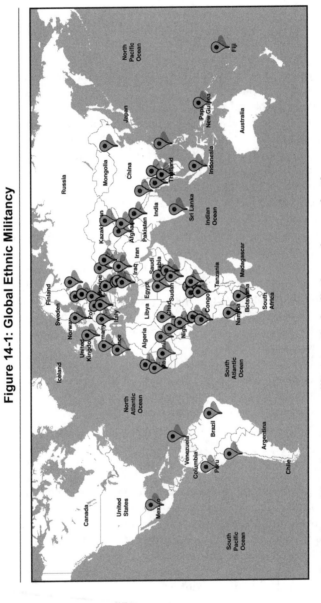

Countries with at least one militant, ethnically based organization

14-2 shows something of a decline in the number of armed conflicts since the end of the Cold War.

While the number of armed interstate conflicts averaged about four per year for the international system as a whole from the end of World War II through the mid-1970s, the data show a remarkable decline thereafter, and in particular after the end of the Cold War era in the early 1990s. However, this decline in interstate conflicts was matched by a sharp increase in the average number of intrastate conflicts in the system, to the point where they are virtually the only form of armed conflict today (see Harbom and Sundberg 2009)—Iraq and Afghanistan are the most spectacular recent examples.

While all this is true, the reality as it relates to conflict resolution is quite different: of the 39 armed conflicts that became active in the last 10 years, 31 or nearly 80 percent were conflict recurrences—instances of resurgent, armed violence in societies where conflict had been largely dormant for at least a year (Hewitt 2010). During this period, the greatest threat of armed conflict has come from countries that recently resolved a serious armed conflict. The current rate of conflict recurrence is at its highest level since World War II.

Figure 14-3 shows the evolution over time of the mix between new and recurring conflicts in the system. As can be seen quite vividly, there has been a clear shift in the balance between new and recurring conflicts over time, dramatically bringing into focus the general failure of the system to deal effectively with conflict in order to prevent its recurrence. Another perspective on this issue is that the pool of recently terminated conflicts contains more conflicts with a history of recurrence than ever before, a trend inherited by President Obama. Simply put, despite the proliferation of institutions, we are not getting it right in terms of conflict resolution (Hewitt 2010).

Nowhere is this administration's beginning recognition of this new reality seen more clearly than in the policies that Secretary of State Hillary Clinton has attempted to implement from the very early days of her leadership of the department. Her emphasis on women's issues on a global scale, her focus on NGOs and community-based initiatives, and linking international development and diplomacy to defense and nation building have all been attempts to begin to address some of the factors that have been at the core of the increasingly prevalent sub-national conflicts (LaFranchi 2010). In her discussion of the Quadrennial Diplomacy and Development Review (QDDR) initiative, Clinton advocates a "wholesale review of the State Department and USAID to recommend how to better equip, fund, train, and organize ourselves to meet current diplomatic and development priorities." The QDDR has resulted in numerous recommendations for connecting national security efforts to diplomacy and development (Clinton 2010).

## State Fragility and Failure: Ignore at Your Own Peril

The third challenge facing President Obama is in the realm of development aid. The international community is on the right track both in increasing the overall

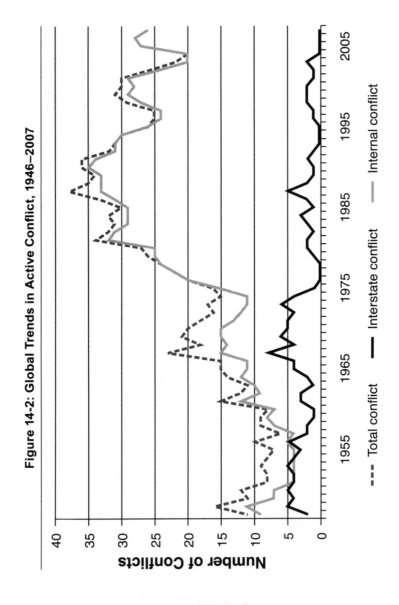

Figure 14-2: Global Trends in Active Conflict, 1946–2007

- - - Total conflict  —— Interstate conflict  —— Internal conflict

Number of Conflicts

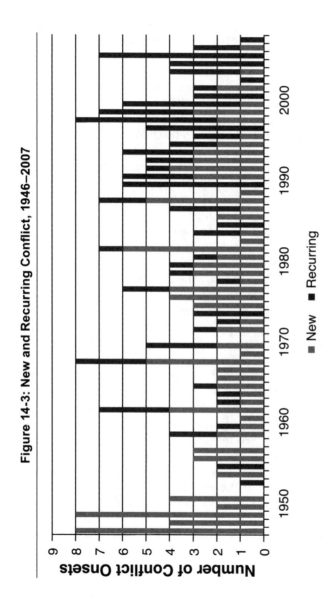

Figure 14-3: New and Recurring Conflict, 1946–2007

total of international development aid funds and in directing those funds to the places and programs where they are needed the most. But development aid from all sources is outpaced by a factor of almost four to one by the economic cost of state instability, fragility, and failure (Hoeffler 2010)—$80 billion in aid per year versus the cost of state failure of $270 billion per year by some estimates. And further, the damage is not just locally to the state experiencing the instability and fragility. A full 87 percent of the economic costs are borne by neighboring states (Chauvet, Collier, and Hoeffler 2006).

One of the little understood realities of state failure is that it is not just a local tragedy, it has widespread negative ramifications through the spread of violence and terrorism beyond the borders of the state that may give rise to the initial grievances. Afghanistan, Yemen, and Somalia, clearly problems for President Obama, are only the most blatant and well-known recent examples. As Figure 14-4 dramatically shows, fragility and failure are "neighborhood" concerns, with states in danger of collapse grouped around each other in instability patterns.

And as if that were not enough, instability is on the rise. Over the past two years, the risk of instability has increased in the regions of the world where those dangers were already high. The top 25 states with the highest risk of failure are at greater risk than they were just two years ago. And more worrisome, 22 of the 25 states at highest risk of failure are in Africa—exceptions are Afghanistan, Iraq, and Nepal (Hewitt 2010).

Reinforcing the notion that state failure is regional rather than local in its consequences, the conflict patterns identified in the map are closely related to patterns of international crisis vulnerability—with crisis involving two or more nation-states. Seventy-seven percent of all international crises in the post–World War II era have had at least one unstable, fragile, or failed state among the parties to the crisis (Wilkenfeld 2008). This disturbing regional and "neighborhood" pattern persists, although crises have a much lower frequency than state instability. Many of these vulnerable states are located in "dangerous neighborhoods" and/or control access to critical natural resources. In attempting to address this stark reality, the Obama administration has proposed an increase of $34 million in 2011 over the 2010 levels for support of the Civilian Response Corps (CRC) of the State Department. The CRC has "become the embodiment of Secretary Clinton's concept of smart power," according to the State Department. This supports the expansion of the civilian response corps, where civilian agencies (Labor, HHS) provide employees to be deployed to crisis zones/war zones in stabilization and capacity building projects (Clinton 2010).

Fortunately, the majority of members of the international community—66 percent—are both stable domestically and not currently or recently involved in international crises. Spread across all regions of the globe, these states constitute the basis for the continued relative stability of the international system. They create neighborhoods of stability—much of Europe and the Western Hemisphere for example—where institutional and informal arrangements are in place to deal with both potential fragility and conflict before they interact to form a lethal dynamic (Wilkenfeld 2008).

Figure 14-4: Risks of Instability, 2008–2010

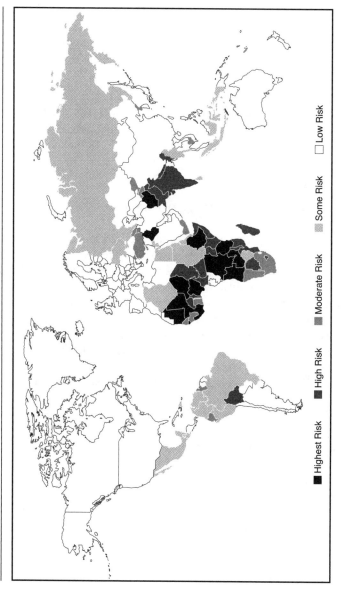

■ Highest Risk    ■ High Risk    ■ Moderate Risk    ▨ Some Risk    □ Low Risk

But the world will not be a secure environment until the cycle of instability and violence is addressed and the linking of human security and international security becomes a priority for the entire international system. As Mohamed ElBaradei, former Secretary General of the International Atomic Energy Agency and 2005 Nobel Peace Laureate, recently stated:

> The modern age demands that we think in terms of *human* security—a concept of security that is people-centered and without borders. A concept that acknowledges the inherent linkage between economic and social development, respect for human rights, and peace. This is the basis on which we must "re-engineer" security. While national security is just as relevant as before, the strategies to achieve it must be much more global than in the past, and our remedies must be centered on the welfare of the individual and not simply focused on the security of the state. Until we understand and act accordingly, we will not have either national or international security (ElBaradei 2010).

## Promotion of Democracy and Regime Consistency

The fourth global challenge facing President Obama focuses on the long-standing policy of all recent US administrations to promote democracy around the world. The significant increase in the number of democracies among the states of the international system, coupled with a decrease in the number of autocracies, bodes well for a more tranquil international system. This phenomenon is sometimes referred to as the democratic peace, wherein we find fully democratic states rarely, if ever, using violence against each other to settle disputes. Indeed, as the data in Figure 14-5 show, there has been a steady increase in the number of democracies in the system, coupled with a steady decrease in the number of autocracies. These two trends crossed in about 1990, and despite some very recent reverses, the trends appear to be stable (Pate 2010).

What is disturbing about this picture is the third line, which plots the number of "anocracies" in the system over time. Anocracies are hybrid regimes, which exhibit some of the characteristics of democracy while retaining some autocratic institutions and practices. In many cases these are regimes in transition from autocracy to democracy. Our research shows that is it these anocratic, transitional regimes that are at the greatest risk for instability. While strong democracies and strong autocracies are best able, obviously through differing means, to control tendencies within their societies to devolve into conflict and violence, anocracies are less able to do this. Some current examples of these states are Niger, Cambodia, and Chad.

So the dilemma for President Obama and the international community is how to promote democratic values in societies emerging from long histories of authoritarian rule, while at the same time keeping these states from slipping into instability and conflict in precisely this transition period. This is particularly true of post-conflict societies because they are vulnerable to the same forces that drive conflict recurrence—poor economic growth, lingering disagreements about power-sharing arrangements, and continued opportunities for insurgencies to organize

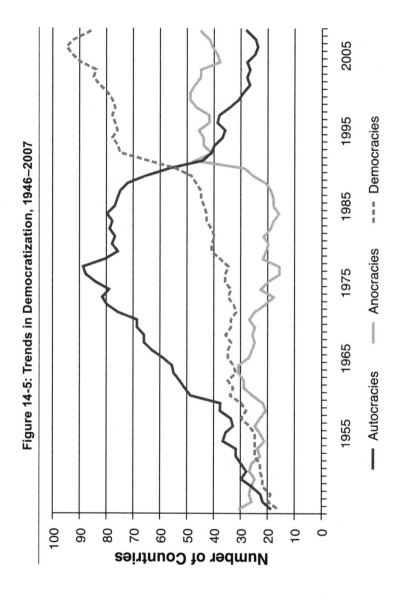

Figure 14-5: Trends in Democratization, 1946–2007

— Autocracies   — Anocracies   ■■■ Democracies

(Hegre and Fjelde 2010). The recent violence in Kenya following the disputed elections in 2007 provides an unfortunate example of this tendency.[1] This is precisely the danger that Egypt faces today as it transitions from autocracy to an emerging form of Egyptian democracy. One of the paradoxes of democracy is a complex relationship between democracy and violence.

One of the sharpest and perhaps most cynical examples of this paradox has been recent Obama administration policy toward Sudan. That country's decades-long civil war between north and south, followed by the more recent complex conflict in Darfur, has resulted in Sudanese president Omar al-Bashir being charged with war crimes by the International Criminal Court (ICC). In the period immediately prior to the January 2011 referendum in which the people of southern Sudan were to decide whether to secede from the north, the US attempted to ensure that the vote went forward by offering to take Sudan off the list of state sponsors of terrorism. This linkage of seemingly unconnected issues is emphatic evidence of a shift toward a more pragmatic and less ideological approach to foreign policy in the Obama administration. Indeed, in his January 2011 State of the Union Address, President Obama used the term political reform instead of democratization to describe US policy in unstable and post-conflict environments. Initial reactions of the American public are encouraging: According to the poll by the Pew Research Center for the People & the Press, 57% say the Obama administration is handling the situation in Egypt about right (Los Angeles Times, February 8, 2011).

## PRESCRIPTIONS FOR STABILITY AND PROSPERITY AND THE OBAMA ADMINISTRATION

Let us turn our attention now to how we might begin to address the long-term challenges that threaten the stability and prosperity of the global community. As the Obama administration begins the second half of its term in office, it has a unique opportunity to meet these challenges. The sections below present an agenda for the development of a comprehensive set of interacting tools that the international community must develop to cope with these challenges. They address these threats at all phases through monitoring and early warning, through conflict management and conflict resolution, and finally in the area of post-conflict reconstruction. Taken together, these tools can be the basis for a forward-thinking approach to international stability and economic development and growth. They can form the basis of a comprehensive global approach to these issues and provide entry points for the Obama administration to impact long-term global trends.

### Monitoring and Early Warning

The rationale behind the development of early warning systems for instability in general and crises in particular lies in the recognition that it is easier to influence global events in their earliest stages, before they become more threatening and less manageable (O'Brien 2010). Such systems, although in their infancy, hold the promise of providing early enough warning so that policy makers can set, calibrate, and adjust their strategies so as to be out ahead of instability events.

The Center for International Development and Conflict Management (CIDCM) at the University of Maryland has been at the forefront of efforts to develop systematic approaches to early warning, particularly as they pertain to the identification of those countries at greatest risk for future civil conflict and instability (Hewitt 2010). Other efforts have been undertaken by the Political Instability Task Force of the US Government (Goldstone et al. 2005; Hegre and Sambanis 2006; Collier and Hoeffler 2004; Fearon and Laitin 2003; US Agency for International Development 2010).

CIDCM's approach has resulted in the production of the *Peace and Conflict Instability Ledger,* a biannual assessment of the risk of future conflict and instability for 162 countries. The ledger is based on a structural model developed from data on a set of factors representing four broad categories of state features and functions drawn from the political, economic, security, and social domains. The specific indicators are institutional consistency, economic openness, infant mortality rate, militarization, and neighborhood security. Based on the model, a risk ratio is produced, which for 2006–2008 (the most recent years for which data on conflict were available) ranked the following countries in the top 10 in terms of risk of instability: Afghanistan, Niger, Burundi, Democratic Republic of the Congo, Djibouti, Ethiopia, Mali, Nigeria, Tanzania, and Zambia (Hewitt 2010). While other approaches to early warning produce some differences in the rank ordering of specific countries, there is a good deal of convergence on membership in the top 25.[2]

Such assessments, particularly where they converge despite differences in data sources and analytic methodologies, have already begun to serve as a basis for policy decisions regarding countries and regions most in need of both development aid and regime stabilization programs. The US Agency for International Development, through its Alert List Reports (USAID 2010), has employed these rankings in making decisions about critical target countries, as well as on the types of aid packages that would be most appropriate for the specific circumstances of those societies. The Obama administration's decision to base such aid on the dual objectives of development and stabilization, rather than solely on the basis of progress toward democratization and strict support for US objectives, has the potential down the road to get us closer to a need-based foreign assistance program. Early-warning monitoring is the key to such decisions.

## INTERVENTION: CRISIS MANAGEMENT AND CONFLICT RESOLUTION

Crisis management is most often thought of as "a set of actions designed to limit or control the level or scope of violence in a given conflict" (Maoz 2004, 13). As Zartman (1997) puts it, management involves "eliminating the violent and violence-related means of pursuing the conflict, leaving it to be worked out on the purely political level." That is, management implies a temporary respite in an otherwise ongoing conflict, a neutralization of the destructive consequences of a conflict. Thought of in this way, crisis management can include any of the following activities: deterrence moves and reactions to them, arbitration, repression of the conflict, containment of the conflict, arms reductions, or any solution that involves the disputants simply arriving at a consensus based on compromise, with or without the assistance of a mediator (Burton 1990). Management nearly always involves the division of power and commonly takes place in a power-bargaining situation. Third parties acting as crisis managers often seek to slow the pace of events occurring between the conflicting parties, to be in constant communication with these parties, and to encourage them to be more flexible regarding their thoughts and actions.

Conflict resolution differs from crisis management most fundamentally in the scope of objectives exhibited by mediators and/or negotiators. Those engaging in conflict resolution are not simply concerned with controlling the negative, violent expressions and side effects of a conflictual relationship. The goal is to move beyond temporary settlements and toward eliminating the roots of the conflict between the parties, which is often an extremely difficult and labor- and time-intensive pursuit. The challenge is to get the parties to redefine or restructure their relations in such a way that their goals no longer conflict or that they realize that they each can achieve their goals without conflict with each other. If the elimination of conflict is not possible, conflict resolution initiatives may attempt to encourage parties to view conflict in an integrated or positive-sum way, rather than in a rigid zero-sum manner.

It is often the case that crisis management is a necessary step that must be taken before trying to find a more deep-seated solution to the conflict, which resolves all of the issues underlying the conflict within which the crisis occurs. Keashly and Fisher (1996) argue for an approach to mediation contingent on the level of conflict intensity at any given point. This allows for the combination of crisis management and conflict resolution objectives, depending on the stage of the conflict. They found conflict resolution in the form of consultation or problem-solving to be especially useful as a precursor or follow-up to more intrusive forms of mediation aimed at management and settlement based on compromise.

As an example of the application of this approach, many observers believe that the Obama administration would be well served if it ratcheted up its involvement in the on-again off-again negotiations between Israel and the Palestinian Authority, and placed a comprehensive peace plan on the table. This approach to conflict resolution, which would combine three types of mediation—the facilitation of the talks, formulation of possible agreements to be considered by the parties, and manipulation through the provision of tangible incentives—would constitute a major change in the US government's approach to the long-running talks, and could provide the necessary bridge between conflict and crisis management and full conflict resolution.

## POST-CONFLICT RECONSTRUCTION

Selecting from a myriad of approaches and suggestions, research reported in *Peace and Conflict 2010* (2010) as focused on four areas where actions taken during the period following active conflict can have the greatest impact.

**Sustained conflict management processes, including development aid and governance.** As noted earlier, it behooves us to think in terms of human security and the linkage between economic and social development, respect for human rights, and peace. We have already discussed the inability of wealthy nations and international and regional organizations to adequately meet the development needs of many nations. But even when we do attempt to address these needs, our efforts have not been sufficiently sustained over the long haul. Put simply, our attention wanders as we are bombarded with new needs that vie for the attention of the international community and the limited resources that have been available. As a consequence, we have been unable to devote the attention and resources that are needed at various stages of recovery from conflict. We know now that targeted international aid programs should be increased, or at least sustained, for five to ten years after the end of war and should aim at promoting social programs as well as economic growth.

Among the additional mechanisms and processes that we need to pay greater attention to as we attempt to systematically address post-conflict reconstruction, the following stand out:

**Tribunals, truth commissions, and other track II processes.** These processes have been employed with increasing success in the post–Cold War era as part of an approach to rebuilding societies and nations that are emerging from conflict. As Meernik et al. (2010) point out, nations that adopt transitional justice tend to begin the post-conflict phase in better political health than those that don't. The Obama administration has expressed strong support for the efforts of the International Criminal Court to arrest President Bashir of Sudan on war crime charges and has supported the UN tribunal that would try suspects in the 2005 assassination of former Lebanese Prime Minister Rafik al-Hariri.

**Women and the post-conflict setting.** Although women are profoundly affected by armed conflict, subject to an array of gender-based abuses both during the violence and in its aftermath, they are often excluded from formal peace-building efforts (Caprioli, Nielsen, and Hudson 2010). Yet women are critically important for the process of creating a more just, sustainable, and durable peace. In many cases, women may be the only remaining vestiges of civil society left after intense conflict. The Obama administration announced on October 26, 2010, a commitment of $44 million to "Women's Empowerment Initiatives," $17 million of which is to be spent in Afghanistan. The funding is in direct response to UN Security Council Resolution 1325, which was adopted in October 2000 and "marked the first time the Security Council required people in conflict areas to respect women's rights and to support the essential role that women play in peacemaking and ending sexual violence in conflicts." The United Nations Development Fund for Women (UNIFEM) is calling for National Action Plans to be enacted in support of 1325. The United States has not yet developed an action plan, but according to Clinton, this funding is an important step (Clinton 2010).

**Paced democratization.** We also know from the discussion above that the building of sustainable democracy is a long-term process. One of the grave dangers of imposing democratic institutions before a full societal comprehension of democratic norms and values is that certain trappings of democracy can actually make the situation worse. For example, in multi-ethnic societies, there have often been historical cultural norms that have kept various ethnic groups in rough balance and some sort of sustainable equilibrium. Imposition of elections in a society not ready for them can mean extreme ethnic voting patterns, which in turn can lead to a more forced division of society along ethnic lines than had heretofore existed, creating tensions and perhaps ultimately conflict.

This discussion has identified critical long-term issues facing President Obama and the global community, with a particular emphasis on conflict prevention, conflict resolution, and post-conflict reconstruction. The question remains whether the Obama administration or any administration has the political will to address issues of a long-term nature, where the payoffs for current investments of both financial and human capital are likely to come long after that administration has faded from the scene. Short-term pain for long-term gain is always tough and usually avoided. But without such investments by President Obama and future presidents, the world may be doomed to live in an environment that will continue to be plagued by inequities in the distributions of wealth, resources, and education, and where ethnic tensions are likely to be exploited by unscrupulous leaders for political and economic gain. This is the ultimate challenge for the Obama administration, which arrived on the international scene facing unparalleled problems and high expectations. Its accomplishments will ultimately be measured by how well it recognizes these long-term challenges and addresses them in unselfish and creative ways.

## Notes

1. Kenya's 2010 vote in support of a new constitution is a hopeful development in the attempt to address some of the structural imbalances of that political and social system and to head off future disputes.

2. Recent political instability in Tunisia and Egypt, two seemingly stable regimes, appears to be stemming from factors beyond those ordinarily tracked by the policy and academic communities. This may call for a drastic restructuring of the models on which some of these early-warning indicator systems have been based.

# CHAPTER 15

# The Obama Administration
# and Counterterrorism

*Martha Crenshaw*

Terrorism is a special challenge for the Obama administration. The president has inherited a set of policies with which he does not entirely agree and in fact some of which he campaigned against in the 2008 elections. Yet he has found it difficult to escape the legacy of his predecessor. Furthermore, dealing with terrorism is complicated because it is both a foreign and a domestic issue. As the threat has evolved since the 9/11 attacks, it is increasingly a mixed one with blurred boundaries. Attacks such as the Christmas bombing attempt in 2009 are instigated by terrorist organizations outside the country, located in Pakistan, Yemen, or other zones of conflict and instability, who seek to radicalize and re-cruit supporters from within the countries they target. Policies directed against the external threat of terrorism have troublesome domestic repercussions, such as the controversies surrounding the questions of where suspects are to be tried or imprisoned terrorists are to be held.

President Obama entered office with the declared intention of reconstitut-ing American policy toward terrorism, but he has continued many of the poli-cies of his predecessor (Lynch 2010). By the time Obama was elected, the Bush administration had already retreated from some of the most extreme positions adopted in the immediate aftermath of the 9/11 attacks. More change occurred during the eight years of the Bush administration than most observers recog-nize, and there is less difference between Obama and Bush than some Obama supporters expected. Taking a long view, the problems that Obama confronts and the constraints on his attempts to break with the past in dealing with them are familiar from previous administrations.

It has become commonplace to refer to the September 11, 2001, attacks on the United States as a watershed in American policy toward terrorism. The changes in policies and institutions caused by that unprecedentedly destructive act of terrorism were indeed substantial and transformative. However, under the Clinton administration, American policy had already begun to shift toward placing a higher priority on the threat of terrorism as well as toward increased willingness to use military force. Both change and continuity characterize American policy, and similar errors of omission as well as inconsistencies and misperceptions have persisted over time and across administrations professing quite different worldviews. The Obama administration inherited a burdensome legacy, and options for change were limited by both the historical record and the ever-present and mutating terrorist threat, which kept the issue salient in the minds of the public and Congress.

Counterterrorism policy broadly construed is an almost unbounded subject. The focus of this chapter is on the American government's recognition of terrorism as a major national security problem, including the significance of the threat of use of weapons of mass destruction or "WMD," the willingness and ability to use military force to counter the threat, respect for the rule of law and restoration of international reputation, and the organization of the government to combat terrorism.

## Recognizing Terrorism as a National Security Threat

Obama's identification of the terrorist threat from al-Qaeda as the primary determinant of his December 2009 decision to escalate combat in Afghanistan is not a departure from the past but a reflection of the Bush administration's priorities, redirected from Iraq to Afghanistan. It is both a rebuttal, in the sense of transferring attention from Iraq to Afghanistan, and a follow-on in that it cites the threat of terrorism as justification for military engagement abroad. As Lynch (2010) noted, both Bush and Obama administrations see the world as the battlefield in the struggle against terrorism. It is ironic in light of the transfer of focus to Afghanistan that in September 2006, the White House had issued a progress report enumerating a long list of successes in the "global war on terror," including the claim that Afghanistan no longer harbored al-Qaeda and had become a partner in the war on terror, and that its people were free (White House 2006b).

Since the beginnings of official American counterterrorism efforts in 1972, with the establishment of the Cabinet Committee to Combat Terrorism under President Nixon in the wake of the Munich Olympics attack, American leaders have reluctantly, even grudgingly, come to recognize that terrorism deserves a place on the national security agenda. Events have typically forced the president's hand; no president except Ronald Reagan ever wanted to put terrorism high on the national agenda or campaigned on the issue until the 2008 presidential contest, when then-candidate Obama criticized the Bush administration's violation of international norms. Terrorism is more likely to derail presidential agendas, as the Iran hostage crisis blocked Jimmy Carter's focus on human rights and aims for a second term, and the 9/11 bombings diverted George W. Bush from his initial interests in immigration reform and great power relationships.

Understandably, neither the Clinton nor the George W. Bush administration initially wished to make terrorism a policy priority (Naftali 2005; Crenshaw 2005). Only Ronald Reagan entered office with terrorism at the top of his presidential agenda, as a reaction to what he believed was the dangerous weakness of the Carter administration in dealing with the Iran hostage crisis. Perhaps in turn as a reaction to Reagan's "proactive" stance (including the 1986 bombing of Libya in retaliation for terrorism against American targets in Germany but also including the withdrawal from Lebanon as a result of the bombing of the US Marine Barracks in 1983), the George H.W. Bush administration played down the threat of terrorism, even though as vice president, Bush had chaired a commission that issued a report on terrorism in 1986, the recommendations of which in many ways foreshadowed those of the 9/11 Commission Report (*Public Report of the Vice President's Task Force on Combating Terrorism* 1986).

The Clinton White House initially wished to treat terrorism as only one among many deadly transnational or border-crossing threats, not as a tool of state aggression or a major national security problem. As the Obama administration does now, the Clinton administration rejected the assumption that terrorism reflected a "clash of civilizations." Instead, it was considered to be a shared and intractable global problem, such as transnational organized crime, epidemics, and environmental disasters. As the Obama national security strategy overview explained in 2010, the 9/11 attacks represented the dark side of a globalized world (Obama 2010a, 1).

In 1993, it was reasonable to think that the risk of terrorism was minor, but events quickly overtook policy. The opening shock for the Clinton administration was the first bombing of the World Trade Center in New York in February 1993. It was during the investigation of this attack, which led to the discovery of a failed plot against American airliners in Asia, that American authorities first discovered traces of the hand of Khalid Sheikh Mohammed and the emergence of Bin Laden's network. A few months later, in April 1993, authorities thwarted a plot to use a car-bomb to assassinate former president Bush during a visit to Kuwait, apparently as revenge for the 1991 Gulf War. Two attacks in 1995 increased apprehensiveness about terrorism, especially the fear of mass casualty attacks on civilian targets and the possibility of the use of weapons of mass destruction. The first, in March, was the sarin gas attack on the Tokyo subways by the Aum Shinrikyo cult, which killed 11 people and injured as many as 5,000. The second frightening attack, in April, was the truck bomb positioned by right-wing extremist Timothy McVeigh in front of the federal building in Oklahoma City, which left 168 people dead, including children at a day care center.

In 1995 and 1996, two bombings targeting American forces in Saudi Arabia were the most serious attacks on US interests outside the country since the 1983 bombing of the US Marines barracks in Lebanon and the 1988 midair bombing of Pan Am Flight 103. In November 1995, an attack on a Saudi National Guard office in Riyadh used by US military trainers killed five Americans. In June 1996, a truck bomb exploded at the Khobar Towers military complex in Dhahran, which housed almost 3,000 personnel participating in Joint Task Force/Southwest Asia, charged with enforcing the no-fly zone in Iraq. The explosion killed 19 US airmen, wounded 372 other US citizens, and injured more than 200 non-Americans.

In August 1998 the American embassies in Kenya and Tanzania were struck by suicide bombers deployed by the al-Qaeda organization, which by 1996 had emerged as a hostile and aggressive foe. Events then moved in a rapid progression, with the Millennium and Ahmed Ressam plots and the bombing of the USS *Cole* in Yemen in 2000. By the summer of 2000, Clinton administration officials realized that international terrorism was a threat, but awareness was unevenly distributed within the administration (Benjamin and Simon 2003).

Terrorism was not a campaign issue in the 2000 elections, and the newly elected Bush administration did not consider it a compelling risk even as warnings of imminent attack mounted through the summer of 2001. It took the appalling catastrophe of 9/11 to jolt the country and policy makers into radical action. The shift or "watershed" was not from one administration to another, more prescient one, but a reaction to crushing disaster.

In the letter of transmission accompanying the Obama administration's first National Security Strategy statement issued in May 2010, terrorism and al-Qaeda were named as threats in the opening paragraphs. However, the tone and emphasis of the Obama national security strategy differ significantly from Bush's, even taking into account the important changes between the 2003 and 2006 versions of the national strategy for combatting terrorism (White House 2003 and 2006b).

The initial post-9/11 strategy statements defined the goal of the United States in expansive terms: "a world in which terrorism does not define the daily lives of Americans and their friends" and the elimination of terrorism as a threat to the American way of life. The national interest was defined in a dual sense: opposing terrorism and preventing irresponsible states from acquiring weapons of mass destruction. This aim was defined not just as a matter of national survival and self-defense, but as a moral necessity in dealing with evil.

In 2006, spreading democracy around the world became the goal of American counterterrorism policy, based on the assumption that democracy would bring terrorism to an end. The stated intent of the United States became the defeat of violent extremism of all sorts, not just Islamist or "jihadist." The aim was to create an international environment that would be inhospitable to extremism. The ultimate goal of American policy, startling in its ambitiousness, was to end tyranny around the world.

Accordingly, the Bush administration emphasized the similarities between the war on terrorism and the Cold War. The war on terrorism was described as a "generational struggle," with victory far in the future. The adversary was equated with the historical precedents of fascism and totalitarianism. Although the war was against "terror," the enemy was an ideology, defined as a murderous movement united by an ideology of oppression, violence, and hate that wished to establish totalitarian rule over a world empire. This enemy threatened "global peace, international security and prosperity, the rising tide of democracy, and the right of all people to live without fear of indiscriminate violence" (White House 2006b).

The means of prosecuting the war on terror also changed over time, even more so than the ends. The early Bush administration statements stressed preemption as "anticipatory self-defense" and bluntly advocated unilateralism. They warned that the United States would seek international support but would act alone if American interests and "unique" responsibilities required. The strategy thus justified in advance the invasion of Iraq in the spring of 2003. It laid the grounds for the claim that the war in Iraq was an integral part of the global war on terrorism and that victory in Iraq was essential to victory over terrorism. American policy makers frequently and vehemently asserted that Saddam Hussein was linked to al-Qaeda. Preemption of emerging threats was a centerpiece of the American position.

The unilateralist approach was renewed in 2006, but its edges were softened. The revisions did not dwell on going alone but referred to "international standards" and strengthened coalitions and partnerships. For example, the Department of Defense's National Military Strategic Plan of February 2006 stressed the importance of the global coalition against terrorism and described the US as leading an international effort. Allies and partners were said to be vital to combating terrorism. The March 2006 strategy statement from the White House contained an entire chapter devoted to the subject of reinforcing alliances and preventing attacks not just against the United States, but against American friends. There was mention of "prevention" in the context of dealing with terrorist networks, not overthrowing regimes.

All the Bush administration statements of strategy called for reliance on both military force (in the short term) and diplomacy or "winning the battle of ideas" (in the long term). However, the 2006 revision stressed that "advancing democracy" was the long-term solution, whereas all other actions were short term. In 2002–2003, the short-term actions required by national strategy were summarized alliteratively as the four "D's," but omitting democracy: defeat terrorists (including cutting off their finances); deny them state support; diminish their strength by addressing "root causes"; and defend the homeland and interests abroad. In 2006, advancing democracy (absent in the earlier statements) took precedence. Next was the prevention of terrorist attacks before they occurred. Then three "D's" followed, including defeat, deny, and defend, as listed in 2002, but omitting the requirement of "diminish" by addressing "root causes." The statement claimed instead that democracy could provide a counter to the causes of terrorism, which were identified as political alienation, grievances that could be blamed on others, subcultures of conspiracy and misinformation, and an ideology that justified murder. The report dismissed other possible causes, such as poverty, hostility to US policy in Iraq, Israel-Palestine issues, and negative reactions to American efforts to prevent terrorism. The official view was that "terrorists are emboldened more by perceptions of weakness than by demonstrations of resolve." In 2006, the US also placed a strong emphasis on denying access to weapons of mass destruction, restricting the support and sanctuary of states, and preventing terrorists from gaining control of a state from which they could launch attacks on the US.

While focusing on the threat of terrorism as opposed to other threats (e.g., from rising great powers), the Obama national security strategy stresses strengthening and building America at home, particularly the economy, and renewing American leadership in the world. Rather than spreading democracy, the US is to set an example for others to follow. Yet the Obama administration's language of "disrupt, dismantle, and defeat" is reminiscent of the Bush administration's 2003 "defeat, deny, diminish" (by addressing "root causes"), and "defend." The trend in the 2006 Bush strategy toward promoting alliances and cooperation is reflected in a stress on international institutions, although the Obama administration emphasizes justice and order as important values. Clearly the Obama administration emphasizes engagement, not unilateralism, and cooperation, not preemption, but the Bush administration was also moving in this direction by 2006.

Continuing the narrowing definition of the adversary, the Obama administration sees the US as at war with a specific network, al-Qaeda and its affiliates, not with Islam or totalitarianism, and it is in order to defeat al-Qaeda, not all terrorism or all tyranny, that the war in Afghanistan is justified. This precision is a far cry from the Bush administration's early adoption of the term "Islamofascism," although in all fairness the usage was dropped quickly. President Obama took steps early in his administration to improve relations with majority Muslim states and with Muslim public opinion and to seek a resolution to the Israeli-Palestinian conflict. These efforts have not so far produced concrete results, but the tone of policy is decidedly different. For example, the Obama administration's concern with resolving the Palestinian-Israeli conflict is not explicitly justified in terms of its relevance to terrorism, but the administration does not deny that the conflict is an impediment to improved relations with majority Muslim countries.

Another point of continuity between Bush and Obama administrations is the concentration on the threat of terrorism using weapons of mass destruction, especially nuclear materials. One of the strategies prominently outlined in the 2006 Bush administration strategy was deterrence of the use of weapons of mass destruction by making it clear that the users of such methods or those who help them would face an "overwhelming response." The statements warned that the United States would ensure that both its determination and its capacity to identify the source of an attack were well known. As under the Bush administration, in the Obama administration the linkage between weapons of mass destruction and terrorism is prominently noted. weapons of mass destruction are named as the greatest threat to security, especially efforts by violent extremists to pursue nuclear weapons and international nuclear proliferation. According to the 2010 National Security Strategy (23), "The American people face no greater or more urgent danger than a terrorist attack with a nuclear weapon."

## The Use of Force to Counter Terrorism

Controversy over the appropriateness and utility of military force as a counterterrorism tool has been a constant feature of the American debate, and this issue, like the others, predates the Clinton administration. The Carter administration considered but rejected the retaliatory use of force during the Iran hostage crisis, and Reagan retaliated against Libya in 1986. Concern about committing ground troops and causing civilian casualties has always led to caution.

The Clinton administration first used force against terrorism in 1993. Convinced that the Iraqi Intelligence Service was behind a plan to assassinate former President Bush, American forces retaliated with cruise missile strikes against Baghdad's intelligence headquarters. This response established a pattern of retaliation via cruise missile or other air strike, although the administration was not always confident enough of the attackers' responsibility to carry out plans to retaliate.

After the Khobar Towers attacks in Saudi Arabia in 1996, the US was said to be actively considering a forceful response, including preemptive strikes and covert operations. However, there were a number of constraints: disagreement over attribution to Iran; need for the help of Iran's ally, Syria, in the Israeli-Palestinian peace process; and Saudi reluctance to share information or to approve of retaliation. In December, more press leaks hinted at possible military action, such as selective strikes to shut down Iran's oil export terminal at Kharg Island, destroy Iran's navy, blockade Iranian ports, impose a selective embargo on shipping, or attack Hezbollah training camps in Lebanon (Lippman and Graham 1996; Wright 1996). Still the government hesitated, and in 1997 the change of regime in Iran toward a more moderate direction (reinforced in the 2000 parliamentary elections) led the US to appear almost apologetic about prior threats of the use of force. Instead, Clinton decided to offer positive incentives: offering a possible improvement in relations in exchange for cooperation in solving the problem of the bombing. Neither threats nor inducements worked.

In response to the August 1998 bombings of the American embassies in Kenya and Tanzania, the US launched Operation Infinite Reach, which deployed cruise missiles against the al-Shifa pharmaceuticals plant in Khartoum, suspected of manufacturing chemical weapons for Bin Laden, and al-Qaeda training camps in Afghanistan (including some camps run by Pakistani intelligence agencies). American officials continued to discuss the use of force, especially against al-Qaeda targets in Afghanistan, but as in the Khobar Towers case, the constraints were too great. These barriers included the need for precision and quick timing, as well as the perception that popular support was lacking for any response beyond limited air power.

Time was a critical factor in decisions about the use of force. Launching bombers from air bases in the Middle East was politically awkward, so in order to satisfy the requirement of targeting precision, cruise missiles would have to be launched from ships. This mission required a minimum of six hours' notice. US policy then, as now, was "decapitation," pinpointing Bin Laden and top al-Qaeda leaders, who were moving targets (Gellman 2002a, b). Clinton had reportedly authorized the CIA or its local recruits to use lethal military force against Bin Laden and associates, to the extent of shooting down civilian aircraft should he attempt to leave Afghanistan. Indeed, in December 1998 CIA director George Tenet issued a written "declaration of war" against Bin Laden.

Not surprisingly, the issue of using ground troops was contentious. The Joint Chiefs opposed using special forces in a limited military operation, rejecting such proposals from Clinton's advisers as too risky and "naïve." Even had the risks been acceptable, a raid by delta force, for example, would have taken 12–14 hours' advance notice. The Clinton administration did not think that the alternative, a major combat commitment that the military would have supported, would be accepted by the public. The provocation simply was not great enough.

The shock of 9/11 led quickly to the invasion of Afghanistan. It is important to recall that after 1998, the Clinton and then the Bush administrations had repeatedly asked the Taliban to turn over Bin Laden for prosecution. The United Nations had agreed on sanctions against the regime. Even after 9/11, the United States repeatedly warned Mullah Omar that he had a last clear chance to avert military action (Crenshaw 2003). In contrast, the Bush administration justified the invasion of Iraq as preemption of Iraqi use of weapons of mass destruction. Although it is impossible to imagine such a decision without the catalyst of 9/11, the threat of terrorism was peripheral to the decision except as it justified preemption across the board. Obama's escalation of combat in Afghanistan in 2009–2010 returned to the original rationale for intervention as an explicit response to terrorism.

In the context of the war in Afghanistan aimed at stopping the al-Qaeda threat, the use of drones is frequently cited as characteristic of the Obama administration (Mayer 2009). The development of unmanned aerial vehicles (UAVs) was initiated under the Clinton administration (Gellman 2001; Bovard 2003). Drones were used successfully for surveillance in the Balkans conflicts of the 1990s. In the spring of 2000, Clinton's national security team, under pressure from the counterterrorism "czar" Richard Clarke, pushed for arming Predator drones with the lightweight Hellfire missiles that were deployed on helicopters. Video technology had improved to the extent that users could feel reasonably confident about the reliability of targeting. The Air Force and the CIA opposed arming the drones, while the Joint Staff supported the idea. A trial phase of CIA deployment of unarmed drones in Afghanistan was conducted in September and October from a secret base in Uzbekistan, but the program was set back when one crashed in early October. At this time drones were still thought of primarily in terms of surveillance: they would identify a target for a subsequent cruise missile attack. In typical bureaucratic politics fashion, the Air Force and the CIA argued over which agency would pay for the program, although both agencies felt that the rival National Security Council staff was out of line in trying to direct the effort. The program was shut down as the Clinton administration left office (a further consideration was bad winter weather in Afghanistan).

Richard Clarke, who made the transition to the Bush administration, urged National Security Adviser Condoleeza Rice to restart the armed drone program but she was hesitant. However, tests were conducted, and on February 16, 2001, a Hellfire missile was successfully fired from the Predator. Ironic in light of present circumstances is the worry at the time that the missiles might not be sufficiently lethal and would merely alert Bin Laden to the fact that he was under surveillance. At a meeting on September 4, 2001, CIA Chief George Tenet argued that the DOD rather than the CIA should operate the armed Predators, but the decision to deploy was still deferred.

After 9/11 both the CIA and the military were authorized to use drones, the DOD within combat zones and the CIA elsewhere for purposes of "anticipatory self-defense." In 2002, an al-Qaeda operative in Yemen was killed in a Predator strike, the first known targeted killing outside a conflict area. This policy has endured, and the use of drones outside war zones has escalated sharply. The New America Foundation estimates that there were 9 drone attacks in Pakistan in the period 2004–2007, 34 in 2008, 53 in 2009, and 104 as of November 22, 2010 (New America Foundation 2010). Apparently the United States has also authorized attacks in Yemen, specifically against Anwar al-Awlaki, an American citizen suspected of having directed or inspired a series of unsuccessful plots against American territory.

## Values and the Rule of Law

In March 2010, State Department Coordinator for Counterterrorism Daniel Benjamin declared (Benjamin 2010):

> Our approach recognizes that our counterterrorism efforts can best succeed when they make central respect for human rights and the rule of law. Because as President Obama has said from the outset, there should be no tradeoff between our security and our values. Indeed, in light of what we know about radicalization, it is clear that navigating by our values is an essential part of a successful counterterrorism effort. We have moved to rectify past excesses of the past few years by working to close the prison at Guantánamo Bay, by forbidding enhanced interrogation techniques, and by eliminating secret detention sites.

Similarly, in August 2009, John Brennan, the president's assistant for homeland security and counterterrorism, emphasized that President Obama rejected the "false choice" between security and civil liberties (Brennan 2009).

Adhering to the rule of law and democratic norms in counterterrorism conforms to the Obama administration's chief national security objective of creating an example at home of promoting democratic values rather than forcibly establishing democracy and ending tyranny abroad. Yet the administration's record is contradictory. The government has been unable to close the prison at Guantánamo or transfer trials to civilian courts, instead continuing reliance on military commissions while trying to move some trials to federal court. Harsh interrogation techniques and secret prisons were immediately outlawed by executive order, although the Bush administration had already moved in this direction. However, both the principle and the practice of indefinite detention without trial of terrorist suspects have been upheld. Domestic political considerations and the Bush administration legacy are serious impediments to change. The inadmissibility of evidence obtained under torture in the past is only part of the problem. Critics of the administration charge that civilian courts are insufficiently rigorous, and some believe that terrorist suspects should not be accorded the same constitutional rights as others detained and prosecuted in the criminal justice system. Partisan politics pervades the issue. Local political objections to trying Khalid Sheikh Mohammed in New York derailed the administration's plans. Human Rights Watch issued an end-of-first-year report card that expressed disappointment in the administration's record on restoring the rule of law (Human Rights Watch 2010).

On the international level, both the press and the United Nations are critical of the reliance on targeted killings via the deployment of drones outside conflict zones (Mayer 2009; United Nations 2010). The UN report did not find the administration's general self-defense justification satisfactory. The report cited as problematic lack of definition of the scope of the conflict, absence of criteria for selecting targets, failure to specify safeguards for ensuring legality and accuracy, and lack of accountability. In light of the Obama administration's determination to restore the American reputation in the eyes of Muslims, it has to be assumed that the administration calculates that the national security benefit of the practice outweighs the legal as well as the political costs, because the drone attacks in Pakistan have generated massive ill will among the Pakistani public.

## THE ORGANIZATION OF THE GOVERNMENT FOR THE CONDUCT OF COUNTERTERRORISM

Controversy and confusion over how best to organize the government bureaucracy to combat terrorism have been familiar refrains in the policy debate since the 1970s. From the early years, rivalries persisted among the State Department, CIA, FBI, and National Security Council over which was to be the "lead agency" in dealing with terrorism (Crenshaw 2001). Despite periodic reforms of the counterterrorism bureaucracy, with the most ambitious and comprehensive reorganization following the recommendations of the 9/11 Commission, the Obama administration is still struggling for clarity, transparency, and efficiency.

The Bush administration established the National Counterterrorism Center (NCTC) in 2004 to coordinate the work of the many intelligence agencies with terrorism portfolios, including the CIA as well as the State Department and the National Security Agency. The NCTC proved to be less than successful in integrating and directing a national effort, according to the Project on National Security Reform, a nonpartisan research and policy organization in Washington, financed by Congress, which issued a critical report in February 2010. Longstanding tensions between the NCTC, the State Department, and the CIA remained unresolved. The decision-making process remains decentralized, which dilutes responsibility and accountability.

The new agency on the domestic side, the Department of Homeland Security, also struggled to consolidate its authority. In February 2010, the department issued the first Quadrennial Homeland Security Review, which was mandated by Congress in 2007. In general, the report was well received even by conservatives (Hsu 2010).

In May 2010, the unclassified version of a Senate Intelligence Committee report summarizing its investigation of the December 2009 "Christmas bombing" attempt noted systemic failures across the entire intelligence community. The committee cited the NCTC specifically as inadequately organized to carry out its mission, and it expressed disappointment in the lack of progress in counterterrorism implementation nine years after the 9/11 attacks. Whether or not the decision was related to the report, the president promptly fired the director of national intelligence.

## LOOKING AHEAD

The Obama administration's aspirations for counterterrorism policy are more novel than the accomplishment. His framing of policy in terms of repudiation of a generalized war on terror, rejection of the idea that security requires weakening of legal and moral standards, and positive outreach to Muslims was a break with the past. However, the implementation of these aims so far has not lived up to promise. It has proved difficult to undo the domestic security apparatus in terms of both structure and practice. Many of these frustrations are to be expected, because every president who had to deal with the threat of terrorism has confronted them. However, the emphasis on military force as a solution to international terrorism has not been explained in terms that make it a logical means to the ends the administration has prescribed.

The road ahead involves complex and daunting challenges. One is how to deal with terrorist organizations, now known as "violent extremist organizations," which are located in fragile states disrupted by serious civil conflict rooted in deep socioeconomic, ethnic, and religious divisions, such as Pakistan, Somalia, and Yemen. These groups, principally al-Qaeda and its affiliates, threaten the stability of the states where they are based as well as the security of the United States. The use of military force might defeat the central core of such an organization, but it might also further destabilize already weak regimes and further radicalize audiences who identify with jihadist claims and aspirations. In addition, the Obama administration's counterterrorism policy is inextricably tied to the conduct of the long war in Afghanistan. The rationale for American involvement is to remove forever a threat from a resurgent al-Qaeda. Thus the ending of that war depends on the success of counterterrorism.

# CHAPTER 16

# Obama's Use of Prerogative Powers in the War on Terrorism

*Richard M. Pious*

President Obama laid out much of the strategy in the struggle against terrorists in a speech at the National Archives Museum on May 21, 2009: "For the first time since 2002, we are providing the necessary resources and strategic direction to take the fight to the extremists who attacked us on 9/11 in Afghanistan and Pakistan." Obama claimed that the decisions of his predecessor had taken the nation "off course" and promised that he would deal with the terrorism threat "with an abiding confidence in the rule of law and due process; in checks and balances and accountability." He noted that he had banned "enhanced interrogation" techniques, ordered the closing of the prison camp at Guantánamo and a review of all pending cases there (involving 240 people), and took credit for developing due-process standards to apply to those the government would wish to detain indefinitely. This chapter presents an in-depth analysis of President Obama's use of prerogative powers within the war on terrorism, whereas Martha Crenshaw's Chapter 15, "The Obama Administration and Counterterrrorism," outlines the general counterterrorism policy of the Obama administration.

A longer version of this article was published in *Presidential Studies Quarterly*, Vol. 41, No. 2, June 2011.

Obama's speech raises the question of whether his policies involved fundamental changes from those of the Bush administration. John Brennan (an assistant to former President George W. Bush) called Obama's decisions "Bush's third term." Bush's CIA director, General Michael Hayden, praised Obama's "continuity" of policy, observing "to President Obama's credit, he has used many of the tools that we used to continue to take the fight to the enemy." He cited renditions to other nations for interrogation, indefinite detention of detainees, limited definition of habeas corpus rights, use of military commissions, and reliance on state secrets defenses in court proceedings (Meyers 2010).

But Vice President Cheney criticized the Obama administration for ending "enhanced interrogation techniques," claiming that they had averted serious terrorist plots. By closing Guantánamo, Cheney observed that "terrorists might soon be relocating" into several states, and that would "be cause for great danger and regret" (Cheney 2009a).

## PREROGATIVE CLAIMS

In some respects Obama chose continuity, and in others he chose significant change in *policy*. But irrespective of policy changes, Obama has not yielded any grounds in his claims of constitutional *prerogatives*, and in some respects he has gone even farther in than his predecessors.

### Detentions

President Obama came into office having voiced approval of a 2008 Supreme Court decision granting habeas corpus rights to detainees at Guantánamo (*Boumediene v. Bush*, 128 S. Ct. 2229) and having championed due process in detainee proceedings. But once in office, Obama found the situation to be complicated: after the *Boumediene* decision, 22 detainees had sued for habeas corpus and had been released by federal district courts. Obama, on January 22, 2009, issued Executive Order No. 13493, "Review of Detention Policy Options," which created a special interagency task force to identify the options for disposition of individuals captured in connection with armed conflicts and counterterrorism operations. On May 20, 2009, Obama told representatives from some human rights organizations that he was thinking about creating a "preventive detention system" on a legal basis to hold indefinitely 75 detainees held at Guantánamo that presented a threat to national security but could not be tried (Stolberg 2009b). Obama would not seek congressional authorization, but would rely on his constitutional powers as commander-in-chief, upholding the laws of war, to continue with indefinite detention.

After the *Boumediene* decision, the Pentagon had sent some prisoners to Bagram Air Force Base in Afghanistan. The Combat Status Review Tribunals that had been put in place in Guantánamo as a result of the 2006 Supreme Court decision in *Hamdan v. Rumsfeld* (127 S. Ct. 2749) had not reviewed these prisoners.

After *Boumediene* their relatives also began filing habeas corpus petitions in the federal courts. Lawyers in Obama's Department of Justice filed briefs in 2009, *al-Maqaleh v. Gates* (U.S.D.C. Civil Action No. 06-1669), claiming that those detained at Bagram had no habeas corpus rights, and these briefs recognized no limit on the categories of detainees that would be denied these rights. Instead, the briefs claimed that the president could detain indefinitely members of al-Qaeda, the Taliban, "associated forces," and those who "substantially support" those groups—wherever they might be located, which meant that the government claimed a presidential "police power" that could operate far from any battlefield and that could allow for indefinite detentions without prospect of trial for anyone, anywhere, on suspicion of providing material support to terrorists.

In another 2009 case, *Gherebi v. Obama* (609 F. Supp. 2nd. 43), the administration changed its position slightly. In its Respondent's Memorandum of March 13, 2009, it argued that authority for indefinite detention is not based on the commander-in-chief clause (as Bush's Department of Justice had argued), but rather on the congressional Authorization for the Use of Military Force (AUMF) and on the laws of war. The administration filed a brief arguing that Bagram was a theater of war, and that to require status determination tribunals or other legal procedures would "divert the military's attention and resources at a critical time for operations in Afghanistan" (Gerstein 2009a).

Federal District Court Judge Bates rejected these arguments in *al-Maqaleh*. For Bates, although *Boumediene* applied only to detainees at Guantánamo, there was a principle at stake that had to be defended: the judiciary and not the executive decides when habeas corpus protections can be invoked. And the key factor in that decision for Bates was the question—as it had been for the Supreme Court in *Boumediene*—of "indefinite Executive detention without judicial oversight." Bates went further and ruled that the congressional statute suspending habeas corpus for detainees who were unlawful combatants was unconstitutional. Thereafter the Obama administration issued new guidelines providing detainees at Bagram with military-appointed representatives (not lawyers) who could challenge their detentions.

In some cases the Department of Justice has taken positions in favor of indefinite detention that have been overturned by federal courts. Razak-al-Ginco, detained at Guantánamo, had been a member of al-Qaeda and had helped the Taliban in Afghanistan. But videos from an al-Qaeda safe house showed that Razak had been tortured by al-Qaeda for several months, evidence that backed his assertion that he had cut ties with the group before being detained by American forces. The government claimed that he still had ties to his torturers, which a US District judge in 2009 in *Razak v. Obama* (626 F. Supp. 2nd 123) characterized as "a position that defies common sense" in ordering Razak's release.

*Enhanced Interrogation and Torture*

Throughout the Bush presidency, "enhanced techniques" to interrogate detainees were authorized by the president and implemented by orders of the Secretary of Defense. In three cases these involved "waterboarding" high-value detainees; in many cases these involved sensory deprivations or painful enhancements (cold conditions, painful noises, etc.) or threats of harm (mock executions, brandishing guns and power drills). Bush administration officials denied these actions constituted torture, distinguishing between actions that would cause permanent injury and those that would cause temporary suffering, with only the latter supposedly authorized.

In his third day in the White House, Obama signed Executive Order 13491: "Ensuring Lawful Interrogations," which revoked Bush Executive Order 13440 that had authorized "enhanced techniques." Obama promulgated standards and practices that would be consistent with statutes and international conventions: the Detainee Treatment Act (banning torture of detainees), the Anti-Torture Statute (making torture a criminal offense), and Article 3 of the Geneva Conventions (dealing with treatment of combatants). His order required that detainees "shall in all circumstances be treated humanely and shall not be subjected to violence to life and person (including murder of all kinds, mutilation, cruel treatment, and torture), nor to outrages upon personal dignity (including humiliating and degrading treatment)...." It also required the CIA to close "as expeditiously as possible" detention facilities that it operated. Obama centralized decisions about interrogation within the White House: he created a unit of the National Security Council called the High-Value Detainee Interrogation Group (HIG) to supervise interrogations that had previously been done by the CIA. The FBI (which had objected to "enhanced measures" during the Bush administration) would now take the lead role in the interrogations, a step that would minimize abuses.

Obama also issued a directive to officials indicating that they could not rely on any memoranda prepared during the Bush administration to justify interrogation methods, and that banned coercive interrogation. CIA Director Leon Panetta stated that waterboarding is torture and prohibited it. The CIA indicated it would go back to traditional methods, i.e., "dialog," without using physical force. It also stopped relying on contractors (such as ex-military psychologists) to handle interrogations, Panetta provided legal cover for interrogators involved in past practices when he circulated the following statement to agency employees: "Officers who act on guidance from the Department of Justice—or acted on such guidance previously—should not be investigated, let alone punished. This is what fairness and wisdom require" (Shane 2009). Panetta's statement glossed over the fact that many of the interrogations occurred before the Department of Justice justified interrogation tactics in an August 2002 memorandum.

The administration came under heavy criticism for its changed positions, most notably from Vice President Cheney, who claimed that these techniques had provided invaluable information, claiming they "were absolutely essential in saving thousands of American lives, in preventing further attacks against the United States, in giving us the intelligence we needed to go find al-Qaeda, to find their camps, to find out how they were being financed" (Cheney 2009b). Cheney strongly defended the use of waterboarding, explaining that the Justice

Department lawyers had been told to write their legal opinions after the White House had decided on its use—in effect admitting to compromising the professionalism of department lawyers (Cheney 2009c). The Obama administration argued not only that torture was unconstitutional and illegal, but also that it didn't work. General David Petraeus observed that whenever the US took these measures, "we end up paying a price for it ultimately" because the enemy uses these actions to inflame and then recruit local populations (Petraeus 2010). FBI director Robert Mueller asserted that he didn't believe that "intelligence gleaned from abusive interrogation techniques had disrupted any attacks on America" (Siebel and Strobel 2009).

Yet Obama authorized a Task Force on interrogation policies to recommend interrogation techniques for the CIA that might go beyond the limitations imposed on the military. The Pentagon's Joint Special Operations Command (JSOC) still operates a detention facility, has maintained secrecy about its activities, and has denied access to the Red Cross, as Obama's Executive Order seemed to require (Rubin 2009).

*Extraordinary Renditions*

Obama opposed extraordinary renditions (sending detainees to other countries) because detainees had been turned over to foreign governments that used torture. He issued an Executive Order ending the practice. Yet his administration shielded the Bush administration from civil liability for its renditions. Two cases involved Binyam Mohamed, an Ethiopian who had been subjected to extraordinary renditions and who claimed he had been tortured in CIA-operated facilities in Afghanistan, Pakistan, and Morocco. According to court papers his lawyers filed, he was "routinely beaten, suffering broken bones and, on occasion, loss of consciousness. His clothes were cut off with a scalpel and the same scalpel was then used to make incisions on his body, including his penis" (Horton 2009). American authorities threatened to end cooperation with Britain in counterterrorism cases if British intelligence authorities provided the American or British courts with information about Mohamed's treatment. The other case involved four detainees (Mohamed among them) incarcerated in Guantánamo, who sued a subsidiary of Boeing (Jeppesen Dataplan, Inc.) for arranging flights in the "extraordinary rendition" program. The government argued that Jeppesen's role was a state secret, even though it had already been reported in the media and been a subject of discussion by Boeing shareholders. The government's secrets claim and its motion to dismiss the case were upheld by the court of appeals in 2010 in *Mohamed et. al. v. Jeppesen Dataplan* (539 F. Supp. 2d 1128).

Although Obama's Executive Order banned extraordinary renditions, there may be a loophole, as CIA detention facilities that must be closed "do not refer to facilities used only to hold people on a short-term, transitory basis." Renditions will be continued, although the administration has developed guidelines based on Obama's order that they "do not result in the transfer of individuals to other nations to face torture," to ensure that prisoners will not be turned over if there is a likelihood that they will be subject to abusive treatment.

*Trials of Detainees*

On November 13, 2001, President Bush issued "Military Order on Detention, Treatment and Trial of Certain Non-Citizens in the War Against Terrorism," (66 *Fed. Reg.* 57831, 2001). Based on his power as commander in chief, it mandated the establishment of military tribunals (either inside or outside US territory), to be implemented subsequently through regulations developed by the Pentagon. Those subject to the tribunals, at the discretion of the president, would be any non-citizen of the US (including a resident alien) who was a member of al-Qaeda, involved in "acts of international terrorism," or had "knowingly harbored" others in the first two categories. US citizens would not be subject to their jurisdiction. Decisions would not be reviewable by federal courts.

The administration claimed the president had constitutional authority to establish such commissions by fusing his power as commander in chief with his oath of office to defend the Constitution. The government also cited the Authorization for the Use of Military Force (AUMF) in which Congress had authorized the president "to use all necessary and appropriate force" against 9/11 terrorists (P.L. 107-40 sec. 2a, 2001). The administration also pointed out that the Articles of War (1920), the Uniform Code of Military Justice (1950), and the War Crimes Act (1996) all refer to the establishment of military tribunals by the president. But Congress had specifically provided in Section 36 of the UCMJ that such tribunals "may not be contrary to or inconsistent with the UCMJ."

In 2004 in *Rasul v. Bush* (542 U.S. 466) Justice Stevens held that in Guantánamo the United States exercises plenary and exclusive jurisdiction, although not ultimate sovereignty, and so the petitioners had the right to habeas corpus review based on a statute granting review. (He also held that in the absence of such a congressional statute, alien detainees would have had no constitutional right to such review.) In 2006 in *Hamdan v. Rumsfeld* (126. S. Ct. 2749), the Supreme Court ruled that the president had authority granted by Congress to establish military commissions. The court ruled that trials in civilian courts were not required for detainees, and none of the justices insisted on closure of Guantánamo or other military detention facilities. The court's decision was not a complete victory for the government, because it then considered and rejected many of the procedures for the commissions established by the president, requiring the Pentagon to make significant changes in its initial reviews of the status of the detainees.

The Obama administration has upended much of the Bush administration's policy, but it has done so not by seeking to put the detention regime on a statutory basis, but rather by relying on presidential prerogative power. In 2009, Obama signed Executive Order 13492, creating a Guantánamo Review Task Force to start planning to shut down the facility "no later than one year from the date of this order." The administration planned to transfer detainees to one of three venues: their home countries (for release or trial), military brigs located in the United States in preparation for regular courts martial, or the federal court jails in preparation for trials in district courts on criminal charges.

But it was difficult to close Guantánamo, and both an interim deadline to report after six months and the final deadline in the Executive Order were not met. Even so, by the deadline the administration managed to release 42 detainees to other countries, and 103 of those still held had been cleared for release by an interagency task force, although the task force did classify at least 50 detainees to be held indefinitely without trial under the laws of war. Defense Department officials were also at work on revisions to the Military Commission procedures as well as a better process to determine whom the commissions would try and who would be tried by federal courts.

The American Bar Association and other professional groups concerned with the rule of law applauded the decision of the administration to move trials to federal courts. The Bush administration, after all, had prosecuted many terrorists in courts rather than use tribunals; it had only convicted three through tribunals, but more than 200 in federal district courts, for an 88.2 percent conviction rate (Center on Law and Security 2009). Before 9/11, it was routine for terrorists to be tried for criminal acts in federal courts, and thus there had never been a need for Guantánamo or the military tribunals. These had included suspects involved in bombings in the World Trade Center in 1995, and in bombings of American embassies in Africa in 1998.

The president and his opponents remained deadlocked and in a fierce debate about the closing of Guantánamo and transfers to courts. Congress passed legislation to modify some of Obama's policies: the National Defense Authorization Act of 2010 (P.L. 111-84) allowed the government to transfer detainees to the US, but it required the administration to provide Congress with 15 days' notice before ordering release, and to certify that the transfer did not present a security risk. And it passed a provision preventing any cleared prisoner awaiting transfer to another nation from being housed in the US mainland. The act also amended the Military Commissions Act of 2006 to revive new trials of detainees under revised evidentiary rules.

*Extra-Judicial Process*

The use of extra-judicial process, otherwise known as "executive action" or "termination with extreme prejudice" or "wet operations" or "targeted killing" is shrouded in secrecy. After CIA assassination attempts against foreign leaders were investigation by several congressional committees, President Ford in 1975 prohibited US government assassination attempts in Executive Order 11905.

During the Bush administration leaders of terrorist organizations were considered to be enemy combatants and were targeted in both Afghanistan and Pakistan. President Bush ordered Osama Bin Laden taken "dead or alive" and the CIA's counterterrorism chief was quoted by an agent as ordering, "Capture Bin Laden, kill him and bring his head back in a box on dry ice" (Stein 2009). In his 2003 State of the Union Address Bush boasted: "All told, more than 3,000 suspected terrorists have been arrested in many countries. Many others have met a different fate. Let's put it this way—they are no longer a problem to the United States and our friends and allies." Bush's counterterrorism adviser

Frances Townsend told Wolf Blitzer in a television interview that government agencies were authorized to kill "less than a hundred" people "who have blood on their hands or are plotting the death and destruction of Americans or American interests around the world" (Stein 2009).

The Obama administration has defended targeted killings—even expanding such actions so that they might be used against American citizens. The Joint Special Operations Command had a list of targets, which as of spring 2010 included three Americans. Director of National Intelligence Dennis C. Blair testified at a congressional hearing in February 2010 that the government may use lethal force against Americans: "We target them for taking action that threatens Americans" (Priest 2010). The State Department's legal adviser, Harold Koh, stated that it was "the considered view of this administration" that drone attacks "comply with all applicable law, including the laws of war" (Koh 2010). The Obama administration has defended the policy in federal court in a case brought by Nasser al-Awlaki, the father of the Islamist cleric Anwar al-Awlaki (born in New Mexico). Awlaki preaches hatred of America from his headquarters in Yemen, and had been in contact via e-mail with Major Nidal Hassan, who allegedly killed 12 soldiers and one civilian at Fort Hood. The administration cited "state secrets" and moved for dismissal of Awlaki's lawsuit, in effect defending a policy that allows the president to order a death sentence on an American citizen who has not been charged or indicted for a crime, and allows the president to keep his reasoning secret, and do so without any judicial review of his decision.

## State Secrets

In some cases in which the government is a defendant in a civil suit, it claims the right to protect state secrets, and also claims that it alone must determine the need, and that the courts must defer when the case involves "a secret of the highest order" (*United States v. Reynolds,* 345 U.S. 1, 1953). Unlike the balancing tests used for executive privilege claims in criminal cases (in which the need of the grand jury or the prosecutors for "every person's evidence" is weighed against the need of the executive for confidentiality), when state secrets privilege is claimed, it prevails if the court is satisfied that such secrets are at stake. In *Reynolds,* Justice Vinson ruled that the lawsuit would then proceed as if the evidence sought by the plaintiffs had never existed.

State secrets doctrine has been used by both the Bush and Obama administrations to protect the government against the international fallout that would ensue if the government were required to provide evidence about renditions and torture of detainees. In *El-Masri v. United States,* a federal district court in 2007 dismissed a case brought by Khaled El-Masri, a German citizen of Lebanese descent who alleged that while traveling in Macedonia he was detained by Macedonian law enforcement officials and then handed over to CIA operatives, who flew him to an agency detention facility near Kabul, Afghanistan. He claimed that he was held against his will, beaten, drugged, bound, and blindfolded during transport; confined in a small, unsanitary cell; interrogated several times;

and prevented from communicating with anyone outside the detention facility, including his family or the German government. He was eventually released from custody in Albania. El-Masri sued then-CIA director George Tenet and 10 unnamed employees of the CIA. The Court of Appeals in 2007 upheld the government's claim of state secrets in dismissing the case (479 F.3d 296; 552 U.S. 947).

During the presidential campaign, Obama indicated that he would limit the use of state secret privilege. After Obama took office, Attorney General Eric Holder announced that he would review every pending court case in which the Bush administration had asserted state secrets. But Holder, in an April 7, 2009, interview with CBS News Anchor Katie Couric, claimed, "On the basis of the two, three cases that we've had to review so far—I think that the invocation of the doctrine was correct." The Obama administration then disappointed its civil libertarian constituencies by expanding the doctrine. In *Mohammed et. al. v. Jeppesen Data Plan,* Obama's Department of Justice took state secret doctrine further than any administration had done before: it argued that "the very subject matter" was entitled to a presumption of state secret privilege, and that any information that the government had classified as "top secret" was entitled to the privilege. The Court of Appeals rejected this assertion, and in its instructions to the district court it ordered that the case proceed, and that classified information would not necessarily be considered a state secret until the court had examined it *in camera* and made its own determination. The government would have to assert the privilege against requests for specific secrets, and only if the court determined (a) that evidence was privileged *and* (b) that it was indispensable to the suit, could the court then dismiss the case—which eventually a court of appeals did.

In 2009 in *Al-Haramain v. Obama,* the Obama administration claimed (Motion 09-15266) that state secret privilege was rooted in the constitutional responsibilities of the presidency and was not just a common-law privilege that could be altered by Congress. For the first time, a president had tied the privilege to presidential prerogative powers. The Justice Department lawyers again affirmed that the entire case should be dismissed if a state secret (as determined by the president) was involved, rather than the narrower view that courts should simply exclude state secrets from a trial. In 2009 in a summary motion to dismiss in *Jewel v. NSA* (No. C:08-cv-4373-VRW), the Obama administration adopted the Bush position that courts could not judge the legality of NSA wiretapping or an NSA dragnet surveillance program because they involved state secrets.

Obama's position led Senate Judiciary Committee Chair Patrick Leahy to introduce the State Secrets Protection Act in the Senate (a similar bill was introduced in the House). It would require judges to inspect all disputed evidence *in camera,* rather than rely on government claims, affidavits, or classifications. The White House responded by seeking to work with Congress to fashion a compromise, and Attorney General Holder issued new guidelines for invoking state secrets: Agencies would now submit an "evidentiary memorandum" to the Department of Justice, which would trigger a high-level review process to see if release would cause "significant harm" to national security. The Department of Justice would try not to move to dismiss the entire case. The guidelines provided that state secrets could not be claimed if the motive was to "conceal violations of the law, inefficiency or administrative error" or to avoid "embarrassment" (Holder 2009a).

## Defending Bush Administration Officials

Attorney General Eric Holder in his confirmation hearings talked of not wishing to "criminalize policy differences" when asked if he would investigate waterboarding and warrantless searches in the prior administration. Obama himself talked of not wanting CIA employees "to suddenly feel like they've got to spend all their time looking over their shoulders and lawyering up" (Lithwick 2009). Obama's Department of Justice defended Bush administration officials against civil suits brought by detainees. One case involved Jose Padilla, arrested in Chicago and charged with plotting to blow up soft targets in the US. Padilla was imprisoned in a Navy brig in Charleston, South Carolina, before being transferred in 2006 to civilian custody (where he was tried and eventually convicted). Padilla brought suit against Bush administration lawyer John C. Yoo, claiming that Yoo's legal opinions encouraged his military jailors to subject him to unlawful interrogation threats and sensory deprivation. Obama's Justice Department filed an amicus brief asking the federal judge handling the case to dismiss, on the grounds that Yoo had absolute immunity from suit. Judge Jeffrey White (a Bush appointee) denied in part Yoo's motion to dismiss in 2009 in *Padilla v. Yoo* (633 F. Supp. 2nd 1005). The court accepted jurisdiction to try Padilla's claims that he was imprisoned without charge, without the ability to defend himself, without the ability to challenge the conditions of his confinement, and that he had suffered gross physical and psychological abuse upon the orders of high-ranking government officials.

A similar pattern of support holds for the possibility of criminal prosecutions. Obama's CIA director Leon Panetta has argued that agents acting in accordance with Bush administration legal opinions should not face any consequences: "I would not support, obviously, an investigation or a prosecution of those individuals. I think they did their job, they did it pursuant to the guidance that was provided them, whether you agreed or disagreed with it" (Miller 2009). President Obama has stated that he would not prosecute government agents who had interrogated detainees. "This is a time for reflection, not retribution," he said, adding "nothing will be gained by spending our time and energy laying blame for the past" (Perrine and Stern 2009).

The Obama administration has not even embraced Senator Patrick Leahy's "middle ground" of constituting a "truth commission." As outlined by Leahy, such a commission would not prosecute high-level Bush administration officials, but would have the power to subpoena testimony and offer immunity from prosecution. At a news conference, President Obama deflected a question about the commission, saying, "I'm more interested in looking forward than I am in looking backwards." (Obama 2009d)

## Obama's Choice

What accounts for Obama's choices? Below are some lines of inquiry that may shed some light on his decisions.

### Personality and Leadership

Stephen Wayne in Chapter 4, "Obama's Personality and Performance," and Garry Wills argue that Obama's political style has always involved being placatory and conciliatory (Wills 2010). From his editorship of the *Harvard Law Review* to the White House, he claims that Obama has always taken ideas from all sides, much as Franklin Roosevelt did. And so on some policies he would be hawkish (escalate in Afghan/Pakistan, step-up drone attacks, order extra-judicial killing) and in some dovish (ban torture, order the closing of Guantánamo) depending on the merits as he assessed them. But attempting to placate and to be conciliatory is more about Obama's *style* and personality than it is about his *substance*. Obama is like George W. Bush, proposing huge new programs in one area after another: he has piled many far-reaching "yes we can" proposals onto the national agenda. This disjunction between style and substance might help explain why Obama tends to pull back from a highly confrontational approach in the war on terrorism, but it also might explain why expanded claims to prerogative powers are buried deep inside the legal briefs and motions filed by administration lawyers.

### Regime, Party, and Public Opinion

Much of Obama's decision-making can be explained in terms of presidential calculations. He offers up the closing of Guantánamo and what seems to be an end to abusive interrogation to protect his reputation on his left flank, and relies on state secrets and protection of former officials to protect his right flank. As the right-wing tendencies in American politics grew stronger during his first two years, so did his positioning on terrorism issues move rightward.

One might have expected Obama in 2009 to repudiate Bush's prerogative claims and to make gestures toward accountability. Yet to do so would have positioned him too far to the left (albeit at a centrist position within his own party). He seems instead to have moved toward the center from the left as he moved from contender to nominee to president. The reasoning might have been that with the left wing of his party having no place to go, a centrist position could retain support on the left while avoiding vulnerability on the right. To placate the left, he could offer tidbits: promises to close Guantánamo, administrative reorganization in DOJ to monitor state secret claims, release of DOJ memos, new guidelines involving military tribunals. Meanwhile, by adopting a "soft prerogative" style (claim to collaborate with Congress but always keep prerogative power in reserve), he could work with Congress on new framework legislation that would allow him to rely on both prerogative power and legislative delegations.

But Obama was walking on eggshellss and not on water. Even as he moved to the center, he remained out of sync with a public sharply divided along partisan lines on key issues. In a Pew poll (February 28, 2009), when asked if torture of suspected terrorists was often or sometimes justified, 65 percent of Republicans agreed, compared with 44 percent of independents and 29 percent of Democrats. Similarly a Fox News/Opinion Dynamics poll (with data from January 10–12, 2009) claimed that almost half of Americans thought torture had saved lives since the 9/11 attacks. Public opinion seemed to move (albeit slowly) away from due-process protections. In an AP-GFK poll (with data from May 28–June 1 2009), 52 percent said torture could be justified sometimes, with 66 percent of Republicans and 33 percent of Democrats agreeing. In the same poll, the public was evenly divided on closing Guantánamo, with a majority of Republicans disagreeing and a majority of Democrats agreeing. Obama's position in the polls on terrorism deteriorated in fall 2009, much as his overall standing diminished, with the "Christmas Bomber" incident precipitating a serious slide for the Democratic party. In a Greenberg Quinlan Rossner Research/Democracy Corps poll (with data from February 20, 2010), Republicans took a lead, 50–33, on the question of which party did a better job on national security, and 51 percent of the public disapproved of the way the Obama administration interrogated and prosecuted terror suspects, with independents favoring the Republicans 56–20 on this issue. By early in Obama's second year in a Quinnipiac poll (data from February 2–4, 2010), 59 percent of respondents favored military courts and 35 percent favored civilian trials for terrorists; with Democrats almost evenly divided, 48 civilian and 45 military, while independents had gone 61 military and 31 civilian, and Republicans were at 73 military and 23 civilian.

These polls have some value, but they cannot explain Obama's decision not to institute mechanisms of accountability, because pluralities of the public have supported investigation, prosecution, or a commission. In a *USA Today/ Gallup Poll* (data from January 30–February 1, 2009), large majorities favored criminal investigation or an investigation by a special panel on the following three issues: attempts to use the Justice Department for political purposes (71 percent), telephone wiretaps without warrants (63 percent), and torture in interrogations (62 percent). Other explanations involving the institutionalized presidency might better account for the protective cover Obama offered to Bush administration officials.

*Clientelism in the Department of Justice*

In the court cases that have carried over from the Bush administration, he seems to be acting in accordance with the observation of Brad Berenson, a former associate counsel in the Bush White House who pointed out that "The dirty little secret here is that the United States government has enduring institutional interests that carry over from administration to administration and almost always dictate the position the government takes" (Gerstein 2009b). Similarly, a law professor at Columbia University, Matthew Waxman, who served as deputy assistant secretary of defense for detainee affairs in the Bush administration, has noted "These are long-standing institutional positions of the executive branch that have historically transcended partisan divides" (Waxman 2010).

## Immunizing Administration Emergency Powers

In post 9/11 America the president is expected to be protector-in-chief. The prospect of more terrorist attacks, let alone the possibility of the use of weapons of mass destruction by terrorists on American soil, raises the stakes for each president and his administration. "We know that organizations like al-Qaeda are in the process of trying to secure a nuclear weapon—a weapon of mass destruction that they have no compunction at using," Obama said on the eve of his Nuclear Security Summit in April 2010 (ABC News 2010). Much as doctors prescribe tests to avoid liability, presidents must create and maintain security systems that demonstrate their efforts to "preserve, protect, and defend." But they also defend themselves: presidents make sure that the war on terrorism doesn't become an issue in congressional or presidential elections or in national agenda politics. And so the Obama White House protects itself on some issues (i.e., indefinite detention), but more important, it protects its predecessors by blunting calls for accountability, so that it too will gain the same protections once out of office.

## The "Deep Structure" of Prerogative Power

Hugh Heclo has analyzed the "deep structure" of the presidency as an institution, i.e., those parts that do not change when an administration changes (Heclo 1999). So too there is a "deep structure" of prerogative claims, which do not change—or change slowly—when partisan control of the White House changes. These include claims of sovereign immunity, official immunities involving duties of officials, testimonial privileges (executive, departmental, lawyer-client, protective service), and state secrets doctrines, all of which the Obama administration has attempted to extend in court filings. And when there is movement, it seems always to be in the direction of extending claims rather than retracting them. The Obama administration, in its court filings involving the Bush administration, has distinguished between *policy* (which is not defended) and *privilege.* The "deep structure" is not substantive as much as it is a set of privileges that prevent accountability. Obama seems to have made a "non-decision" about most of these privileges, with extensions of some—which not only help the Bush officials, but also may help members of his administration once they leave office.

It is important to consider the behavior of politicians from their own perspective and to follow them as they see things prospectively rather than to analyze their decisions retrospectively (Fenno 1986). A *propaedeutic* view provides us with a "vantage point" of the future as Obama might have seen it in the first months of his presidency: it may have been that Obama's willingness to promote significant changes was sapped by an eroding political position. He wound up taking the low-hanging policy fruit (torture), stalling on what had seemed low-hanging fruit but turned out to be poisonous apples (Guantánamo and military tribunals), and turning away from change that could ultimately bite him and others in his administration (mechanisms for accountability). This strategic and tactical flexibility kept the war on terrorism from becoming an important theme in the subsequent midterm elections of 2010. Yet the resounding Republican victory in recapturing control of the House of Representatives and thinning the Democratic margin of control in the Senate certainly points toward a continuation of Obama's stance—a "no drama Obama" strategy on these issues, for the remainder of his presidential term.

As yet these remain speculations, but they point the way for presidency scholars to determine the validity of each factor as the historical record emerges.

CHAPTER 17

# Reclaiming and Rebuilding American Power

*Lawrence J. Korb and Alexander H. Rothman*

With his inauguration in January 2009, Barack Obama inherited a host of domestic and foreign policy challenges unmatched by any president in recent history. Stretched nearly to the breaking point by two bloody, prolonged, and deeply unpopular wars, the American military was mired in Iraq and Afghanistan. In both of these conflicts, "victory" remained difficult to define, and, as a result, nearly impossible to achieve. Our invasion of Iraq had alienated not only the Muslim world, but also traditional allies, such as Germany and Turkey. Waterboarding, Guantánamo Bay, and Abu Ghraib had compromised US credentials on human rights. US-Russian relations were at their lowest point since the end of the Cold War. At a time when Iran and North Korea appeared determined to continue their nuclear weapons programs, the Bush administration's incoherent nonproliferation policy had seriously undermined the global nonproliferation regime. And in the midst of a global recession, the United States faced record deficits, fueled by the cost of the wars and a tax policy that had neither grown the economy nor created jobs. These deficits compelled and continue to compel the US to borrow 40 cents of every dollar it spends. Propelled into office by an electorate frustrated with the disastrous policies of the Bush administration, President Obama now faced the prospect of picking up the pieces.

Two years later, as Democrats and the Obama administration regroup from an Election Day "shellacking," this chapter will assess Obama's record thus far on foreign policy. Since taking office, in crafting his foreign policy agenda, President Obama has been forced to balance his own signature foreign policy goals—such as focusing international attention on the threat of nuclear terrorism—and his responses to unexpected crises—such as provocations from North Korea—with a need to address the serious national security threats inherited from his predecessor.

In large part, Obama's foreign policy efforts have focused on four major initiatives: winding down the US military presence in Iraq, refocusing American attention and resources on the war in Afghanistan, combating the spread of weapons-usable nuclear material and technology, and crafting a defense policy that sustains, rather than simply expends, American political, economic, and military power. Change has been neither quick nor easy, and significant challenges remain in all four of these arenas. Nevertheless, before looking to the work that remains, it is important to take a moment to appreciate the Obama administration's impressive list of foreign policy accomplishments. Now halfway through his first term, President Obama deserves credit for fulfilling his campaign promises in Iraq and Afghanistan, recommitting the United States to nuclear disarmament, and reorienting US defense policy to better handle the threats of the twenty-first century.

## IRAQ

When President Obama assumed office in January of 2009, Iraq presented perhaps the lone bright spot in an extraordinarily bleak international landscape. Over the previous three years, the Sunni Awakening movement, which brought former Iraqi insurgents into the fight against al-Qaeda, had achieved resounding successes, reducing violence to levels far below their peak in 2006 and changing the course of the war. Moreover, faced with the expiration of the UN mandate authorizing the US occupation of Iraq, in its final days in office the Bush administration had negotiated and signed the US-Iraq Security Agreement, laying out a framework for complete US withdrawal from Iraq by December 31, 2011 (United States Department of State 2008).

For Obama, this bright spot could not have been better located. Given his history of vocal opposition to the war in Iraq and the prominence of the war as a campaign issue, Obama faced intense pressure to deliver on what had become one of his signature campaign promises: the withdrawal of all US combat troops from Iraq within 16 months of taking office.

In the two years since his inauguration, President Obama has expertly guided US policy in Iraq, demonstrating a clear commitment to complete troop withdrawal—as dictated by the Security Agreement—while also working pragmatically to ensure that hard-won US gains in Iraq are not squandered. To a large extent, Obama has been able to deliver on his campaign promise simply by adhering to the timeline for withdrawal put in place by the Security Agreement, signed before his tenure as president. Nevertheless, the Obama administration deserves credit for ending the US combat mission in Iraq, withdrawing more than 100,000 American troops from the country, and working to close the door on a catastrophic chapter in both American and Iraqi history.

The Security Agreement and Status of Forces Agreement (SOFA), both signed by the Bush administration, coupled with declining violence in Iraq, greatly facilitated the Obama administration's success, allowing Obama to meet his campaign pledge without significantly altering the timeframe for US withdrawal. While the UN Security Council never authorized the Iraq War, between 2003 and 2007, the council passed yearly resolutions approving the presence of foreign troops in Iraq, thereby effectively legitimizing the US occupation. When the Security Council allowed this mandate to expire in 2008 at the request of the Iraqi government, the United States and the government of Iraq negotiated a bilateral agreement that authorized the continued presence of US troops in Iraq but also outlined a specific timeline for their complete withdrawal. This agreement—the US-Iraq Security Agreement—required all US troops to withdraw from Iraqi cities to their bases by June 30, 2009, and set a deadline of December 31, 2011, for complete US withdrawal (United States Department of State 2008).

When Obama took office in early 2009, he announced that he would honor the deadlines in the Security Agreement, and he also added a third date to the timetable: the withdrawal of all US combat troops from Iraq by August 31, 2010. In doing so, Obama followed through on his campaign pledge to end US combat operations in Iraq, but he extended his timeframe from 16 months to 19 months. This three-month extension was made at the request of the General Ray Odierno, the commanding general of US forces in Iraq, in order to maximize security during the Iraqi parliamentary elections in spring of 2010 (Associated Press 2009).

In reality, Obama's August 31 deadline did little to alter the pace of US withdrawal from Iraq. When American troops withdrew to their bases in summer of 2009, as dictated by the SOFA, their combat operations largely ended, paving the way for Obama to officially end the US combat mission in Iraq in summer of 2010 without significantly altering the situation on the ground. After the 2009 withdrawal to their bases, American troops remained available to support their Iraqi counterparts but no longer led operations and could only go out on missions with the permission of the Iraqi government: American combat troops were still stationed in Iraq, but their combat role was extremely limited. As a result, Obama's August 2010 deadline officially ended a combat mission that had, for all practical purposes, ended the year before.

While Obama's decision to end the US combat mission in Iraq did little to change the situation on the ground, it sent an unmistakable message that the United States is committed to a sovereign Iraq and to ending US military involvement in the country. The US troops that remain in Iraq, less than 50,000, are composed primarily of advisory and assistance brigades, which carry more engineers, military police, and civil affairs professionals than combat brigades and are designed to support, rather than lead, their Iraqi counterparts (Miles 2009). Moreover, by demonstrating our commitment to leave, Obama has also taken an essential step in rebuilding trust with the Iraqi government and people, refashioning the US's reputation on the international scene, and undermining the al-Qaeda narrative that the US seeks to control Muslim countries.

It would be inaccurate to say that President Obama has fashioned a victory out of disaster in Iraq. Iraq is not the "model for democracy" envisioned by the Bush administration. Many would argue that it is not even particularly stable. Nevertheless, the US combat mission in Iraq is over, and we are on track for complete withdrawal by December 2011. American troops are no longer dying every day in a war that never should have begun. And the future of Iraq is, finally, in the hands of the Iraqi people. What more could one ask of the successor to George W. Bush?

## AFGHANISTAN

As President Obama has scaled back military operations in Iraq, he has reallocated American troops and resources to the war in Afghanistan. On the campaign trail, Obama cited the growing insurgency in Afghanistan as a reason for the US to withdraw from Iraq, arguing that the war in Iraq sapped resources from the far more important conflict in Afghanistan. Candidate Obama defended Afghanistan as the "good war"—the war that was justified on national security grounds, legitimized by the support of the international community, and begun in response to the deadliest terror attack in the history of the United States. Calling Afghanistan the "central front in the war on terror," Obama pledged to rededicate American resources to Afghanistan and "make the fight against al-Qaeda and the Taliban the top priority that it should be" (Obama 2008a). The first step in this strategic rebalancing: a campaign promise to send at least two additional combat brigades to Afghanistan.

Since taking office, President Obama has more than delivered on his pledge to refocus American resources on Afghanistan, tripling the number of US troops in the country to more than 100,000 and augmenting this increased military commitment with a "civilian surge" of engineers, teachers, and agricultural specialists (Northam 2009). Despite this renewed focus on Afghanistan, however, the current US counterinsurgency strategy does not appear likely to create a stable, sustainable solution. The US-backed Karzai government is viewed as illegitimate by many of its own people and has been either unable or unwilling to crack down on rampant corruption within its ranks. Moreover, American public support for the war continues to fall, with an October 2010 poll finding that 60 percent of respondents viewed Afghanistan as a lost cause (Dorning 2010).

Afghanistan may very well be the defining foreign policy challenge of Obama's presidency. Two years in, however, it is too early to assess Obama's efforts in Afghanistan. Rather, history will judge Obama based on his ability to shift gears in order to achieve three key goals in Afghanistan: 1. Begin withdrawing American troops by July of 2011, as promised in his 2009 speech at West Point, 2. Transition to a counterterrorism strategy in order to prevent al-Qaeda from reestablishing its presence in Afghanistan as this troop drawdown continues, and 3. Achieve complete withdrawal of US combat forces by 2014.

To prevent al-Qaeda from regaining a safe haven in Afghanistan, the Obama administration has implemented a costly counterinsurgency strategy designed to prevent the Taliban from maintaining and regaining control of significant segments of the country. As part of this strategy, President Obama poured troops, money, and civilian aid into the US's long under-resourced war in Afghanistan. Despite this influx of resources, however, Obama's counterinsurgency strategy faces two obstacles likely to be insurmountable in the short term: the ineptness of the Afghan National Security Forces (ANSF) and corruption of the Karzai government.

Having surged troop levels in Afghanistan, the US and coalition forces launched clearing operations into Taliban-controlled areas in the eastern and southern areas of the country, most prominently in Marja and Kandahar. These offenses aim to use US and coalition troops to clear the Taliban out of major population centers and hold these areas until control can be transferred to Afghan authorities. The problem: the strategy is stuck at the "hold" phase—the ANSF are still too weak to maintain control of these territorial gains, so coalition troops are forced to remain indefinitely. Only 14 percent of Afghan security forces are capable of reading or writing at a third-grade level (Chivers 2010). A recent Council on Foreign Relations report observes that "drug abuse, desertion, and violence remain persistent challenges" among the Afghan National Police, and even the better trained Afghan National Army is widely reported to suffer from corruption, uneven levels of commitment, and infiltration by the Taliban (Bruno 2010). As a result, this strategy of "clear, hold, build, and transfer" has become an endless cycle of "clear, hold, hold, hold, hold."

Even more significantly, in supporting the Karzai government, the US is fighting the insurgency on behalf of a government that has lost legitimacy in the eyes of most of its people. Tainted by reports of widespread fraud and the eventual withdrawal of President Karzai's opponent, Abdullah Abdullah, the 2009 Afghan presidential elections exemplified the high-level corruption that plagues the current Afghan government. Whether or not the coalition clearing operations are successful, long-term stability will be impossible in Afghanistan if the US cannot provide the Afghan people with a viable alternative to Taliban rule. At the moment, the Karzai government does not appear to present such an alternative.

Given the frailties of the Karzai government, the Obama administration's counter-insurgency strategy appears unlikely to produce a stable Afghanistan capable of functioning without indefinite American military and economic aid. As a result, President Obama must recalibrate his approach in Afghanistan to switch to a more limited counterterrorism approach aimed at combating al-Qaeda. Taliban interests are largely confined to Afghanistan; al-Qaeda's are not. By focusing on containing and combating al-Qaeda, not the Taliban, the US would be able to draw down its military presence in Afghanistan while still effectively working to protect the US from the most direct military threat stemming from Afghanistan: al-Qaeda and other terrorist organizations. Moreover, such an approach would free up American military and economic power—principally the $100 billion a year being spent on Afghanistan and the 100,000 American troops tied down in the country—to address other national security threats, such the spread of al-Qaeda in Yemen, and the deficit. The Obama administration's obligation to American people in Afghanistan is to prevent the rebirth of al-Qaeda and prevent Afghanistan from destabilizing the region, not to reverse Taliban momentum. While allowing the Taliban to regain control of some parts of Afghanistan may have serious consequences for the Afghan people, nation-building in Afghanistan is not possible without a viable partner, and the Karzai government has proven itself to be fatally flawed. As a result, President Obama should stick to his July 2011 deadline to begin troop withdrawals from Afghanistan and end the US combat mission in Afghanistan by 2014 at the latest.

While on the campaign trail, candidate Obama spoke of how the war in Iraq had undermined the US's position in the world:

> What has been missing since before the war began—is a discussion of the strategic consequences of Iraq and its dominance of our foreign policy. This war distracts us from every threat that we face and so many opportunities we could seize. This war diminishes our security, our standing in the world, our military, our economy, and the resources that we need to confront the challenges of the 21st century. By any measure, our single-minded and open-ended focus on Iraq is not a sound strategy for keeping America safe (Obama 2008a).

The question for Obama today is to what extent does this same statement now apply to his tremendous commitment in Afghanistan?

## Nonproliferation

In a May 2009 speech in Prague, President Obama famously proclaimed that, as the only country to have used a nuclear bomb, the United States has a moral responsibility to lead efforts toward creating a world without nuclear weapons (Obama 2009b). During his tenure as president, Obama has lived up to this pledge, crafting a cohesive nonproliferation agenda that has focused international attention on the threat of nuclear terrorism, reaffirmed the US's commitment to the Nuclear Nonproliferation Treaty (NPT), and provided "rogue" countries, such as Iran and North Korea, with strong incentives to abide by their NPT commitments. The centerpieces of this agenda—the 2010 Nuclear Posture Review (NPR), Nuclear Security Summit, and New START Treaty—have updated US nuclear policy to address the threats of the twenty-first century while allowing the United States to maintain a viable nuclear deterrent to protect itself and its allies.

### The 2010 Nuclear Posture Review

Released by each presidential administration since 1993, the Nuclear Posture Review (NPR) defines the role of nuclear weapons in US security strategy. Departing from the hyper-aggressive rhetoric of the Bush administration, President

Obama's NPR limits the situations in which the US will consider using nuclear weapons, stating explicitly that the United States will not use nuclear weapons against non-nuclear states that are in compliance with their NPT obligations. Critics argue that this new doctrine increases the likelihood that the United States will be attacked by a non-nuclear state using chemical or biological weapons. In reality, however, the 2010 NPR allows the US to maintain a robust deterrent for defensive purposes while also providing countries with strong incentives to abide by the NPT.

Arguing that the "fundamental purpose" of nuclear arms is to "to deter nuclear attack on the United States, our allies, and partners," the 2010 NPR states that the US "will not use or threaten to use nuclear weapons against non–nuclear weapons states that are party to the NPT and in compliance with their nuclear non-proliferation obligations," even in response to chemical or biological attacks (United States Department of Defense 2010). By explicitly limiting the scenarios in which the US will consider using nuclear weapons, the Obama administration broke with the Bush administration's policy of "strategic ambiguity," under which the United States retained the option of using nuclear weapons in response to chemical, biological, and large conventional attacks, and even "surprising military developments" (Young and Gronlund 2002). Instead, the Obama administration has adopted a policy that utilizes the US nuclear arsenal to deter not just a direct attack on the United States, but also nuclear proliferation, which the NPR identifies as "today's most immediate and extreme danger" (United States Department of Defense 2010). Proliferation increases the chances that nuclear material will fall into the hands of a rogue state or terrorist organization and, as a result, arguably presents a greater threat to the United States than traditional state-to-state warfare. With its negative security assurances, the Obama administration's Nuclear Posture Review encourages good behavior from non-nuclear states, which know they can neutralize the American nuclear arsenal by adhering to their responsibilities under the NPT, and thereby discourages proliferation.

Moreover, in pledging not to use a nuclear weapon in response to a chemical or biological attack, the 2010 NPR does little to change the options available to American military officials. In an April 2010 interview, Secretary of Defense Gates explained the Obama administration's shift in policy, stating, "[T]ry as we might, we could not find a credible scenario where a chemical weapon could have the kind of consequences that would warrant a nuclear response" (United States Department of State 2010). US conventional weapons are becoming so devastating that a nuclear response, even to a chemical or biological attack, is no longer necessary.

Instead, the 2010 NPR promises that "any state ... that uses chemical or biological weapons against the United States or its allies and partners would face the prospect of a devastating conventional military response" (United States Department of Defense 2010). In many ways, this threat of massive conventional retaliation is more credible than the threat of a nuclear response: American policymakers refused to use nuclear weapons in both Korea and Vietnam, where more than 100,000 American servicemen and -women were killed. By dropping the implausible threat of nuclear retaliation, the Obama administration strengthens the global norm against nuclear use and nuclear weapons without undermining American security. General Charles Horner, the Allied Air Force Commander during the First Gulf War, put it most explicitly some 14 years ago when he said, "I came to the realization that nuclear weapons had little utility when I realized that even if Saddam Hussein had used a nuclear weapon on us, we would have to retaliate on a conventional basis" ("Questioning Nuclear Arms" 1996).

With an increased focus on combating global proliferation and nuclear terrorism, the Obama administration's NPR updates US nuclear policy to address the most pressing threats to the United States in the twenty-first century. The NPR encourages good behavior by promising that non-nuclear states in compliance with their NPT commitments will not be threatened or attacked with nuclear weapons. Additionally, the NPR pledges to "hold fully accountable any state, terrorist group, or other non-state actor that supports or enables terrorist efforts to obtain or use weapons of mass destruction" (United States Department of Defense 2010). The Obama administration's Nuclear Posture Review supports the global nonproliferation regime, provides strong incentives to states to keep nuclear material out of the hands of terrorists, and allows the United States to maintain a viable nuclear and conventional deterrent, thereby strengthening America's national security in both the short and long term.

*The 2010 Nuclear Security Summit*

Bringing together the heads of 47 different countries, the 2010 Nuclear Security Summit in Washington, DC continued the Obama administration's efforts to focus international attention on the threat of loose nuclear material and nuclear terrorism. Individual countries—ranging from nuclear behemoths such as Russia to non-nuclear states such as Canada, Mexico, and Chile—pledged to eliminate, stop producing, or better safeguard their nuclear material. Even more significantly, the summit reinforced the global nature of the threat of nuclear terrorism and the need for international cooperation on this issue. All 47 attending countries endorsed the goal of securing all weapons-usable nuclear material within four years, and a follow-up summit was scheduled for 2012 in South Korea (Ploughshares Fund 2010). By spearheading the 2010 summit, the Obama administration bolstered its nonproliferation credentials and demonstrated its commitment to a safer and more peaceful world.

*The New START Treaty*

Ratified in by the US Senate and Russian Duma, the New Strategic Arms Reduction Treaty—or New START—requires the United States and Russia to make modest reductions in their nuclear arsenals, with deployed strategic warheads limited to 1,550 and delivery vehicles limited to 800 (Gard and Isaacs 2010). In doing so, New START continues a decades-old process of cooperative arms control between the US and Russia, the two countries that possess about 95 percent of the world's nuclear weapons (Gard and Isaacs 2010). Moreover, as the successor to the START I agreement, which expired in December 2009,

New START replaces the now-expired verification provisions of the START I agreement, thereby allowing the US and Russia to inspect each other's nuclear arsenals and thus providing a measure of security and transparency to the US-Russian relationship. By eliminating excess nuclear warheads, demonstrating the US's commitment to its obligations under the NPT, promoting international cooperation on nuclear disarmament, and strengthening US-Russia relations, the New START treaty furthers the security interests of the United States and the world.

During the height of the arms race, the US nuclear stockpile peaked at nearly 32,000 warheads (Mount 2010). A remnant of this Cold War hysteria, the US's current nuclear arsenal—5,113 weapons as of September 2009—is expensive to maintain, in need of constant protection, and seriously disproportionate to our security needs (Mount 2010). The nation's top military leadership—including Secretary of Defense Robert Gates, Chairman of the Joint Chiefs of Staff Admiral Michael Mullen, Vice Chairman of the Joint Chiefs of Staff Marine Corps General James Cartwright, and STRATCOM Commander General Kevin Chilton—endorsed New START and its limit of 1,550 deployed strategic nuclear weapons (Isaacs 2010). A May 2010 article by two Air Force strategists argued that the US could draw down to 311 nuclear weapons without negatively impacting our security (Schaub and Forsyth 2010).

By pledging to eliminate some of these surplus weapons, the US has demonstrated its commitment to its obligations under the Nuclear Nonproliferation Treaty, thereby strengthening its hand in tackling the threat of global nuclear proliferation, arguably the greatest long-term threat to US national security. First enacted in 1968, the Nuclear Nonproliferation Treaty, or NPT, was essentially a compromise between the states that possessed nuclear weapons in 1968 and those that did not: the non-nuclear states pledged to forgo developing nuclear weapons, and, in return, the nuclear states pledged to work toward "general and complete [nuclear] disarmament" (United States Department of State 1968). Over the past four decades, the non-nuclear states have largely kept their side of the deal: since the NPT entered into force in 1970, only five states—Israel, India, Pakistan, South Africa, and North Korea—have developed nuclear weapons. Three of these—Israel, India, and Pakistan—never signed the NPT. South Africa developed its nuclear weapons before it signed the NPT; it has since given up its small nuclear stockpile and become party to the Nuclear Nonproliferation Treaty. As a result, North Korea stands as the only state to have signed the NPT and then developed nuclear weapons (North Korea withdrew from the treaty in 2003).

The nuclear weapon states, on the other hand, have made slow progress toward upholding their side of the bargain. None of the treaty's nuclear states (the United States, China, Russia, the United Kingdom, and France) have given up their arsenals. Moreover, the non-nuclear states have watched three countries—India, Israel, and Pakistan—develop and maintain significant nuclear stockpiles in defiance of the international community without suffering long-lasting consequences. If the United States is going to expect the rest of the world to abide by the NPT, it must do so itself by working to reduce its own nuclear stockpile.

New START reduces the US nuclear stockpile to levels somewhat more appropriate to the threats of the twenty-first century. It demonstrates American support for the NPT, thereby strengthening one of the US's key tools in discouraging nuclear proliferation, and it provides a foundation for further arms control negotiations involving the world's two largest nuclear powers.

Over the past two years, President Obama has made nuclear disarmament one of his signature foreign policy endeavors. Beginning with his Prague speech and continuing through his strong support for New START, Obama has breathed new life into the global nonproliferation regime and focused international attention on the threat of nuclear terrorism. In doing so, the Obama administration has expertly crafted a nuclear policy that protects American security in both the short and long term.

## NATIONAL SECURITY POLICY

In his National Security Strategy (NSS), released in May 2010, President Obama outlines a national security policy that attempts to sustain, rather than simply expend, American political, economic, and military power. The NSS begins with a call for the US to "pursue a strategy ... that rebuilds the foundation of American strength and influence" (Obama 2010a). In the document, Obama is quick to acknowledge that this "strength and influence" stem from far more than American military might. Rather, the NSS argues that American power is founded in multiple sources, including the US economy, education system, and scientific base.

Moreover, in the NSS, the Obama administration acknowledges that the threats of the twenty-first century differ markedly from those of the twentieth. Rather than direct state vs. state warfare, the NSS argues that the greatest threats facing the United States today are largely asymmetric: most significantly, the spread of nuclear and biological weapons, al-Qaeda and extremist groups, and cyberwarfare.

In identifying ways to address these threats, Obama's NSS is a direct rejection of the foreign policy of the Bush administration. Having learned from the disaster in Iraq, the NSS warns that unilateral action has the potential to "overextend our power" and thereby undermine American influence. Obama writes that while "the United States remains the only nation able to project and sustain large-scale military operations over extended distances," military force must be used appropriately, and "America has not succeeded by stepping outside the currents of international cooperation" (Obama 2010a). Instead, the NSS endorses a national security policy characterized by cooperation and engagement.

Additionally, in the wake of the US's costly nation-building efforts in Iraq and Afghanistan, Obama's NSS recognizes the need for an integrated approach to dealing with threats to American security. President Obama argues that while the armed forces will always be a "cornerstone" of American security, US security is best protected by a military force "complemented" with diplomats, development experts, intelligence officers, and law enforcement officials (Obama

2010a). Finally, in response to the disasters of Abu Ghraib and Guantánamo Bay, the NSS asserts the importance of maintaining the US's moral credibility on human rights, arguing "the most effective way for the United States of America to promote our values is to live them."

In many ways, Obama's NSS appears to be a rhetorical repudiation of the Bush-era principles. However, the document also accomplishes the far more important goal of modernizing US national security policy to meet the threats of the twenty-first century. With his National Security Strategy, President Obama has laid the foundation for defense and foreign policies intended to protect American interests in both the short and long term.

## THE NEXT TWO YEARS

This chapter does not aim to paint too rosy a picture of Obama's first two years or gloss over the work that remains to be done. President Obama's rhetorical support for closing the US's detention camp at Guantánamo Bay has been stymied not only by legislative roadblocks but by his own unwillingness to expend political capital. Despite the legislative repeal of "Don't Ask, Don't Tell," implementing a move away from this discriminatory policy—one of Obama's signature campaign promises—could take months if not years. The military budget still funds many unneeded and unwanted systems. The American economy, which impacts not only US political and military power but also Obama's own reelection prospects, continues to grow at a glacial pace. And there is no readily apparent way forward in addressing climate change, either domestically or globally.

Furthermore, due to the Bush administration's misguided invasion of Iraq, mishandling of the war in Afghanistan, and failure to raise taxes to pay for the costs of these wars, the Obama administration's military options are sharply constrained in responding to unexpected crises. North Korea's 2010 sinking of a South Korean warship and shelling of the South Korean island of Yeonpyeong illustrates the lingering effects of the Bush administration's policy of military and economic overreach. The United States responded to North Korea's unprovoked artillery attack, which killed two South Korean civilians, by issuing a verbal condemnation of the attack, holding joint military exercises with South Korea and Japan, and asking China to lean on North Korea to change its behavior. However, a more aggressive military response was rendered impossible in part because US military might is tied down in the Middle East and South Asia, just as it was tied down in Vietnam during the 1968 *Pueblo* crisis with North Korea. Moreover, America's leverage with China is constrained because China holds nearly one trillion dollars in US debt. While the Obama administration has worked admirably to rededicate American resources to face the threats of the twenty-first century, significant obstacles remain before the United States will be completely free of the shadow the Bush administration.

Nevertheless, before looking to the future, it is important to stop to appreciate President Obama's numerous foreign policy accomplishments. In his first two years in office, the Obama administration has made significant progress in undoing the damage of the Bush years. Obama has delivered on his campaign promises to the American people in both Iraq and Afghanistan. The US military is on track toward complete withdrawal from Iraq by December 31, 2011. Afghanistan is finally receiving the resources and attention that it deserves, although a satisfactory end game remains in doubt. President Obama's commitment to nuclear disarmament has been nothing short of historic. He has established a commission to deal with the burgeoning budget deficit. And, most importantly, President Obama has crafted a national security strategy that focuses on not only defending American interests in the short term, but also shoring up the foundations of American power, thereby preparing the nation to face the threats of the future. If Obama sticks to this strategy for the rest of his presidency, be it one term or two, perhaps his successor will be able to enter office with both eyes trained firmly on the possibilities of the future, rather than on the mistakes of the past.

# References

"2008 Stimfulus: Putting Money in Peoples' Pockets." 2009. *CQ Weekly Online,* February 23, 397.

"A Balanced Approach to Restoring Fiscal Responsibility." 2008 (July). http://www.cbpp.org/files/7-9-08bud.pdf.

Abbate, Janet. 1999. *Inventing the Internet.* Cambridge, MA: MIT Press.

ABC News. 2010. "Al Qaeda Is Seeking a Nuke—and They Will Use It." April 11.

Abramowitz, Alan I. 2008. "It's About Time: Forecasting the 2008 Presidential Election with the Time-for-Change Model." *International Journal of Forecasting* 24: 209–217.

———. 2010. *The Disappearing Center: Engaged Citizens, Polarization and American Democracy.* New Haven, CT: Yale University Press.

Abramowitz, Alan I., and Kyle L. Saunders. 2008. "Is Polarization a Myth?" *Journal of Politics* 70: 542–555.

Abramson, Jill. 2009. *Obama: Historic Journey.* New York: New York Times/Callaway Arts and Entertainment.

Aldrich, John H., and David W. Rohde. 2000. "The Consequences of Party Organization in the House: The Role of the Majority and Minority Parties in Conditional Party Government." In *Polarized Politics: Congress and the President in a Partisan Era,* eds. Jon R. Bond and Richard Fleisher. Washington, DC: CQ Press, 31–72.

———. 2001. "The Logic of Conditional Party Government: Revisiting the Electoral Connection." In *Congress Reconsidered,* 7th ed., eds. Lawrence C. Dodd and Bruce I. Oppenheimer. Washington, DC: CQ Press, 269–292.

Alexander, Andrew. 2010. "Behind the Rahm Emanuel 'Conspiracy.'" *Washington Post,* March, A15.

Alter, Jonathan. 2010. *The Promise: President Obama, Year One.* New York: Simon & Schuster.

Ambinder, Mark. 2009. "The White House Takes on *Politico.*" *theatlantic.com,* November 30. http://www.theatlantic.com/politics/archive/2009/11/the-white-house-takes-on-politico/31033.

American Enterprise Institute. 2010. "Election 2010: How the Results Stack Up Historically." http://www.aei.org/docLib/Political-Report-Nov-2010.pdf.

The American Presidency Project. 2010. "Presidential Elections Data." http://www.presidency.ucsb.edu/elections.php (November 30, 2010).

Ansolabehere, Stephen. 2009a. *2008: Common Content.* Cooperative Congressional Election Survey, February 2. Cambridge, MA: MIT Press.

———. 2009b. "Guide to the 2008 Cooperative Congressional Election Survey." Harvard University, February 9.

Applewood, J. Scott. 2008. "Interview with Howard Dean." Associated Press. March 7.

281

Asal, V., C. Johnson, and J. Wilkenfeld. 2008. "Ethnopolitical Violence and Terrorism in the Middle East." In *Peace and Conflict 2008*, eds. J. J. Hewitt, J. Wilkenfeld, and T. R. Gurr. Boulder, CO: Paradigm Publishers.

Associated Press. 2009. "Obama Will Say Iraq Combat Mission to End Aug. 31, 2010." February 24. http://www.usatoday.com/news/washington/2009-02-26-obama-iraq_N.htm (November 16, 2010).

Auletta, Ken. 2010. "Non-Stop News: With Cable, the Web and Tweets, Can the President or the Press Still Control the Story?" *The New Yorker*, January 25.

Bai, Matt. 2009. "Taking the Hill." *New York Times Sunday Magazine*, June 7, MM30.

———. 2010. "Do It Yourself Populism, Left and Right." *New York Times*, October 30, WK1.

Baker, Peter. 2008. "With His Cabinet Appointments, Obama Puts the Campaign Behind Him." *Washington Post*, December 2, A20.

———. 2009b. "How Obama Came to Plan for 'Surge' in Afghanistan." *New York Times*, December 6.

———. 2009c. "With Pledges to Troops and Iraqis, Obama Details Pullout." *Washington Post*, February 27.

———. 2010a. "Education of a President." *New York Times Sunday Magazine*, October 17, MM40.

———. 2010b. "Interview Excerpts: President Obama." *New York Times Magazine*, October 12.

———. 2010c. "Obama's War on Terror." *New York Times Magazine*, January 17, 30.

———. 2010d. "One Subject Pushes Talk of Any Other to the Margins." *New York Times*, March 20, A11.

———. 2010e. "The Limits of Rahmism." *The New York Times Magazine*, March 8.

Baker, Peter and Scott Shane. 2009. "Obama Seeks to Reassure U.S. After Bombing Attempt." *New York Times*, December 28. http://www.nytimes.com/2009/12/29/us/29terror.html.

Baker, Peter, and Jeff Zeleny. 2010. "Staff Chief Wields Power Freely, But Influence Comes With Risk." *New York Times*, August 16, 1.

Balz, Dan, and Haynes Johnson. 2009. *The Battle for America 2008*. New York: Viking, 119–121.

Barone, Michael. 2009. Profiles of Pelosi and Reid. *The Almanac of American Politics 2010*, 162–167, 927–930.

Barstow, David. 2010. "Tea Party Lights Fuse for Rebellion on Right." *New York Times*, February 16.

Bartels, Larry M. 2008. "The Study of Electoral Behavior." In *The Oxford Handbook of American Elections and Political Behavior*, ed. J. E. Leighley.

Baum, Matthew A. 2010. "Preaching to the Choir or Converting the Flock: Presidential Communication Strategies in the Age of Three Medias." http://www.hks.harvard.edu/fs/mbaum/documents/Baum_3Medias_LMU.pdf.

Baumann, David. 2009. "Blue Dogs vs. Red Ink: Softer Lines in the Sand." *CQ Weekly Online*, January 19, 111–112.

Baumgartner, Frank R., Timothy M. LaPira, and Herschel F. Thomas. 2008. "The Structure of Washington Lobbying Networks: Mapping the Revolving Door." Paper presented at the Annual Meetings of the Midwest Political Science Association, Chicago, April 4–7.

Beckmann, Matthew N., and Anthony McGann. 2008. "Navigating the Legislative Divide: Polarization, Presidents, and Policymaking in the US." *Journal of Theoretical Politics*, 20 (2): 201–220.

Bendery, Jennifer. 2010. "Axelrod: We Didn't Do Enough to Sell Agenda." *Roll Call*, October 21, 1. http://www.rollcall.com/issues/56_40/-50882-1.html.

Benjamin, Daniel. 2010. "International Counterterrorism Policy in the Obama Administration: Developing a Strategy for the Future." Address to the International Peace Institute, New York, March 1.

Benjamin, Daniel, and Steven Simon. 2003. *The Age of Sacred Terror: Radical Islam's War Against America*. New York: Random House.

Berners-Lee, Tim. "Information Management: A Proposal." W3C, May 1990. http://www.w3
.org/History/1989/proposal.html.
Bettelheim, Adriel. 2009a. "Four Keys to a New Presidency." *CQ Weekly Online*, April 27, 958–960.
———. 2009b. "Obama's Cautious Cheerleading." *CQ Weekly Online*, May 25, 1204–1211.
———. 2009c. "Overhaul Hard to Steer Using Hands-Off Approach." *CQ Weekly Online*, August 10, 1894–1895.
"Big Plans, Big Costs, Big Deficits." 2009. *CQ Weekly Online*, March 2, 472–481.
Binder, Sarah. 1999. "The Dynamics of Legislative Gridlock, 1947–1996." *American Political Science Review* 93: 519–536.
———. 2003. *Stalemate: Causes and Consequences of Legislative Gridlock*. Washington, DC: Brookings Institution Press.
Binder, Sarah A., and Steven S. Smith. 1997. *Politics or Principle? Filibustering in the United States Senate*. Washington, DC: Brookings Institution Press.
Birnbaum, Jeffrey H. 2000. *The Money Men: The Real Story of Fund-Raising's Influence on Political Power in America*. New York: Crown Publishers.
"Bloomberg National Poll." 2010. *Bloomberg*, July 14. http://mediabugs.org/peoplepods/files/docs/57.original.pdf.
Blumenthal, Sidney. 1982. *The Permanent Campaign*. New York: Simon & Schuster.
Boehner, John. 2010. "Bloodhounds." http://www.youtube.com/watch?v=tl_q0afUl0E.
Bond, Jon R., and Richard Fleischer. 1990. *The President in the Legislative Arena*. Chicago: The University of Chicago Press.
Bovard, James. 2003. "Déjà Vu Five Years Before Iraq." *Washington Times*, August 31.
Bowman, Karlyn. 2008. *Attitudes Toward the Federal Government*. Washington, DC: American Enterprise Institute.
Boyd, Richard W. 1974. "Electoral Trends in Postwar Politics." In *Choosing the President*, ed. J. D. Barber. Englewood Cliffs, NJ: Prentice-Hall.
Branigin, William. 2010. "Obama Reflects on 'Shellacking' in Midterm Elections." *Washington Post*, November 3.
Brennan, John. 2009. "A New Approach for Safeguarding Americans." Speech to the Center for Strategic and International Studies, Washington, DC, August 6.
Bresnahan, John. 2008. "Pelosi Lays Down the Law with Rahm." *Politico*, December 16.
———. 2009. "Byrd: Obama in Power Grab." *Politico*, February 25.
Broadband. Broadband USA Broadband Initiative Program portal, http://www.broadbandusa
.gov/BIPportal/index.htm, and Broadband Technology Opportunities Program portal, http://www.ntia.doc.gov/recovery/BTOP/BTOP_QuarterlyReport_11172010.pdf, p. 3.
Broder, John M. 2009. "White House Official Resigns After G.O.P. Criticism." *New York Times*, September 7, 1.
Brooks, David. 2010a. "Getting Obama Right." *New York Times*, March 12.
———. 2010b. "The Soft Side." *New York Times*, October 5.
Brownstein, Ron. 2010. "Barack Obama May Be Too Cool." *National Journal*, October 30.
Bruno, Greg. 2010. "Afghanistan's National Security Forces." Council on Foreign Relations, August 18. http://www.cfr.org/publication/19122/afghanistans_national_security_forces
.html.
Bureau of the Census. 1975. "Historical Statistics of the United States: Colonial Times to 1970." September. http://www2.census.gov.
Bureau of Economic Analysis. 2010. "National Income and Product Accounts; Gross Domestic Product, 3rd Quarter 2010." October 29. http://www.bea.gov/newsreleases/national/gdp/2010/gdp3q10_adv.htm.
Bureau of Labor Statistics. Economic News Release. http://www.bls.gov/news.release/empsit
.toc.htm (November 30, 2010).
———. "Labor Force Statistics from the Current Population Survey."
Burke, John. 1992. *The Institutional Presidency*. Baltimore, MD: The Johns Hopkins University Press.

————. 2009a. *Honest Broker? The National Security Advisor and Presidential Decision Making.* College Station: Texas A&M University Press.

————. 2009b. "The Obama Presidential Transition: An Early Assessment." *Presidential Studies Quarterly* 39 (3): 574–618.

Burns, James MacGregor. 1978. *Leadership.* New York: Harper & Row.

Burton, J. W. 1990. *Conflict: Resolution and Prevention.* New York: St. Martin's Press.

Caliendo, Stephen Maynard, and Charlton McIlwain. 2009. "The Racial Context for Joe Wilson's Outburst." The Project on Race in Political Communication, September 9. http://www.opednews.com/articles/The-Racial-Context-for-Joe-by-The-Project-on-Rac -090910-824 .html.

Calmes, Jackie. 2009. "House Passes Stimulus Plan With No G.O.P. Votes." *New York Times,* January 28.

————. 2010a. "Panel Seeks Social Security Cuts and Higher Taxes." *New York Times,* November 10.

————. 2010b. "Obama Offers Hope for Debt Panel's Plan." *New York Times,* December 3.

Calvert, Randall L., and John A. Ferejohn. 1983. "Coattail Voting in Recent Presidential Elections." *American Political Science Review* 77 (2): 407–419.

Campbell, Angus, Philip E. Converse, Warren E. Miller, and Donald E. Stokes. 1960. *The American Voter.* New York: John Wiley & Sons.

Campbell, Colin, and Bert Rockman, eds. 1996. *The Clinton Presidency: First Appraisals.* Chatham, NJ: Chatham House Publishers.

Campbell, Colin, Bert Rockman, and Andrew Rudalevige, eds. 2008. *The George W. Bush Legacy.* Washington, DC: CQ Press.

Campbell, James E. 2008. "An Exceptional Election: Performance, Values, and Crisis in the 2008 Presidential Election." *The Forum* 6 (4): 1–20.

————. 2010. "The Exceptional Election of 2008: Performance, Values, and Crisis." *Presidential Studies Quarterly* 40 (2): 225–246.

Caprioli, M., R. Nielsen, and V. M. Hudson. 2010. "Women and Post-Conflict Settings." In *Peace and Conflict 2010,* eds. J. J. Hewitt, J. Wilkenfeld, and T. R. Gurr. Boulder, CO: Paradigm Publishers.

Carroll, Royce, Jeff Lewis, James Lo, Nolan McCarty, Keith Poole, and Howard Rosenthal. 2008. "Who is More Liberal, Senator Obama or Senator Clinton?" http://voteview.com/ Clinton_and_Obama.htm.

Carter, Bill. 2010. "CNN Fails to Stop Fall in Ratings." *New York Times,* March 29, B1. http:// www.nytimes.com/2010/03/30/business/media/30cnn.html.

Center for Congressional and Presidential Studies. 2008. Cooperative Congressional Election Study (CCES) Voter Opinion Survey Results on President Obama and Lobbying Reform. November 15.

Center on Law and Security. 2009. *Terrorist Trial Report Card 2001–2009: Lessons Learned.* New York: New York University School of Law.

Center for Responsive Politics. 2010a. "Lobbying Database" http://opensecrets.org.

Center for Responsive Politics. 2010b. "Revolving Door Database." http://opensecrets.org.

Chaddock, Gail Russell. 2009. "Town-Hall Meetings: Facing Voter Wrath on Healthcare." *Christian Science Monitor,* September 4.

Chainon, Jean Yves. 2010. "*Politico*: Multimedia and Niche, A Model for Future Newspapers?" February 13, 16.

Chauvet, L., P. Collier, and A. Hoeffler. 2006. *The Cost of Failing States and the Limits to Sovereignty.* UN-WIDER. WP.

Cheney, Dick. 2009a. "The United States Has Never Lost Its Moral Bearings." Speech delivered at the American Enterprise Institute, May 21. http://www.politico.com/news/ stories/0509/22823.html.

————. 2009b. Interview on *Fox News Sunday,* August 30. http://www.foxnews.com/ politics/2009/08/30/raw-data-transcript-cheney-fox-news-sunday.

————. 2009c. Interview on *ABC This Week,* February 14. http://abcnews.go.com/ThisWeek/ week-transcript-vice-president-dick-cheney/story?id=9818034.

Chivers, C. J. 2010. "Gains in Afghan Training but Struggles in War." *New York Times,* October 12.

Cho, David. 2010. "Timothy Geithner's Realm Grows with Passage of Financial Regulatory Reform." *Washington Post,* July 17.

Cho, David, and Lori Montgomery. 2009. "New Bailout May Top $1.5 Trillion: Plan Aims to Aid Banks, Spur Lending, Push Private Investors to Buy Toxic Assets." *Washington Post,* February 10.

Clarke, David. 2009. "Earmarks: Here to Stay or Facing Extinction?" *CQ Weekly Online,* March 16, 613.

———. 2010a. "Fiscal Hawks Urge Holistic Treatment." *CQ Weekly Online,* January 18, 160–162.

———. 2010b. "Fiscal Commission as Cornerstone." *CQ Weekly Online,* April 19, 944–945.

Clarke, David, and Edward Epstein. 2010. "Earmark Bans Get a Frosty Reception." *CQ Weekly Online,* March 15, 634.

Clarke, David, and Greg Vadala. 2010. "Senate Passes Debt Limit Increase After Commission, Pay-As-You-Go Agreements." *CQ Weekly Online,* February 1, 288.

Clarke, David, and Kerry Young. 2009. "In Hearings, Orszag Gives Only a Few Specifics on OMB, Stimulus Plans." *CQ Weekly Online,* January 19, 140.

Clinton, Hillary. 2010. "Leading Through Civilian Power: Redefining American Diplomacy and Development." *Foreign Affairs* 89 (6): 13–24.

Clinton staffer. 2009. Interview by Owens. October 30. Washington, DC.

Clinton, William J. 1997. Second Inaugural Address. January 20.

CNN Politics. 2009a. "White House Focuses on Stimulating the Stimulus."

———. 2009b. "CNN Poll: Double-Digit Post-Speech Jump for Obama Plan." *CNN Political Ticker,* September 9.

Cohen, David. 2010. "The White House Chief of Staff in the Obama Administration: A Six Month Review."

Cohen, Jeff, Rick Pearson, John Chase, and David Kidwell. 2008. "Blagojevich Arrested on Federal Charges." *Chicago Tribune,* December 10, 1.

Collier, D., and A. Hoeffler. 2004. "Aid, Policy, and Growth in Post-Conflict Countries." *European Economic Review* 48: 1125–1145.

Colvin, Ross. 2009. "Obama Sets Qaeda Defeat as Top Goal in Afghanistan." Reuters, March 27.

*Comcast Corporation v. Federal Communications Commission.* 2010. United States Court of Appeals for the District of Columbia Circuit, No. 08-1291.

Compton, Ann. 2010. Interview with Ron Elving. October 8.

Condon, Stephanie. 2010. "Poll: Economy Brings Down Obama's Job Approval Rating." February 11. http://www.cbsnews.com/8301-503544_162-6199106-503544.html?tag=contentMain%3bcontentBody.

Conference Report. 1996. Telecommunications Act of 1996. House of Representatives, 104th Congress, 2nd Session. House Rept. 104–458.

Connolly, Ceci. 2010. "How Obama Revived His Health-Care Bill." *Washington Post,* March 23.

Connor, James L. 2002. "Principles for the Ethical Conduct of Lobbying." Woodstock Theological Center, Georgetown University.

Conroy, Scott. 2008. "Palin: Obama's Plan Is 'Experiment With Socialism.'" CBS News, October 19. http://www.cbsnews.com/8301-503443_162-4532388.html.

Converse, Philip E. 1972. "Change in the American Electorate." In *The Human Meaning of Social Change,* eds. A. Campbell and P. E. Converse. New York: Russell Sage.

Cook, Corey, 2002. "The Permanence of the Permanent Campaign: George W. Bush's Public Presidency." *Presidential Studies Quarterly* 32 (4): 753.

Cook, Rhodes. 2009. "Obama and the Redefinition of Presidential Coattails." Larry J. Sabato's Crystal Ball. http://www.centerforpolitics.org.

CQ.com. http://www.cq.com/ (2008).

*CQ Weekly.* 2010. January 4, 31–32. http://library.cqpress.com/cqweekly/.

Cranford, John. 2009. "Renegotiating the Social Contracts." *CQ Weekly Online,* January 19, 118–124.

———. 2010a. "Congress Sticks With Obama on Votes He Cares About." *CQ Weekly,* October 11, 2327.

———. 2010b. "Political Economy: Earmarks, Shmearmarks." *CQ Weekly Online,* March 15, 650.

Crenshaw, Martha. 2001. "Counterterrorism Policy and the Political Process." *Studies in Conflict and Terrorism* 24 (5): 329–338.

———. 2003. "Coercive Diplomacy and the Response to Terrorism." In *The United States and Coercive Diplomacy,* eds. R. J. Art and P. M. Cronin. Washington, DC: U.S. Institute of Peace Press.

———. 2005. "Counterterrorism in Retrospect: Chronicle of a War Foretold." *Foreign Affairs* 84 (July–August): 187–193.

Cutler, David. 2010. "How Health Care Reform Must Bend the Cost Curve." *Health Affairs* 29 (6): 1131–1135.

Daou, Peter. 2010. "How a Handful of Liberal Bloggers Are Bringing Down the Obama Presidency." September 27. http://peterdaou.com/2010/09/liberal-bloggers-are-bringing-down-the-obama-presidency.

Davenport, Coral, and Avery Palmer. 2009. "A Landmark Climate Bill Passes." *CQ Weekly,* June 29, 1516–1517.

Davis, Susan. 2010. "Polarized Congress May Be Here to Stay: Congress Is Evolving into an Institution Where Combative Rules of Engagement Are the Norm, Not the Exception." *National Journal,* October 16.

Dennis, Steven T., and Tory Newmyer. 2009. "Democrats Clash on Climate Change." *Roll Call,* May 4.

DeYoung, Karen. 2009. "Obama's NSC Will Get New Power." *Washington Post,* February 8, 1.

Dick, Jason. 2010. "Skepticism, Lack of Consensus on Government Efforts." *National Journal,* June 21.

Dickinson, Tim. 2010. "The Spill, the Scandal and the President." *Rolling Stone.* June 24. http://www.rollingstone.com/politics/news/the-spill-the-scandal-and-the-president-20100608.

Dorning, Mike. 2010. "Obama Loses Support in Poll as Joblessness Prompts Growing U.S. Discontent." *Bloomberg,* October 12.

Downie, Leonard, and Michael Schudson. 2010. "The Reconstruction of American Journalism." *Columbia Journalism Review,* October 19. http://www.cjr.org/reconstruction/the_reconstruction_of_american.php.

Drew, Elizabeth. 2010. "Is There Life in Health Care Reform?" *New York Review of Books,* March 11, 49–52.

Drogan, Bob, and Mark Barabak. 2008. "McCain Says Obama Wants Socialism." *Los Angeles Times,* October 19.

Dulio, David A., and James A. Thurber. 2001. "The Symbiotic Relationship Between Political Parties and Political Consultants: Partners Past, Present and Future." October. Washington, DC: Center for Congressional and Presidential Studies, American University.

*The Economist.* 2010. "Welcome to the Tea Party." http://www.economist.com/node/17035460.

"Economists Chop U.S. GDP Forecast: Blue Chip Survey." 2008. Reuters, December 10.

"Economy, Jobs Trump All Other Policy Priorities in 2009; Environment, Immigration, Health Care Slip Down the List." 2009. Survey Report, Pew Research Center for the People & the Press.

Edwards, George C. 1989. *At the Margins: Presidential Leadership of Congress.* New Haven, CT, and London: Yale University Press.

———. 1998. "Bill Clinton and His Crisis of Governance." *Presidential Studies Quarterly* 28 (Fall): 754–760.

———. 2009. *The Strategic President: Persuasion and Opportunity in Presidential Leadership.* Princeton, NJ: Princeton University Press.

———. 2010. "Barack Obama's Leadership of the Public." Paper delivered at the Annual Meeting of the Midwest Political Science Association, Chicago, April 22–25.

Edwards, George C., and Andrew Barrett. 2000. "Presidential Agenda Setting in Congress." In *Polarized Politics: Congress and the President in a Partisan Era,* eds. Jon R. Bond and Richard Fleischer. Washington, DC: CQ Press.

Edwards, George C., Andrew Barrett, and Jeffrey Peake. 1997. "The Legislative Impact of Divided Government." *American Journal of Political Science* 41 (2): 545–563.

Edwards, George C., and Stephen J. Wayne. 1994. *Presidential Leadership: Politics and Policy Making.* New York: St. Martin's Press.

Eilperin, Juliet. 2006. *Fight Club Politics: How Partisanship Is Poisoning the House of Representatives.* Lanham, MD, and Oxford: Rowman & Littlefield.

ElBaradei, M. 2010a. "Human Security and the Quest for Peace in the Middle East." In *The Sadat Lectures: Words and Images on Peace, 1997–2008,* ed. Shibley Telhami. Washington, DC: U.S. Institute of Peace Press.

———. 2010b. "Sadat Lecture 2006." In *The Sadat Lectures: Words and Images on Peace, 1997–2008,* ed. Shibley Telhami. Washington, DC: U.S. Institute of Peace Press.

"Election 2010." *New York Times.* http://elections.nytimes.com/2010/results/senate.

Elliott, Phillip. 2009. "Anita Dunn Stepping Down as White House Communications Director." *Huffington Post,* November 10. http://www.huffingtonpost.com/2009/11/10/anita-dunn -stepping-down-_n_352298.htm.

Emanuel, Ezekiel J. 2008. *Healthcare, Guaranteed: A Simple, Secure Solution for America.* New York: Public Affairs.

Emanuel, Rahm. 2008. "In Crisis, Opportunity for Obama." *Wall Street Journal,* November 21, A1.

Epstein, Edward. 2010. "Earmarking in an Anti-Earmark World." *CQ Weekly Online,* May 3, 1068.

Eshbaugh-Soha, Matthew. 2005. "The Politics of Presidential Agendas." *Political Research Quarterly* 58 (2): 257–268.

Espo, David. 2009. "Stimulus Bill Survives Senate Test." Associated Press, February 10.

"Exit Polls: Economy, Voter Anger Drive Republican Victory." *ABC News.* http:// abcnews.go.com/Politics/vote-2010-elections-results-midterm-exit-poll-analysis/story?id= 12003775&page=3.

Fearon, James D., and David D. Laitin. 2003. "Ethnicity, Insurgency, and Civil War." *American Political Science Review* 97: 75–90.

Federal Communications Commission. 2008. The FCC's Rural Health Care Pilot Program. http://www.fcc.gov/cgb/consumerfacts/RuralHealthProgram.html.

Federal Election Commission. 2009. "2008 Official Presidential General Election Results." January 22. http://www.fec.gov/pubrec/fe2008/2008presgeresults.pdf.

Fenno, Richard. 1986. "Observation, Context, and Sequences in the Study of Politics." *American Political Science Review* 80: 3–15.

Fiorina, Morris P., Samuel J. Abrams, and Jeremy Pope. 2006. *Culture War? The Myth of a Polarized America.* 2nd ed. New York: Pearson Longman.

"Fiscal Responsibility Summit." 2009. The White House, March 20. http://www.whitehouse .gov/assets/blog/Fiscal_Responsibility_Summit_Report.pdf.

Fox News. 2009. "White House Urges Other Networks to Disregard Fox News." October 19. http://foxnews.com/politics/2009/10/19/white-house-urges-networks-disregard-fox-news.

Frantzich, Stephen E. 2009. "E-Politics and the 2008 Presidential Campaign: Has the Internet 'Arrived?'" In *Winning the Presidency 2008,* ed. William J. Crotty. Boulder, CO: Paradigm Publishers, 135–151.

Free, Lloyd A., and Hadley Cantril. 1967. *The Political Beliefs of Americans: A Study of Public Opinion.* New Brunswick, NJ: Rutgers University Press.

Freeland, Chrystia. 2010. "Obama Should Call a Truce with Wall Street." *Washington Post,* September 10. http://www.washingtonpost.com/wp-dyn/content/article/2010/09/09/ AR2010090905239.

Frumin, Ben. 2009. "Obama's Sunday Show Blitz: How'd He Do?" http://tpmlivewire .talkingpointsmemo.com/2009/09/president-barack-obama-appeared-on.php.

Gallup Poll. 2009. "Gallup Daily: Obama Job Approval." http://www.gallup.com/home .aspx.

———. 2010a. "Tea Party Supporters Overlap Republican Base." http://www.gallup.com/ poll/141098/tea-party-supporters-overlap-republican-base.aspx.

———. 2010b. "Topics A-Z: Most Important Problem." http://www.gallup.com/poll/1675/ Most-Important-Problem.

———. 2010c. "Topics A-Z: Presidential Ratings—Issues Approval." http://www.gallup.com/ poll/1726/Presidential-Ratings-Issues-Approval.

———. 2010d. "Topics A-Z: Presidential Ratings—Personal Characteristics." http://www.gallup .com/poll/1732/Presidential-Ratings-Personal-Characteristics.

———. 2010e. "Gallup Daily: U.S. Health—April 2009–October 2010." http://www.gallup .com/poll/110128/Gallup-Daily-Health.aspx.

Galston, William A. 2010. "Can a Polarized American Party System Be 'Healthy?'" In *Issues in Governance Studies*. Washington, DC: Brookings Institution Press.

Gamson, William A. 1968. *Power and Discontent*. Homewood, IL: Dorsey Press.

Gard, Robert G., and John Isaacs. 2010. "New START and the Obama Nuclear Agenda." *Huffington Post*, April 27. http://www.huffingtonpost.com/lt-general-robert-g-gard-jr-/ new-start-and-the-obama-n_b_554264.html.

Garin, Geoff. 2010. Non-Broadcast Group Interview at NPR. October 5.

Garrett, Garet. 2002. *Salvos Against the New Deal*. Caldwell, ID: Caxton Press.

Garrett, Major. 2010. "Within His Grasp." *National Journal*, October 30, 16–22.

Gelb, Leslie H. 2010. "Replace Rahm." *Daily Beast*, February 15.

Gellman, Barton. 2001. "Broad Effort Launched After '98 Attacks." *Washington Post*, December 19.

———. 2002a. "Clinton's Covert War." *Washington Post*, National Weekly Edition, January 7–13.

———. 2002b. "Terrorism Wasn't a Top Priority." *Washington Post*, National Weekly Edition, January 14–20.

Gelman, Andrew. 2008. *Red State, Blue State, Rich State, Poor State: Why Americans Vote the Way They Do*. Princeton, NJ, and London: Princeton University Press.

Gerstein, Josh. 2009a. "DOJ: Courts Could Harm Afghan Effort." *Politico*, April 11.

———. 2009b. "Obama Lawyers Set to Defend Yoo." Associated Press, January 28.

Giroux, Greg. 2009. "Split Districts of '08 Key to GOP Rebound Hopes." *CQ Weekly*, March 21, 658–660.

Goidel, Robert K., Donald A. Gross, and Todd G. Shields. 1999. *Money Matters*. Lanham, MD: Rowman & Littlefield.

Goldstone, Jack A. Robert H. Bates, Ted Robert Gurr, Michael Lustik, Monty G. Marshall, Jay Ulfelder, and Mark Woodward. 2005. "A Global Forecasting Model of Political Instability." Presented at the Annual Meeting of the American Political Science Association, Washington, DC.

Goodwin, Doris. 2005. *Team of Rivals: The Political Genius of Abraham Lincoln*. New York: Simon & Schuster.

Gottlieb, S. 2010. "War on Terror: Obama Softened the Language, but Hardened Muslim Hearts." *Christian Science Monitor*, October 14.

Greenstein, Fred I. 2009. *The Presidential Difference: Leadership Style from FDR to Barack Obama*. 3rd ed. Princeton, NJ, and London: Princeton University Press.

Greenstein, Robert. 2010. "Statement of Robert Greenstein, Executive Director, on the Tax-Cut Unemployment Insurance Deal." Center on Budget and Policy Priorities, December 8. http://www.cbpp.org/files/12-7-10tax-stat.pdf.

Greenwald, Glenn. 2010. "The Obama Administration's War on Privacy." September 27. http:// www.salon.com/news/opinion/glenn_greenwald/2010/09/27/privacy.

Groeling, Tim. 2010. *When Politicians Attack: Party Cohesion in the Media*. Cambridge, MA: Cambridge University Press.

Hacker, Jacob S. 2010. "The Road to Somewhere: Why Health Reform Happened." *Perspectiveson Politics* 8 (3): 861–876.

Hafner, Katie. 1998. *Where Wizards Stay Up Late: The Origins of the Internet.* New York: Simon & Schuster.

Hagey, Keach. 2010. "White House Scorecard: MSNBC Up, Bloggers Down." *Politico,* September 29. http://www.politico.com/news/stories/0910/42864.html.

Harbom, L., and R. Sundberg, eds. 2009. *States in Armed Conflict 2008.* Uppsala, Sweden: Department of Peace and Conflict Research.

Hargrove, Erwin C. 2003. "Presidential Leadership in Context." In *Leadership in Context,* eds. Erwin C. Hargrove and John E. Owens. Lanham, MD, and Oxford: Rowman & Littlefield, 17–42.

———. 2008. *The Effective Presidency. Lessons on Leadership from John F. Kennedy to George W. Bush.* Boulder, CO: Paradigm Publishers.

Hart, John. 1995. *The Presidential Branch.* 2nd ed. Chatham, NJ: Chatham House.

Harris, John F., and J. VandeHei. 2010. "Why Obama Loses by Winning." *Politico,* July 15.

Heclo, Hugh. 1999. "The Changing Presidential Office." In *The Managerial Presidency,* ed. James P. Pfiffner. College Station: Texas A&M University Press.

———. 2000. "Campaigning and Governing: A Conspectus." In *The Permanent Campaign and Its Future,* eds. Norman Ornstein and Thomas Mann. Washington, DC: American Enterprise Institute and the Brookings Institution.

Hegre, H., and H. Fjelde. 2010. "Democratization and Post-Conflict Settings." In *Peace and Conflict 2010,* eds. J. J. Hewitt, J. Wilkenfeld, and T. R. Gurr. Boulder, CO: Paradigm Publishers.

Hegre, H., and N. Sambanis. 2006. "Sensitivity Analysis of Empirical Results on Civil War Onset." *Journal of Conflict Resolution* 50: 508–535.

Heilemann, John, and Mark Halperin. 2010. *Game Change: Obama and the Clintons, McCain and Palin, and the Race of a Lifetime.* New York: HarperCollins, 395–416.

Herszenhorn, David M. 2008. "Senators Begin Setting Agenda on Health Care." *New York Times,* November 19.

Herszenhorn, David, and Jackie Calmes. 2010. "Tax Deal Suggests New Path for Obama." *New York Times,* December 7.

Herszenhorn, David M., and Carl Hulse. 2008. "Democrats in Congress Vowing to Pursue an Aggressive Agenda." *New York Times,* January 20.

Hess, Stephen. 2010. Interview with Ron Elving. August 30.

Hess, Stephen, and James Pfiffner. 2002. *Organizing the Presidency.* Washington, DC: Brookings Institution Press.

Hetherington, Marc J. 2005. *Why Trust Matters: Declining Political Trust and the Demise of American Liberalism.* Princeton, NJ, and Oxford: Princeton University Press.

———. 2009. "Review Article: Putting Polarization in Perspective." *British Journal of Political Science* 39 (2): 413–448.

Hetherington, Marc J., and Jonathan Daniel Weiler. 2009. *Authoritarianism and Polarization in American Politics.* New York: Cambridge University Press.

Hewitt, J. J. 2010. "Trends in Global Conflict, 1946–2007." In *Peace and Conflict 2010,* eds. J. J. Hewitt, J. Wilkenfeld, and T. R. Gurr. Boulder, CO: Paradigm Publishers.

Hewitt, J. J., J. Wilkenfeld, and T. R. Gurr, eds. 2010. *Peace and Conflict 2010.* Boulder, CO: Paradigm Publishers.

*The Hill.* 2009. December 13. http://thehill.com/.

Hirsch, Michael. 2010. "The Partners," *National Journal,* October 23, 31–35. http://www.nationaljournal.com/member/magazine/joe-biden-second-to-none-among-vice-presidents—20101023?page=1.

Hoeffler, A. 2010. "State Failure and Conflict Recurrence." In *Peace and Conflict 2010,* eds. J. J. Hewitt, J. Wilkenfeld, and T. R. Gurr. Boulder, CO: Paradigm Publishers.

Hofstadter, Richard. 1964. "The Paranoid Style in American Politics." *Harper's Magazine,* November.

Holder, Eric. 2009a. "Memorandum from the Attorney General: Policies and Procedures Governing Invocation of the States Secrets Privilege." United States Department of Justice, September 23. http://www.talkingpointsmemo.com/documents/2009/09/holder-memo -on-state-secret.php?page=1.

———. 2009b. "New CIA Docs Detail Brutal 'Extraordinary Rendition' Process." *Huffington Post,* September 28.

Honest Leadership and Open Government Act of 2007. Pub. L. 110-81, 121 Stat. 735, September 14.

Hook, Sidney. 1943. *The Hero in History. A Study in Limitation and Possibility.* New York: John Day Co.

Horney, James. 2010. "Bowles-Simpson 2.0: How Does It Compare to the Original?" Center on Budget and Policy Priorities, December 3. http://www.offthechartsblog.org/bowles -simpson-2-0-how-does-it-compare-to-the-original.

Hornick, Ed. 2008. "Obama's Top Priorities for '09." *CNN Political Ticker,* October 31.

Horowitz, Jason. 2010a. "Obama's 'Enforcer' May Also Be His Voice of Reason." *Washington Post,* March 2, 1.

———. 2010b. "Press Secretary Gibbs, Ready to Speak for Himself." *Washington Post,* April 13.

Horsley, Scott. 2010. Interview with Ron Elving. August 15.

Horton, Scott. "New CIA Docs Detail Brutal 'Extraordinary Rendition' Process." *Huffington Post,* September 28.

"House Vote Caps Long Legislative March." 2010. *CQ Weekly Online,* March 29, 752–753.

Hsu, Spencer. S. 2010. "Obama Officials Present a Strategic Redefining of Homeland Security's Mission." *Washington Post,* February 2.

Hulse, Carl, and Avery Palmer. 2009. "Sweeping Health Care Plan Passes House." *The New York Times,* November 8.

Hulse, Carl, and David Herszenhorn. 2008. "Obama Team Makes Early Efforts to Show Willingness to Reach Out to Republicans." *New York Times,* November 5.

Hulse, Carl, and Robert Pear. 2009. "Sweeping Health Care Plan Passes House." *New York Times,* November 7, A1.

Hult, Karen, and Charles Walcott. 2004. *Empowering the White House.* Lawrence: University Press of Kansas.

Human Rights Watch. 2010. "Counterterrorism and Human Rights: A Report Card on President Obama's First Year." January.

Ignatius, David. 2010. "Foreign Policy at Cruising Speed." *Washington Post,* April 15.

Isaacs, John. 2010. "Key U.S. Military Leaders and Influential Moderates and Republicans Strongly Support New START." http://www.armscontrolcenter.org/policy/nuclearweapons/ articles/031009_conservatives_for_nuclear_weapons_cuts.

Isenstadt, Alex. 2009. "Senate Denies ACORN Funding." *Politico,* September 14. http://politico .com/news/stories/0909/27153.html.

Jacobs, Lawrence R., and Theda Skocpol. 2010. *Health Care Reform and American Politics. What Everyone Needs to Know.* New York: Oxford University Press.

Jacobson, Gary C. 2001. *The Politics of Congressional Elections.* New York: Longman.

———. 2008. *A Divider, Not a Uniter: George W. Bush and the American People, Great Questions in Politics Series.* New York: Pearson Longman.

———. 2009a. "The 2008 Presidential and Congressional Elections: Anti-Bush Referendum and Prospects for the Democratic Majority." *Political Science Quarterly* 124 (Spring): 1–30.

———. 2009b. "The Effects of the George W. Bush Presidency on Partisan Attitudes." *Presidential Studies Quarterly* 39 (June): 172–209.

———. 2010a. "Barack Obama and the American Public: From Candidate to President." Paper prepared for delivery at the Conference on the Early Obama Presidency, Centre for the Study of Democracy, University of Westminster, London, May 14.

———. 2010b. "George W. Bush, the Iraq War, and the Election of Barack Obama." *Presidential Studies Quarterly* 40 (June): 207–224.

———. 2010c. "A Tale of Two Wars: Public Opinion on the U.S. Military Interventions in Afghanistan and Iraq." *Presidential Studies Quarterly* 40 (December).

————. 2011a. "Obama and the Polarized Public." In *Obama in Office*, ed. James A. Thurber. Boulder, CO: Paradigm Publishers.

————. 2011b. *A Divider, Not a Uniter: George W. Bush and the American People*. 2nd ed. New York: Pearson Longman.

————. 2011c. "The Obama and Anti-Obama Coalitions." In *The Barack Obama Presidency: First Appraisals*, eds. Bert A. Rockman and Andrew Rudalevige. Washington, DC: CQ Press (forthcoming).

Jamieson, Kathleen Hall. 2010. Interview with Ron Elving. October 7.

Johnson, Alex. 2008. "McCain Hammers Obama on Ayers Ties." MSNBC, October 23. http://www.msnbc.msn.com/id/27343688.

Johnson, Haynes, and David S. Broder. 1996. *The System: The American Way of Politics at the Breaking Point*. Boston: Little Brown.

Jones, Charles O. 1988. *The Trustee Presidency: Jimmy Carter and the United States Congress*. Baton Rouge, LA, and London: Louisiana State University Press.

————. 1998. *Passages to the Presidency: From Campaigning to Governing*. Washington, DC: Brookings Institution Press.

————. 1999a. *Separate But Equal Branches: Congress and the Presidency*. New York: Chatham House.

————. 1999b. *Clinton and Congress, 1993–1996: Risk, Restoration, and Reelection*. Norman: University of Oklahoma Press.

————. 2005. *The Presidency in a Separated System*. Washington, DC: Brookings Institution Press.

Jones, Jeffrey M. 2009. "Most Americans Still Credit Obama for Bipartisan Efforts." Gallup Poll, September 18.

————. 2010. "Voters Rate Economy as Top Issue for 2010." Gallup, April 8.

Jost, Timothy S., and Joseph White. 2010. "Cutting Health Care Spending: What Is the Cost of an Excise Tax That Keeps People from Going to the Doctor?" Institute for America's Future Discussion Paper, January 13. http://www.ourfuture.org/files/Jost-White_Excise_Tax.pdf.

"Kaiser Health Tracking Poll." 2010. The Henry J. Kaiser Family Foundation, November. http://www.kff.org/kaiserpolls/upload/8120-F.pdf.

Kamarck, Elaine C. 2009. "The Evolving American State: The Trust Challenge." *The Forum* 7 (4): 1–22.

Kane, Paul. 2008. "GOP Leaders Oppose Haste on Stimulus. Extensive Vetting of Proposal Sought." *Washington Post*, December 30.

————. 2009a. "Gregg's Withdrawal Becomes a Partisan Issue." *Washington Post*, February 13. http://www.washingtonpost.com/wp-dyn/content/article/2009/02/12/AR2009021203841.html.

————. 2009b. "Pelosi Says She Will Not Seek Votes for Troop Surge." *Washington Post*, December 17.

Kantor, Jodi, and Charlie Savage. 2010. "Getting the Message." *New York Times*, February 15.

Keashly, L., and R. J. Fisher. 1996. "A Contingency Perspective on Conflict Intervention: Theoretical and Practical Considerations." In *Resolving International Conflicts*, eds. J. Bercovitch and J. A. Rubi. Boulder, CO: Lynne Reinner.

Keating, Stephen. 2010. "President Obama's Remarks at Greenwich Fundraiser." *Hartford Courant*, September 1. http://blogs.courant.com/Capitol_watch/2010/09/president-obamas-remarks-at-gr.html.

Kennedy, Robert C. 2010. "Can He Make the Donkey Drink?" *Harper's Weekly*. http://www.harpweek.com/09Cartoon/RelatedCartoon.asp?Month=September&Date=15.

Kernell, Samuel, and Samuel L. Popkin. 1986. *Chief of Staff: Twenty-Five Years of Managing the Presidency*. Berkeley: University of California Press, 91, 146.

Key, V. O., Jr. 1964. *Politics, Parties, & Pressure Groups*. 5th ed. New York: Crowell.

Kinder, Donald R., and Lynn M. Sanders. 1996. *Divided by Color*. Chicago: University of Chicago Press.

King, Gary. 1993. "The Methodology of Presidential Research." In *Researching the Presidency:*

*Vital Questions, New Approaches,* eds. George C. Edwards, John H. Kessel, and Bert A. Rockman. Pittsburgh, PA, and London: University of Pittsburgh Press, 287–314.

Kingsbury, Alex. 2008. "David Lawrence: A Profile." *U.S. News & World Report,* May 16.

Klaidman, Daniel. 2009. "Independent's Day." *Newsweek,* July 20.

Klein, Ezra. 2009. "Phil Schiliro." *Washington Post,* October 5.

Knoller, Mark. 2010. "Obama's First Year: By the Numbers," *CBSNews,* January 20. http://www.cbsnews.com/8301-503544_162-6119525-503544.html.

Koh, Harold. 2010. "Keynote Address." American Society of International Law Annual Meeting, March 25. http://www.state.gov/s/l/releases/remarks/139119.html.

Kornblut, Anne E. 2010. "Emanuel's Replacement Is Known as a Fixer." *Washington Post,* October 1, 1.

Kornblut, Anne E., and Scott Wilson. 2010. "Two of Obama's Closest Advisers Among Those Likely to Leave in White House Shuffle." *Washington Post,* September 23.

Kornblut, Anne E., Scott Wilson, and Karen De Young. 2009. "Obama Pressed for Faster Surge." *Washington Post,* December 6, A1.

Koszczuk, Jackie, and Martha Angle, eds. 2007. Profiles of Pelosi and Reid. *CQ's Politics in America 2008: The 110th Congress,* 87–88, 616–617.

Kroft, Steve. 2008. "Interview with Barack Obama." CBS News, *60 Minutes,* September 17. http://www.cbsnews.com/story/09/24/60minutes/main4476095.

———. 2010. "Interview with President Obama." CBS News, *60 Minutes.* November 7. http://www.wisepolitics.com/obama-on-60-minutes-november-7-2010-interview-2277.html.

Krugman, Paul. 2009. "The Stimulus Trap." *New York Times,* July 9.

Kumar, Martha Joynt, and Terry Sullivan, eds. 2003. *The White House World: Transitions, Organization, and Office Operations.* College Station: Texas A&M University Press, 259–265.

Kurtz, Howard. 2009. "Emanuel's Master of Reading Reporters." *Washington Post,* June 23.

LaFranchi, Howard. 2010. "Hillary Clinton: A Quiet Brand of Statecraft." *Christian Science Monitor,* September 25.

Lee, Frances E. 2009. *Beyond Ideology. Politics, Principles, and Partisanship in the U. S. Senate.* Chicago: University of Chicago Press.

Leibovich, Mark. 2008. "Between Obama and the Press." *New York Times Sunday Magazine,* December 21.

———. 2010a. "The First Senator from the Tea Party?" *New York Times Magazine,* January 6.

———. 2010b. "The Man the White House Wakes Up To." *New York Times Magazine,* April 25.

Lewis, David. 2009. *The Politics of Presidential Appointments.* Princeton, NJ: Princeton University Press.

Light, Paul C. 1999. *The President's Agenda.* Baltimore, MD, and London: The Johns Hopkins University Press.

Limbaugh, Rush. 2009. "I Hope He Fails." *RushLimbaugh.com,* March 3. http://www.rushlimbaugh.com/home/daily/site_011609/content/01125113.guest.html.

Linkins, Jason. 2009. "Obama 'Overexposed': The Media's New New Obsession." *Huffington Post,* March 24. http://www.huffingtonpost.com/2009/3/24/obama-overexposed-the-med_n_178569.html.

Lippman, Thomas W., and Bradley Graham. 1996. "U.S. Mulls Possible Response to Iran in Saudi Bombing." *Washington Post,* December 22.

Lithwick, Dahlia. 2009. "Obama, Bush Secret-Keeper." *Slate.com,* March 6.

Lizza, Ryan. 2009a. "Inside the Crisis: Larry Summers and the White House Economic Team." *The New Yorker,* October 12.

———. 2009b. "The Gatekeeper." *The New Yorker,* March 2.

———. 2010. "As the World Burns: How the Senate and the White House Missed Their Best Chance to Deal With Climate Change." *The New Yorker,* October 11.

Loomis, Burdett. 2001. "The Industry of Politics." Unpublished manuscript. Department of Political Science, University of Kansas.

Luce, Edward. 2010. "America: A Fearsome Foursome." *Financial Times,* February 3.

Luce, Edward, and Daniel Dombey. 2010. "US Foreign Policy: Waiting on the Sun King." *Financial Times,* March 30.

Luntz, Frank I. 2006. *Words That Work: It's Not What You Say, It's What People Hear.* New York: Hyperion.

Lux, Mike. 2009. "One More Step." *The Huffington Post,* November 9. http://www .huffingtonpost.com/mike-lux/one-more-step_b_351269.html.

Lynch, Marc. 2010. "Rhetoric and Reality: Countering Terrorism in the Age of Obama." Washington, DC: Center for a New American Security.

MacFarquhar, Larissa. 2007. "The Conciliator. Where Is Barack Obama Coming From?" *The New Yorker,* May 7.

Madison, James. [1788] 1962a. "No. 10." In *The Federalist Papers.* 2nd ed. New York: A Mentor Book, New American Library.

———. [1788] 1962b. "No. 45." In *The Federalist Papers.* 2nd ed. New York: A Mentor Book, New American Library.

Magleby, David, and Candice J. Nelson. 1990. *The Money Chase: Congressional Campaign Finance Reform.* Washington, DC: Brookings Institution Press.

Makinson, Larry. 2002. "What's Ethics Got To Do With It?" In *Shades of Gray: Campaign Ethics,* ed. Candice J. Nelson, David Dulio, and Stephen K. Medvic. Washington, DC: Brookings Institution Press.

Malbin, Michael J., and Thomas J. Gais. 1998. *The Day After Reform: Sobering Campaign Finance Lessons from the American States.* Albany, NY: Rockefeller Institute Press.

Mann, Thomas E., and Norman J. Ornstein. 2008. *The Broken Branch: How Congress Is Failing America and How to Get It Back on Track.* New York: Oxford University Press.

Maoz, Zeev. 2004. "Conflict Management and Conflict Resolution." In *Multiple Paths to Knowledge in International Relations,* eds. Zeev Maoz, Alex Mintz, T. Clifton Morgan, Glenn Palmer, and Richard J. Stoll. Lanham, MD: Lexington Books.

MarketWatch.com. Stock Quotations for Gannet, *The New York Times,* and *The Washington Post,* 2004–2010.

Markus, Gregory B., and Philip E. Converse. 1979. "A Dynamic Simultaneous Equation Model of Electoral Choice." *American Political Science Review* 73: 1055–1070.

Marmor, Theodore R., and Jonathan Oberlander. 2010. "The Health Bill Explained at Last." *New York Review of Books* LVII (13): 61–63.

Marmor, Theodore R., Jonathan Oberlander, and Joseph White. 2009. "Cost Control Options for the Obama Administration: Hope vs. Reality." *Annals of Internal Medicine* 150 (7): 485–489.

Mason, R. Chuck. 2008. "U.S.-Iraq Withdrawal/Status of Forces Agreement: Issues for Congressional Oversight." *Congressional Research Service,* December 12.

Mayer, George H. 1966. "Alf M. Landon, as Leader of the Republican Opposition, 1937–1940." *Kansas Historical Quarterlies* 32 (3): 325–333.

Mayer, Kenneth R., and David T. Canon. 1999. *The Dysfunctional Congress? The Individual Roots of an Institutional Dilemma.* Boulder, CO: Westview Press.

Mayer, Jane. 2009. "The Predator War." *The New Yorker,* October 26.

———. 2010. "The Trial." *The New Yorker,* February 15.

Mayhew, David R. 1991. *Divided We Govern: Party Control, Lawmaking, and Investigations, 1946–1990.* New Haven, CT, and London: Yale University Press.

———. 2008. "Major White House Legislative Proposals During First Two Years of Presidential Terms, 1949–2006." http://pantheon.yale.edu/~dmayhew/data5.html.

McCarthy, Daniel. 2003. "Mencken and His Enemies." *The American Conservative,* March 24.

McCarty, Nolan, Keith Poole, and Howard Rosenthal. 2006. *Polarized America: The Dance of Ideology and Unequal Riches.* Cambridge, MA, and London: MIT Press.

———. 2010. "Party Polarization: 1879–2009." http://voteview.com/polarizedamerica .asp#POLITICALPOLARIZATION.

McCutcheon, Chuck, and Christina L. Lyons, eds. 2009. Profiles of Pelosi and Reid. *CQ's Politics in America 2010: The 111th Congress,* 85–87, 619–621.

McGillis, Alec. 2010. "The Price Problem That Health-Care Reform Failed to Cure." *Washington Post,* October 24.

McGreal, Chris. 2009. "Americans Stick to Their Guns as Firearms Sales Surge." *The Guardian,* April 13.

McLoughlin, Glenn J. 2006. The National Telecommunications and Information Administration (NTIA): Budget, Programs, and Issues. Congressional Research Service, The Library of Congress. Updated August 29, 2006. (Order Code RS21469.)

Meacham, Jon. 2009. "A Conversation with Barack Obama." *Newsweek,* May 16. http://www.newsweek.com/id/19788/page/1.

Medvic, Stephen K. 2001. *Political Consultants in U.S. Congressional Elections.* Columbus: The Ohio State University Press.

Meernik, James, Rosa Aloisi, Marsha Sowell, and Angela Nichols. 2010. "The Impact of Tribunals and Truth Commissions on Post-Conflict Peace Building." In *Peace and Conflict 2010,* eds. J. J. Hewitt, J. Wilkenfeld, and T. R. Gurr. Boulder, CO: Paradigm Publishers.

Melber, Ari. 2009. "Caught on Tape: Obama Adviser Explains How to Control Media." *Huffington Post,* October 19. http://www.huffingtonpost.com/ari-melber/caught-on-tape-obama-advi_b_325782.html.

Memoli, Michael A. 2010. "The President Tapes an Appearance on 'The View.'" *Los Angeles Times,* July 29. http://articles.latimes.com/2010/jul/29/nation/la-na-obama-view-20100729.

Meyers, Jim. 2010. "Ex-CIA Director Hayden Praises Obama for 'Continuity' in the War on Terror." *NEWSMAX TV,* February 28.

Milbank, Dana. 2010a. "Obama Needs Rahm at the Top." *Washington Post,* February 21, A17.

———. 2010b. "Rep. Norm Dicks is About to Go from Mr. Boeing to Mr. Spending." *Washington Post,* May 9.

Miles, Donna. 2009. "New Advisory Brigades to Deploy to Iraq During Troop Rotations." American Forces Press Service, July 14.

Miller, Arthur H. 1974. "Political Issues and Trust in Government, 1964–1970." *American Political Science Review* 68.

Miller, Dale E., and Stephen K. Medvic. 2002. "Chapter 2—Campaign Ethics: A Framework." In *Shades of Gray: Perspectives on Campaign Ethics,* eds. Candice J. Nelson, David A. Dulio, and Stephen K. Medvic. Washington, DC: Brookings Institution Press.

Miller, Greg. 2009. "Senate to Investigate CIA's Actions Under Bush." *Los Angeles Times,* February 27.

Miller, Warren E., and J. Merrill Shanks. 1996. *The New American Voter.* Cambridge, MA: Harvard University Press.

Minorities at Risk Project. 2010. "Minorities at Risk: Monitoring the Persecution and Mobilization of Ethnic Groups Worldwide." University of Maryland, Center for International Development and Conflict Management. http://www.cidcm.umd.edu/mar.

Montgomery, Lori. 2010. "Economist Christina Romer Regrets Saying Jobless Rate Would Stay Below 8 Percent." *Washington Post,* August 7.

Montopoli, Brian. 2010. "White House: Obama Can Walk and Chew Gum." *CBSNews,* January 4. http://www.cbsnews.com/8301-503544_162-6054148-503544.html.

Mount, Mike. 2010. "U.S. Reveals It Has 5,113 Nuclear Weapons." CNN, May 3.

Mundy, Liza. 2007. "A Series of Fortunate Events." *Washington Post,* August 12.

Murray, Shailagh. 2008. "Looking Ahead, Obama Builds Ties With 'Blue Dogs.'" *Washington Post,* October 14.

Naftali, Timothy. 2005. *Blind Spot: The Secret History of American Counterterrorism.* New York: Basic Books.

Nagourney, Adam, and Jeff Zeleny. 2007. "Obama and Clinton Duel for Iowa Democrats." *New York Times,* November 11. http://www.nytimes.com/2007/11/11/us/politics/11cnd-dems.html.

Nather, David. 2008. "Obama's Next Task: Quick Rise to a Steep Challenge." *CQ Weekly,* November 10, 2960–2967.

———. 2009a. "Early Hope for a 'Grand Bargain.'" *CQ Weekly Online,* March 2, 462–470.

———. 2009b. "Information Age Has Fringe on Top." *CQ Weekly,* August 2.

————. 2009c. "Selling the Greater Good." *CQ Weekly Online,* July 6, 1576–1582.

National Broadband Plan. *Connecting America: The National Broadband Plan.* Federal Communications Commission. http://www.broadband.gov.

National Commission on Fiscal Responsibility and Reform. 2010. "The Moment of Truth." December. http://graphics8.nytimes.com/packages/pdf/politics/TheMomentofTruth12_1_2010.pdf?scp=2&sq=national%20commission%20on%20fiscal%20responsibility%20and%20reform&st=cse.

National Committee to Preserve Social Security and Medicare (NCPSSM). 2010. "Entitled to Know." December 10. http://www.ncpssm.org/entitledtoknow.

National Conference of State Legislatures. 2010. "Republicans Exceed Expectations in 2010 State Legislative Elections." November 3. http://www.ncsl.org/?tabid=21634.

Neustadt, Richard E. 1990. *Presidential Power and the Modern Presidents: The Politics of Leadership from Roosevelt to Reagan.* New York: Free Press.

Next Generation Internet. 2010a. Home Page. http://web.archive.org/web/19971210184945/http://www.ngi.gov.

————. 2010b. "Draft Implementation Plan Executive Summary." http://web.archive.org/web/19990502011102/www.ccic.gov/ngi/implementation-Jul97/exec_summary.html.

New America Foundation. 2010. "The Year of the Drone." 2004–2010, compiled by P. Bergen and K. Tiedemann. http://www.newamerica.net/drones.

Newhall, Marissa. 2009. "All Atwitter at Correspondents' Dinner, Minus Twitter." *Washington Post,* June 20.

Newport, Frank. 2009a. "Many Gun Owners Think Obama Will Try to Ban Gun Sales." Gallup News Service, October 20.

————. 2009b. "Obama Has Upper Hand in Stimulus Fight." *Gallup.com,* February 9.

————. 2009c. "More in U.S. Say Health Coverage Is Not Gov't. Responsibility: Marks Significant Shift from the Attitudes of the Past Decade." *Gallup.com,* November 13.

Nivola, Pietro S., and David W. Brady. 2006. *Red and Blue Nation? Characteristics and Causes of America's Polarized Politics.* Washington, DC: Brookings Institution Press.

————. 2008. *Red and Blue Nation? Characteristics and Causes of America's Polarized Politics.* Vol. 2. Washington, DC: Brookings Institution Press.

Nobel Prize Committee. 2009. "Peace Prize Citation for Barack Obama." http://nobelprize.org/nobel_prizes/peace/laureates/2009/press.html.

Northam, Jackie. 2009. "'Civilian Surge' Plan for Afghanistan Hits a Snag." *National Public Radio,* September 20.

"NSFNET: A Partnership for High-Speed Networking Final Report 1987–1995." http://www.merit.edu/about/history/pdf/NSFNET_final.pdf.

Nutting, Rex. 2008. "U.S. Economy Expected to Contract in 2009." *MarketWatch,* November 10.

Nyhan, Brendan. 2010. "Beware Context-Free Election Analysis." *Huffington Post,* November 4. http://www.huffingtonpost.com/brendan-nyhan/beware-context-free-elect_b_778921.html?view=screen.

Obama, Barack. 1995. *Dreams From My Father.* New York: Times Books.

————. 2006. *The Audacity of Hope.* New York: Crown Publishers.

————. 2007. Speech. August 17.

————. 2008a. "Obama's Remarks on Iraq and Afghanistan." *New York Times,* July 15.

————. 2008b. "Turn the Page." Speech to the California Democratic Party Convention, San Diego, CA, May 2.

————. 2008c. Speech—The Change We Need. Detroit, MI. September 28. http://www.barackobama.com/2008/09/28/remarks_of_senator_barack_obam_123.php.

————. 2009a. Executive Order No. 13490. January 21.

————. 2009b. "Obama Prague Speech on Nuclear Weapons: Full Text." *Huffington Post,* April 5.

————. 2009c. White House News Conference. February 9. http://www.nytimes.com/2009/02/09/us/politics/09text-obama.html?_r=1.

———. 2009d. "News Conference by the President." July 22. http://www.whitehouse.gov/the-press-office/news-conference-president-july-22-2009.

———. 2009e. "News Conference by the President." March 24. http://www.whitehouse.gov/the-press-office/news-conference-president-march-24-2009.

———. 2009f. "News Conference by the President." February 9. http://www.whitehouse.gov/the-press-office/news-conference-president-february-9-2009.

———. 2009g. Transcript: President Obama Delivers Remarks at Georgetown University. April 14. http://www.washingtonpost.com/wpsrv/politics/documents/Obama_Economy_Georgetown.html.

———. 2009h. "George Stephanopoulos' Exclusive Interview with President-Elect Barack Obama." *ABC News/This Week,* January 11. http://abcnews.go.com/ThisWeek/Economy/story?id=6618199&page=1.

———. 2010a. "National Security Strategy." May. http://www.whitehouse.gov/sites/default/files/rss_viewer/national_security_strategy.pdf.

———. 2010b. Speech at George Mason University Patriot Center. March 19.

———. 2010c. State of the Union Message. January 19.

"Obama Will Say Iraq Combat Mission to End Aug. 31, 2010." 2009. Associated Press, February 24.

Oberlander, Jonathan, and Joseph White. 2009. "Public Attitudes Toward Health Care Spending Aren't the Problem; Prices Are." *Health Affairs* 28 (5): 1285–1293.

O'Brien, S. 2010. "Crisis Early Warning and Decision Support: Contemporary Approaches and Thoughts on Future Research." *International Studies Review* 12 (1): 87–104.

OCI. 2003. *Revolutionizing Science and Engineering Through Cyberinfrastructure: Report of the National Science Foundation Blue-Ribbon Advisory Panel on Cyberinfrastructure.* January.

Office of the Clerk, U.S. House of Representatives. "Party Divisions of the House of Representatives (1789 to Present)." http://clerk.house.gov/art_history/house_history/partyDiv.html.

Office of Management and Budget. 2009. *A New Era of Responsibility: Renewing America's Promise.* February 26. http://www.gpoaccess.gov/usbudget/fy10/pdf/fy10-newera.pdf.

Oleszek, Walter J. 2007. *Congressional Procedures and the Policy Process.* 7th ed. Washington, DC: CQ Press.

Ornstein, Norman J. 2010. "Obama: A Pragmatic Moderate Faces the 'Socialist' Smear." *Washington Post,* April 14.

Osnos, Evan. 2009. "The Daley Show: Letter from Chicago." *The New Yorker,* March 8.

Ota, Alan K. "Obama's Go-To GOP Senators." *CQ Weekly,* January 26, 180–181.

Owens, John E. 2004. "Challenging (and Acting For) the President: Congressional Leadership in an Era of Partisan Polarization." In *New Challenges for the American Presidency,* eds. George C. Edwards and John Philip Davies. New York: Longman, 123–143.

Owens, Simon. 2009. "May '09 Political Blog Readership 53% Lower Than It Was in October '08," *Bloggasm.com,* June 11. http://www.bloggasm.com/may-09-political-blog-readership-53-percent-lower-than-it-was-in-october-08.

Pace, Julie. "Obama Seeks to Return to Campaign-Style Discipline." Associated Press, February 16.

Packer, George. 2010a. "The Era of the Disappearing Era." *The New Yorker,* November 2. http://www.newyorker.com/online/blogs/georgepacker/2010/11/tom-perriello-went-down-to.html.

———. 2010b. "Obama's Lost Year." *The New Yorker,* March 15.

Page, Benjamin I., and Calvin C. Jones. 1979. "Reciprocal Effects of Policy Preferences, Party Loyalties, and the Vote." *American Political Science Review* 73: 1071–1089.

Page, Susan. 2010. Interview with Ron Elving. October 14.

Palmer, Anne. 2009. "Legislative Affairs Team Gets to Work: Full Plate Awaits Hill Vets Staffing Office." *Roll Call,* January 21.

Panagopoulos, Costas, and Peter L. Francia. 2009. "Grassroots Mobilization in the 2008 Presidential Election." *Journal of Political Marketing,* October 8 (4): 315–333.

Parsons, Chris, and Peter Nicholas. 2010. "Obama Transition Bumps Up Against Congress' Egos." *Los Angeles Times,* January 12.

Pate, A. 2010. "Trends in Democratization: A Focus on Minority Rights." In *Peace and Conflict 2010*, eds. J. J. Hewitt, J. Wilkenfeld, and T. R. Gurr. Boulder, CO: Paradigm Publishers.

Patterson, Bradley. 2000. *The White House Staff.* Washington, DC: Brookings Institution Press.

Patterson, Bradley, and James Pfiffner. 2001. "The White House Office of Presidential Personnel." *Presidential Studies Quarterly*, September.

Peabody, Robert L. 1977. "House Party Leadership in the 1970s." In *Congress Reconsidered*, 2nd ed., eds. Lawrence C. Dodd and Bruce I. Oppenheimer. Washington, DC: CQ Press.

Pear, Robert. 2010. "Health Official Can't Guarantee Openness in Talks." *New York Times*, February 4.

Pelosi, Nancy. 2009. Speech given at John F. Kennedy School of Government, November 13, 2009.

Perrine, Keith, and Seth Stern. 2009. "Obama Says No Prosecutions." *CQ Today Online News*, April 16.

Peterson, Mark A. 1990. *Legislating Together: The White House and Capitol Hill from Eisenhower to Reagan*. Cambridge, MA, and London: Harvard University Press.

Petreaus, David. 2010. *NBC Meet the Press*. February 21.

Pew Research Center for the People & the Press. 2009. "Economy, Jobs Trump All Other Policy Priorities in 2009: Environment, Immigration, Health Care Slip Down the List." Pew Research Center for the People & the Press Survey Report.

———. 2010a. "A Clear Rejection of the Status Quo, No Consensus About Future Policies." Pew Research Foundation, November 3.

———. 2010b. "Americans Spending More Time Following the News." September 12. http://pew-press.org/report/652.

Pew Research Center Project for Excellence in Journalism. 2009. "Confrontational Health Care Coverage." Pew Research Center Publications, August 18. http://pewresearch.org/pubs/1314/cable-news-coverage-town-hall-confrontations.

———. 2010. "The New News Landscape: Rise of the Internet—Understanding the Participatory News Consumer." Pew Research Center Publications, March 1. http://pewresearch.org/pubs/1508/internet-cell-phone-users-news-social-experience.

Pfiffner, James. 1993. "The President's Chief of Staff: Lessons Learned." *Presidential Studies Quarterly*, Winter.

———. 1996. *The Strategic Presidency: Hitting the Ground Running.* 2nd ed. Lawrence: University Press of Kansas.

———, ed. 1999. *The Managerial Presidency.* 2nd ed. College Station: Texas A&M University Press.

———. 2009a. "Decision Making in the Bush White House." *Presidential Studies Quarterly*, June.

———. 2009b. "Presidential Use of White House 'Czars.'" Testimony before the Senate Committee on Homeland Security and Governmental Affairs, October 22.

———. 2010a. *Torture as Public Policy.* Boulder, CO: Paradigm Publishers.

———. 2010b. *The Modern Presidency.* 6th ed. Belmont, CA: Wadsworth Thomson.

Pildes, Richard H. [Forthcoming.] "Why the Center Does Not Hold: The Causes of Hyperpolarized Democracy in America." *California Law Review*.

Ploughshares Fund. 2010. "Nuclear Security Summit." January 29. http://www.ploughshares.org/news-analysis/publications/nuclear-security-summit-fact-sheet.

Plouffe, David. 2009. *The Audacity to Win.* New York: Viking Penguin.

*Politico*/George Washington University. 2010. "Battleground Poll." September 27. http://www.politico.com/pdf/PPM156_bg-41-questionnaire_092410.pdf.

"Poll: October 21–26, 2010." *The New York Times*/CBS News Survey. http://s3.amazonaws.com/nytdocs/docs/503/503.pdf.

Polsby, Nelson. 1983. "Some Landmarks in Modern Presidential-Congressional Relations." In *Both Ends of the Avenue*, ed. Anthony King. Washington, DC: American Enterprise Institute.

Pomper, Gerald M. 2010. "The Presidential Election: Change Comes to America." In *The Elections of 2008*, ed. M. Nelson. Washington, DC: CQ Press.

"President Bush's Hill-Savvy Lobbying Team." 2002. CQ Weekly, December 14, 3252.

"Presidential Elections Data." The American Presidency Project. http://www.presidency.ucsb.edu/elections.php

"The President's Budget for Fiscal Year 2011." http://www.whitehouse.gov/omb/budget.

Preston, Mark. 2009. "Steele and Limbaugh Speak." CNN.com, March 3. http://politicalticker.blogs.cnn.com/2009/03/03/steele-and-limbaugh-speak.

Priest, Dana. 2010. "U.S. Military Teams, Intelligence Deeply Involved in Aiding Yemen on Strikes." *Washington Post*, January 27.

Project on National Security Reform. 2010. *Toward Integrating Complex National Missions: Lessons from the National Counterterrorism Center's Directorate of Strategic Operational Planning.* http://www.pnsr.org/data/files/pnsr_nctc_dsop_report.pdf.

Przybyla, Heidi. 2009. "Obama Campaign Activists Find Health Care Harder Sell." *Bloomberg*, June 17. http://www.bloomberg.com/apps/news?pid=20670001&refer=&sid=arSw7zOwyxKo.

Przybyla, Heidi, and John McCormick. 2010. "Poll: Americans Don't Know Economy Expanded With Tax Cuts." *Bloomberg*, October 19.

Public Report of the Vice President's Task Force on Combating Terrorism. 1986. February. Washington, DC: U.S. Government Printing Office.

Puzzanghera, Jim. 2010. "Estimate of TARP Losses Falls to $25 Billion." *Los Angeles Times*, November 30.

Quelch, John. 2009. "Quantifying the Economic Impact of the Internet." *Harvard Business School Working Knowledge*, August 17.

"Questioning Nuclear Arms." 1996. PBS, December 4. http://www.pbs.org/newshour/bb/military/nuclear_debate_12-4.html.

Rampell, Catherine. 2009. "Economists' Letter to Obama on Health Care Reform." *The New York Times* Economix website, November 17. http://economix.blogs.nytimes.com/2009/11/17/economists-letter-to-obama-on-health-care-reform.

Remnick, David. 2010a. *The Bridge: The Life and Rise of Barack Obama.* New York: Alfred A. Knopf.

———. 2010b. "Obama Has a Considerable Ego." *Der Spiegel*, October 8. http://www.spiegel.de/international/world/0,1518,721922,00.html.

Renshon, Stanley A. 2008. "Psychological Reflections on Barack Obama and John McCain: Assessing the Contours of a New Presidential Administration." *Political Science Quarterly* 123 (Fall): 391–433.

Reynolds, Katherine Lewis. 2010. "Treasury Reports Larger-Than-Expected Returns on TARP." *The Fiscal Times*, February 12.

Richardson, Elliot. 1996. *Reflections of a Radical Moderate.* New York: Pantheon.

Rivers, Douglas. 2006. "Sample Matching: Representative Sampling from Internet Panels." Palo Alto, CA: Polimetrix White Paper Series.

Rockman, Bert A. 2009. "Does the Revolution in Presidential Studies Mean 'Off with the President's Head'?" *Presidential Studies Quarterly* 39 (4): 786–794.

Rogin, Josh. 2009. "Disputes in House Delay War Funds." *CQ Weekly Online*, June 8, 1318–1319.

Rohde, David. 1991. *Parties and Leaders in the Postreform House.* Chicago: University of Chicago Press.

*Roll Call.* 2009. March 20, June 12, June 18, December 23. http://www.rollcall.com/.

Romano, Lois. 2010. "Hillary Rodham Clinton Widens Her Circle at State Department." *Washington Post*, March 10.

Rosen, Jay, 2004. "'Nobody heard what you said.' Lesley Stahl's Fable About Reagan and the Press." Pressthink.org, June 9. http://archive.pressthink.org/2004/06/09/reagan_words.html.

Rubin, Alissa. 2009. "Afghans Detail a Secret Prison Still Operating on a U.S. Base." *New York Times*, November 28.

Rubin, Richard, and Niels Lesniewski. 2010. "Extenders Bill Stalls Over Deficit Effect." *CQ Weekly Online*, June 21.

Rucker, Philip, and Dan Eggen. 2009. "Protests at Democrats' Health-Care Events Spark Political Tug of War." *Washington Post*, August 6.

Rutenberg, Jim. 2008. "Pundits Pronounce Judgment: It's Over." *New York Times*, May 8.

Saad, Lydia. 2009. "Public Support for Stimulus Package Unchanged at 52%: Seven in 10 Favor Some Type of Stimulus Legislation." http://www.gallup.com/poll/114184/public-support -stimulus-package-unchanged.aspx (February 6).

Sabato, Larry J. 2000. *Feeding Frenzy: Attack Journalism and American Politics*. Baltimore, MD: Lanahan Publishers, Inc.

Savage, James D. 1990. *Balanced Budgets and American Politics*. Ithaca, NY: Cornell University Press.

Schatz, Joseph J. 2009. "Obama's Budget Proposal Alters the Typical 'Tax and Spend' Equation." *CQ Weekly Online*, March 2, 480–481.

———. 2010. "Murphy's Law and the Stimulus." *CQ Weekly Online*, October 11, 2342–2344.

Schaub, Gary, Jr., and James Forsyth, Jr. 2010. "An Arsenal We Can All Live With." *New York Times*, May 23. http://www.nytimes.com/2010/05/24/opinion/24schaub.html (November 8, 2010).

Schram, Martin. 1987. *The Great American Video Game: Presidential Politics in the Television Age*. New York: William Morrow & Company.

Scheiber, Noam. 2010. "The Chief." *The New Republic*, March 3.

Seabrook, Andrea. 2009. "House Vote on Stimulus Follows Partisan Lines." *NPR*, January 28. http://www.npr.org/templates/story/story.php?storyId=99974987.

Seelye, Katherine Q. 2009a. "Fighting Heath Care Overhaul, and Proud of It." *New York Times*, August 30.

———. 2009b. "Obama Wades Into a Volatile Racial Issue." *New York Times*, July 23.

Senior, Jennifer. 2009. "The Message Is the Message." *New York Magazine*, August 2. http:// nymag.com/news/politics/58199.

Shane, Scott. 2009. "C.I.A. to Close Secret Overseas Prisons for Terrorism Suspects." *New York Times*, April 10.

Shear, Michael, and Ceci Connolly. 2009. "Obama Assembles Powerful West Wing." *Washington Post*, January 8.

Shear, Michael, and Carol Leonning. 2009. "Commerce Pick Richardson Withdraws." *Washington Post*, January 5.

Sherif, Muzafer, and Carl I. Hovland. 1961. *Social Judgment: Assimilation and Contrast Effects in Communication and Attitude Change*. New Haven, CT: Yale University Press.

"Sickly U.S. Economy Set for 2nd Half Rebound: Survey." 2009. Reuters, March 10.

Siebel, Mark, and Warren P. Strobel. 2009. "CIA Official: No Proof Harsh Techniques Stopped Terror Attacks." McClatchy, April 24.

Sifry, Micah L. 2009. "The Obama Roadblock: Why He's Sagging Online." techpresident.com, September 21. http://techpresident.com/blog-entry/obama-roadblock-why-hes-sagging -online.

Silver, Nate. 2010. "2010: An Aligning Election." http://fivethirtyeight.blogs.nytimes.com/ 2010/11/08/2010-an-aligning-election.

Sinclair, Barbara. 1995. *Legislators, Leaders and Lawmaking*. Baltimore, MD: The Johns Hopkins University Press.

———. 2006. *Party Wars: Polarization and the Politics of National Policymaking*. Norman: University of Oklahoma Press.

———. 2007a. "Living (and Dying?) by the Sword: George W. Bush as Legislative Leader." In *The Bush Legacy*, eds. Colin Campbell and Bert Rockman. Washington, DC: CQ Press.

———. 2007b. *Unorthodox Lawmaking: New Legislative Processes in the U.S. Congress*. Washington, DC: CQ Press.

———. 2008. "Orchestrators of Unorthodox Lawmaking: Pelosi and McConnell in the 110th Congress." *The Forum*, 6 (3): 1–15.

Singletary, Michelle. 2010. "Like Most of Us, Velma Hart Just Wanted a Little Reassurance." *Washington Post,* September 25. http:www.washingtonpost.com/wp-dyn/content/article/2010/09/24/AR2010092401762.html.

Siroker, Dan. 2010. Interview with Ron Elving. August 26.

Skowronek, Stephen. 1993. *The Politics Presidents Make, Leadership from John Adams to George Bush.* New Haven, CT, and London: Yale University Press.

Smith, Steven S. 1993. "Forces of Change in Senate Party Leadership and Organization." In *Congress Reconsidered,* 5th ed., ed. Lawrence C. Dodd and Bruce I. Oppenheimer. Washington, DC: CQ Press.

Sniderman, Paul M., and Edward H. Stiglitz. 2008. "Race and the Moral Character of the Modern American Experience.: *The Forum* 6 (4): 1–15.

Social Security Administration. "Father Charles E. Coughlin." http://www.ssa.gov/history/cough.html.

Solomon, Deborah. 2010. "Bailout Looking Much Less Pricey." *Wall Street Journal,* April 12.

Soraghan, Mike. 2009. "Dem Centrists Press Pelosi to Shelve Climate Bill." *The Hill,* May 6.

Standard & Poor's 500 Index. 2009 and 2010. "S&P 500 INDEX,RTH (^GSPC)." http://finance.yahoo.com/echarts?s=^GSPC+Interactive#chart4:symbol=^gspc;range=2y;indicator=volume;charttype=line;crosshair=on;ohlcvalues=0;logscale=on;source=.

Stein, Jeff. 2009. "What's the Big Deal About Hersh's Assassinations' Claim?" *CQ Politics,* April 2.

Steinhauser, Paul. 2009. "Poll: Obama Rating Slips, but Still High." *CNN Politics,* February 20.

Stimson, James A. 1999. *Public Opinion in America: Moods, Cycles, and Swings.* 2nd ed. Transforming American Politics. Boulder, CO: Westview Press.

Stolberg, Sheryl Gay. 2009a. "Democrats Raise Alarms Over Health Bill Costs." *New York Times,* November 9.

———. 2009b. "Obama Is Said to Consider Preventive Detention Plan." *New York Times,* May 21.

———. 2010. "Filling an Aide's Shoes With Very Different Feet." *New York Times,* October 1.

Stolberg, Sheryl Gay, and Helene Cooper. 2009. "Obama Adds Troops, but Maps Exit Plan." *New York Times,* December 1.

Stolberg, Sheryl Gay, Shaila Dewan, and Brian Stelter. 2010. "With Apology, Fired Official Is Offered a New Job." *New York Times,* July 21.

Stolberg, Sheryl Gay, and David M. Herszenhorn. 2010. "Obama Weighs a Paring of Goals for a Health Care Bill." *New York Times,* January 21.

Stolberg, Sheryl Gay, Jeff Zeleny, and Carl Hulse. 2010. "The Long Road Back." *New York Times,* March 21.

Sullivan, Terry, ed. 2004. *The Nerve Center.* College Station: Texas A&M University Press.

Sundquist, James L. 1968. *Politics and Policy. The Eisenhower, Kennedy and Johnson Years.* Washington, DC: Brookings Institution Press.

Talev, Margaret. 2009. "Obama Sets New Standard for Managing the News." McClatchy Washington Bureau, March 27. http://w3.nexis.com/new/results/docview/docview.do?docLinkInd=true&risb=21_T10605916226&format=GNBFULL&sort=BOOLEAN&startDocNo=1&resultsUrlKey=29_T10605916229&cisb=22_T10605916228&treeMax=true&treeWidth=0&csi=247820&docNo=3.

Talley, Ian, and Stephen Power. 2009. "House Panel Clears Plan to Cut Greenhouse Gases: U.S. Bill Moves a Step Closer, but a Global Deal on Climate Change Presents a Bigger Challenge for Obama Administration." *Wall Street Journal,* May 22.

Tapper, Jake. 2008. "ABC Evening News," ABC Transcripts, abcnews.com, "Napolitano: System Like 'Clockwork ' After Attack, Not So Sure About Before." December 27. http://blogs.abcnews.com/politicalpunch/2009/12/napolitano-system-like-clockwork-after-attack-not so-sure-about-before.html.

Teixeira, Ruy. 2010. *The Public Opinion Paradox: An Anatomy of America's Love-Hate Relationship with Its Government.* Washington, DC: Center for American Progress.

Telecommunications Act of 1996. Public Law No. 104–104, 110 Stat. 56 (1996).

Tesler, Michael, and David O. Sears. 2010. *Obama's Race: The 2008 Election and the Dream of a Post-Racial America*. Chicago: University of Chicago Press.

Theriault, Sean M. 2008. *Party Polarization in Congress*. New York: Cambridge University Press.

Thomasson, Lynn. 2009. "U.S. Stocks Slide in Dow's Worst Drop Since April on Jobs Data." *Bloomberg,* July 2.

Thomma, Steven. 2010."Michelle Obama Hits Trail to Help Vulnerable Democrats." McClatchy, October 13. http://www.mcclatchydc.com/2010/10/13/v-print/102002/michelle-obama -hits-trail-to-help.html.

Thrush, Glenn. 2009. "With 111th, the Age of Pelosi Dawns." *Politico,* January 6. http://www .politico.com/news/stories/0109/17105.html.

Thurber, James A. 1996. "Political Power and Policy Subsystems in American Politics." In *Agenda for Excellence: Administering the State,* eds. B. Guy Peters and Bert A. Rockman. Chatham, NJ: Chatham House, 76–104.

———. 2002. "From Campaigning to Lobbying." In *Shades of Gray: Perspectives on Campaign Ethics.* Washington, DC: Brookings Institution Press, 151–170.

———. 2009. "Corruption and Scandal in Washington: Have Lobbying and Ethics Reform Made a Difference? Exploring the Relationship Among Candidates, Campaign Consultants, Lobbyists, and Elected and Appointed Public Officials." Paper for Conference on Political Corruption in America at Loyola Marymount University, Institute for Leadership Studies, February 23.

———. 2010. "President Obama, Congress and the Battle with Interest Groups and Lobbyists." Paper for Conference on American Government, Politics and Policy.

Thurber, James A., and Samantha Durst. 1993. "The 1990 Budget Enforcement Act: The Decline of Congressional Accountability." In *Congress Reconsidered,* 5th ed., eds. Lawrence C. Dodd and Bruce I. Oppenheimer. Washington, DC: CQ Press.

Thurber, James A., and Candice J. Nelson, eds. 2000. *Campaign Warriors: Campaign Consultants in Elections.* Washington, DC: Brookings Institution Press.

Thurber, James A., Candice J. Nelson, and David A. Dulio. 2000. *Crowded Airwaves: Campaign Advertising in Elections.* Washington, DC: Brookings Institution Press.

Toner, Robin. 2008. "Obama's Test: Can a Liberal Be a Unifier?" *New York Times,* March 25.

Tumulty, Karen, and Michael Scherer. 2009. "An Enforcer Named Emanuel." *Time,* January 21. http://www.time.com/time/printout/0,8816,1873120,00.html, 48.

Turner, S. Derek. *Dismantling Digital Deregulation: Toward a National Broadband Strategy.* Freepress. http://www.freepress.net/files/Dismantling_Digital_Deregulation.pdf.

United Nations. 2010. *Human Development Report 2004: Cultural Liberty in Today's Diverse World.* New York: United National Development Program.

United Nations. General Assembly, Human Rights Council. 2010. "Report of the Special Rapporteur on Extrajudicial, Summary or Arbitrary Executions, Philip Alston."

United States Agency for International Development. 2005. "Measuring Fragility: Indicators and Methods for Rating State Performance." Washington, DC.

———. 2010. "Alert List Reports." Washington, DC.

United States Congress, Congressional Budget Office. 2008. "Key Issues in Analyzing Major Health Insurance Proposals." December. http://cbo.gov/ftpdocs/99xx/doc9924/12-18 -KeyIssues.pdf.

———. 2009a. "The Troubled Asset Relief Program: Report on Transactions Through December 31, 2008." January. http://www.cbo.gov/ftpdocs/99xx/doc9961/01-16-TARP.pdf.

———. 2009b. "The Budget and Economic Outlook: Fiscal Years 2009 to 2019." http://cbo .gov/ftpdocs/99xx/doc9957/01-07-Outlook.pdf.

———. 2009c. "Estimated Macroeconomic Impacts of the American Recovery and Reinvestment Act of 2009: Letter to the Honorable Charles E. Grassley." http://cbo.gov/ftpdocs/100xx/ doc10008/03-02_Macro_Effects_of_ARRA.pdf.

———. 2009d. "A Preliminary Analysis of the President's Budget and an Update of CBO's Budget and Economic Outlook." http://cbo.gov/ftpdocs/100xx/doc10014/03-20-PresidentBudget .pdf.

————. 2009e. "The Economic Effects of Legislation to Reduce Greenhouse Gas Emissions." http://cbo.gov/ftpdocs/105xx/doc10573/09-17-Greenhouse-Gas.pdf.

————. 2010a. "Estimated Impact of the American Recovery and Reinvestment Act on Employment and Economic Output from October 2009 Through December 2009." CBO Report, February 10.

————. 2010b. "The Budget and Economic Outlook: An Update." http://cbo.gov/ftpdocs/117xx/doc11705/08-18-Update.pdf.

————. 2010c. "Estimated Impact of the American Recovery and Reinvestment Act on Employment and Economic Output from April 2010 Through June 2010," August. http://www.cbo.gov/publications/collections/collections.cfm?collect=12.

————. 2010d. "Estimated Impact of the American Recovery and Reinvestment Act on Employment and Economic Output from July 2010 Through September 2010." http://cbo.gov/ftpdocs/119xx/doc11975/11-24-ARRA.pdf.

————. 2010e. "The Budgetary Impact and Subsidy Costs of the Federal Reserve's Actions During the Financial Crisis." http://cbo.gov/ftpdocs/115xx/doc11524/11524_Summary.pdf.

————. 2010f. "The Individual Alternative Minimum Tax." http://cbo.gov/ftpdocs/108xx/doc10800/01-15-AMT_Brief.pdf.

United States Department of Defense. 2006. *National Military Strategic Plan for the War on Terrorism.* February.

————. 2010. *Nuclear Posture Review Report.* April.

United States Department of State. 1968. *Treaty on the Nonproliferation of Nuclear Weapons.*

————. 2008. "Agreement Between the United States of America and the Republic of Iraq on the Withdrawal of United States Forces from Iraq and the Organization of Their Activities During Their Temporary Presence in Iraq." http://www.usf-iraq.com/images/CGs_Messages/security_agreement.pdf (February 2, 2011).

————. 2010. "Clinton, Gates Interview on CBS's 'Face the Nation.'" April 11. http://www.america.gov/st/texttrans-english/2010/April/20100412150641xjsnommis0.1368372.html.

United States General Accounting Office. 1996. "Financial Audit: Resolution Trust Corporation's 1995 and 1994 Financial Statements." July. http://www.gao.gov/archive/1996/ai96123.pdf.

United States Office of the Director of National Intelligence. 2010. *Annual Threat Assessment of the US Intelligence Community for the Senate Select Committee on Intelligence.* February 2.

United States Senate. "Party Divisions in the Senate, 1989–Present." http://www.senate.gov/pagelayout/history/one_item_and_teasers/partydiv.htm.

United States Senate. Select Committee on Intelligence. 2010. *Attempted Terrorist Attack on Northwest Airlines Flight 253.* 111th Congress, 2nd Session. Report 111–199.

"U.S. Revises Offer to Take Sudan off Terror List." 2010. *New York Times,* November 8.

Van de Water, Paul N. 2010. "Changes to Excise Tax on High-Cost Health Plans Address Criticisms, Retain Long-Term Benefits." Center on Budget and Policy Priorities Special Series: Health Reform Issues, January 26. http://www.cbpp.org/files/1-26-10health2.pdf.

Vargas, Jose Antonio. 2008. "On the Web, Supporters of McCain Wage an Uphill Battle." *Washington Post,* June 26, C1.

————. 2009. "Web-Savvy Obama Team Hits Unexpected Bumps." *Washington Post,* March 2, A3.

Villalobos, Jose D., and Justin Vaughn. 2010. "More Czars Than the Romanovs? Barack Obama's Czars in Historical and Legal Context." Paper presented at the American Political Science Association Convention, September 2.

Waitz, Nancy. 2008. "Economic Slide to Extend into 2009: Blue Chip." Reuters, August 11.

————. 2009. "Recession Likely to End in Q3 2009: Blue Chip Survey." Reuters, July 10.

Walcott, Charles E., Shirley Anne Warshaw, and Stephen J. Wayne. 2001. "The Chief of Staff." *Presidential Studies Quarterly,* 464–489.

Wallace-Wells, Ben. 2008. Interview: "Dreams of Obama." *Frontline.* PBS/2009 WGBH Educational Foundation, October 14.

Walsh, Ken. 1996. *Feeding the Beast: The White House Versus the Press.* New York: Random House.

Warshaw, Shirley Anne. 1996. *Powersharing.* Albany, NY: SUNY Press.

Waxman, Matthew. 2010. "Faculty Q and A: Matthew Waxman." *The Record,* Columbia University, February 22, 7.

Wayne, Alex, and Edward Epstein. 2010. "Obama Seals Legislative Legacy with Health Insurance Overhaul." *CQ Weekly Online,* March 29, 748–753.

Wayne, Stephen J. 1978. *The Legislative Presidency.* New York: Harper & Row.

*Webster's New Ninth Collegiate Dictionary.* 1983. Springfield, MA: Merriam-Webster.

Weisberg, Herbert F., and Christopher J. Devine. 2009. "Racial Attitude Effects on Voting in the 2008 Presidential Election: Examining the Unconventional Factors Shaping Vote Choice in a Most Unconventional Election." Presented at the Mershon Conference on the Transformative Election of 2008, Columbus, OH, October 1–4.

Weisman, Jonathan. 2009. "Geithner Tax History Muddles Confirmation." *Wall Street Journal,* January 14.

Weisman, Jonathan, and Naftali Bendavid. 2009. "Obama Eyes $300 Billion Tax Cut." *The Wall Street Journal,* January 5.

Weisman, Jonathan, Laura Meckler, and Naftali Bendavid. 2009. "Obama on Defense as Daschle Withdraws." *Wall Street Journal,* February 4, 1.

Wenner, Jann. 2010. "Obama in Command: The Rolling Stone Interview." *Rolling Stone,* September 28. http: www.rollingstone.com/politics/news/17390/209395.

White, Joseph. 2003. *False Alarm: Why the Greatest Threat to Social Security and Medicare Is the Campaign to "Save"Them.* Baltimore, MD: The Johns Hopkins University Press.

———. 2009. "The President's Budget vs. Congressional Budgeting: Institutionalizing the Adversarial Presidency?" In *Rivals for Power: Presidential-Congressional Relations,* 4th ed., ed. James A. Thurber. Lanham, MD: Rowman & Littlefield.

———. 2011. "Muddling Through the Muddled Middle." *Journal of Health Politics, Policy and Law* 36 (3).

White, Joseph, and Aaron Wildavsky. 1991. *The Deficit and the Public Interest: The Search for Responsible Budgeting During the 1980s.* Berkeley and New York: University of California Press and The Russell Sage Foundation.

White House. 2003. *National Strategy for Combating Terrorism (NSCT).* February.

White House. 2006a. "9/11 Five Years Later: Successes and Challenges." September.

———. 2006b. *National Strategy for Combating Terrorism (NSCT).* September.

———. 2009. Transcripts. May 10. http://whitehouse.gov.

White House Office of the Press Secretary. 2009a. "Statements and Releases." January–July 2009. http://www.whitehouse.gov/briefing-room/Statements-and-Releases/2009/01.

———. 2009b. "Remarks by the President after Meeting with Energy CEOs," July 2. http://www.whitehouse.gov/the-press-office/remarks-president-after-meeting-with-energy-ceos (December 2, 2010).

———. 2009c. "ADVISORY: Conference Call with Senior Administration Officials to Discuss President Obama's Trip Next Week." July 1. http://www.whitehouse.gov/the-press-office/advisory-conference-call-with-senior-administration-officials-discuss-president-ob-0 (December 2, 2010).

———. 2009d. "President Obama to Meet with Business Leaders to Discuss Innovation and Job Creation." July 2. http://www.whitehouse.gov/the-press-office/president-obama-meet-with-business-leaders-discuss-innovation-and-job-creation (December 2, 2010).

———. 2009e. "Weekly Address: Recovery and the Jobs of the Future." July 10. http://www.whitehouse.gov/blog/2009/07/10/weekly-address-recovery-and-jobs-future (December 2, 2010).

Wickham, DeWayne. 2008. "Obama Insider Paints Portrait of 'Pragmatic' President-Elect." *USAToday,* November 11.

Wilkenfeld, J. 2008. "Unstable States and International Crises." In *Peace and Conflict 2008,* eds. J. J. Hewitt, J. Wilkenfeld, and T. R. Gurr. Boulder, CO: Paradigm Publishers.

Wilkenfeld, J., A. Pate, and V. Asal. 2009. "Mosaic of Minority Violence." In *START 2009 Research Review,* National Consortium for the Study of Terrorism and Responses to Terrorism. College Park: University of Maryland.

Willis, Bob. 2010. "Forecasting the U.S. Economy." *Bloomberg Markets,* January.

Wills, Gary. 2010. "Behind Obama's Cool." *New York Times Book Review,* April 11.

Wilson, Reid. 2009. "Big Tent or 'Blurring the Lines'? Reagan Words, Meaning Drive GOP Debate." *The Hill,* October 24.

Wilson, Scott. 2009. "Obama Team Derides Cheney's Criticisms." *Washington Post,* March 17.

———. 2010a. "Biden vs. Cheney on Terror Policy." *Washington Post,* February 15.

———. 2010b. "The Making of a Wartime Commander in Chief." *Washington Post,* January 19.

Winters, Jeffrey A., and Benjamin I. Page. 2009. "Oligarchy in the United States?" *Perspectives on Politics* 7 (December): 731–752.

Witwer, David. 2005. "Westbrook Pegler and the Anti-Union Movement." *Journal of American History* 92 (2).

Woellert, Lorraine, and Simon Lomax. 2009. "Waxman Seeks Bipartisan Help in Passing Climate Bill." *Bloomberg,* May 18.

Wolffe, Richard. 2009. *Renegade: The Making of a President.* New York: Crown Publishing Group.

Woolf, Michael. 2009. "Politico's Washington Coup." *Vanity Fair,* August.

Woodward, Bob. 2010. *Obama's Wars.* New York: Simon & Schuster.

Wright, Robin. 1996. "Iran Braces to Get Blamed for Bombing." *Los Angeles Times,* December 25.

Young, Kerry, Brian Friel, and Joseph Schatz. 2010. "Democrats' Play: 'CR and See You.'" *CQ Weekly Online,* September 27, 2228–2229.

Young, Stephen, and Elizabeth Gronlund. 2002. "A Review of the 2002 U.S. Nuclear Posture Review." Union of Concerned Scientists Working Paper. May 14.

Youngman, Sam. 2010. "White House Unloads Anger Over Criticism from 'Professional Left.'" *The Hill,* August 10, 1.

Zartman, I. W. 1997. "Toward the Resolution of International Conflicts." In *Peacemaking in International Conflict: Methods and Techniques,* eds. I. W. Zartman and J. L. Rasmussen. Washington, DC: U.S. Institute of Peace Press.

Zeleny, Jeff. 2009. "Health Debate Fails to Ignite Obama's Grass Roots." *New York Times,* August 14. http://www.nytimes.com/2009/08/15/health/policy/15ground.html?src=sch.

Zeleny, Jeff, and David Stout. 2009. "Daschle Withdraws As Cabinet Nominee." *New York Times,* February 4.

Zernike, Kate. 2010. "With No Jobs, Plenty of Time to Tea Party." *New York Times,* March 27.

# Index

Abortion, 102, 204
Abramoff, Jack, 127
Absolutism, 68
Accountability, 9, 14, 80–81, 139
Administrative Procedures Act (APA), 202
Affordable Care Act, 190–192, 207–208. *See also* Health care reform
Afghanistan war, 7–8; approval of Obama's job performance, 33(table); cause of, 250; Clinton's support of, 79; Emanuel's stance, 82; Guantánamo detainees, 256–257; justification for, 248; Obama inheriting, 269–270; Obama's counterterrorism policy, 244; Obama's policy on, 34–35, 70, 272–274; political polarization over, 34; 2008 voters' views on troops abroad, 51; war supplemental appropriations bill, 95–97
Afghanistan war, 14
Africa: state fragility and failure, 234
African Americans, 23, 36, 46–47, 66, 164(n2)
Age: 2008 voter demographics, 48, 60–61(n10)
Ailes, Roger, 151
Al-Qaeda, 244, 246, 248, 250, 257, 273
Alternative Minimum Tax (AMT), 186–187, 189–190
Amazon.com, 212
American National Election Studies (ANES), 22–23, 25, 33(table), 38(n16), 40(n39)
American Recovery and Reinvestment Act (2009), 114, 217, 220
*The American Voter* (Campbell et. al.), 42–43

Angle, Sharon, 58–59
Anocracies, 236, 237(fig.)
Approval rating, 31–32, 34–35, 40(n42), 41–42, 60(n2), 177, 179
*The Audacity of Hope* (Obama), 67–68
Autocracies, 237(fig.)
Axelrod, David, 82–84, 112, 117, 120–121, 134, 160

Bailouts. *See* Troubled Assets Relief Program (TARP)
Banking reform, 15, 52
Baucus, Max, 122, 195
Bauer, Bob, 136
Beck, Glenn, 21, 38(n9), 152
Beliefs, Obama's, 66–69
Benjamin, David, 251
Bennett, Bob, 58
Berenson, Brad, 266
Berners-Lee, Tim, 212
Biden, Joe, 83, 125(n6), 125(n9), 159
Bin Laden, Osama, 245, 249
Biological weapons, 275–276
Blagojevich, Rod, 148, 164(n2)
Blair, Dennis C., 262
Blitzer, Wolf, 262
Bloggers, 156, 166(n12)
Bloomberg, Michael, 77, 155
Boehner, John, 29, 117, 178
Bowles, Erskine, 196
Bradley, David, 155
Brennan, John, 251, 256
Broadband Technology Opportunities Program (BTOP), 219–220

Brown, Scott, 29, 102, 123, 190–191
Browner, Carol, 80, 118, 120
Buck, Ken, 58–59
Budget, 2–3; baselines for, 186–187; challenges posed by, 10–11; congressional politics, 193–196; diminishing resources challenging administration, 5; health care reform, 190–193; influencing the economy, 183–184; midterm elections' impact on, 196–198; partisan perspectives on, 56–57; preferences, 185–186; stimulus bill, 187–190; 2008 voters' policy views, 50–51
Budget Act (2009), 103
Bureaucracy, federal, 199
Burns, Robert, 79
Bush, George H.W., 175; legislative achievements, 116(table); midnight regulations, 204; midterm approval rating, 42; terrorism and, 249; voter sentiment, 54
Bush, George W., 4–5, 35; absolutism, 68; blocking Democrats' legislation, 93; bloggers, 156; circumventing the media, 153; communication style, 70–71; counterterrorism policy, 245; damaging Republican Party image, 36; Democrats' legislative goals under, 92; detainee trials, 260; Internet policy, 211, 216–217; legislative achievements, 116(table), 126(n12); media exposure, 150; midnight regulation, 204–205; midterm approval rating, 42; political change, 42; tax cuts, 187, 189; war funding, 95
Bush administration, 14; counterterrorism policy, 243–244, 246–248, 252; disapproval affecting voter sentiment, 53; enhanced interrogation and torture, 257–259; extraordinary rendition, 259; Obama's counterterrorism policy, 256; Obama's defense of counterterrorism policy, 264; polarization sources, 32–33; state secrets doctrine, 262–263; targeted killing, 261–262; TARP, 184
Byrd, Robert, 80, 104

Cabinet secretaries, 77, 83–84, 85(n1), 148
Cable television, 155, 172–173, 212–213, 220–221
Campaigns, 6–7; conservative attacks on Obama, 22; federal funding, 65; governance and, 15–16; Internet use, 12, 157, 164(n1), 211; lobbying expenditures associated with, 134–135; lobbying scandals

associated with, 127–128, 132–133; meaning of change, 7; media impact, 165(n7); message and impact of, 2–3; Obama's stand on Iraq, 274; political change, 43; proposed tax cuts, 187; reciprocity, 137–138; setting up unreal expectations, 145–147; shaping anti-Obama public opinion, 23; stakeholder advocates, 133–134; state secrets doctrine, 263
Cao, Joseph, 94
Cap-and-trade legislation, 119–120, 205
Carter, Jimmy, 53; circumventing the media, 153; counterterrorism policy, 245, 249; legislative achievements, 116(table); midnight regulations, 204; midterm approval rating, 42
Cartwright, James, 277
Center for Responsive Politics, 134, 136–137
Central Intelligence Agency (CIA), 249–252, 258–259, 261–262, 264
Character, 63–64. *See also* Personality, Obama's
Chemical weapons, 275–276
Cheney, Dick, 68, 256, 258–259
Chief of Staff, 75–76, 78, 81–84, 111
Children's health insurance program (SCHIP) reauthorization, 93, 115(table)
Chilton, Kevin, 277
Christmas Day bomber, 166(n11), 243, 253, 266
Chu, Steven, 159
Clarke, Richard, 250–251
Clientelism, 266
Climate change bill, 99, 101, 104–105, 115(table), 118–121
Clinton, Bill, 29; cabinet and staff, 76; circumventing the media, 153; counterterrorism policy, 245, 249–250; Democrats' failure to cooperate with, 109; dependence on congressional Democrats, 72; Internet policy, 211, 214–215; legislative achievements, 116(table), 126(n12); media exposure, 150; midnight regulations, 204; midterm approval rating, 42, 165(n5); midterm elections, 167; smart power, 234; temperament, 71; voter sentiment, 54
Clinton, Hillary Rodham, 76, 79, 96, 121, 124, 148, 159, 231
Clyburn, James, 90, 95, 98–99
CNN, 155–156, 165(n6), 172
COBRA coverage, 208

Cognitive processes, Obama's, 69
Cold War, terrorism and, 246–247
Collins, Susan, 65, 95, 170
Communication style, Obama's, 8, 10, 16, 70–71, 174, 177, 179
Communications, 149. *See also* Internet policy and use
Communism, 20
Competence, political, 44
Compromise, 66–67
Compton, Ann W., 150
Conflict, 232(fig.)–233(fig.), 235(fig.). *See also* Afghanistan war; Foreign policy; Iraq war
Conflict management/conflict resolution, 229–231, 240–241
Congress: action on Obama's legislative proposals, 115(table); budgetary preferences and processes, 185–186, 193–198; climate change bill, 104–105, 118–121; Democratic leadership, 89–92; divided government, 4–5; eroding trust in government, 59–60; financial regulatory reform, 103–104, 126(n17), 207; health care reform, 29, 30(fig.), 121–125; Internet policy, 213–214, 221–222; leadership styles and strategies, 97–101; legacy legislation, 101–105; legislative achievements in 2009, 93; lobbying scandals, 127–128; midterm elections, 42, 105–106, 163, 166(n10), 173; 1932 election, 169–170; Obama's dependence on Democrats in, 72; Obama's election, 170; Obama's legislative priorities and accomplishments, 113–114, 116(table); Obama's legislative standing entering office, 108–109; Obama's lobbying and ethics reforms, 129; Obama's political background, 27, 112; Obama's post-election approach to, 110–111; Obama's strategic plan for legislative achievement, 114–115; polarization limiting cooperation, 57–58; president's rivalry with, 3–4, 19–22; productiveness of, 15; stimulus bill, 93–95; strategic context, 9; TARP bill, 39(n29), 116–118, 188; 2001 tax cuts, 186–187; vacating federal agency rules, 203; war funding, 95–97
Congressional Budget Office (CBO), 184, 186, 190
Congressional Review Act (CRA), 203–205
Conrad, Kent, 190, 195
Constitution, US, 3, 13–14, 80–81
Cooperative Congressional Election Study

(CCES), 23, 29, 31, 33(table), 37, 40(n38); Bush administration performance, 51–53; gender voting, 60(n9); lobbying and ethics, 140–141; partisan and ideological identifications, 48–49; partisan polarization, political change, and trust in government, 53–58; political and moral policy preferences, 49–53; social, economic, and demographic characteristics, 46–48
Corker, Bob, 104
Corruption: Afghanistan, 273
Counterterrorism policy, 13, 244–253
Couric, Katie, 263
Crawford, Susan, 223(n11)
Cunningham, Duke, 127
Czars, policy, 75–76, 79–81, 84, 130

Daley, Richard M., 111
Daou, Peter, 166(n12)
Daschle, Tom, 70, 78, 83, 97, 121, 133, 148
Dawes, Charles, 77
Decision-making process, Obama's, 69–70
Defense Advanced Research Projects Agency (DARPA), 212
Defense policy, 13–15. *See also* Foreign policy
Deficit, 184. *See also* Budget
DeLay, Tom, 127
Delivery system reform, 191–192
DeMint, Jim, 29, 58
Democracy promotion, 229–231, 237(fig.), 241–242, 246, 251–252, 272
Democrats: budget policy views, 57; budgetary preferences, 185–186; climate change bill, 105; congressional leadership after 2008 wins, 90–92; Guantánamo detainees, 96; health care reform, 29–32, 32(table), 101–102; increasing polarization with Republicans, 19–22; legislative achievements in 2009, 93; midterm elections, 8–9, 35–36, 42; party unity, 4; voter turnout in 2008, 23; White House communications failure, 174; white voter support, 47. *See also* Congress; Midterm elections
Demographic groups, political change and, 43
DeParle, Nancy-Ann, 78, 80
Detainee policy, 77, 260–261
Detentions, 256–257
Development aid, 231, 234, 239, 241
Dicks, Norm, 127
Disaffection, political, 44–46
Discrimination, ethnic, 229
Diversity, 66, 228–229

Divided government, 4–5
Dodd, Chris, 104
Dodd-Frank Wall Street Reform and Consumer Protection Act, 114, 115(table)
"dog" journalism, 171–172
Domestic policy, 9–11, 13, 15, 45. *See also* Economy
Donilon, Thomas, 78–79, 84
"don't ask, don't tell" policy, 15, 59
*Dreams From My Father* (Obama), 64
Drone technology, 250–252
Drug czars, 81
Due-process standards, 255–257
Dunn, Anita, 153
Durbin, Dick, 90

Early warning indicators, 238–239, 242(n2)
Economic crisis (2008): Democratic win in 2008 raising expectations, 89–90; Democrats' legislative goals after, 92; midterm elections of 2010, 8–9; Obama's inheritance of, 2; Obama's pragmatic and conciliatory response to, 116–118; public and party expectations after 2008 elections, 109; roots of polarization, 22; timing of, 168–169, 183–184; White House media message, 160. *See also* Stimulus bill
Economy: approval of Obama's job performance, 33(table); budget decisions influencing, 183–184; growth under Obama, 175; midterm elections, 35; policy czar appointments, 80; political change, 42–43; public perception of Obama's political failure, 175–176; right-wing populist antipathy to Obama, 26–27; 2008 voters' perspective on, 51–52. *See also* Budget
Education, 48, 115(table), 158–159, 164(n1), 217–219
Egypt, 82, 242(n2)
Ehrlichman, John, 76
Eisen, Norm, 130, 136
Eisenhower, Dwight D., 42, 116(table), 126(n12)
ElBaradei, Mohamed, 236
Elections, Afghanistan, 273
Elections (1932), 169–170
Elections (2008), 22–26; bad timing of, 168–169; CCES analysis, 46–53; Democratic triumph, 89; gender gap, 60(n9); lobbying expenditures, 135; Obama's criticism of Bush's counterterrorism policy, 245; partisan polarization, political change, and trust

in government, 53–58; policy moderates and extremists, 58–59; political and moral policy preferences, 49–53; setting up unreal expectations, 145–147; trust in government, 59–60; voters' partisan and ideological identification, 48–49; voters' perspectives on performance and expectations, 51–53
Elections (2010). *See* Midterm elections (2010)
Emanuel, Rahm, 75–76, 78–79, 81–84, 95, 97, 111, 113, 117–121, 126(n19), 160–161
Emergency powers, 267
Enforcement of law, 9
Enhanced interrogation techniques, 255–259
Environmental legislation, 45, 202, 204–206. *See also* Climate change bill
Environmental Protection Agency (EPA), 119–120, 126(n15), 200(table), 202, 205–206
Estate tax, 186–187
Ethics, 9, 127–133, 139–141
Ethnicity, 46–47, 229, 230(fig.)
Executive Office of the President (EOP), 75
Executive Orders, 208–209, 209(n9), 256, 258–259
Extra-judicial process, 261–262
Extraordinary rendition, 259
Extremists, policy, 58–59

Failed states, 231–236
Federal agencies, 200–202, 201(table)
Federal Bureau of Investigation (FBI), 258
Federal Communications Commission (FTC), 213–214, 216–218, 221
*Federal Register,* 203–204
*Federalist Paper Number 10* (Madison), 128
*Feeding Frenzy* (Sabato), 171
Feeling thermometers, 26(table), 38(n16)
Financial Reform Act (2010), 207
Financial regulatory reform, 101, 103–104, 126(n17), 207
*Firedoglake,* 156
Fletcher, Henry, 169–170
Flight of the Independents, 57–58
Food safety legislation, 105, 115(table)
Ford, Gerald, 261
Foreign policy, 13–15; achievements, 15; Afghanistan, 272–274; Bush's polarization, 33; Clinton's role in, 79; conflict management/conflict resolution, 229–231; democracy and regime consistency promotion,

236–238; diversity and state stability, 228–229; four initiatives of, 270; fragile and failed states, 231–236; intervention, 239–240; Iraq, 270–272; long-term issues, 227–228; national security policy, 278–279; post-conflict reconstruction, 240–242. *See also* Afghanistan war; Counterterrorism policy; Iraq war

Foreign-born conspiracists, 21, 152, 165(n4)

Fox News, 21, 151–153, 163, 165(n6), 171–172

Fragile states, 231–236

Frank, Barney, 103–104

Franken, Al, 99, 125(n4)

Gates, Henry Louis, 66

Gates, Robert, 76, 79, 84, 96, 159, 275, 277

Geithner, Timothy, 78, 80, 96, 148

Genachowski, Julius, 218

Gender gap: 2008 elections, 46, 60(n9)

Gibbs, Robert, 82–83, 153, 159–160

Global ethnic militancy, 230(fig.)

Global warming, 21, 80. *See also* Climate change bill

Gonzales, Alberto, 77

Goolsbee, Austan, 84

Gore, Al, 214, 216, 222(n1)

Governance, 15–16, 136–137, 179–180, 241

Government, Obama's view of, 67–68

Graham-Lieberman amendment, 96–97

Gregg, Judd, 148, 195

Groeling, Tim, 158

Guantánamo detainees, 96, 156, 193, 255–257, 260–261

Habeas corpus rights, 256–257

Halperin, Mark, 147

Hamsher, Jane, 156

Harkin, Tom, 102

Hart, Velma, 163

Hassan, Nidal, 262

Hate crimes legislation, 115(table)

Hatzius, Jan, 168

Hayden, Michael, 14, 256

Health care reform, 8–9, 15; approval of Obama's job performance, 33(table); budgetary politics, 190–193; climate change legislation and, 119; congressional action, 115(table); congressional negotiation and campaign for, 101–103; congressional polarization, 170; costs of, 32(table); CRA, 203; Emanuel's media message, 160–161;

health czar, 78; House support distribution, 30(fig.); increasing political and ideological polarization, 28–32; Internet policy, 216, 219; legal challenges to, 209(n7); midterm elections, 36; Obama-Congress strategy, 121–125; Obama's achievements, 114; public opinion, 126(n18); Republican opposition to, 37(n1); reserve fund, 189; *Rolling Stone* interview, 161–162; Tea Party response to, 151

Hispanic voters, 46

Holbrooke, Richard, 79

Holder, Eric, 77–78, 84, 166(n11), 263–264

Homeland Security, Department of, 252

Honest Leadership and Open Government Act (HLOGA; 2007), 129, 139

Hoover, Herbert, 169–170

Horner, Charles, 276

House rules, 92

Hoyer, Steny, 90, 98, 190

Huffington, Arianna, 155

Hughes, Chris, 157

Hughes, Karen, 153

Human rights, 256

Ideology: ideological conservatives with liberal policy views, 44, 49; moderates and extremists, 58–59; partisan response to health care reform, 32; policy mood cycles, 60(n3); public perception of, 24(figs.); 2008 elections, 23, 25; 2008 voter demographics, 48–49. *See also* Polarization

Immigration law, 45–46, 112, 114, 115(table)

Independents, 30–32, 32(table)–33(table), 38(n13), 55–58

Industrial policy, 216

Infinite Reach, Operation, 249

International Monetary Fund (IMF), 96

Internet policy and use, 12; challenges of divided government, 221–222; Clinton and Bush administrations, 213–217; growth of, 166(n9); history of, 211; multiple media platforms, 166(n8); new media, 154; Obama administration, 217–221; public and political dynamics of Internet development, 212–213; social networking, 156–158

Intervention, military, 239–240

Iran, 14

Iraq war, 14; approval of Obama's job performance, 33(table); Obama inheriting, 269–270; Obama's policy and, 270–272;

Iraq war (continued): political polarization
over, 33–34; 2008 voters' views on, 52–53;
2008 voters' views on troops abroad, 51;
war supplemental appropriations bill,
95–97
Israel/Palestine negotiations, 240

Jarrett, Valerie, 82–83, 111
Job-approval ratings, 20(fig.)
Johnson, Lyndon, 116(table), 123, 126(n12)
Joint Special Operations Command (JSOC),
259, 262
Jones, James, 76, 78–79, 84

Karzai government, 273
Kennedy, Edward, 29, 65, 102, 121–122, 149
Kennedy, John F., 42, 54, 107, 116(table)
Kenya, 238, 242(n1), 246, 249
Keyes, Alan, 68
Khalid Sheikh Mohammed, 83, 245
Kissel, Larry, 94
Kissinger, Henry, 76
Knoller, Mark, 149, 165(n3)
Koh, Harold, 262
Krugman, Paul, 179

Lame Duck Congress, 5, 15, 195
Leahy, Patrick, 263–264
Legal principles, 77–78
Leno, Jay, 150
Lethal force, 261–262
Lew, Jack, 84
Lieberman, Joseph, 96, 99, 102, 119–121,
125(n4)
Lilly Ledbetter Fair Pay Act, 93, 100,
115(table)
Limbaugh, Rush, 152
Lincoln, Abraham, 81
Lobbying, 9; campaign contributions,
134–135; campaigning and governance,
136–137; CCES questions, 141; declining
public trust in government, 138; defining,
142(n1); effectiveness of reforms, 131–133;
expenditures from 1998–2009, 132(table);
interest groups, 135–136; necessity for,
133–134; Obama's reforms, 129–131,
138–140, 142(n4); reciprocity, 137–138;
scandal associated with, 127–128
Lobbying Disclosure Act (LDA; 1995), 129,
139
Luntz, Frank, 179

Madison, James, 128
McCain, John, 21, 23, 25–26, 47, 52,
125(n5), 140–141, 142(n2), 157
McChrystal, Stanley, 70
McConnell, Mitch, 7, 100
McVeigh, Timothy, 245
Media, 9–10; campaign and election coverage,
146; circumventing, 153–154; conservative
factions, 21, 151–153, 171–173; fighting
the professional left, 161–162; Fox News,
21, 151–153, 163, 165(n6), 171–172;
hostility toward Obama, 171–173; journalistic periods, 171–172; midterm elections, 162–164, 167; multiple platforms,
166(n8); new media, 154–156, 166(n8);
Obama's early visibility, 149–151; Obama's
economic policy, 178–179; post-election
change in Obama's relationship with,
147–149; Reagan criticism, 165(n7); social
networking, 156–158; White House messengers, 158–161
Message, campaign, 2–3
Messina, Jim, 82, 84
Midterm elections (2010), 8–9, 19–20; causes
of Democrats' losses, 173–177; Flight
of the Independents, 58; foreign policy
impact, 228; impact on congressional
function, 105–106; lobbying expenditures,
135; lobbying reform, 128; media coverage,
162–164; Obama's approval rating decline,
42; Obama's response to, 167; Pelosi and
Reid's reelection, 166(n10); reflection
Obama's political failure, 145–147; White
House staff changes, 76
Militancy, ethnic, 230(fig.)
Military intervention, 239–240, 248–251. *See
also* Afghanistan war; Foreign policy; Iraq
war
Mining regulation, 206
Minorities at Risk Project, 229
Mitchell, George, 78
Mohamed, Binyam, 259
*Mohammed et. al. v. Jeppesen Data Plan,* 263
Monitoring systems, 238–239
Moral policy, 49–53
Moral traditionalism, 49–50, 55,
56(fig.)–57(fig.)
Moran, Ellen, 153
Moran, Jim, 127
Mullen, Michael, 277
Murdoch, Rupert, 151

Murkowski, Lisa, 58
Murtha, John, 127

National Ambient Air Quality Standards
Program, 205
National Military Strategic Plan (2006), 247
National Science Foundation (NSF), 216
National Security Council (NSC), 78–79
National Security Strategy statement, 246
National Telecommunications and Informa-
tion Administration (NTIA), 216, 220
Native American voters, 47
Nelson, Ben, 95, 102
Networking and Information Technology
Research and Development (NITRD)
Committee, 218
*New York Times,* 41, 152, 158, 164, 179
Next Generation Internet Program (NGI),
215
Ney, Bob, 127
Nixon, Richard, 42, 71, 76, 116(table), 153,
244
Nobel Peace Prize, 146, 236
Nonproliferation regime, 14, 274–278
North Korea, 14
Notice of Proposed Rulemaking (NPRM),
203
NSFNET project, 212
Nuclear Nonproliferation Treaty (NPT), 274,
277
Nuclear Posture Review (2010), 274–276
Nuclear programs, 13–15. *See also* Nonprolif-
eration regime
Nuclear Security Summit, 276
Nunes, Devin, 29

Obama, Michelle, 65, 158–159
Obey, David, 93–94, 96
Occupational Safety and Health Administra-
tion (OSHA), 204, 206
O'Donnell, Christine, 58–59
Office of Communications, 153–154
Office of Cyberinfrastructure (OCI), 216
Offshore drilling, 45, 115(table), 120,
126(n16)
Oklahoma City bombing, 245
Olympic Games (Munich), 244
Operational policy liberals, 60(n3)
Optimism, Obama's, 68–69
Organization, White House, 5, 8, 76–85,
85(n1), 252–253

Orszag, Peter, 80, 84, 95, 97, 191

Page, Susan, 147–148
Palin, Sarah, 23, 58
Palmer, Alice, 65
Panetta, Leon, 125(n8), 258, 264
Patient Protection and Affordable Care Act
(2010), 114, 203
Pawlenty, Tim, 28
Pelosi, Nancy, 90–91, 93–94, 97–98; budget
resolution, 190; centrist agenda, 108;
climate change mitigation bill, 104–105;
health care legislation, 101–103, 123;
media message, 159; midterm elections,
166(n10); Social Security cuts, 196; TARP
legislation, 116–117
Personality, Obama's, 7–8; character for-
mation, 64–65; chief of staff Emanuel
contrasted with, 82–83; cognitive processes,
69; communication style, 70–71; decision-
making process, 69–70; enthusing Democrats and independents, 108; importance
in decision-making, 63–64; political and
cultural beliefs, 66–69; pragmatic conciliatory style, 111–113; prerogative powers use,
265; presidential performance and, 72–73;
Rouse's personality and, 84; temperament,
71; 2008 election image, 23–25
Persuasion, 99
Petraeus, David, 259
Pfeiffer, Dan, 154
Plouffe, David, 84, 157–158
Pluralist democracy, 131–132
Podesta, John, 111, 133–134
Polarization, congressional: Bush administration, 32–33; Democrat-controlled Congress,
92; economic crisis fueling, 26–28; evidence
for voter polarization, 44–45; health care
reform, 28–32; increase in, 19–20; increasing
conservatism, 20–22; Iraq and Afghanistan
wars, 34; limiting cooperation, 57–58; midterm elections, 35–37, 105–106; Obama's
cross-party appointments, 37(n1); Obama's
post-partisan agenda, 109–110; Obama's
public approval decline, 44–46; policy
extremists, 58–59; root causes of, 22; stimulus
bill, 94; Tea Party movement influencing,
6–7; trust in government, 59–60; 2008 voter
sentiment, 53–54
Policy, 73–74; calls for political change,
42–43; character and personality, 63–64;

Policy (continued): climate change bill, 118–121; Democratic congressional leadership after 2008 wins, 90–92; Democratic win in 2008 raising expectations, 89–90; environmental regulation, 205–206; governance and, 15–16; ideological conservatives with liberal policy views, 44, 49; immigration law, 45–46, 112, 114, 115(table); leading to good governance, 179–180; lobbying reform, 130, 138–140; moderates and extremists affecting voter disaffection, 58–59; Obama sharing crafting of, 97–98; Obama's beliefs and values influencing, 66–69; Obama's flexibility, 65; Obama's legislative priorities and achievements, 113–114; Obama's operating style, 69; policy mood contributing to Obama's decline, 44–46; political and moral policy preferences in 2008 elections, 49–53; political change, 43; public opinion on Obama's, 33(table), 175–177; rulemaking, 202; 2008 voters' perspective on performance and expectations, 51–53; White House staff role in, 76–84. *See also* Budget; Counterterrorism policy; Domestic policy; Foreign policy; Internet policy and use; Personality, Obama's; Prerogative powers; Stimulus bill
Policy mood cycle, 54, 54(fig.), 55–56, 60(n3)
*Politico,* 154–155
Post-partisanship, 3; climate change legislation, 118–120; health care bill, 121–125; lobbying reform, 136; Obama's approach to Congress, 110–111; Obama's failure to achieve congressional harmony, 19; Obama's promise of, 107; Obama's strategic context, 107–110; pragmatic conciliatory style, 111–113; strategic context, 9; TARP legislation, 117–118
Powell, Colin, 79
Pragmatic conciliatory style, Obama's, 111–113, 116–118
Preemption strategy, 96
Pre-existing conditions, health care and, 31
Prerogative powers, 13–14, 255–256; deep structure of, 267–268; defending the Bush administration, 264; detainee trials, 260–261; detentions, 256–257; enhanced interrogation and torture, 257–259; extra-judicial process, 261–262; extraordinary rendition, 259; factors in the use of, 265–268; state secrets doctrine, 262–264
Progressive pragmatism, 68

Propaedeutic view of prerogative powers, 267–268
Public mood, 7; disappointment over Obama support, 41; health care reform, 29–30, 126(n18); increasing polarization, 19–20; lobbyists, 127–128; media change, 9–10; midterm elections, 35–37; Obama ideology, 33(table); party polarization, policy moods, and public trust contributing to Obama's decline, 44–46; political change, 43; prerogative powers use, 265–266; racial resentment scale, 39(n19); racial resentment scale in 2008 elections, 25; ratings of Obama on the Thermometer Scale, 26(table); TARP bailout, 27–28, 39(n24); Tea Party movement, 38(n5); 2008 elections, 22–26; 2008 voters' perspective on the economy, 51–52

Quadrennial Diplomacy and Development Review (QDDR) initiative, 231
Quinnipiac poll, 31, 38(n6)

Racial component of 2008 election, 25, 27, 149
Racial resentment scale, 25, 39(n19)
Rangel, Charles, 127
Reagan, Ronald, 42, 53–54, 69, 71, 116(table), 126(n12), 153, 165(n7), 167, 173, 185–186, 244–245
Reciprocity, 137–138
Recovery and Reinvestment Act (2009), 15, 174, 177, 197. *See also* Stimulus bill
Regime consistency, 229–231
Regulation, 11–12; benefits and costs of major federal rules October 1999–September 2009, 200(table); benefits and costs of major federal rules October 2008–September 2009, 201(table); federal bureaucracy, 199–200; Internet policy, 12, 213–216; legal requirements for, 202–203; major rules by federal agency, 201(table); midnight regulations, 203–205; Obama's new initiatives, 205–209; process of, 203
Reid, Harry, 90–91, 95, 99–100, 102, 104, 108, 119, 121, 123, 159, 166(n10)
Religion: 2008 voter demographics, 47–48
Reno, Janet, 77
Republicans: budget policy views, 57; climate change bill, 105; confronting Obama in 2008, 170; conservative media coverage, 152; financial reform bill, 103–104; Fox News, 172; Guantánamo detainees, 96;

health care bill, 29–32, 32(table), 103,
123; increasing polarization with Democrats, 19–22; midterm elections, 36–37,
42; Obama's Afghanistan policy, 34–35;
Obama's cross-party appointments, 37(n1);
opposing Democratic agenda, 100; party
unification, 4; recovering from 2006 and
2008 losses, 28–29; reversing Obama's
accomplishments, 7; stimulus bill, 94–95;
TARP, 117; Tea Party movement, 20–22,
58–59; 2008 elections, 22–26. *See also*
Congress; Midterm elections (2010)
Revolving Door project, 136–137
Rich, Marc, 77
Richardson, Bill, 148
Rivlin, Alice, 196
*Rolling Stone* magazine, 161–162
Romer, Christina, 80, 84
Roosevelt, Franklin, 168–171
Rospars, Joe, 157
Ross, Dennis, 79
Rouse, Peter, 82–84, 97, 111
Rule of law, 251–252
Rulemaking, 199–202. *See also* Regulation
Russia: START treaty, 276–278

Sabato, Larry, 171
*Saturday Night Live,* 83
Schiliro, Phil, 111, 117
Schumer, Charles, 90, 108–109
Sebelius, Kathleen, 78, 80
Security, 13, 79, 244–248, 278–279. *See also*
Foreign policy
Selzer, Ann, 162, 176
Senate Intelligence Committee report, 253
Senate rules, 92
Senior, Jennifer, 150
September 11, 2001, 77, 244, 246, 250
Shelby, Richard, 104
Simpson, Alan, 196
Siroker, Dan, 157
Snowe, Olympia, 65, 95, 123, 170
Social networking, 154, 156–158
Social welfare, 49–50, 55–56, 56(fig.)–57(fig.)
Socialism, 20, 26, 29, 39(n20)
Special interests, 9, 135–136
Specter, Arlen, 65, 95, 99, 125(n4), 170
Stakeholder advocates, 133–134
State Department, US, 76, 79, 234
State of the Union message (2010), 130–131,
151
State secrets doctrine, 262–264
State-based parties, 4

Status of Forces Agreement (SOFA), 271
Steele, Michael, 152
Stevens, Ted, 127
Stimulus bill, 28, 40(n31), 65, 72, 93–95,
115(table), 116–118, 187–190
Stock market, 27, 175, 178
Strategic Arms Reduction Treaty (START),
15, 114, 115(table), 124, 126(n11), 274,
276–278
Strategic context of Obama's post-partisan-
ship, 107–110, 124
Sudan, 238
Summers, Lawrence, 80, 84
Sustainable Growth Rate (SGR) formula,
186–187
Sutphen, Mona, 82
Swine flu, 95, 193

Talev, Margaret, 150
Taliban, 250, 257, 273
Tanzania, 246, 249
Targeted killing, 261–262
Taxation, 31, 32(table), 94, 117, 148, 174,
186–188
Tea Party movement, 6–7, 20–22, 29, 32,
36–37, 38(n5), 52, 58–59, 151
Telecommunications Act (1996), 214–216, 221
Temperament, Obama's, 71, 82
Tenet, George, 249–251, 263
Terrorism, 51, 229, 234, 244–248. *See also*
Counterterrorism policy
Terrorism, war on, 13–14, 247. *See also* Pre-
rogative powers
Thermometer Scale, 26(table), 38(n16)
Thompson, Robert, 151
Tiahrt, Todd, 127
Torture, 257–259
Townsend, Frances, 262
Transition team, 111, 121, 125(nn6, 7)
Transparency, 9, 130, 138–139
Troubled Assets Relief Program (TARP),
15, 27–28, 39(n24), 39(n26), 52, 72,
116–118, 162, 174–175, 184, 188
Truman, Harry, 81
Trust in government, 44–46, 59–60, 138
Truth commissions, 241, 264
Tunisia, 242(n2)

UN Security Council, 271
Unanimous consent agreements (UCAs), 100
Unemployment, 27–28, 40(n31), 106, 175,
178, 194
Unified government, 4–5

Universal health care coverage, 31
Unmanned aerial vehicles (UAVs), 250
US Agency for International Development
(USAID), 239

Values, 66–69, 251–252
Van Hollen, Chris, 99
Visclosky, Peter, 127
Volcker, Paul, 80

Walsh, Ken, 155–156
War funding, 95–97
War supplemental appropriations bill, 93,
95–97
Wars. *See* Afghanistan war; Iraq war

Waterboarding, 258–259, 269
Waxman, Henry, 105, 118–119
Wenner, Jann, 161–162
White House staff, 76–79, 111, 220. *See also*
Organization, White House
Wilderness protection, 207
Wilson, Joe, 151
Women: post-conflict reconstruction, 241
Worker protection, 206–207
World Trade Center bombing (1993), 245
World Trade Center bombing (2001). *See*
September 11, 2001
Wright, Jeremiah, 27, 65

Yemen, 251

# About the Contributors

**Richard W. Boyd** is Professor of Government Emeritus at Wesleyan University, where he taught from 1969 to 2006. His research fields are American politics, public opinion and electoral politics, and public opinion and foreign policy. Boyd was Vice President for Academic Affairs and Provost at Wesleyan from 1994 to 2000.

**Martha Crenshaw** is a Senior Fellow in the Center for International Security and Cooperation at the Freeman Spogli Institute for International Studies and Professor of Political Science by courtesy at Stanford University. She taught at Wesleyan University in Connecticut from 1974 to 2007 and was a Guggenheim Fellow in 2005. She is a Lead Investigator at the National Consortium for the Study of Terrorism and Responses to Terrorism (START), a Center of Excellence of the Department of Homeland Security based at the University of Maryland. Her recent work includes an edited volume, *The Consequences of Counterterrorism* (Russell Sage Foundation, 2010).

**Ron Elving** is Senior Washington Editor for NPR News. He was previously political editor for Congressional Quarterly. He was a Congressional Fellow with the American Political Science Association and worked as a staff member in the House and Senate. He received his bachelor's degree from Stanford University and master's degrees from the University of Chicago and the University of California, Berkeley. He has taught at American University, George Mason University, and Georgetown University. He is the author of *Conflict and Compromise: How Congress Makes the Law* (Simon & Schuster, 1995).

**Gary C. Jacobson** is Distinguished Professor of Political Science at the University of California, San Diego. He specializes in the study of US elections, parties, interest groups, public opinion, and Congress. He is the author of *Money in Congressional Elections, The Politics of Congressional Elections,* and *The Electoral Origins of Divided Government,* and co-author of *Strategy and Choice in Congressional Elections,* and *The Logic of American Politics.* His most recent book is *A Divider, Not a Uniter: George W. Bush and the American People.*

**Lawrence J. Korb** is a Senior Fellow at the Center for American Progress and an adjunct professor at Georgetown University. Dr. Korb served on active duty for four years as a naval flight officer and retired from the Naval Reserve with the rank of captain. From 1981 to 1985, he served as assistant secretary of defense (manpower, reserve affairs, installations, and logistics). Prior to joining the Center for American Progress he was director of National Security Studies at the Council on Foreign Relations. He has also served as director of the Center for Public Policy Education and senior fellow in the Foreign Policy Studies Program at the Brookings Institution; dean of the Graduate School of Public and International Affairs at the University of Pittsburgh; vice president of corporate operations at the Raytheon Company, and director of defense studies at the American Enterprise Institute. Dr. Korb has authored, co-authored, edited, or contributed to more than 20 books and written more than 100 articles on national security issues.

**Scott Lilly** is a Senior Fellow at American Progress, specializing in governance, federal budgeting, national security, and the economy. He joined the center in March of 2004 after 31 years of service with the United States Congress. He served as clerk and staff director of the House Appropriations Committee, minority staff director of that Committee, executive director of the House Democratic Study Group, executive director of the Joint Economic Committee, and chief of staff in the Office of Congressman David Obey (D-WI). He is also an adjunct professor in the Public Policy Institute at Georgetown University.

**John E. Owens** is Professor of United States Government and Politics in the Centre for the Study of Democracy at the University of Westminster and a Faculty Fellow in the Centre for Congressional and Presidential Studies at the American University in Washington, DC, and the Institute for the Study of the Americas in the University of London's School of Advanced Study. He is the author of numerous articles on congressional-presidential relations, the United States Congress, and comparative legislative politics, including his most recent book, co-edited with Ricardo Pelizzo, *The "War on Terror" and the Growth of Executive Power? A Comparative Analysis* (2010). Other publications include *Congress and the Presidency: Institutional Politics in a Separated System* (1996), co-authored with Michael Foley; *Leadership in Context* (2003), co-edited with Erwin C. Hargrove; *America's "War" on Terrorism: New Dimensions in United States Government and Foreign Policy* (2008), co-edited with John W. Dumbrell; and *The Republican Takeover of Congress* (1998), co-edited with Dean McSweeney.

**James P. Pfiffner** is University Professor and directs the doctoral program in the School of Public Policy at George Mason University. He has written or edited 12 books on the presidency and American national government, including *Power Play: The Bush Administration and the Constitution* (Brookings, 2008) and *Torture as Public Policy* (Paradigm Publishers, 2010).

**Richard M. Pious** is Adolph and Effie Ochs Professor at Barnard College and professor at the Graduate School of Arts and Sciences at Columbia University. His books include *The American Presidency* (Basic Books, 1979); *The President, Congress and the Constitution* (The Free Press, 1984); *Why Presidents Fail* (Rowman & Littlefield, 2008); *The Constitution Under Siege* (Carolina Academic Press, 2010); co-authored with Christopher Pyle; and *The War on Terrorism and Rule of Law* (Oxford University Press, 2006). He has published articles in many anthologies, as well as in *Political Science Quarterly, The Wisconsin Law Review,* the *Journal of International Affairs,* the *Journal of Armed Forces* *and Society,* and *Presidential Studies Quarterly.* In addition, he has co-authored a widely used print and online reference work, *The Oxford Guide to American Government.*

**Alexander H. Rothman** is a Special Assistant with the National Security and International Policy team at Center for American Progress. His work at CAP is focused primarily on US military and defense policy and nonproliferation issues.

**Barbara Sinclair** is Professor Emerita of Political Science at UCLA. She specializes in American politics and primarily does research on the US Congress. Her publications include articles in the *American Political Science Review,* the *American Journal of Political Science,* the *Journal of Politics,* and *Legislative Studies Quarterly* and the following books: *Congressional Realignment* (1982), *Majority Leadership in the U.S. House* (1983), *The Transformation of the U.S. Senate* (1989), *Legislators, Leaders and Lawmaking: The U.S. House of Representatives in the Postreform Era* (1995), *Unorthodox Lawmaking: New Legislative Processes in the U. S. Congress* (1997, 2000, 2007), and *Party Wars: Polarization and the Politics of National Policy Making* (2006). She has served as chair of the Legislative Studies Section of the American Political Science Association, president of the Western Political Science Association, and vice president of the American Political Science Association. She is an elected member of the American Academy of Arts and Sciences.

**Claudia Hartley Thurber, Esq.** is a Consultant in Occupational Safety and Health Policy and Former Counsel for Health Standards, Office of the Solicitor, US Department of Labor. Ms. Thurber continues to work on occupational health and safety standards. She is an expert on the regulatory process, from proposals to promulgation of rules. She has spoken on current issues in federal regulation at professional conferences and to academics, government managers, graduate students, and practitioners in the US and abroad, including Fudan University, China; Conference of Canadian Administrators, Ottawa, Canada; American University at Sharjah, UAE, Dubai; and ILLUM Milan, Italy. She has taught *Evidence Based Thinking and Writing and Research* to OSHA professionals and published a three-part recorded course, *The Regulatory Process* (The Capitol Net, 2009). She has also taught political science courses, including *Film and Politics,* at American University.

**James A. Thurber** is University Distinguished Professor of Government and Founder (1979) and Director of the Center for Congressional and Presidential Studies at American University, Washington, DC. He is an author or editor of 16 books and 80 articles on Congress, the president, campaigns and elections, and lobbying, including *Rivals for Power: Presidential-Congressional Relations* (2009, 4th ed.), *Campaigns and Elections, American Style* (with Candice Nelson, 2009, 3rd ed.), *Congress and the Internet* (with Colton Campbell, 2002), *The Battle for Congress: Consultants, Candidates, and Voters* (2001), *Crowded Airwaves: Campaign Advertising in Elections* (with Candice J. Nelson and David A. Dulio, 2000), *Campaign Warriors: Political Consultants in Elections* (with Candice J. Nelson, 2000), *Remaking Congress: The Politics of Congressional Stability and Change* (with Roger Davidson), and *Divided Democracy: Cooperation and Conflict Between Presidents and Congress.* He is editor of the journal *Congress and the Presidency.*

**Douglas E. Van Houweling** is Professor and Associate Dean for Research and Innovation in the School of Information at the University of Michigan and former President and CEO of Internet2. With James Duderstadt and Daniel Atkins, he authored *Higher Education in the Digital Age.* Van Houweling is the recipient of the EDUCAUSE 2002

Excellence in Leadership Award and Iowa State University's John V. Atanasoff Discovery Award, and currently serves on the boards of Altarum, Advanced Network & Services, and Merit Network. Dr. Van Houweling played a major role in Internet development in the United States.

**Stephen J. Wayne** is an expert on the American presidency. He has written 12 books, several in multiple editions, and more than 100 articles, chapters, and book reviews. His major works include *The Road to the White House,* 9th edition, *The Legislative Presidency,* and *Presidential Leadership* (with George C. Edwards), 8th edition. His latest book, published in 2011, is *Personality and Politics: Obama For and Against Himself.* Professor Wayne has served as President of the Presidency Research Group and the National Capital Area Political Science Association. He regularly lectures to international visitors, senior federal executives, and college students in the United States and abroad on the presidency and electoral politics.

**Joseph White** is Luxenberg Family Professor of Public Policy in the Department of Political Science at Case Western Reserve University. In 2010–11, he was on leave at the Conservatoire National des Arts et Metiers in Paris and at Oxford University. He is the author of many articles on budget politics and policy as well as on entitlements and health care policy and politics. His books include *The Deficit and the Public Interest: The Search for Responsible Budgeting in the 1980s* (University of California Press and the Russell Sage Foundation, 1991), with Aaron Wildavsky.

**Jonathan Wilkenfeld** is Director for the Center for International Development and Conflict Management as well as a professor and prior chair of the Department of Government and Politics at the University of Maryland. Since 1977, Wilkenfeld has served as co-director (with Michael Brecher) of the International Crisis Behavior Project, a cross-national study of international crises in the 20th century. His most recent books include *A Study of Crisis* (1997 and 2000, with Michael Brecher), *International Negotiation in a Complex World* (2009, with Brigid Starkey and Mark Boyer), and *Mediating International Crises* (2005, with Victor Asal, David Quinn, and Kathleen Young).